# THE OFFICIAL® PRICE GUIDE TO POLITICAL MEMORABILIA

## RICHARD FRIZ

**First Edition**

**House of Collectibles**
**New York, New York 10022**

© 1988 by Random House, Inc.

All rights reserved under International and
Pan-American Copyright Conventions.

Published by: The House of Collectibles
201 East 50th Street
New York, New York 10022

Distributed by Ballantine Books, a division of Random House, Inc., New York and simultaneously in Canada by Random House of Canada Limited, Toronto.

Manufactured in the United States of America

ISBN: 0-876-37744-4

10 9 8 7 6 5 4 3 2 1

*This book is dedicated to my son Josh and all the other fledgling political collectors. May all your finds be unlisted.*

# CONTENTS

# ACKNOWLEDGMENTS

For their invaluable assistance in a multitude of ways, including sharing with us their material, time, and knowledge, we would like to extend a sincere appreciation to the following: Bernard Barenholtz, Marlboro, New Hampshire; Ken Smith, Greenwich, Connecticut; Rex Stark Auctions, Bellingham, Massachusetts; Robert A. Fratkin, Washington, D.C.; David Frent Auctions, Oakhurst, New Jersey; Fred Jorgensen, Santa Rosa, California; Ginger Sawyer, Skinner Auctions, Bolton, Massachusetts; Frank Corbeil, Unionville, Connecticut; Richard Maxson, Enfield, Connecticut; Ken Florey, Hamden, Connecticut; Riba-Mobley Auctions, Wethersfield, Connecticut.

An extra-special thanks is due the following: Bruce and Yvonne DeMay, Keene, New Hampshire; Dr. Edmund Sullivan, Suffield, Connecticut; Theodore L. Hake, Hake Americana & Collectibles, York, Pennsylvania; U. I. Chick Harris, St. Louis, Missouri. We are also grateful to Geary Vlk, president of American Political Items Collectors, for permission to quote from their *Keynoter;* and last, our appreciation to artist Barbara Smullin of Hancock, New Hampshire, who produced the drawings of pinback designs from the Golden Era.

## PHOTOGRAPHIC ACKNOWLEDGMENTS

Our appreciation goes to those generous individuals, institutions, and auction houses who granted us permission to use photographs. They are properly credited under their respective illustrations and photographs throughout this guide. It is to Madaline Friz, however, that words fail us, for her contribution in terms of photographing the majority of items pictured is immeasurable.

# GETTING ON THE BANDWAGON

# THE PRICES IN THIS BOOK

Whenever political memorabilia dealers and collectors caucus—at bourses, antique shows, auctions, national conventions—when the smoke clears and the tumult and the shouting abates, the inevitable question arises: "What's it worth?"

To arrive at an answer to this multifaceted question, we have attended countless live auctions; pored over mail auction catalogs, dealer listings, and trade magazine ads; roamed endless aisles at shows; and accomplished a fair share of buying and selling on our own.

We sought advice from acknowledged specialists in the hobby whose credentials are impeccable. The more immersed we became, the clearer the realization that assessing value is truly an inexact science. Even the "pros" often voiced highly subjective, sometimes conflicting opinions. (Now we know how the pollsters felt in '48 in predicting a Dewey landslide over Truman.)

We hope we can persuade you to eliminate the obviously negative connotations of "price" from your mind. Accentuate instead the positive aspects of the word "guide." Roget cites an idiom, "set one on one's way," "guide safely through the mine fields," which strikes us as appropriate here.

We have attempted to pack this guide with as much information as possible to assist you in identifying and dating thousands of political artifacts—from the magnificent to the mundane. In so doing, we hope to alert you to at least a few political treasures that you might never have laid eyes on before, or even knew existed. To paraphrase "His Honor Duh Mayor," James Daley of Chicago, the late, great political pundit, "This is for your enlightenment, edification, and hallucination."

3

# HOW TO USE THIS GUIDE

How often have you been frustrated when attempting to research a particular political artifact, resorting to pulling down half a shelf of books to extract information? Frequent index checks, cross-referencing, and even decoding certain symbols to determine a price range can further complicate matters. With this all-inclusive guide to political memorabilia we've tried to take the "search" out of "research."

We set out (paraphrasing a 1930s Hoover slogan pinback) "to do an elephant's job and no time for donkey business." Material is organized in logical sequence. Categories are amassed alphabetically, and descriptive data instantly matches up with a value range. Under "Adams, John," for example, memorabilia can be checked off beginning with *A*, as in "Advertising and Packaging," to *T*, as in "Trays, Serving and Tip."

Political/patriotic memorabilia is presented in two sections:

*Section I.* A chronological (1789–1984), campaign-by-campaign highlighting of classic artifacts that best exemplify specific candidates, their respective party affiliation and platforms, and campaign strategies.

*Section II.* An alphabetical listing by candidate, winner or loser, from "Adams, John," to "Wilson, Woodrow." While space prohibits our listing them all, certain third-party candidates, "Hopefuls and Locals," are also included.

4

# GRADING OF POLITICAL ITEMS

## CONDITION GRADING OF CAMPAIGN RIBBONS

Originally made of silk, and later of cotton and other fabrics, campaign ribbons are the most fragile of all campaign memorabilia. Produced as bookmarks and lapel items, the majority of early ribbons were printed on a "white" background, which may actually be off-white, cream, or a number of other colors, depending on original fabric, weave, dye fading, and state of preservation.

Most early ribbons (pre-1870) were cut from bolts of material by hand. Therefore, lengths of individual ribbons may differ. This should not concern a collector as long as there are adequate margins at the top and bottom. The fragile nature of the ribbons and their vulnerability to such perils as staining, tearing, and rubbing make each a special case. Certain varieties are practically unobtainable in any condition.

The "unique" condition of each ribbon stems from the combination of factors mentioned. However, ribbons fall into six basic grades. The following is a definition of our grading terms.

MINT: Clean and crisp with no noticeable defects interfering with content.

EXCELLENT: Very few defects, extremely clean, an above-average example.

GOOD: Defects blend into item or don't materially affect the appearance.

AVERAGE: Defects noticeable and detract from appearance.

FAIR: Several serious, highly visible defects.

POOR: Numerous defects, extremely low quality. It is best to pass by specimens in this condition, unless you desire to merely fill a void until you can upgrade.

*Note:* This section was compiled from criteria prepared by David Frent in the catalog for the Don Warner sale, New England Rare Coins Auction, NYC, 1981.

## CONDITION GRADING OF PINBACKS

Condition as it affects value must include mention of deep scratches or lines, celluloid cracking, surface bumps, structural damage and staining, flaking of celluloid, serious oxidation of metal parts, and similar conditions.

Items are graded by a system ranging from A+ to E.

A: Grade A items are not usually described at all. In each case, a judgment was made that the visual impact of the item and its physical condition are of high quality, that no obvious marks or flaws are visible on the face that would detract from the collector's enjoyment of the piece, and that no flaws exist, except as noted. Condition ranges from Essentially Perfect (A+) and Excellent (A) to Nearly Excellent (A—).

B: Having defects that would prevent an A grade but not necessarily faults that are immediately apparent on the item's face. Within a range of B+ to B—, these items would be regarded as Very Good.

C: These items have more serious flaws but in some cases may achieve the high prices due to rarity and desirability.

D: These items would have to be considered in poor condition for the reasons noted.

E: Fails to make grade in acceptability.

## CONDITION GRADING OF TOKENS AND MEDALS

Political tokens and medals are coinlike in nature, and traditionally they are graded on a scale similar to that used for coins. Grading criteria here corresponds to the American Numismatic Association standards for coins.

UNCIRCULATED: Has no trace of wear but may show a moderate number of contact marks, and surface may be spotted or lack some luster.

ABOUT UNCIRCULATED: Has traces of light wear on many of the high points. At least half of the mint luster still present.

EXTREMELY FINE: Design is lightly worn throughout, but all features are sharp and well defined.

VERY FINE: Shows moderate wear on high points of design; all major details clear.

VERY GOOD: Well worn, with main features clear and bold although rather flat.

GOOD: Heavily worn, with design visible but faint in areas. Many details are flat.

POOR: Numerous defects that substantially alter appearance of tokens.

# MARKET OVERVIEW

One inescapable truism about campaign pinbacks in the hobby is that they rank supreme on the covetability scale. To be sure, there are distant rumblings over such categories as three-dimensional artifacts, textiles, and political paper (now classified under the more prestigious aegis of "Ephemera"). Go to any regional or national APIC show, check out the political mail auction catalogs, however, and you're clearly in "button heaven."

Until just recently, any ultimate rarities among lapel devices that surfaced on the market, were invariably pounced upon by those who became known as "the Big Four." There was always an aura of awe and mystery about these obviously affluent individuals; and when this writer asked around, rather innocently, as to to their identity, the answers varied. We eventually learned their names: Morton Rose of Bethesda, Maryland; Paul Purlin, who recently donated his collection to the University of Louisville; Merill Berman of Westchester, New York, whose bounty of campaign treasures was exhibited at the Hudson River Museum in Yonkers, New York, in 1984; and Don Warner, whose collection of over 850 items was sold at the only auction of a major political collection to date, the New England Rare Coins Auction of Don Warner Political Memorabilia in New York City and Carlisle, Pennsylvania.

Times sure have changed. A market once dominated by a few free spenders now boasts a broad, solid base, attesting to the landsliding growth and vitality of the hobby.

After leveling off over the past two or three years, the stability for four-figure pinbacks has ended dramatically. In 1987, as we write this, five items have sold for over $2,000, and three crossed the $3,000 threshold. Jeff Pressman, in a recent "Button Beat" column in *The Political Bandwagon,* reported that most items, with few exceptions, have doubled since the Warner sale in 1981. (Exceptions were specimens that were bitterly contested, for example, the $33,000 Cox–Roosevelt jugate.)

7

Dave Frent, a leading mail auctioneer, attests that there is also intense competition as of the past two years in the $50 to $100 range. In fact, at a panel discussion* on market trends at the APIC National Convention in Louisville in August, 1987, questions from the audience seemed to focus on how their chances might be enhanced to snare those elusive auction entries.

While political ephemera and three-dimensional items are still generally undervalued, particularly when offered at regional shows within the hobby, they have risen to rather astounding price levels on the auction block at Phillips, Skinners, Bourne and Riba-Mobley recently. The following comprise a few of the blockbusting top bids, many of which were won not by political collectors but by a new breed that prizes these artifacts more for their exceptional graphics or historical value.

- A quarter plate daguerreotype of Abraham Lincoln, pre-presidency, the only known dag still in private hands—$17,600.
- A small Lincoln–Johnson campaign flag banner—$8,250.
- An engraved plaque on metal with gold relief busts of Grant and Colfax on silver, "The People's Choice, 1868"—$2,090.
- Ship's papers, dated July 6, 1795, and signed by George Washington—$3,630.
- Zachary Taylor Bennington pottery pitcher, ca. 1850—$4,620.
- "Old Hickory Forever" pierced-tin lantern, Andrew Jackson—$935.
- Full-bodied copper eagle 1860 Lincoln campaign torch—$3,080.
- Eight-inch Liverpool pitcher decorated with black transfer of George Washington sold at David Arman Auctions in Woodstock, Connecticut, for $5,720.
- Martin Van Buren campaign ribbon inscribed "New York Must and Shall Be Redeem'd, New York's Favorite Son," with bust portrait, guided at $450–$550 at Riba-Mobley, closed at $2,420.
- A presentation black bass T. H. Chubb fishing reel from Grover Cleveland, 1895 (so engraved), was gaveled down at $2,750, or five times pre-sale estimate.

Enough said!

---

*Panelists were Dave Frent, Bob Coup, Al Anderson, and Rex Stark, all successful mail auctioneers. Jeff Pressman, one of the most knowledgeable assessors of value ranges in the hobby, acted as moderator.

# POLITICAL MEMORABILIA TREND SETTERS TO KEEP AN EYE ON IN THE '80s

The following political categories reflect intensified activity and interest on the part of dealers, collectors, and museum people at recent auctions, shows, and exhibitions.

## *Presidential Campaign Posters, Prints*

Can someone offer a logical explanation as to why most political collectors can go weak at the knees at the sight of a tiny campaign jugate pinback yet stifle a yawn when a visually stunning poster, fine print, or cartoon passes in review?

Vastly underrated, these "sleeping giants," especially posters and broadsides with knockout graphics, vibrant colors, and a degree of scarcity, are beginning to create a stir in auction circles.

Jugate campaign posters from 1880 through 1908, particularly the chromolithographic specimens, cleverly embellish candidates' portraits with winged eagles, scepters, shields, draped flags, wispily clad Miss Liberty and other deities. An 1856 poster featuring Republican nominee John Fremont and his wife, Jessie Benton Fremont, cavorting on horseback has all the whimsy and charm of a folk art oil on canvas by Edward Hicks or Mathew Pryor.

In the modern political arena, collectors should be on the alert for the George McGovern posters created by Peter Max in 1972; several pop art posters for Eugene McCarthy in 1968; the classic Uncle Sam "I Want You F.D.R." by James Montgomery Flagg in 1944; Harry Truman at the keyboard with Thomas Dewey atop the piano singing in a 1948 study by Ben Shahn, and from 1984, a FREEZE poster, "Only One Earth/Don't Blow It!" for Mondale–Ferraro.

Hand-colored Currier & Ives prints, clearly abetted by crossover competition, have already moved up into the respectable $400–$500 range at auction houses such as Riba-Mobley and Skinners for such examples as the Zachary Taylor–Millard Fillmore Grand National Whig banner of 1853; even higher for a Lincoln–Johnson 1860 Currier & Ives with full margins and minimal wear and tear. A more common Lincoln–Hamlin Currier & Ives print recently topped $800 at a Riba-Mobley auction.

## *Political Pinback Subcategories*

Collectors who zero in on one favorite presidential front runner almost always develop an affinity for pinbacks relating to holding public offices that were springboards to the national scene. A "Harry Truman For Judge" cello, for example, is highly desirable and elusive, now listing in the $300-plus range. In recent mail auctions, an "Alton B. Parker For Judge" item brought $166, making it the most expensive of Parker ⅞-inch cellos. One of the highlights of a Dave Frent auction (#14) a few years back was what Jeff Pressman in *The Bandwagon* hailed as "the ultimate pre-presidential button," the New York State Senator piece from FDR's 1910 campaign. Four bidders locked horns at the $1,000-plus level, and the hammer price was $1,200!

Other so-called Locals that are increasingly in demand feature those who have been in the national spotlight or have a strong tie-in with the national ticket. Popular names in these categories include William Randolph Hearst, Huey Long, Douglas MacArthur, Champ Clark, Robert and Edward Kennedy, Michael James Curley, and Boss Tweed.

## Women's Suffrage

The emergence of the New Left female activists of the 1960s, the pioneer lib organizations such as WITCH, Red Stockings, and the broader-based NOW created instant collectibles via awareness-raising pinbacks, banners, flyers, and other ephemera. The movement has also aroused and rekindled interest in memorabilia relating to the Woman Suffrage movement from the late 19th century to finally winning the right to vote in 1920. At a recent Riba-Mobley auction, a six-piece place setting in ironstone lettered "Votes For Women" that a wealthy Newport, Rhode Island, dowager had specially made up for a Suffrage benefit (ca. 1913) doubled estimates at $770, while a lot of nine Dunston-Wheeler Anti-Suffrage postcards, 1909, brought $275. At the U. I. "Chick" Harris Auction held in conjunction with the APIC National Convention in Louisville in August 1987, a black Suffragette statuette, allegedly depicting famed rights advocate Sojourner Truth, soared past the $300 mark, about twice the asking price for this rather bizarre ceramic knickknack, in previous mail auctions. "Old Guard" Woman Suffrage collectors may well have mixed emotions about this sudden upsurge in related artifacts. On the one hand, many women are finding equal status in the hobby, which previously had been almost exclusively a man's domain. On the other hand, what happens to "mad money" for future acquisitions when the distaff side of the family also gets the collecting fever?

Anti-nuke and Anti-Vietnam Cause
pinbacks.

### Other Cause Items—Anti-War, Civil Rights, the Environment

While there has been ongoing interest among collectors in "cause" material associated with great political, social, and economic upheaval, prices tend to remain stable. Most contemporary "cause" material can still be purchased for just a few dollars (a recent mail auction offered 55 different "cause" pinbacks, for example, for only $50). Reasonable prices, plus a certain romantic appeal to some collectors, has attracted a new wave of young people to the hobby.

Temperance-Prohibition material, as well as previously mentioned Suffrage items from the 19th century, are already climbing in price. Contemporary "cause" pinbacks, posters, and pamphlets often have powerful graphic appeal and vibrant colors that clearly outclass much of the humdrum material generated by major political parties in recent years. Dr. Edmund Sullivan,

One of the very latest of the highly
collectible Cause items.

in *Collecting Political Americana,* estimated (this was in 1980, mind you) that "over four thousand buttons had been issued since the early 1960s in support of student and anti-war activities, radical militants, and the feminist movement." Robert Fratkin, in "Political Souvenirs" in *The Time-Life Encyclopedia of Collectibles,* classifies "among the more desirable, those from the early days of the Civil Rights movement, and those from the mid-'60s protesting the United States involvement in the Vietnam War."

*All of this talk about ultimate rarities and industrial strength prices is not intended to discourage collectors, particularly newcomers. On the contrary, one of the enticements of political memorabilia is that it exists in abundance and infinite variety, and one may specialize on many different levels.*

*We do feel it is important to mention and illustrate, when possible, certain classic beauties that set the standard in collectibility.*

*As Fred Jorgenson, a Santa Rosa, California, collector emphasizes, however, "most collections are made up primarily of good strong items of considerable appeal, but* modestly priced. *The 'high tariff' pieces don't make up even 1 percent of the hobby. To represent it otherwise is misleading and does the hobby a disservice."*

# ATTRIBUTION—DATING AND IDENTIFYING POLITICAL MEMORABILIA

Part of the joy, as well as the frustration, of collecting political memorabilia is identifying and dating artifacts that, at first glance, yield scarcely a clue. Like the hieroglyphics and runes of ancient civilizations, they pose a real challenge to decipher. Bob Cutter, a fellow APIC member from Bridgeport, Connecticut, made a major contribution recently in *The Bandwagon* by decoding innumerable initialisms or acronyms. Meanwhile, here is a poser for you to decipher: What do the initials W.C.R.P.O. signify in the "Willkie For President" cartoon pinback (Hake 205)?

The jury is still out, and there probably always will be conflicting opinions on any number of political artifacts. The following examples give some clues as to our dilemma.

- A recently discovered cartoon pinback, "Democracy/White Man And Indian Against Negro and Carpetbagger," although documented by collector Marty Hauser of Berkeley, California, as associated with William Jennings Bryan, still fails to connect with many collectors because Bryan's name isn't "up there in lights."

- "Teddy's Our Iceman" pins—there are several clever versions including one with a piece of crystal, to simulate ice, held between tiny ice tongs. As much as we'd like to attribute them to Teddy Roosevelt, no amount of sleuthing has been able to verify these pins as anything but an advertising gimmick.

- A china figurine, "Votes For Women" (ca. 1912), is generally regarded as a caricature of black suffragette Sojourner Truth. Dr. Ed Sullivan tells us, however, that he has been unable to unearth any evidence that Truth went around in her underwear brandishing a club. An activist in the 1850s and 1860s, she was long in her grave by the time the figurine was issued.

13

"Votes for women" bisque statuette, ca. 1912 ($150–$175). *(Frank Corbeil Collection)*

Much closer ties to Sojourner Truth could be claimed for an ingenius clockwork toy "Suffragette" by Automatic Toy Works, 1875. When activated, the figure in blue-check dress and bonnet bends forward and bangs her fist on a tiny rostrum to emphasize a point. (The windup is valued well up in the four figures.)

- Over the years a number of figural canes have cropped up bearing a carved handle shaped like a water faucet and believed to be inspired by a candidate of that name. Just recently we heard from a collector, Jon Zoler of Ridgewood, New Jersey, who was fortunate in locating a faucet cane with the label intact. The cane was made by Kilmer & Reynolds of Elmira, New York, and boosted the candidacy of Jacob Sloat Fassett (read Faucet; hence the word play) for governor of New York in 1891. He lost anyway.

- A lithographed tin figural puzzle, "The Boodle Alderman," which the author acquired recently, was a puzzler indeed until a bit of research in Jerry Slocum's and Jack Boterman's *Puzzles Old and New* (see Bibliography) unmasked the villain as a member of the New York Board of Aldermen who in the late 1890s was "charged with accepting bribes in connection with granting a franchise for a street railroad on Broadway." (The term "boodle" thus came into common usage to signify bribery in general.)

- For many years a small cast-iron frog embossed with "I Croak For The Jackson Wagon" was deemed a treasure from the campaign of Andrew Jackson. Then in 1980 Herbert Collins of the Smithsonian, writing in the APIC *Keynoter,* debunked the myth and indicated the frog to be an advertising giveaway from a wagon company in Jackson, Michigan, in the 1880s. The deglamorized frog, which once commanded prices as high as $700, is now valued at far less as an advertising doorstop.

- A dealer at an antiques show recently tried in vain to convince a collector friend that a small cigar-shaped liquor flask was inspired by the famous quote of Woodrow Wilson's running mate, John Marshall: "What this country needs is a good five-cent cigar." (Close—but no cigar!)

- Some stories of attribution have happier endings. A few years ago, collector Bruce DeMay of Keene, New Hampshire, bought at auction a 19th-century wooden mantel clock with reverse painting on glass of a military figure on horseback. There was no immediate clue as to who the figure might be, and the clock sold rather reasonably despite the presence of a number of political collectors in the audience. After several months of careful research, DeMay found at a flea market an item of ephemera that featured the identical figure and verified it as being General Winfield Scott, Whig candidate for president in 1852! (Other clocks of this type are known, with reverse paintings on glass of William Henry Harrison and Zachary Taylor, and are valued in the $1,000-plus range.)

So take heart. By learning as much as you possibly can about each presidential candidate, you may find a real buy perhaps *because* it's missing an apparent name, date, or other signs of identification. Attribution may come to you in a sudden flash of recognition.

# GLOSSARY

*Acetate*—a clear synthetic filament derived from acetic ester of cellulose, noted for its totally light-reflective surface, typically featured in World War II buttons.

*Albumen*—the first paper photographic print, which by the 1880s had supplanted ferrotypes in presidential portraiture and on lapel devices. Invariably sepia in color.

*Altered*—a pinback, ribbon, or other item recognizable in one form, which may be transformed or "doctored" into still another incarnation, usually surfacing long after the actual campaign.

*Amalgam*—paper or tin celluloid sandwiched together in political shell badges.

*Ambrotype*—positive photo on glass, backed by a dark color, patented in 1843; had its major impact in the 1860s campaigns.

*Back-printing*—messages or company logos printed directly on the reverse of lithographed buttons, designating them as reproductions, in compliance with Hobby Protection Act, PL 19-367. Unscrupulous entrepreneurs, however, have been known to remove back-printing ink with solvents, in an attempt to pass off the items as original. Examples of back-printing include the Kleenex repro series of 1968 and Crackerbarrel series of 1972.

*Bartender's Delight*—pinbacks depicting candidates from rival parties as a token of impartiality. Advertisers were known to produce them, but more commonly, button manufacturers provided them as samples; a 1940 version depicts both Willkie and FDR and is designated as a "Salesman's Safety Pin."

*Browntone*—lighter shade or texture of brown in a photograph or illustration, popular on buttons in the late 19th century, replacing the sepiatone.

*Brummagem* (brum/-i-jem)—alternate form of Birmingham, England, notorious as a hotbed for counterfeit groats, or coins, in 17th-century England. Term has come to apply to any cheaply contrived object having a showy quality; a reproduction and not the genuine article.

16

*Celluloid*—or "cello"; generic term for buttons featuring clear plastic-like layer as protective coating over paper or metal disks; reflects light unevenly. Common button material from 1896 to 1920. *Solid celluloid* buttons are known for Cleveland, Blaine, Hayes, Tilden, and Harrison, although they proved impractical and short-lived.

*Centerpiece*—usually designates an oversize, dynamic pinback, medallion, or paper hanger that stands out in a grouping or special display of political items. The Taft–Bryan "My Hobby" pinbacks are prime examples.

*Clasp-back*—as name implies, a locking catch or clasp that firmly secures pin as an option to the more common spring-wire pin.

*Classic*—political item that clearly qualifies as one that is representative of any given campaign, irrespective of rarity.

*Collet*—the inner metal ring on a pinback that locks the celluloid disk into the paper or metal (the amalgam).

*Curl*—in political button vernacular, the rim or edge, not visible head on, between outer edge of the face and the collet. Union labels, logos, and other identifying marks often appear on the curl.

*Daguerreotype*—the first presidential photographs to appear on lapel devices; introduced in the 1848 campaign of Zachary Taylor and later replaced by ferrotypes. Political photophiles are also known to favor "dags," particularly those mounted in decorative thermoplastic or papier-mâché cases.

*Fantasy*—items not campaign-related or of the period but usually commemorative in nature, for example, a John Fremont celluloid ribbon badge issued by the Republican League in 1906 to celebrate the 50th anniversary of the GOP. While qualifying as originals, fantasies lack the popular appeal of campaign material.

*Jugate* (jü/ gāt)—images of a pair of party candidates, the most common portraying the presidential and vice-presidential entries. Whether on pinbacks, posters, or other campaign items, they are eagerly pursued, as evidenced by prices paid recently for F.D. Roosevelt–Cox, Davis–Bryan, and T. Roosevelt–Johnson jugates.

*Key item*—an elite artifact that ranks in the top 5 percent among collectors in terms of desirability, rarity, and graphic appeal, with major focus on pinbacks.

*Lithograph*—in the hobby the reference is not only to a landslide of prints, posters, broadsides, and flyers but to virtually all political buttons after 1920 that were produced by this printing method. The process was introduced in 1798 and soon supplanted the woodcut; finest political examples are posters and trade cards from the golden age of chromolithography, which peaked in the 1870s.

*Lithopane*—a semitransparent porcelain plaque with incised design or image, appearing in varying thicknesses. When back-lit, there are thick areas that restrict light and thin areas that transmit light, creating an interesting effect. Lithopanes are found as lamp shades and fireplace screens; most commonly they were hung in windows, much the same as stained glass. Lithopanes enjoyed a brief popularity from 1850 to 1870, and examples are known for candidates Henry Clay, Winfield Scott, and Zachary Taylor.

*Litho under glass*—engraved paper portrait of leading candidates, appeared under a glass disk secured by a pewter frame. The first campaign example known is for the 1828 Jackson–Quincy Adams tilt. Early versions featured a small mirror on the reverse with a brass loop atop the frame, suiting it for hanging as a wall plaque. In later versions the vice-presidential running mate replaced the mirror. By the 1848 Taylor–Cass campaign, interest had quickly waned in lithos under glass.

*Multicolor*—term used in hobby to denote *any* full-color item; portraits even included flesh tones.

*Patch box*—novel little container of cardboard and glass resembling a miniature book; so called because it held small cosmetic patches favored by ladies in the first half of the 18th century. Presidential portraits often appeared in the glass lid, although the item was probably commemorative rather than campaign-oriented. Most patch boxes appear to be of French manufacture.

*Pinback*—a blanket term applied to the modern campaign lapel device; features a spring wire pin.

*Planchet*—flat metal disk that takes the engraving or stamping of a design as a lapel device.

*Rebus button*—a favorite among collectors due to clever juxtaposition of pictures and symbols to punch out a slogan or a favorite candidate's name. Among the most coveted rebus buttons in the hobby are the "I Would Row Wilson" (a play on words, as Wilson and running mate Marshall are pictured being rowed in a boat to the White House, towering in the background); also a classic was "Land-On Washington" showing Alf Landon leaning out of an airplane as it soars above the Capitol dome, a 1936 GOP entry.

*Ribbon badge*—a political ribbon to which a medal or pinback is attached or suspended; typical of national convention and presidential inaugural artifacts.

*Shank button*—clothing button with metal loop on the reverse, through which thread is passed to attach to wearer's sleeve or lapel.

*Slogan button*—any pinback that punches out a campaign message. It may simply express the wearer's party or candidate preference, the most succinct and alliterative being "I Like Ike," or espouse a cause or plank in the party platform, for example, Bryan's "Free Silver" rallying cry in 1900.

*Sulfide*—a cameo visualization of a candidate or party symbol set on an enameled surface; enjoyed a vogue in campaign brooches during the Jackson, Van Buren, and William Henry Harrison contests. Although most popular as badges, campaign examples include a paperweight-type doorknob and a perfume bottle. Sulfide playing marbles are known for Teddy Roosevelt, William McKinley, Grover Cleveland, and William Howard Taft.

*Thread box*—probably the first real campaign items to be issued, they originated in the John Quincy Adams–Andrew Jackson campaign of 1824; of cardboard with gilt-paper trim, sides of rainbow-colored paper, and a velvet pincushion mounted atop the lid, they contained a paper engraving of the candidate inside, usually mounted under glass. Extremely uncommon, thread boxes enjoy elevated status among advanced collectors.

*Three-dimensional*—any political artifact having more than two sides, including statuary, toys, figural canes, ceramic and glassware objects.

# HISTORY OF POLITICAL MEMORABILIA COLLECTING

The retention of old political memorabilia, almost a reflex action with countless Americans, probably began as early as 1789 when the first "GW" inaugural button was struck. The actual purposeful collecting of political material in general, or campaign material specifically, has its origins in the late 1860s following the assassination of Abraham Lincoln. Politics, as opposed to baseball and football, was then the national pastime, and commercial lithographers and engravers produced single-sheet political prints that soon lined the walls of Victorian homes. Ironically, it was not until 34 years after Lincoln's death that a retrospective of Lincoln prints was exhibited at New York City's Grolier Club.

A handful of affluent collectors had quietly amassed all manner of Lincolniana by that time, and eventually their vast, priceless collections were donated to the National Archives, the Library of Congress, the Smithsonian, and other leading institutions for all to view and enjoy.

Further stimulation for collecting political memorabilia came much, much later; Robert T. King's *Lincoln in Numismatics,* comprising a listing of over 1,000 medalia issues honoring Lincoln, appeared in February 1924. Two other volumes made an impact on the hobby as we know it today: Bessie M. Lindsey's *American Historical Glass* in 1948 and 1950 (see Bibliography) and J. Doyle DeWitt's *A Century of Campaign Buttons* in 1959.

Large-scale international events, notably the Centennial Exposition in Philadelphia in 1876 and the Columbian Exposition in 1892, played a major role in rekindling our patriotic spirit. Chromolithograph posters, prints, and trade cards appeared; ceramic, glassware, and textile commemorative souvenirs honored our presidents, statesmen, and military heroes of the past and instilled a collecting mania that is with us to this day.

20

In 1945 The American Political Items Collectors, the first organization of its kind, was initiated and was maintained through its first 15 years via the U.S. mail. As U. I. "Chick" Harris, one of the early members and APIC historian relates:

> Monroe D. Ray, then living in Belmont, New York, had been putting on displays of his items at banks and other businesses throughout upstate New York . . . attracted the attention of newspapers and *Hobbies Magazine. Hobbies* then forwarded letters from other political collectors to Monroe, allowing him to develop correspondence with many of them, resulting in APIC, originated by Monroe and named by Joe Fuld of Hailey, Idaho, who was "declared" . . . first president. Other charter members were John W. Barkley (recently deceased), Agnes Gay, Walter Sanders and Louis Foster. John Barkley donated his collection to Cleveland's Case–Western Reserve University. This was the early APIC, held together by a few (15–30) active members who did a lot of corresponding and trading with only infrequent personal contact. Not until 1960 were the first steps taken that directly led to the active, nationally recognized APIC we share today.

Membership in the APIC has grown to over 2,000 and now serves the entire spectrum of political collecting: presidential, local, third-party, woman's suffrage, and cause-type artifacts. This nonprofit organization today includes over 30 local chapters and clubs across the United States.

# HOUSING YOUR COLLECTION

"Finding a home" for your political memorabilia is far more than a figure of speech. These relics from past campaigns assume a very intense personal meaning, and how the material is stored or displayed is limited only by the individual's taste, personality, imagination, or creative flair.

There are two extremes: the collector who transforms his or her home into a museum or shrine, perhaps even losing touch with the real world, and the compulsive accumulator who sequesters his or her collection away in safe deposit boxes, bank vaults, and packing crates.

Our middle-of-the-road credo is that political memorabilia—originally created to excite the eye, stir the soul, and influence voters—were meant to be studied and admired.

The necessity of applying certain constraints is undeniable. There are inherent dangers in risking exposure of artifacts to excessive handling, dust, humidity, and direct sunlight; also, it is obvious that the ever-menacing problem of security must be addressed.

To avoid extended exposure to environmental elements, many collectors wisely rotate their collection, keeping certain items displayed and others carefully packed away and protected.

A preference among many collectors is display cases, which are available through a number of museum and exhibit supply houses. Another, more costly, alternative is to have cases custom-made. (We have long admired the handsome mahogany file display cases in the DeWitt Collection.) Still another possibility is to convert old printer's cases with shallow drawers, originally designed to accommodate type fonts but readily adaptable for buttons, medals, tokens, etc. (Our personal choice is a Lorillard Tobacco cabinet from the 1890s with 20 flat drawers, once used for storing tobacco cut plugs and twists. It's certainly in keeping with the period, our favored "Golden Era.")

For displaying three-dimensional artifacts, resurrected barber or dental cabinets with heavy glass shelves come highly recommended.

22

Deterioration and rapid fading is particularly high with 19th-century pin-backs, ribbons, and other items, with ultraviolet rays posing a real menace. Fluorescent lighting affords less opportunity of fading favorite objects, but purists argue that this type of lighting distorts colors and tones, making it difficult to distinguish certain varations. Low-wattage incandescent mini-shelf lights, arranged in tandem, are a suitable compromise and show off artifacts to great advantage.

Lithographed paper items are especially vulnerable to moisture and other elements, including silverfish and other pests seemingly addicted to glue or paste used as binding agents. They can swiftly be reduced to confetti. Prints, ribbons, trade cards, ballots all benefit when interleaved between acid-free paper or matting and protected by Mylar.

By giving political artifacts the special care and attention they deserve, you are better assured of their being preserved for future generations to enjoy.

# HOW TO DETECT FAKES AND FANTASIES

Copies or reproductions of political memorabilia have been known to exist at least since 1889, the centennial of George Washington's First Inaugural.

Over 90 percent of all bogus material is confined to political buttons. Invariably, they were issued as commemorative items, with no intent to deceive. They tend to surface in special sets as advertising premiums in election years, when recollections of past campaigns intensify.

Primarily, it is the more inexpensive, commonplace button that is reproduced, such as an Adlai Stevenson portrait pin; FDR "Our President," starred portrait litho; a number of Landon Sunflower variations, etc. Most repros are of lithographed tin, although some cello copies have also been issued.

Extreme rarities to date have attracted no known imitators (perhaps because they might invite too close a scrutiny). This hobby, through the auspices of the APIC, has done a thorough job of policing. Led by two prominent APIC members, Senators Barry Goldwater (AZ) and George McGovern (SD), P.L. 93-167, the Hobby Protection Act, was signed in 1973, the final act prior to Richard Nixon's resignation. The law calls for imitations of buttons and other objects of Americana to be clearly marked "Reproduction," or a similar term, in a prominent place on the item itself.

The APIC has been instrumental in setting up its own self-policing mechanism by establishing a Committee on Ethics. One of the best investments any political collector, particularly newcomers to the hobby, can make is to send for the APIC Brummagem Project Report ($6 ppd.) to APIC Mailing Supply Service, P.O. Box 340339, San Antonio, TX 78234.

To describe a complete range of objectionable material, APIC uses "brummagem" as a noun denoting a showy but inferior and worthless thing. Other definitions lend further clarification, as follows:

24

*Reproduction*—similar in many aspects to originally produced item but issued *subsequent* to a campaign for which original was distributed.

*Restrike*—a metallic lapel device such as medalet or token struck from original dies, subsequent to its date of original issue. Restrikes produced since 1900 are universally condemned; earlier medalets (e.g., those restruck in the 1850s), justify a qualification and are treated on an individual basis.

*Fantasy*—an original item, not a copy of a prexisting artifact, giving all appearances of dating back to a specific period or campaign but issued much later. While most fantasies are regarded as intentionally deceptive, examples exist that were merely commemorative, for example, an engaging fantasy badge issued by the National Republican League in 1906 to commemorate the party's 50th anniversary. (This item is collectible in its own right.)

*Repin or Retin*—applies most generally to celluloid buttons that were partially manufactured at the time of the campaign but entailed additional manufacture subsequent to that time. An example: A button supplier, who might already have a supply of original decals, applies (conceivably many years later) a metal ring, backing, and pin to be sold *complete* to the collector's market. This poses a "gray area" because all components *are* original. The APIC Ethics Committee takes a hard line, finding them objectionable, since they were only partially manufactured and not available for the campaign for which they were obviously intended.

*Rerun*—an item completely remanufactured at a date subsequent to the original issue. Also condemned, as its sole purpose is to exploit the collector market.

*Altered*—an artifact recognizable in one form, which may be "doctored" or transformed into another incarnation or state, again subsequent to the campaign in question: making a shell badge out of one half of a Harrison match safe; adding a ribbon and/or bar onto a pinback for which it was not originally intended; gluing manufacturer's papers inside the backs of buttons (usually to cover up some flaw); cutting out small candidate's photos to replace ferrotypes germane to that shell badge, paper hanger, etc.

The following checkoff list is intended to help you avoid fakes and fantasies.

1. Promotional premiums offered by various manufacturers (see pages 212–224 of Edmund Sullivan's *Collecting Political Americana* for detailed descriptions) most often stamp the caveat that said item is a reproduction either on the bottom curl or inside back of button. These IDs can readily be erased, however, by chemicals, filing off, or overpainting. Be alert for strange abrasions or color differences on curls of litho buttons.

2. Look for signs of cover-up with old backpapers, designed to add authenticity or conceal shiny or Venetian backs (so called because same white steel sheets were used in manufacture of Venetian blinds). If in doubt, remove paper. If paper is glued, tampering is almost a certainty. Early manufacturers did not glue in backpapers.

3. New fakes rarely feature old pins. The differences are quite obvious compared to pins made 30, 60, and 80 years ago. Certain recent sets also have other telltale signs: Kleenex buttons are higher domed on the face and usually come with pin-lock back pin. Most usurpers have a wider collar; Proctor & Gamble sets have outer curl of red, white, blue stripes; Liberty Mint sets lack the brightness and sharp contrasts of originals. Images in repros often appear to be out of focus; this is due to a moiré effect (a distortion in dot pattern caused when negative is made from an original halftone photograph). Also, fake buttons often appear in the wrong size or vary considerably in color from originals.

4. Washington Inaugural button repros are usually in silver, lead, or bright white brass; originals are known only on copper, deep yellow brass, and pewter. (See also Sullivan's *American Political Badges and Medalets 1789–1892* for discrepancies in size.)

5. There were no presidential pinback buttons prior to 1896, lithograph or celluloid. (A cello premium set produced by a tobacco company from the early 1900s, depicting presidents from Washington to McKinley, would automatically eliminate all but McKinley as originals.)

6. Almost all celluloid fakes are actually acetate-covered. Acetate was developed in the late 1930s and after a crossover period has been employed rather exclusively since 1952. To determine the difference, use an incandescent light; tilt the pinback so light is reflected off the surface to your eyes. Celluloid has an irregular surface and absorbs light; acetate is almost 100 percent light-reflective.

Fortunately, as mentioned earlier, most other categories of political artifacts, thus far at least, have been bypassed by devious entrepreneurs. There are a few obvious exceptions:

- A number of 1840s Sandwich cup plates have been copied (at least since the 1920s), W. H. Harrison and Henry Clay being most frequently imitated. Fakes are often heavier and lack that pleasant "ping" when lightly tapped at the plate's edge.

- A number of jackknife fantasies with white plastic handles made their flea market debut in the early 1970s. Versions exist for Thurmond and Wright (States Rights Party) 1948; McGovern–Shriver, Nixon–Agnew, and a George Wallace/Confederate flag jackknife dated 1972.

- A pair of cast-iron matchbox figurals depicting 1872 candidates Horace Greeley and U. S. Grant have been reproduced. Telltale signs: busts attached to backplate by wires as opposed to being riveted in original; surface has a grainy rather than a smooth feel. "LB 77/3" is stamped on reverse.

- The most oddball of all three-dimensional fantasies is a 6-inch-high opaque white glass flask with "Keep Cool & Keep Coolidge With Near Beer" inscribed in red and blue. Dave Frent indicated that the item was Japanese-made and first appeared in gift shops in the mid-1970s.

Fewer examples of tampering with campaign posters, ballots and other ephemera exist, as one might have anticipated. But note the following:

- Beware of reproductions of an admission ticket to Andrew Johnson impeachment proceedings; printed in black ink on heavy blue stock, as is the original, it is truly authentic in appearance, belied by "Reproduction, July 1974" printed in tiny letters below the lower margin. If you are offered a Johnson ticket with lower edge trimmed tight to the margin, it is most probably a repro.

- A highly desirable "Workingman's Banner" campaign poster for Ulysses S. Grant and Henry Wilson from the 1872 campaign, featuring the pair as "The Galena Tanner" and "The Natick Shoemaker," has inspired a rash of copies that are unlikely to be discernible without a trained eye. A Van Buren mechanical trade card and a W. H. Harrison song sheet repro were gift shop items at Sturbridge Village Museum in conjunction with a Presidential Exhibition in 1984. The trade card is immediately obvious and would fool no one, but the Harrison song sheet, put in an old frame, may someday pose a challenge to unsuspecting collectors.

As Robert Fratkin and Christopher Hearn point out in a *Keynoter* article, *How to Use the Brummagem Project,* "the most important facet of collecting is also the most important facet in recognizing brummagem: education."

To prepare yourself for any curves fakers might throw at you, the best remedy is to become familiar with as many original artifacts as possible; scrutinize them closely as to how they look and how they are put together. At a certain point this visual and tactile information becomes assimilated, and your sense of whether any given item is "wrong" or "right" becomes almost intuitive.

# BUYING AND SELLING AT AUCTION

## LIVE AUCTIONS

The one and only major cataloged political memorabilia auction, the Don Warner Collection, was held in two sessions: April 4, 1981, in New York City and August 8, 1981, in Carlisle, Pennsylvania, by New England Rare Coins Auctions.

The sale of a Cox–Roosevelt jugate pinback from the 1920 campaign to FDR collector Joe Jacobs for $33,000, a record in the hobby, overshadowed many other significant rarities. Prices realized at the Warner sale are still used as a barometer of value in the hobby to this day. (Note that in our listing of lapel devices, Warner catalog numbers are included.)

Other auctions have been held in recent years that have devoted special sessions to political items. In March 1987 Richard A. Bourne, Hyannisport, Massachusetts, auctioned off a collection of rare buttons from the collection of Mrs. Robert Szmollko of Doylestown, Pennsylvania, and the Just Buttons Museum in Southington, Connecticut, which included George Washington inaugurals as well as a number of ferros and shell badges from the last half of the 19th century. Riba-Mobley of South Glastonbury, Connecticut, devoted well over 100 lots of political items and Lincolniana in their June 1987 auction. They invariably include a special segment of political items in their quarterly outings.

In 1985 G. C. Sloan & Sons, a Washington, D.C., auction gallery sold a Dolley and James Madison cut-glass decanter with presidential seal for $1,100 in a bidding snafu (a $4,350 left bid by White House curator Clement Conger had gone astray). Meanwhile, a *second* decanter has been discovered, which is expected to bring $15,000 to $20,000.

28

In buying at auction, the following suggestions may prove helpful:

Always get to the preview as early as possible so that you can give any entries of interest a thorough inspection, without being rushed or distracted by the crowd. If you have any questions regarding condition or provenance, or wish to have the item put up at a certain time (providing it is not a cataloged sale), you will have time to discuss it with the auction manager.

Be sure to find a seat or a place to stand where you can be readily spotted by the auctioneer. Make positive bidding motions. Some bidders we know go through all manner of method-acting machinations, such as eye twitchings, shoulder tics, and head scratchings, to indicate a bid (as if to disguise their identity from others while bidding). What generally happens is that the auctioneer is the one who misses your bid and you may be "out" a very desirable item.

Try to contain your excitement by taking a few deep breaths between bids, and don't raise your own bid. Most auctioneers are charitable about this, but we do know of a few who will have you up there well beyond what you should be paying. If you are not certain who has the high bid, don't be shy about asking the auctioneer.

This advice is easier to give than to follow, but decide *beforehand* the very maximum you'd be willing to pay, and hold to it.

Above all, don't be intimidated by any bidding "pool" that may be working in the audience. Remember, those involved in the pool are usually dealers who still have to hold their little "side auction" and be able to resell the item at a profit. As long as they are in there bidding with you, in all probability the item remains within the realm of reason.

The consignor's role in an auction is often clouded in mystique, and most auction-goers find it more complex to comprehend than the buyer's role. Usually this is because the seller is the silent partner in the auction process. Once the would-be seller has consigned his property to the auction house, his participation ends. Unless a single item is of significant value, an auction house usually elects not to accept one item, preferring, of course, sizable lots of items. The latter balances things out; an item might go disappointingly low, but the law of averages dictates that other items will correspondingly top off beyond expectations.

Auction houses charge varying rates to consignors and for different services, including transportation, insurance, photography, advertising, and repairs. There is also a seller's commission to be exacted. Rates vary from house to house, according to how the contract is negotiated. You pay the house a 10 to 21 percent fee, depending on whether there is a buyer's premium. There have been, of course, auction houses that have accepted extremely coveted properties without charging a seller's fee.

Before choosing an auction house, it pays to check out their commission arrangement thoroughly. Also, most houses assume complete responsibility as to how the consignments are described in the catalog or advertisements. Be certain to touch bases with your auction house to make sure that the item will be accurately described. Resolve any differences before committing yourself to anything.

To protect your investment, you may also want to discuss selling your consignment subject to reserve. This price is usually determined by the seller and ranges from 50 to 80 percent of the low estimate. On items of higher value, the reserve is usually mid-range between the low and high estimate. If perchance your consignment fails to meet reserves, you still may be money-out-of-pocket. At many big auction houses, the contract stipulates that the consignor authorize the house to act as exclusive agent for 60 days following the auction to sell the property privately for the previously agreed reserve price.

Consignors can expect to be paid, minus seller's commission and set fees, as soon as the buyers have paid *them.* Usually this is 35 days after the gavel falls.

This may sound like an awful headache, considering the negotiating that is required, but there are those who swear by selling at auction as the best way to get their maximum return on investment.

## MAIL AUCTIONS

In terms of ultimate rarities, as well as the best variety of political items available today, the real action seems to be generated by the mail auction folks.

### Bidding in Mail Auctions

Bidding in a mail auction has a lot of little nuances. For one thing it's not like a "live" auction, where you learn in a hurry whether you've won a particular cherished lot. With mail auctions, the suspense may drag out over a period of days, even weeks. You can opt to mail in your bid sheet or wait until the final night deadline and participate in the telephone marathon, or do both. At deadline time you can phone and be told what the current high bid may be and will have the privilege of raising that bid, but it must be raised by an increment of at least 10 percent. Calls are generally accepted up to midnight, but we have been able to make calling bids as late as 2 A.M. on occasion.

The problem is that even if yours is the top bid when you retire to bed that closing night, you may still be preempted by a mail bid that arrives days later. (One cynic calls them Yogi Berra "It's Not Over Till It's Over" auctions.) Mail auction people *do* specify that mail bids be postmarked on or before closing date.

Rex Stark reports that approximately 90 percent of the bidders in his sale bid only by mail. All mail auctioneers reserve the right to reject any or all bids.

*Note:* If you spot an item in one of the mail auction catalogs that you sense is going to attract a lot of bidders, and you really want the item, you can place a ceiling on that item in your bid sheet to enhance your chances.

Most auction houses offer their catalogs by subscription for approximately $5 to $6 a year. See listing of major mail auction and "live" auction houses in the back of this guide.

## Mail Auction Consigning

Commission arrangements with mail auctions are structured similarly to those of major live auction houses. Ted Hake and Rex Stark prefer to buy items outright, as opposed to taking them on consignment. On items that *are* consigned, anticipate a slightly longer delay with mail auctioneers, as there are added steps in notifying winners, receiving *their* checks, and in some cases holding merchandise until checks clear.

# MANUFACTURERS

## BUTTON MANUFACTURERS

Literally hundreds of manufacturers and jobbers have produced political buttons since Whitehead & Hoag took out the first patent in 1894 and began production in 1896. The following comprises some of the major button manufacturers with years in active production. For the most comprehensive listing of button manufacturers and guidelines to identifying by backpapers, consult Ted Hake's and Russ King's *Price Guide to Collectible Pin-Back Buttons, 1896–1986*, published by Hake's Americana and Collectibles Press, P.O. Box 1444, York, PA 17405.

American Art Works, Cochocton, OH: 1904–1981

All Metal Products Co., Springfield, OH (reputed manufacturer)

Baltimore Badge Co., Baltimore, MD

Bastian Bros.,* Rochester, NY: 1895–1983

Bainbridge (Chas.) Button & Badge, Syracuse, NY: 1907–1959

Bainbridge (H.C.), Syracuse, NY: 1961–1985

Geraghty & Co., Chicago, IL: 1909–1944

Greenduck Co., Chicago, IL: 1912–1925

Green Duck Corp., Hernando, MI: 1977–1985

Nodel Bros., New York, NY

Novelty Supply Co., Pittsburgh, PA: 1927–1931

Oppenheimer and Shaw, Washington, DC

Parisian Novelty Co., Chicago, IL: 1905–1985

St. Louis Button Co., St. Louis, MO: 1895–1915

St. Louis Button & Mfg., St. Louis, MO: 1918–1965

*Bastian Bros. purchased Whitehead & Hoag in the late 1950s.

32

Schwaab, S & S Co., Milwaukee, WI: 1938–1968
Scovill Mfg. Co., Waterbury, CT: 1850–1985
Western Button & Badge, Los Angeles, CA: 1915–1961
Waterbury Button Works, Waterbury, CT: 1944–1985
Whitehead & Hoag, Newark, NJ: 1894–1958

# TEN WAYS TO GAIN GREATER SATISFACTION FROM COLLECTING POLITICAL MEMORABILIA

1. Many collectors in the hobby tend to gravitate to a category that somehow relates to their own realm of experience, or to a leader they particularly admire. In many instances, specialization is an extension of one's trade or profession. This writer, for example, has been in the advertising/graphics arts business for over 25 years. Advertising and packaging that feature presidents as pitchmen hold a particular fascination. We even know one collector whose specialty is TR, who even *looks* like Teddy Roosevelt. While it may sound simplistic, it is essential, and a lot more fun, to collect what *you* like and not what is considered trendy. Make certain that the category you choose encompasses items that are within your financial grasp and buy the best you can afford. Many beginners make the mistake of collecting anything and everything and quickly become discouraged. At a recent national show, Richard Maxson, a fellow dealer/collector, was approached by a leading corporation executive who wanted to put in his order for "one of each for every campaign from Washington to Reagan!"

2. Sharpen your visual and tactile skills. Visit as many museums and private collections as possible. Just recently, we were privileged to view the fabled J. Doyle DeWitt Collection, as its curator, Dr. Edmund Sullivan, gave us a guided tour. We came away charged with a far deeper appreciation of the vastness, the variety, and the visceral appeal of political treasures.

34

A fascinating spinoff, pursued by many
ephemerists, is advertisements and display
cards that promote political items.

3. Do your homework. Surround yourself with as many political books, reference guides, trade catalogs, auction listings, newspaper clippings, and photographs as possible, and don't let this material gather dust in your files and library shelves. Consult your sources frequently; these refresher courses will come in handy sooner and more often than you think.

4. Get to know your fellow collectors. An organization such as the American Political Items Collectors (APIC) sponsors research projects and has established a free loan audiovisual library for members' use. In addition, you're afforded the opportunity to attend or exhibit at regional and national meetings or bourses where intensive buying, selling, and swapping is assured. In policing its own hobby, the APIC periodically lists fakes and restrikes that inevitably appear on the market through a quarterly publication, *The Keynoter.*

Most important is the interfacing with others who are possessed with the same unbounded enthusiasm for political collecting as you are. What's more, you'll be exposed to more quality political artifacts than you are likely to come across in a lifetime of searching. The most important reason to collect may not be intrinsic to the political items themselves but to the interesting people you meet, the friendships you strike up with those whose paths you might never had crossed were it not for sharing of this special interest.

5. Expect the unexpected. Political relics often turn up in the most unlikely places, as in the following examples:

   - A Hartford, Connecticut, policeman was directing traffic recently when a construction crew putting in a new traffic signal standard inadvertently uncovered an old dumping site. What appeared to be a 50-cent piece rolled across the pavement to the policeman's feet. It turned out to be a previously unknown, unlisted George Washington Inaugural button.

   - This writer had been checking out a local group shop center for over ten years without finding anything more exciting than a Willkie slogan button. Then one day, tucked away in the corner of a display case, a Henry Clay carved wooden cane head was discovered.

   - Bruce DeMay of Keene, New Hampshire, tells about the time he attended an area Antiques Benefit Show. A dealer in colonial lighting fixtures had a rather battered figural campaign torch on one of her tables, but her price seemed way out of line. DeMay checked out a number of other exhibits, then headed back to see if the lady would dicker on the price. Somebody apparently had beat him to it. DeMay sidled up to listen in on the bargaining repartee and, in order to appear inconspicuous, pretended to be examining a Revere-type pierced lantern from the display. "That's signed," the lady dealer remarked to Bruce as an aside, just as he was unlatching the lantern door, and the light shone through the pierced letters C-L-A-Y. This time the price was right!

   - A Martin Van Buren campaign ribbon was picked up at a local flea market by Frank Corbeil of Unionville, Connecticut, for $15 a few years ago. It recently fetched $2,400 at a Mobley-Riba auction.

6. Despite all of the how-to articles and books that talk of "collecting for fun and profit," approaching political rarities as blue-chip investments has its perils. Ten years ago Merrill Lynch, Shearson Hayden Stone and other Wall Street brokers considered investment programs in the fields of rare coins, Chinese ceramics, and oil paintings. Investors soon found less secu-

rity than in securities, and the bottom dropped out of the coin market. A handful of our peers, obviously, have shown they can make a comfortable living auctioning and dealing in political items, but admittedly, the business is not for dabblers.

Even if your interest in the hobby is purely therapeutic, it still pays to have a thorough understanding of the value of the political treasures you own. Many collectors keep a complete inventory of memorabilia on file cards or computer disk and maintain a photographic record of each item.

Building up a collection with one eye on aesthetic appeal and the other on investment quality is a middle-of-the-road approach that appeals to those moderates in our ranks. Many observers still feel that the often overlooked $7/8$-inch pinbacks from the Golden Era are still priced modestly enough to make the plunge. We know of one fellow collector who concentrates exclusively on TR–Johnson jugates from the 1912 race. If he eventually collects all 23 known designs, he will have a tidy little nest egg indeed.

7. Take a conservative approach to new issues of campaign material.

   As election years approach, the question is invariably posed: how one determines what the rare and potentially valuable pieces might be for this and future campaigns. Dealer/collector Dave Frent states:

   > Track records from '72, '76, '80, and '84 show an election fever buying panic which breaks sharply six months or so following the election. Interest diminishes (as does the price) for the next two years until a realistic level is reached. Some of the "hot" McGoverns and '76 Carters originally went from 5–10 times what they sell for today. Personally, I wait until eight or nine months after an election before focusing on what I want for my collection. I see a better selection, and my dollar goes further. We all collect history, so let's use it to avoid the pitfalls of the past.

8. It is always important to sit back occasionally and determine what direction your collection is to take and what limitations need to be set. It's like the old Yogi Berra quote, "If you don't know where you're going, you'll wind up somewhere else." Avoid whenever possible the so-called real "buys"—the badly foxed cello, the tattered ribbon; remember that in most cases this deterioration is irreversible. Examine each speciman carefully and determine what you *don't* like about it—the little things that may detract from its presentation should you wish to resell the item. Don't let the fact that you may have gone through a recent "dry spell" influence your decision.

9. Resign yourself to the prospect that sooner or later you will make errors of judgment. Take heart; mistakes often pay for themselves if they remain indelibly etched on your mind. This can only heighten your perception in future transactions and keep you humble.

10. Be patient. The FDR dynasty wasn't built in a day, and the same holds true for your collection. Learn as much as you can, keep your eyes open, and above all have fun. That's really what it's all about.

# CAMPAIGN BY CAMPAIGN,
## 1789–1984

The American presidential campaign has been called a quadrennial carnival of buncombe, an incredible national popularity contest. Harry Truman termed it "our four-yearly spasm."

To "hit the campaign trail" with the leading candidates and the memorabilia that best typify their ability to win over voters, here is a brief synopsis—from George Washington to Ronald Reagan.

# THE WINNERS AND LOSERS

The following listing is intended as a guide to help you associate or identify each presidential and vice-presidential candidate with their appropriate campaigns, appearing chronologically from 1789 through 1984. We have further added what we consider to be the key pieces—the classics that represent each of the 50 (or 51 if you count the 1861 Confederate States of America candidacy) campaigns waged between 1789 and 1984.

Although we basically have a two-party system, there have been any number of parties over the years who have received electoral votes. They include the following:

A—American Party  
AF—Anti-Federalist  
AM—Anti-Masonic  
CU—Constitution Party  
D—Democratic Party  
DN—Democratic Northern  
DR—Democratic Republican  
DS—Southern Democratic  
F—Federalist  
G—Greenback Party  

I—Independent  
ID—Independent Democratic  
NR—National Republican  
P—Populist  
PG—Progressive  
PR—Prohibition  
R—Republican Party  
STR—States Rights Party  
W—Whig Party  

## FIRST ELECTION—1789

*President:* George Washington  
*Vice President:* John Adams  
*Uncontested*

George Washington was a unanimous choice of the first Electoral College, which convened February 4, 1789, garnering all 69 votes. There was no competition, therefore no campaigning, no oratory, and no rush to the polls by

41

the populace of our fledgling nation. It was never to be like this again. John Adams, however, as vice president, received no such vote of confidence. Adams tallied only 34 votes by the College, although it may have been that some electors supported another candidate so that Adams could not possibly upstage The Father of Our Country.

Purist collectors who seek only campaign-related relics must compromise in the case of Washington. As some consolation, there are a number of inaugural clothing buttons, brooches, cuff links, and medalets associated with his two-term presidency; but the vast proportion of Washington items are memorial or commemorative in nature.

Standout inaugurals: Among the 27 to 30 varieties (depending on which authority you talk to), the best known is the linked state within a wreath of incised circles, the "G.W." monogram in a depressed center encircled by "Long Live the President" ($650–$750).

One of the more graphically stunning examples is the spread-eagle button inscribed, "March the Fourth/1789/Memorable Era ($700–$800.) Most uncommon is the bust-of-Washington inaugural, or the spread eagle with an added sunburst above—both of which rate in rarefied ($1,000 plus) company.

Battersea curtain tiebacks of the period, showing bust caricatures of General Washington, find ready buyers ($700–$800) on those rare occasions when they surface. There is simply not enough great material relating to our founding fathers to go around.

George Washington miniature on ivory, ca. 1796, signed W. B., presented by Washington to Abiel Foster; sold for $3,850 at Winter Gallery in 1983.

## SECOND ELECTION—1792

*President:* George Washington (F)*
*Vice President:* John Adams

Although alarmed by the rift between his Secretary of State, Thomas Jefferson, and Secretary of the Treasury, Alexander Hamilton, and longing for retirement, Washington was nevertheless coaxed to run again, and again he was a unanimous choice. Adams, his running mate came in a poor second, as there was a lot of support for Governor George Clinton of New York.

Unaccountably a medal struck for the second Washington Inaugural, showing a bust of the first president, has increased tenfold in value over the past ten years. Rated at $175 in *Hake's Political Buttons Book III* (1978 edition), a 1984 updating by a panel of experts appraised it at $1,200. All Washington artifacts are uncommon, and the competition for such items comes from museums as well as collectors.

## THIRD ELECTION—1796

*President:* John Adams (F)
*Vice President:* Thomas Jefferson (DR)

*Defeated candidates:*
Thomas Pickney (F)
Aaron Burr (DR)

The first true presidential campaign in American history proved to be a raucous shouting match. "On both sides, handbills, pamphlets, and articles in party newspapers denounced, disparaged, damned, decried, denigrated and declaimed," wrote Paul F. Boller, Jr., in *Presidential Campaigns.* Republicans harped on Adams's lack of faith in the people and preference for high-toned government. Federalists cited Jefferson's sympathy with the French Revolution and claimed he was the tool of a foreign power. Adams edged out Jefferson by a slim three-vote margin, 71 to 68. Presidential electors were chosen by legislatures in some states and by popular vote in others. This marks the only term of office in which president and vice president were of opposing parties, with Jefferson, as runner-up, occupying the second slot.

If anything, Adams artifacts are even more difficult to come by than those honoring George Washington. From the period is a small English token of Thomas Paine (at that time a refugee from the United States living in France) hanging from a gallows ($100–$125). A possibly unique leather bridle rosette

*Federalist Party—please note code above.

inscribed "John Adams M. 4. 1797," used on a horse that pulled Adams's inaugural carriage, has been priced as high as $1,500 but could probably write its own ticket.

An engraved portrait of John Adams in a two-piece frame under glass (see *Litho under glass* in *Glossary*) exists ($500–$600), as does a pair of cuff links with Adams's bust incised along with JO ADAMS ($600–$700). Both are probably memorial items issued some years following his death in 1826.

What may well aspire as the prime piece of Adamsiana is a slate-blue and white rose jar with black transfers of John Adams and James Monroe and the tender sentiment: "Kindly take this Gift of Mine,/Full of Love for Thee and Thine," ca. 1798–1799 ($800–$900.) Little 2½-inch-high ceramic picture mugs, with his image and name on one and an eagle and floral border surrounding "ADAMS" on the other, rate in the $1,000-plus and $750–$800 range, respectively; although again, they were probably memorial items. A very uncommon ($1,000-plus) Liverpool creamware jug in blue enamel with black-and-white checked borders shows a gilded bust portrait of Adams on the obverse and the warship *Orono* on the reverse.

## FOURTH ELECTION—1800

*President:* Thomas Jefferson (DR)
*Vice President:* Aaron Burr (DR)

*Defeated candidates:*
John Adams (F)
John Jay (F)
Charles Pickney (F)

Adams's defeat at the hands of his vice president, Jefferson, was attributed as much to the disruption within his own party (the high Federalists, or Hamiltonians, had disowned him) as to Republican opposition. Adams's presidency was an unpopular one, and major issues were his sponsorship of the Alien and Sedition Acts in 1798 and his appeasement tactics with France following the disgraceful "XYZ Affair." Final tally was 73 for Jefferson, 73 for Burr, and 65 for Adams. The deadlock was settled in the House of Representatives, with Jefferson squeaking by as victor amid much controversy. Just as Jeffersonians had jeered Adams as "President by three votes" in 1896, Federalists retaliated with "President by no votes" in 1800. Nonetheless, the 1800 contest proved there could be a peaceful exchange of parties without shaking the foundations of the new republic.

Leading off the Jefferson trinkets was an inaugural medalet picturing a bust of the third president. John Matthias Reich is said to have engraved this medalet as a model for a number of later Jefferson medals ($1,000 plus). Also in this rarefied range were a Liverpool pitcher with bust figure of Jefferson surrounded by laurel wreath; creamware tankards by Liverpool with similar bust figure transfer pictures ($1,500–$2,000).

Probably the ultimate prize from the Jefferson era is a flag banner with the third president's portrait topped by a winged eagle ($4,000 plus). As evidence that coveted Jefferson artifacts tend to exceed one's financial grasp, an autographed letter, penned prior to his becoming president, was gaveled down for $17,600 at a Riba-Mobley auction several years ago.

## FIFTH ELECTION—1804

*President:* Thomas Jefferson (DR)
*Vice President:* George Clinton (DR)

*Defeated candidates:*
Charles Pinckney (F)
Rufus King (F)

Peace, prosperity, reduction in national debt, and the stupendous Louisiana Purchase of 1803 made Jefferson unbeatable.

## SIXTH ELECTION—1808

*President:* James Madison (DR)
*Vice President:* George Clinton

*Defeated candidates:*
Charles Pinckney (F)

When the Royal Navy attacked an American vessel, the *Chesapeake,* off the American coast in 1807, Jefferson resorted to peaceable coercion with the Great Embargo that cut off trade with England and France. The unpopular act, which Federalists called the "Dambargo," was a major campaign issue, and Pinckney and King again were defeated. Again, as with all of the Founding Fathers, campaign artifacts are scarce indeed. A Liverpool creamer with black transfer portrait of Madison is valued at over $2,000; a Scottish chintz with a medallion portrait of Madison, at $1,100–$1,200. Lapel devices had not as yet been developed by the time of Madison's administration.

## SEVENTH ELECTION—1812

*President:* James Madison (DR)
*Vice President:* Elbridge Gerry (DR)

*Defeated candidates:*
DeWitt Clinton*
Jared Ingersoll

The central issue was the War of 1812, "Mr. Madison's War." No president has ever failed of reelection in wartime; and he won comfortably, 128 votes to Clinton's 89. Madison is pictured on numerous bandannas commemorating the War of 1812. An 1815 bandanna, "A Geographical View Of All The Post Towns," bears medallion likenesses of Madison and his three predecessors ($1,200–$1,300).

## EIGHTH ELECTION—1816

*President:* James Monroe (DR)
*Vice President:* Daniel Tompkins (DR)

*Defeated candidates:*
No real presidential campaign, although Rufus King was backed by some Federalists.

The War of 1812, the sponsorship of a national bank by Madison, and higher duties on imports to protect America's industries all boded well for the Republicans and heir-apparent James Monroe, who swamped Rufus King 183 to 34 and sounded the death knell for the Federalists.

One of a set of English gaming tokens inscribed "Munro" *(sic)* with displayed eagle and olive branches is one of a few items of remembrance for the 1816 campaign ($1,000 plus). A Monroe bust-portrait ceramic mug, only 2½ inches high, is the most prized of a number of Monroe ceramic items ($2,100–$2,200).

---

*Ran as Clintonians, a coalition of Republicans and Federalists.

## NINTH ELECTION—1820

*President:* James Monroe (DR)
*Vice President:* Daniel Tompkins

*Uncontested*

James Monroe, now 62, won perhaps the most lopsided election in history, with 231 of 232 electoral votes. William Plumer, a former New Hampshire senator and governor, cast a single vote for Secretary of State John Quincy Adams. A Vieux Paris porcelain demitasse cup picturing Monroe is a cherished commemorative item ($1,000 plus)

## TENTH ELECTION—1824

*President:* John Quincy Adams (NR)
*Vice President:* John Calhoun

*Defeated candidates:*
Andrew Jackson (D)
Henry Clay (DR)
William H. Crawford (DR)

In a close election, in which the Senate and House in joint session announced that no candidate had received a majority for first place, Adams was declared winner by only one ballot. Jacksonians were infuriated, as they felt that Adams and Henry Clay had struck a corrupt bargain, and Clay tilted the House vote. Adams appointed Clay as Secretary of State. Jackson soon resigned from the Senate; in 1825 he began campaigning toward 1828 in his quest for vindication.

John Q. Adams collectors have a little more variety in their choice of artifacts, with the recent discovery of a papier-mâché portrait snuffbox; the first known example of lithographs under glass disks in plain pewter frame; and at least four varieties of whimsical stenciled-slogan thread boxes—all of which command four-figure prices.

## ELEVENTH ELECTION—1828

*President:* Andrew Jackson (D)
*Vice President:* John C. Calhoun

*Defeated candidates:*
John Quincy Adams (NR)
Benjamin Rush (NR)

Jackson supporters saw the 1828 fray as a struggle "between the democracy of the country on one hand, and a lordly purse-proud aristocracy on the other." Both parties agreed that henceforth there would be more popular participation in American politics. Over three times as many voters went to the polls than in 1824. Jackson bested J. Q. Adams by 178 electoral votes to 83.

Many ribbons and bandannas from 1828 picture Andrew Jackson's victory at New Orleans, the final crucial battle ending the War of 1812. A favorite is "The Gallant Gen'l Jackson Animating His Troops," a brown and white bandanna also depicting vignettes of War of 1812 naval battles ($1,200–$1,300). A lithograph under glass in pewter frame, matching the J. Q. Adams version mentioned earlier, shows Jackson with flowing mane and coat collar up and wide open ($1,150–$1,200). Other popular campaign items include an "Old Hickory Forever" thread box, and a "Gen. Andrew Jackson" trinket box, both imported from France and in the $1,000 range. Adams forces sought to discredit Jackson's military background with "Bloody Deeds of Gen. Jackson," an anti-Jackson broadside showing coffin silhouettes representing six militiamen "murdered by Jackson for desertion" ($425–$450). A superb bronze statue of a very youthful Andrew Jackson sold for over $800 at a Riba-Mobley auction in 1987. Lusterware pitchers with "Gen. Jackson at New Orleans" themes are as scarce as they are beautiful ($1,500 plus).

## TWELFTH ELECTION—1832

*President:* Andrew Jackson (D)
*Vice President:* Martin Van Buren

*Defeated candidates:*
Henry Clay (DR) and John Sargeant
William Wirt (AM) and Amos Ellmaker
John Floyd (D) and Henry Lee

For the first time in American history, a president took a strong stand on a social issue (his veto of a bill rechartering the Second Bank of the United States) and then asked the approval of the voters at the polls. Old Hickory believed that specie (gold or silver), not paper money, should be the standard medium of exchange. "No Bank! Down With The Rag Money" was a typical Jackson campaign slogan in 1832. Jackson triumphed over Clay, 219 electoral votes to 49. Wirt, the first third-party candidate (Anti-Masonic), won 7 percent of the votes.

A classic anti-Jackson broadside—"King Andrew The First/Born To Command/Shall He Reign Over Us, Or Shall The People Rule"—typifies the campaign strategy of Clay forces in 1832 ($600–$650). A "National Currency Revenue and Protection" flag banner with Clay portrait in red, white, and blue clearly states the National Republicans' platform ($1,500 plus).

## THIRTEENTH ELECTION—1836

*President:* Martin Van Buren (D)
*Vice President:* Richard Johnson

*Defeated candidates:*
William Henry Harrison (W) and Francis Granger
Hugh White (W), Daniel Webster (W), Willie Mangum (I)

Jackson's firm stand against South Carolina's bid to nullify the tariff laws alienated Southern states-righters. The National Republicans were still smarting over his war against the banks and high tariffs. Southerners distrusted Jackson's choice for nominee in 1836, dismissing him as a slick New Yorker. The Whigs, meanwhile, were too disorganized even to hold a national convention and eventually placed three favorite sons from various sections of the country on the ticket. W. H. Harrison, the strongest of the three Whigs, pulled 73 of the 124 electoral votes for the losers, while Van Buren was victorious with 170 votes.

A nice piece of ephemera is a Van Buren–King Democratic election ballot from 1836 ($65–$75), and the sucessful nominee is portrayed impeccably attired on a papier-mâché snuff box ($850–$900). A satirical cartoon, "Political Race Course," depicts W. H. Harrison as a horse with human face leading the 1836 contenders ($250–$300).

## FOURTEENTH ELECTION—1840

*President:* William H. Harrison (W)
*Vice President:* John Tyler

*Defeated candidates:*
Martin Van Buren (D)
Ricard Johnson
James G. Birney (L)*

Harrison's "Tippecanoe and Tyler Too" campaign set a new style of Presidential image-building that remains a practical model even today. For the first time, the masses were treated to barbecues, rallies, songfests, and parades. All manner of ribbon badges, walking sticks, kerchiefs, and broadsides reshaped Harrison's personna while portraying incumbent Van Buren as an effete, high-falutin' Easterner. When the Whigs passed over Henry Clay for Harrison at the party's national convention in 1839, an offhand slur by a Clay supporter was transformed into a slogan that established Harrison as the "log-cabin-hard-cider candidate." The Whigs popularized the expression "keep the ball rolling" as they actually rolled huge Harrison balls, ten or twelve feet in diameter, down streets and from town to town chanting "Van is a used-up man. We'll beat you, little Van!" Harrison edged Van Buren by a narrow margin in the popular vote, but his electoral triumph was overwhelming, with 234 votes to 60. A month after the inauguration Harrison died of pneumonia, and John Tyler became the first "accidental" president.

Harrison Log Cabin sulfides abound, with one lone Van Buren counterpart, "The Temple Of Liberty"; three portrait varieties are known for each candidate, and one of the Van Burens features an unusual blue background. They run the gamut from $400 to $1,700!

A "Martin Van Buren And The Independent Treasury/No Property Qualification And No White Slavery" campaign ribbon and a hand-embroidered apron championing "Van Buren, The Warm And Zealous Advocate Of The People's Rights" range from $900–$1,000 and $450–$500, respectively.

Among the favorite Harrison three-dimensional treasures is a "Cider Extra" 7-inch-high wooden keg, holed for a stick to carry in a political parade ($700–$750). Another item that had its heyday in the 1840s was the Sandwich glass cup plate. As many as 14 Log Cabin varieties exist and two Harrison portrait designs; all are still fairly common and sell at $60–$70. Two seldom seen artifacts are the "North Bend" cabin mantel clock, reverse painting on glass ($1,600–$1,700), and a folk art–type yellow, green, and brown hairbrush with black-and-white Harrison portrait ($900–$1,000). A prized advertising

---

*Liberty Party, a tiny antislavery party, a forerunner of the Free Soil Party of the 1840s and the Republican Party of the 1850s.

novelty is the Old Cabin Whiskey figural bottle put out by Philadelphia distiller E. C. Booz, thus introducing "booze" as a synonym for whiskey into the lexicon.

John Tyler relics pose a real challenge as they verge on being non-existent: a single flask probably harks back to his days as a U.S. senator from Virginia ($500–$600); a presidential ribbon ca. 1841 ($1,000–$1,200) and a snuffbox of comparable value.

## FIFTEENTH ELECTION—1844

*President:* James K. Polk (D)
*Vice President:* George Dallas

*Defeated candidates:*
Henry Clay (W) and Theodore Frelinghuysen
James G. Birney (L)

In 1844, for the first time, the key campaign issue was territorial expansion. Reannexation of Texas, originally part of the Louisiana Territory, could mean war with Mexico; it met with considerable Northern opposition because it entailed adding a sizable slave territory. The Democrats shrewdly linked Texas with Oregon as a national versus sectional expansionist objective, claiming all of Oregon up to Alaska's southern boundary and inspiring the stirring slogan "Fifty-four Forty or Fight!" Polk took 170 electoral votes to Clay's 105, and many blamed the Whig defeat on James Birney and the Liberty Party, who siphoned off votes that might have gone to Clay.

A Polk–Dallas jugate ribbon showing the Lone Star of Texas and the slogan "Alone But Not Deserted" best exemplifies the Democrats' stand on expansion ($800–$850). A rather crude woodblock Polk–Dallas ribbon, "Oregon, Texas And Democracy" now commands four figures. A possibly unique gem from the Abby Rockefeller Folk Art Collection is a large, brightly colored, painted banner with Polk–Dallas ovals sheltered by an eagle's outspread wings, which appears to have been copied by an untutored artist from a Currier print. Not all Polk treasures require an unlimited bank account. A nice little Polk–Dallas songster by Turner & Fisher sells for less than $100. Clay is represented by a real treasure trove of arcana: reverse painting of Clay on mantel clock front ($1,600–$1,700); bas-relief portrait ivory cane head ($900–$1,000); several full-color, painted-leather cigar cases ($1,000–$1,100 each); "Clear The Way For Old Kentucky. I'm That Same Old Coon" (cartoon poster of a sly raccoon sitting on a fence rail), which proved prophetic as Clay straddled the slavery issue ($650–$700). A Clay–Frelinghuysen flag banner proved to be a stunner at a Riba-Mobley auction last year when it topped $3,500.

## SIXTEENTH ELECTION—1848

*President:* Zachary Taylor (W)
*Vice President:* Millard Fillmore

*Defeated candidates:*
Lewis Cass (D) and William Butler
Martin Van Buren and Charles Francis Adams (Free Soil Party)

"Old Zack" Taylor boasted far better military credentials than did "Old Tippecanoe," but only a skilled orator such as Abraham Lincoln, then in the House of Representatives, could make a virtue out of Taylor's vagueness on issues. By 1848 the subject of slavery was clearly a ticking time bomb. Lewis Cass advocated "squatter sovereignty," the right of federal territory settlers to decide the slavery question for themselves. Taylor was opposed to the expansion of slavery in the West. The Whigs proved victorious, 163 to 127. Van Buren and his Free Soil Party did surprisingly well with approximately 10 percent of the total and probably took enough antislavery votes away from Cass (especially outside New York) to assure his defeat.

General Taylor's prowess in the Mexican War was played up heavily in the 1848 race. A colorful ribbon of Taylor on horseback, and the slogans "A Little More Grape, Capt. Bragg" and "General Taylor Never Surrenders" embossed on an amber flask, both rate at $650 to $700.

More like a magnificently carved piece of sculpture than a parlor stove, a cast-iron heater bears a bas-relief likeness of Old Rough & Ready ($4,000 plus). Many regard "Gen. Z. Taylor Rough & Ready/Palo Alto" as the most stunning of all campaign bandannas. The red, white, blue, and brown textile with Old Glory as focal point and Taylor and other military heroes in cameo portraits ranks in the $1,100–$1,200 range. Taking the prize for the most unflattering of all campaign portraits—a lithograph under glass of Lewis Cass with pewter frame (running mate William O. Butler appears on the reverse)—may run as high as $2,200 to $2,300. Another elusive Cass item (aren't they all?) is a small brass shell with profile portrait ($600–$625).

Zachary Taylor served only a year in office before being fatally stricken with gastroenteritis and was succeeded by Vice-President Millard Fillmore. One of the few treasures from Fillmore's presidency is a 2½-inch silver Indian Peace Medal dated 1850 ($3,000 plus).

## SEVENTEENTH ELECTION—1852

*President:* Franklin Pierce (D)
*Vice President:* William King

*Defeated candidates:*
Winfield Scott (W) and William Graham
John P. Hale

"Dark horse" Franklin Pierce supported the Compromise of 1850, with its notorious Fugitive Slave Act, more forthrightly than his opponent, citizen-soldier Winfield Scott did, and voters decisively settled the matter with Pierce the victor, 254 electoral votes to 42. "We Polked 'em in '44" went a popular Democratic slogan; "We'll Pierce 'em in '52."

Pierce's campaign is distinguished by several outstanding ribbons: a 6½-inch jugate version of Pierce and King with facsimile signatures ($2,000 plus) and "We Honor the Citizen and Soldier General Franklin Pierce" portrait ribbon ($1,200–$1,500). A Pierce pennant medallion with embossed full torso image shows the nominee brandishing a rolled-up document ($800–$850). "Old Fuss 'n' Feathers" Scott, enamored of fancy uniforms, strikes a classic pose holding the reins of a prancing steed in a prized red, white, and brown cotton bandanna ($1,000–$1,100). A brass match safe portrays Scott in profile wearing a cockade hat ($650–$700), and the grizzled Mexican War hero seems out of place on a 5-inch-diameter ABC plate ($200–$250).

## EIGHTEENTH ELECTION—1856

*President:* James Buchanan (D)
*Vice President:* John C. Breckinridge

*Defeated candidates:*
John C. Fremont (R) and William Dayton
Millard Fillmore (A) and Andrew Donelson

The Kansas-Nebraska Act of 1854 and a bloody civil war in Kansas between free-soilers and proslavery settlers precipitated the breakup of the two major parties in this pivotal campaign. On February 28, 1854, the Republican Party as we know it today was born. The first major sectional party (it had no Southern support), the Republicans pledged to oppose further extension of slavery and protested the Kansas-Nebraska Act. The Democrats took the opposite position and vowed to resist all attempts at renewing, in Congress or out of it, the agitation of the slavery question. Another party, the "Know-Nothings," which grew out of a secret society organized in New York in 1849, directed its prejudices against aliens, particularly Irish immigrants, and was anti-Catholic as well. The "Know-Nothings" were weakened by defections to the Republican Party at their national convention in 1855 but succeeded in nominating ex-president Millard Fillmore and Andrew J. Donelson to run under a new banner, The American Party. John Fremont, "The Pathfinder," a popular hero and explorer of the Far West, was the Republican frontrunner, and his name was in sync with the party slogan, "Free Soil, Free Speech, Free Men, Fremont." James Buchanan, the Democratic nominee, was deemed the least objectionable choice, being far less controversial than Franklin Pierce and Stephen A. Douglas. Buchanan pulled 174 electoral votes versus 114 for Fremont, and the ominous part was that all but a handful of the Republican votes came from non-slave-holding states. Fillmore won 25 percent of the popular vote but carried only one state, Maryland, with eight electoral votes.

One of the most graphically appealing banners from the 1856 race is an anti-Buchanan "Buck & Breck/Border Ruffian/Democracy & Slavery," which shows a chained black slave astride a lamb ($2,000 plus). Another stunning Buchanan relic is a huge broadside with oval portraits of Buchanan and Breckinridge flanking George Washington, topped by a large eagle and Miss Liberty; small vignettes border the entire broadside, which lists a full slate of Democratic office seekers ($1,350–$1,400). There is also an unusual tiny brass pillbox with embossed Buchanan portrait ($300–$325). A rebus uniface brass shell showing a deer (as in Buck) and a cannon barrel (as in Cannon) rates as one of the most desirable mid-19th-century campaign pieces ($500–$550).

Two ribbons personify the Fremont candidacy: a black on pale mint green Fremont portrait ribbon (with name misspelled "Jonn") and the previously mentioned "Free Soil, Free Speech ..." slogan ($225–$250); and the "Fremont–Dayton Black Republican," illustrating a runaway slave and skull and crossbones ($800–$825). A fitting centerpiece item for the American Party entry is a Fillmore–Donelson paper badge in red, white, blue, and black, 3½ inches in diameter ($400–$450). A parade lantern, with "Fillmore–Donelson" in pierced letters on the door, is a three-dimensional standout ($1,400–$1,500).

"Lost Cause" poster with large Confederate flag as a focal point; cameo portraits of R. E Lee, CSA President Jefferson Davis, and Stonewall Jackson, with Confederate money and novel border; black and white ($250–$275). *(Photo courtesy of Riba-Mobley)*

## NINETEENTH ELECTION—1860

*President:* Abraham Lincoln (R)
*Vice President:* Hannibal Hamlin

*Defeated candidates:*
Stephen Douglas (DN) and Herschell Johnson
John C. Breckinridge (DS) and Joseph Lane
John Bell (CU) and Edward Everett

*Confederate States of America:* 1861
Jefferson Davis and Alexander Stephens

The Dred Scott decision by the Supreme Court in 1857, ruling that slavery was legal in all territories, angered Republicans, split the Democratic party asunder, and further fueled the heat of sectional tensions. The Democrats' northern wing was headed by Stephen Douglas, who refused to endorse a pro-slavery platform. The southern wing walked out of the convention and later nominated John C. Breckinridge, with the support of former presidents Buchanan, Tyler, and Pierce. Republicans chose Abraham Lincoln, who had a strong appeal for the plain people of the West and who came from Illinois, a pivotal state for the party to carry. William Seward of New York was also a contender, but Lincoln prevailed on the third ballot. The Constitutional Party, with the preservation of the Union their one fervent concern, chose former House Speaker John Bell.

There are matching ferrotype tokens for all four candidates—Lincoln, who outpulled the other three candidates combined, with 180 electoral votes; Douglas, 12; Breckinridge, 72; Bell, 39. Running mates appeared on the reverse of the tokens, which were pierced for hanging ($275–$300 each). One of the truly impressive artifacts from the Douglas candidacy is a large flag banner in red, white, blue, and black with "The Little Giant's" portrait within a starred shield. "Vice President/Herschel V. Johnson" is also imprinted along one of the horizontal stripes ($2,500–$3,000). A jugate John Bell–Edward Everett uniface ferrotype (Hake 3008; Warner 99) brass shell with "Steele–Johnson, 1860, Star, Waterbury" on reverse has soared in value to the $1,250–$1,300 range in recent years. A similar Breckinridge–Lane version (Warner 101) is scaled a bit higher. An ornate glazed-ceramic pin tray in rich brown with John Bell portrait ($1,000 plus) and a Lincoln "Wide Awake" ribbon with bright red, white, and blue attached shield carrying Abe's portrait above and a charging buffalo below ($1,000–$1,200) enliven an otherwise somber array of 1860 arcana.

## TWENTIETH ELECTION—1864

*President:* Abraham Lincoln (R)
*Vice President:* Andrew Johnson

*Defeated candidates:*
George McClellan and George Pendleton (D)

Ironically, as the 1864 campaign began, Lincoln appeared destined for defeat at the hands of his ex-Commander-in-Chief of the Union forces, George McClellan, whom Lincoln replaced because of lack of decisiveness. Decisive victories on the battlefield by Generals Grant and Sherman and the taking of Mobile Bay by Admiral Farragut transformed the political picture. Lincoln won 212 electoral votes to McClellan's 21. Lincoln deemed the results a mandate for restoration of the Union and the cessation of slavery. A favorite *Harpers Weekly* cartoon proclaimed: "Long Abraham Lincoln A Little Longer." Actually, Lincoln's second term was all too brief, as he was assassinated in 1865. Andrew Johnson finished out the term (1865–69).

Symbolic of Lincoln's 1864 campaign is a cotton red, white, blue, and brown bandanna with portrait based on a Brady photo and clasped hands in each corner symbolizing unity ($1,500–$1,700). A glass-sided tin parade lantern with McClellan portrait in uniform and "Union And The Constitution" ($1,000–$1,300) and a fragile, square paper lantern picturing the general with the slogan "The Union/It Was!" ($350–$400) are highly sought after three-dimensional mementos. A three-sided, glass-paneled lantern with Lincoln photograph by Alexander Gardner and slogan is also known ($1,500–$1,600).

## TWENTY-FIRST ELECTION—1868

*President:* Ulysses S. Grant (R)
*Vice President:* Schuyler Colfax

*Defeated candidates:*
Horatio Seymour (D)
Gen. Francis P. Blair

The 1868 campaign focused on the ending of the Civil War and its impact on Reconstruction and was one of the most lackluster in history. Horatio Seymour, "The Great Decliner," did very little barnstorming for votes. U. S. Grant refused to make any campaign speeches. He traveled only once, on a Western tour with Generals Sherman and Sheridan, but merely waved as thousands honored the three great Union military heroes. The black vote proved to be critical as Grant faced formidable sectional opposition (he was accused of trying to Africanize the South). Final tally in the electoral college: Grant, 214; Seymour, 80.

Enriching the material culture relating to the 1868 campaign among the Grant forces are a number of whimsical novelties and toys. A match to the Seymour and Blair round, gutta-percha, embossed jugate snuffbox also exists for Grant–Colfax ($450–$500). There are at least three varieties of figural canes, with a cast-iron example painted brown, one of the most elusive at $235 to $265. Noted antique toy authority Bernard Berenholtz regards a 14-inch-high U. S. Grant clockwork toy by Ives (ca. 1876) as probably the largest and finest automatic clockwork toy made in America. When activated, Grant actually places a small cigar in his mouth and exhales real smoke ($5,000 plus). Another Grant toy, dated 1868, is a glass bowl novelty that features a jiggling Grant lithographed figure on a spring, by A. A. Davis, Nashua, New Hampshire ($650–$700). The showpiece Seymour artifact is the black, red, and blue on silver Stevengraph ribbon (see Seymour listing) for $350–$400. One of the most unusual and striking of the flag banners bears an overstamp of currency in black and green, with a statue of Freedom at left, Seymour's portrait at right. The legend on the note cites "The People Demand of The United States Payment of the Bonds in Greenbacks and Equal Taxation One Currency . . ." ($2,500 plus).

## TWENTY-SECOND ELECTION—1872

*President:* Ulysses S. Grant (R)
*Vice President:* Henry Wilson

*Defeated candidates:*
Horace Greeley (D) and George Pendleton

Often considered by historians as one of the most embarrassing elections in history, the choice between Grant and Greeley, lamented Georgia's Alexander Stephens, was a choice between "hemlock and strychnine." Grant captured 286 of 349 electoral votes. The death of Greeley's wife shortly before the election, plus his decisive defeat at the polls, played heavily on his mind. Shortly thereafter he was institutionalized and died three weeks later.

Grant's first term in office introduced the derogatory word "Grantism" to the lexicon. It meant nepotism, the spoils system, shocking corruption in high office. Actually, Grant himself was honest, as politicians go, but his choice of appointees was another matter. A semimechanical bank, "The Tammany," produced just prior to the second election, capitalized on the headlines being made by Boss Tweed and the Tammany politicians involving graft and bribery. When a coin is inserted in the Tammany, he quickly slips it into his coat pocket and nods his head in thanks. He wears a yellow vest, gray pants, and black jacket ($135–$150).

Collector's choice for the classic Grant campaign item for 1872 would probably be a Grant–Wilson flag banner in red, white, and blue with jugate oval portraits surrounded by stars in field of blue ($2,000 plus). Greeley's plight in the race is made clear in a McLoughlin Bros. caricature fan with scathing cartoons on the reverse side. Under "What I Know About Farming" a pair of mules is kicking him over the plowshare ($175–$200). More pleasing to the eye is "The People's Choice For President/Horace Greeley/1872" with oval portrait; purple and gold banner is mounted on a wooden pole with acorn finials ($1,200–$1,300).

## TWENTY-THIRD ELECTION—1876

*President:* Rutherford Hayes (R)
*Vice President:* William Wheeler

*Defeated candidates:*
Samuel Tilden (D) and Thomas Hendricks

Samuel Tilden, a New York district attorney who had sent Boss William Tweed and his hoodlums to jail, led the reform-minded Democrats, with Indianan Thomas Hendricks as running mate. Republicans, meanwhile, matched

"Tilden and Reform!" with "Hurrah! For Hayes and Honest Ways." What followed was the bitterest, longest, and most controversial presidential election in history. One very sought after Hayes campaign book assails Tilden as a criminal, disgraceful to New York State and a menace to the United States ($50–$65). When the mud-slinging ceased, voters went to the polls and gave Tilden a quarter of a million more popular votes than Hayes, and Tilden topped Hayes by 184 electoral votes to 165, only one shy of victory. The struggle over 20 disputed votes and the investigation of ballot stuffing and intimidation of voters lasted over four months. Hayes was declared the winner, and copies of the *Indianapolis Journal*'s announcement of Tilden's victory on election day became a collector's item; a copy now is valued at $85 to $100. An amusing Republican rebus ribbon issued soon after Hayes's victory reads: "Hayes Elected (portrait of strutting rooster) Tilden (picture of dejected-looking donkey) Nuf Said" ($125–$150.)

The Hayes candidacy inspired the last presidential papier-mâché snuffbox to appear in the post–Civil War era. Only 2½ inches in diameter, it reflects a naive interpretation of Hayes and Wheeler, embossed busts on lid and bottom, respectively ($1,200–$1,300). An uncommon celluloid campaign button (the material had been invented only in the early 1870s) features Hayes and Wheeler in embossed portraits issued in various pastels ($700–$725). Solid celluloids enjoyed a brief vogue before giving way to celluloid-layered tin versions. Matching red, white, and black jugate campaign banners are topped with a "Centennial" portrait of George Washington ($250–$300 each). Centerpiece items include matched "Centennial Candidates For 1876" shield pins with jugate portraits on field of diagonal stripes ($325–$350 each).

## TWENTY-FOURTH ELECTION—1880

*President:* James Garfield (R)
*Vice President:* Chester A. Arthur

*Defeated candidates:*
Winfield Scott Hancock (D) and William H. English
James Weaver (GL) and James Field

Ohio congressman James Garfield, a "dark horse," was picked to be the candidate for the Republicans on the thirty-sixth ballot to head the ticket with Chester Allan Arthur, a New York "gentleman boss." Civil War military leader Winfield Scott Hancock was nominated by the Democrats, with wealthy Indiana banker William H. English, in the second slot. Ironically, in a contrastingly dull contest as compared with the fireworks of '76, the only specific proposals for bettering America's industrial climate, i.e., curtailment of child labor, an eight-hour day, came from James B. Weaver of the Greenback Labor party. Garfield prevailed with a stunning 214 to 155 electoral victory. Only a few months following his inauguration, the twentieth president was felled by an assassin's bullet and was succeeded by Arthur.

A practical campaign memento in the days of the detachable collar in men's wardrobes was a series of four 1880 wooden collar boxes with gutta-percha covers molded in the likenesses of Garfield, Arthur, Hancock, and English ($125–$150 each). "Hurrah For Garfield and Arthur," a vibrant orange, brown, green, and yellow banner, hand-painted by noted carriage decorator Edward Bergum, rates high with collectors ($1,000–$1,100), and a poster version is also known. Hancock inspired one of the most coveted of all 3-D objects, an 1880 glazed mustard-colored rebus design clay pipe with figural hand and rooster along the top of the shank (Hand·cock) ($250–$300).

The Democratic rooster strutting his stuff and wearing an oversized saber is one of the classic gilt brass shells ($85–$100). The Handcock rebus theme is also carried out in a fascinating die-cut advertising trade card, with a tiny rooster and a calling card, "The Next President," tucked between thumb and forefinger of a large hand ($35–$50).

## TWENTY-FIFTH ELECTION—1884

*President:* Grover Cleveland (D)
*Vice President:* Thomas Hendricks

*Defeated candidates:*
James G. Blaine (R) and John Logan
Belva Lockwood*
Benjamin Butler (P)
John St. John (PR)

Governor Grover Cleveland of New York confined his campaigning to a few brief speeches championing civil service reform, preferring to pursue his duties at the Governor's office in Albany. Blaine, meanwhile, toured the nation, delivering over 400 speeches praising protectionism. An advertising trade card focuses on a Repubican mud-slinging tactic in 1884 with the revelation that Cleveland had fathered an illegitimate child. The card shows Cleveland with his arm around his lady friend, Bunny Halpin, the baby smiling in his cradle, with the lines:

---

*National Equal Rights Party.

If Bunny had only waited,
It might have come to this.
But she preferred forty-five thousand*
To Baby Bunting's Hug and Kiss.

The colorful trade card is valued at $65 to $75.

Democrats retaliated with the "Mulligan Letters," damaging papers that exposed Blaine as having received a bribe for killing a bill that would have deprived an Arkansas railroad of a federal land grant. The *Nation*'s E. L. Godkin insisted that the talented but wayward Cleveland would make a far better president than a "wheeler-dealer like Blaine." The voters concurred: Cleveland, 219 electoral votes; Blaine, 182. In response to the Republican campaign ditty: "Ma! Ma! Where's My Pa?" the Democrats rejoined, "Up in the White House. Ha! Ha! Ha!"

Collector's choice for the *Cleveland* candidacy: etched glass jugate tray with Cleveland–Hendricks portraits in relief, stippled leaf borders, designed by P. J. Jacobus of Gillinder & Sons, Philadelphia ($225–$250); parade banner, approximately 6 feet by 4 feet, velvet and silk, multicolored with bust portrait of Cleveland on silk, "Cleveland & Hendricks/1884" in metallic thread ($1,200–$1,300).

*Blaine* candidacy: double-cover cigar box with Blaine–Logan portrait cards inserted in slots of covers ($200–$225); also has Cleveland–Hendricks match. Tops among numerous "Plumed Knight" gilt-edge variants: die-stamped jugate ferro features plumed helmet, draped flags, and pine tree shield ($475–$500).

## TWENTY-SIXTH ELECTION—1888

*President:* Benjamin Harrison (R)
*Vice President:* Levi Morton

*Defeated candidates:*
Grover Cleveland (D) and Allan Thurman
Clinton B. Fisk (PR)
A. J. Streeter (LP)
Belva Lockwood (NER)

Republicans for the first time came to be called the GOP (Grand Old Party); they nominated Benjamin Harrison, former Indiana senator, and Levi Morton, wealthy New York banker, both all-out protectionists. Incumbent Cleveland added former Ohio senator Allan Thurman and took a strong stand

---

*The alleged "hush money."

on tariff revision. Harrison conducted a successful "front porch" campaign in his home town of Indianapolis, receiving strong backing from big business. Cleveland declined to campaign, and it was left to running mate Thurman to convey to voters that the slate favored moderate tariff reductions, not free trade. Harrison bested Cleveland in the Electoral College by 233 to 168, yet pulled almost 100,000 fewer votes than Cleveland in the popular vote.

Collector's choice for 1884 campaign: three-dimensional novelties of Harrison and Cleveland, bisque figures suspended on a balance scale and swathed in American flags ($600–$700); Harrison or Cleveland matching campaign eggs with brass rooster pop-up ($300–$350); papier-mâché and wood Cleveland–Harrison articulated toy, arm-wrestling their way to White House ($600–$700); matching figural cologne bottles ($350–$400).

## TWENTY-SEVENTH ELECTION—1892

*President:* Grover Cleveland (D)
*Vice President:* Adlai Stevenson

*Defeated candidates:*
Benjamin Harrison (R) and Whitelaw Reid
James B. Weaver (PR)
John Bidwell (P)

Grover Cleveland, unseated in 1888, came storming back in 1892, denouncing Republican protectionism as a fraud and favoring economic conservatism with special attachment to the gold standard. Harrison, unpopular with party leaders and preoccupied with an ailing wife (she died shortly before the election), barely put up a struggle. Final tally: Cleveland, 277 electoral votes; Harrison, 145. The Populists made a good showing, entering the fray for the first time with 22 votes. Their proposals for currency expansion and higher farm prices found receptive voters in the rural Midwest and South.

Collector's choice for 1892: "Harrison and Reid" stenciled red, white, and blue three-foot-long parade horn ($300–$325). Clear glass and milk glass mini 2¼-inch-high "The Same Old Hat" Harrison beaver hat, evoking memories of his grandfather, William H. Harrison ($75–$85); "Our Choice" ballot box torch with Harrison–Reid jugate portraits ($250–$275); "Cleveland–Stevenson" red and white silk bandanna; bale of hay with crossed pitchforks and ram between jugate portraits and "Tariff Reform" slogan in bold letters below ($225–$250); pair of wooden ratchet noisemakers, "One Good Term Deserves Another" with figural beaver hat cutout for Harrison; "Cleveland and Victory" portrait with draped flag cutout ($250–$300 each).

## TWENTY-EIGHTH ELECTION—1896

*President:* William McKinley (R)
*Vice President:* Garrett Hobart

*Defeated candidates:*
William Jennings Bryan and Arthur Sewell
James Weaver (P) and James Field
John Palmer (ND)
Joshua Levering (PR)

The 1896 McKinley versus Bryan "Battle of Standards" pivoted on GOP advocacy of the gold standard versus that of the Democrats for unlimited coinage of silver at a 16–1 ratio of ounces to gold. In the liveliest race since 1864, McKinley's campaign chairman, Mark Hanna, unleashed over 120 million posters, including some 275 versions. Young Teddy Roosevelt, then president of the Board of Police Commissioners of New York City, was appalled, "He (Hanna) has advertised McKinley as if he were a patent medicine." Borrowing a page from Harrison in 1888, McKinley staged his own "front porch" campaign from his Canton, Ohio, home. Over 750,000 supporters in some 300 delegations from 30 states paid a visit. Bryan, meanwhile, traveled over 18,000 miles by train and delivered more than 600 speeches about everything from farm prices to railroad regulation. A record 14 million people went to the polls, with McKinley winning, 271 versus 176 electoral votes.

From the collector's viewpoint, the 1896 campaign bears special significance. It not only popularized the celluloid pinback, the most desirable of all campaign memorabilia, but ushered in a "Golden Age" of exciting designs, combining pictures, slogans, and bright colors, that remain unmatched in quality to this day. Choice pinbacks include McKinley–Hobart pedaling a tandem bicycle to the White House; "People's Air Line" with Bryan in clouds riding a bicycle on a high wire to Washington, D.C. ($1,000–$1,100); and for stark simplicity, the illustrated Bryan keynote slogan "Cross with Crown of Thorns" in rose and green on white ($75–$80). "My Hobby A Winner" 2-inch cartoon classics—McKinley riding a hobbyhorse and wearing a cockade hat; a Bryan mate with "the Great Commoner" astride what appears to be an ostrich—invariably are included among the top 10 most desirable specimens in the hobby ($1,500–$2,000). Enthusiasts of three-dimensionals go for matched pairs of Bryan–McKinley soap babies ($35–$45), figural canes ($100–$125), and even Heisey sugar glasses with bust portraits ($65–$75) from the 1896 race.

## TWENTY-NINTH ELECTION—1900

*President:* William McKinley (R)
*Vice President:* Theodore Roosevelt

*Defeated candidates:*
William Jennings Bryan (D) and Adlai Stevenson
Eugene Debs (SD)
Job Harriman
Wharton Barker (P) and Donnely
John Wooley (PR)
Metcalf

The 19th century's last presidential campaign was hardly a rip-snorter. Republicans trotted out a "full dinner pail," and Bryan raised the issue of imperialism, already a fait accompli since the Senate had ratified the Treaty of Paris, ceding the Philippines to the United States. Ultimately, the wave of prosperity that swept the nation at the turn of the century probably assured a McKinley victory, 292 electoral votes to Bryan's 155.

A recent "discovery" in the hobby, a multicolor "Expansion" pinback showing McKinley and TR preventing Bryan from taking down Old Glory over the outline of the Philippines ($2,000 plus), rates at or near the top of a bumper crop of 1900 gems. The resplendent art nouveau Bryan–Stevenson Double Eclipse multicolor forecasting a total blackout for McKinley and TR and a similar McKinley 1½-inch "Imaginary Eclipse" multi ($1,000–$1,200); a classic Bryan "16 to 1" clockface in 1¼- and 1¾-inch sizes have recently soared in value ($200–$300 and $450–$500, respectively; an unlisted ⅞-inch variant sold for $275 at the 1981 Warner auction). "Do You Smoke/Yes Since 1896" is at 2 inches the largest and most graphic of the lunch-bucket McKinleys ($400–$425). Bryan's clever counter, "No Dinner-Pail Lunch For Me," pictures a sumptuous feast of turkey and all the trimmings—"I Am For Bryan And a Square Meal" ($500–$525). A die-stamped, elephant-head "Capital–Labor–G.O.P." mechanical badge opens to McKinley portrait and "His Policy Brings Prosperity" on a yellow disk, with a red disk of TR on bucking broncho, "He Never Was Thrown" ($150–$175).

## THIRTIETH ELECTION—1904

*President:* Theodore Roosevelt (R)
*Vice President:* Charles W. Fairbanks

*Defeated candidates:*
Alton B. Parker (D) and Henry Davis
Silas C. Swallow (PR)
Thomas Watson (P)
Eugene Debs (S) and Harriman

After McKinley's assassination in 1901, Teddy Roosevelt was upset by snide references to "His Accidency" upon becoming president. Although eager to earn a full term on his own, Roosevelt ran a surprisingly passive campaign, as did his Democratic opponent, Judge Alton Parker. TR won by the biggest landslide since the Jackson–Clay race in 1832: 336 electoral votes to 140.

TR's "Square Deal," which included conservation of national resources, regulation of big corporations in the public interest, and friendliness to labor unions, drew widespread support.

Although the 1904 race may have been lackluster, TR and Parker campaign items proved vibrant and colorful. A favorite poster shows TR in a straw hat sowing seeds of prosperity and combines bucolic appeal with a quote from Goethe's *Faust* ($300–$350); also "T.R. at the gate" with Uncle Sam—the most uncommon and graphically exciting of the "Equality" buttons ($1,800–$1,900); "Rose•veldt/Fair•banks" jugate rebus multicolor—in a class by itself ($2,500 plus); "Teddy and the Bear" black and white pinback based on Berryman cartoon ($1,500–$1,700). A "Parker Nit/Knock Him Out/We Want Roosevelt" wood pop-up novelty toy rates high ($450–$500) among three-dimensional treasures.

In the scarce but available class are the Parker "Shure Mike" multicolor jugate with cartoon of rooster in Uncle Sam's costume ($125–$150) and "Uncle Sam's White Elephant" atop football, which takes a swipe at TR's "Safety Standpatism" ($135–$150). The notorious Parker "Wedding Cake" contrasts a white married couple appearing under the Parker portrait and a black and white "mixed" couple under TR's photo, with caption "It's Up To You" ($1,850–$1,900).

Among the embarassment of riches from 1904, if we had to choose *one* specimen that best embodies a personality and platform, it would be the superb "Equal Protection" multi with TR as the just mediator between a capitalist and laborer carrying lunch bucket party symbol ($1,700–$1,800).

## THIRTY-FIRST ELECTION—1908

*President:* William Howard Taft (R)
*Vice President:* James S. Sherman

*Defeated candidates:*
William Jennings Bryan (D) and John W. Kern
Thomas Watson (P)
Eugene Debs (S) and Ben Hanford
Thomas Hisgen (I)

Teddy Roosevelt declined to run again in 1908, but there was no doubt that he was pulling the strings for William Howard Taft and shaping party policy. One of the campaign jokes was that T-A-F-T meant "Take Advice From Theodore." Bryan resurrected an old theme from campaigns past: a choice between a government devoted to people's rights and government by privilege. Taft countered that Bryan's views were "full of sophistries" and would paralyze business. Taft won a popular majority of over a million and bested Bryan 321 to 162 in electoral votes, the worst of his three defeats.

Collector's choices from 1908 include matched Maxfield Parrish art nouveau portrait pinbacks with trumpeting heralds ($250–$275 each); Taft–Sherman "Elephant Ears" jugate with oval portraits appearing in flapping ears of stylized GOP elephant ($900–$1,000); "Our Candidates," Taft–Sherman jugate in sepia, red, white, and blue mirror ($800–$900); Taft "U-N-I-T-E-D ("You and I, Ted" play on words), a clever cartoon with Taft and TR shaking hands ($75–$100); Bryan–Kern prize multi with eagle's wings framing shield portraits ($800–$850); Bryan "Ear of Corn" oval, also issued as badge, watch fob, and stickpin ($450–$500). Collectors of three-dimensionals would happily settle for a J. & E. Stevens Taft "The Egg" cast-iron still bank ($900–$1,000); a Bryan "The White House Or Bust" colorful lithograph-on-tin dexterity puzzle, ($400–$500); a Taft–Sherman painted-tin rattle noisemaker ($450–$500); Uncle Sam milk-glass penny hat bank with Bryan paper litho at coin slot, with Taft–Sherman jugate match ($125–$135).

## THIRTY-SECOND ELECTION—1912

*President:* Woodrow Wilson (D)
*Vice President:* Thomas Marshall

*Defeated candidates:*
William Howard Taft (R) and James Sherman
Theodore Roosevelt (PG) and Hiram Johnson
Eugene Debs (S) and Emil Seidel
Eugene Chafin (PR) and Watkins

A three-cornered race kept the populace agitated throughout the 1912 election. Republicans were split asunder; the regulars renominated incumbent Taft; the insurgents, led by TR, created a new Progressive, or Bull Moose, Party. The Democrats chose New Jersey Governor Woodrow Wilson. A TR "New Nationalism" program called for regulation of big business in the national interest. Wilson took it a step further in his "New Freedom" concept, calling for breaking up monopolies and restoring freedom of competition.

Wilson tallied only 41.9 percent of the popular vote, less than Bryan had won in each of his three tries, and it was evident he needed the split in Republican ranks to be elected. Wilson's victory in the Electoral College was decisive, carrying 40 of 48 states, with 435 votes to TR's 88 and Taft's meager 8.

The Progressive Party in 1912 was woefully short of campaign funds. Later, in defeat, TR would lament: "There were no loaves and no fishes." Consequently, jugates of TR and running mate Hiram Johnson were in short supply and rank high on the rarity scale among 20th-century memorabilia. One of the most graphic entries shows a bull moose straddling a U.S. map while TR and Johnson shake hands in the foreground; black and white ($2,000 plus). Others include jugate ovals nesting in a bull moose's antlers, sepiatone ($1,600–$1,800); William H. Taft Statue of Liberty jugate multicolor with oval portraits extending as beams from torch ($550–$600); unlisted "Winners" jugates for both Taft and Wilson, multicolor with scepter and scroll design ($1,000–$1,100 each); "I Wood Row Wilson and Marshall To Victory," the penultimate visual pun pinback multicolor ($3,000 plus); Wilson "Man Of The Hour" portrait pinback in yellow, blue, and black with slogan used in New Jersey gubernatorial and both presidential races ($200–$225).

## THIRTY-THIRD ELECTION—1916

*President:* Woodrow Wilson (D)
*Vice President:* Thomas Marshall

*Defeated candidates:*
Charles E. Hughes (R) and Charles Fairbanks
Allen Benson and Kirkpatrick (S)
James F. Hanley (PR) and Landrith

Preserving American neutrality in the wake of the savage conflict that erupted in Europe in 1914 was the dominant campaign issue in 1916. The Democrats adopted one of the most famous slogans in campaign history: "He kept us out of war."

The Republicans chose Supreme Court Justice Charles Evans Hughes, former governor of New York and a moderate Progressive. TR's old vice-president, Charles Fairbanks, won a second spot. Hughes often vacillated, sometimes accusing Wilson of not taking a hard line with Germany, at other times favoring a strictly neutral policy. Meanwhile, TR's hawkish pronouncements in Hughes's behalf during the campaign proved to be Hughes's undoing. The election was so close, and Hughes had picked up such overwhelming support in the east on election night, that the *New York Times* and *New York World* conceded him the election. When all returns were in at the week's end, however, Wilson had swept the entire west as well as the solid South. Final tally: Wilson, 277 electoral votes; Hughes, 254. One month after Wilson took his oath of office the United States declared war on Germany.

Collector's choices for the 1916 race include "Wilson's 8-Hour Club," figure-eight Wilson portrait oval in blue, brown, and black, one of over a dozen pinbacks reminding voters of enactment of the eight-hour work day in Wilson's first term ($500–$525); "American For America/Preparedness," Wilson portrait with eagle atop cannons ($450–$500); "Remember Your Friends/Defeat Your Enemy/Union Meeting—Five Brotherhoods," one of hobby's premier slogan pinbacks ($150–$175); Hughes–Fairbanks jugate sepiatone in brass frame with colorful ribbon ($700–$750); Hughes–Fairbanks "no-name" jugate with furled flag and mechanical spinner ($1,750–$1,800). Many feel that spinner may have been added later. The Hearst–Hughes fighting roosters, a red and white cartoon pinback, although a New York gubernatorial item and not germane to the 1916 race, is still a classic ($250–$275). One of the often slighted ⅞-inch classics is a Hughes "no-name" portrait button with bust inset on a patriotic shield ($100–$125).

## THIRTY-FOURTH ELECTION—1920

*President:* Warren Harding (R)
*Vice President:* Calvin Coolidge

*Defeated candidates:*
James D. Cox (D) and Franklin D. Roosevelt
Eugene Debs (S) and Seymour Stedman

Two Ohioans, Warren Harding, a senator and publisher, for the Republicans and Governor James Cox for the Democrats, locked horns in 1920. Cox's running mate was Assistant Secretary of the Navy Franklin Roosevelt; Massachusetts Governor Calvin Coolidge ran with Harding. The choice, said the *Nation,* "was between Debs and dubs." (Debs, of course, was Eugene Debs, the Socialist frontrunner, recently out of the Atlanta Penitentiary where the Wilson administration had put him for antiwar speeches during World War I.) Harding by and large conducted a front-porch campaign from his home town of Marion. His campaign theme was "Back to Normalcy." Cox campaigned actively, traveling over 22,000 miles, but all in vain. Harding won 60.2 percent of the popular vote and 404 electoral votes to Cox's 127. Although women were enfranchised to vote for the first time (thanks to the 19th Amendment), their turnout was surprisingly small.

Collector's choices: Harding–Coolidge jugate sepiatone ($575–$600); "Harding & Coolidge Junior Booster/America First" jugate with red, white, and blue background ($1,500–$1,700); "Warren Harding" oval portrait on shield supported on either side with elephant heads, a red, white, blue, and black pocket mirror ($1,150–$1,200); "For President/G.O.P. Warren G. Harding" cartoon elephant pinback with circle inset photo ($900–$1,000); "For Vice President/Gov. Calvin Coolidge," red, white, and sepiatone bull's-eye portrait pinback ($850–$900).

Any of the dozen known Cox–Roosevelt jugate varieties are beatified in the hobby, ranking supreme for their ultimate scarcity as opposed to aesthetic beauty; only the St. Louis Button Co. Cox–Roosevelt "Sunburst Eagle" qualifies in that department ($4,000–$5,000), also, only the "Cox–Roosevelt Club" jugate (Hake 1) departs from the monotonous black and white. The button that gets all the notoriety, a Hake unlisted $1\frac{1}{4}$-inch jugate with conjoining bleed Cox–Roosevelt bust images, set the record of $33,000 at the 1981 Warner Auction. What is generally overlooked is that an equally impressive Cox–Roosevelt sold a few minutes later at the Warner session to Malcolm Forbes, underbidder to Joe Jacobs on the first blockbuster entry. The second jugate sold for exactly one-tenth that of its predecessor! A significant $\frac{7}{8}$-inch Cox–Roosevelt "Americanize America" has been construed to have extreme rightist Ku Klux Klan overtones ($4,500–$5,000). A Cox donkey-head fob matches the Harding elephant pocket mirror ($1,450–$1,500). A Cox raised-dome design portrait in patriotic colors was unknown until 1982 when a matched Harding–Cox set was offered in a Mark Jacobs mail auction ($1,500–$2,000).

## THIRTY-FIFTH ELECTION—1924

*President:* Calvin Coolidge (R)
*Vice President:* Charles Dawes

*Defeated candidates:*
John Davis (D) and Charles Bryan
Robert LaFollette (PG) and Burton Wheeler
William Z. Foster (C)

"Silent Cal" Coolidge became president in August 1923 when Harding died of a heart attack amid shocking revelations of the Teapot Dome oil scandals. Coolidge himself was not implicated, although corruption became a main issue in 1924. John Davis, a Wall Street lawyer, and "Fightin' Bob" LaFollette, the Progressive candidate, put Collidge on the defensive, but the stoic Vermonter lived up to his slogan "Keep Cool With Coolidge." To millions, Coolidge meant continued prosperity, and the result was a Republican landslide, 382 electoral votes to 136 for Davis and 8 for LaFollette.

Collector's choices for 1924 include "Our President/Deeds Not Words," browntone 3¾-inch portrait centerpiece ($400–$450); "Coolidge–Dawes" jugate with Capitol dome, 2⅛-inch black and white pocket mirror ($850–$900); Coolidge–Dawes 1¾-inch black and white classic jugate ($375–$400); Coolidge "Square Deal" ⅞" portrait pinback ($225–$250); "Home Town Coolidge Club," red, white, and blue ⅞-inch portrait ($100–$110); Davis–Bryan conjoining portraits, black and white 1¼-inch jugate ($4,000 plus); medium blue cello fob, mate to Coolidge and LaFollette portrait items ($500–$525); "For President/John W. Davis" sepia circle inset with flag background ($2,000 plus; may well be unique); "Honest Government" Davis portrait pinback ($3,500–$4,000). "Doom" slogan pinback reverses out of blue teapot, one of the most graphically succinct message pinbacks ($150–$175). "Honest Days With Davis," black and white ⅞-inch pinback carries key Democratic campaign theme ($325–$350).

## THIRTY-SIXTH ELECTION—1928

*President:* Herbert Hoover (R)
*Vice President:* Charles Curtis

*Defeated candidates:*
Alfred E. Smith (D) and Joseph T. Robinson
Norman Thomas (S) and Maurer

Herbert Hoover, an engineer, an Iowan and former head of the Department of Commerce, headed the Republican ticket with Charles Curtis, a Kansas senator as vice-presidential nominee. Alfred E. Smith, the popular governor of New York and the first Catholic nominee for president, and Senator Joseph G. Robinson of Arkansas ran on the Democratic slate. Democrats pledged tax revisions and farm relief measures.

Republicans called for a continuation of prosperity, but it was Prohibition and the religious issue that figured prominently in giving Hoover a lopsided victory: 58 percent versus 41 percent in the popular vote; 444 to 87 in the Electoral College. Political pundit H. L. Mencken summed it up: "Those who fear the Pope outnumber those who are tired of the Anti-Saloon League."

Collector's choices include the Hoover-Curtis "My Country Tis of Thee" Statue of Liberty jugate, generally conceded a top-10 rating ($1,500–$2,000); a centerpiece Hoover browntone portrait 4-inch pinback ($325–$350); Al Smith "*A*merican *L*iberty Smith" with the statue opposite portrait ($425–$450); Smith–Robinson jugate centerpiece pinback with oval portraits inside crown of Smith's trademark derby hat ($525–$550); "Hello Al, Goodby Cal," reddish-brown crowing rooster, slogan pinback ($250–$275); Smith–Robinson sepiatone portraits in brass-rim eyeglass-lenses stickpin ($200–$225).

## THIRTY-SEVENTH ELECTION—1932

*President:* Franklin D. Roosevelt (D)
*Vice President:* John N. Garner

*Defeated candidates:*
Herbert Hoover (R) and Charles Curtis
Norman Thomas (S)
William Z. Foster (C)

In a rare understatement, Hoover later acknowledged in his *Memoirs,* "General Prosperity had been an ally in 1928; General Depression was a major enemy in 1932." The Roosevelt–Garner ticket won over 7 million more popular votes than did Hoover and Curtis and pulled 472 versus 59 electoral votes. William Allen White wrote that the election represented a "firm desire on the part of the American people to use government as an agency for human welfare."

Collector's choices: *FDR*—FDR–Garner slogan jugate promising to end Prohibition and the Depression, red, white, and black ($400–$450); "We Will Protect Our Flag/Prosperity with Roosevelt" portrait multicolor from Western Badge Co., Minnesota ($275–$300); "Work and Wages," FDR–Curley jugate, 2¼ inches, red, white, blue, and black ($125–$150); *Hoover*—"Hoover–Curtis" jugate with classic red, white, and blue border popular during 1928–1948 era ($200–$225); "Have Faith In God And Hoover," provocative slogan with vivid light blue and gold colors ($125–$150).

## THIRTY-EIGHTH ELECTION—1936

*President:* Franklin Roosevelt (D)
*Vice President:* John N. Garner

*Defeated candidates:*
Alfred Landon (R) and Frank Knox
Norman Thomas (S)
Earl Russell Browder (C)
William Lemke (U)

By 1936, FDR, as far as millions of Americans were concerned, was (according to Democratic Chairman Jim Farley) "more popular than the New Deal itself." The Republicans resorted to a few scare tactics, such as their allegation that the Social Security Act, scheduled to go into effect on January 1, 1937, was a gigantic swindle. There was little that Landon and his forces could do to stem the tide. FDR carried every state but Maine and Vermont and swamped Landon 523 to 8 in electoral votes! One of the Democrats' more cryptic slogan buttons had come true: "On The Rocks With Landon and Knox."

Collector's choices: *Landon*—a 1-inch "Landon-Knox" jugate, the elite among sunflower variations, in crisp red, yellow, black, and white, manufactured by Cruver ($900–$950); Landon GOP elephant squashing Democratic donkey, "Landon On The New Deal," black, blue, and white cartoon classic ($325–$350); Landon in airplane over Capitol dome, "Land On Washington," classic visual pun in blue and red ($300–$350); *Roosevelt*—"Railway Employees Roosevelt Club/Stark County, Ohio," red and black on light green, with FDR portrait inset in circle above cowcatcher on train engine ($800–$850); "Victory 1936" 4-inch sepiatone portrait centerpiece

($375–$400); FDR "You Can't Eat Sunflowers/Disgusted Republican/Let's Lose With Landon," the ultimate put-down to GOP's flurry of Landon sunflower pinbacks ($250–$275).

## THIRTY-NINTH ELECTION—1940

*President:* Franklin D. Roosevelt (D)
*Vice President:* Henry A. Wallace

*Defeated candidates:*
Wendell Willkie (R) and Charles McNary
Norman Thomas (S)
Earl Russell Browder (C)

Wendell Willkie launched his crusade against "the third-term candidate, a President bent on perpetuating one-man rule." This issue evoked little response among the populace, and it was only after he pooh-poohed FDR's promise to stay out of war that the Republicans, keeping the peace campaign, really caught fire. FDR, in a ringing speech in Boston responded, "I have said this before, but I shall say it again and again and again: Your boys are not going to be sent into any foreign wars." Roosevelt overwhelmed Willkie at the polls, 449 electoral votes to 82. One small Republican victory came later, in 1951, when belatedly they succeeded in passing the 22nd Amendment to the U.S. Constitution, prohibiting third terms.

Collector's choices: *Willkie*—"Willkie For President," red, white, and blue 2½-inch bull's eye portrait pinback from Midwest Badge Co. ($150–$200), up dramatically from its $77 showing at Warner; "Out At Third," cartoon pinback of FDR being tagged out by Willkie at third, both in baseball uniforms; umpire animatedly signals "out" call; black, red, and white ($575–$600); "I'm For Willkie/Joe Louis," 1 inch, black and white ($150–$175); "On Our Way," smiling GOP elephant sliding to victory at polls on an arrow extending from Maine to California, red, white, and black 2½-inch cartoon classic ($75–$100); Willkie 1¼-inch multicolor "Chemurgy" pictorial and one of the best among literally hundreds of Willkie slogan pinbacks ($115–$125); "I'm Against The Third Term. Washington Wouldn't/Grant Couldn't/Roosevelt Shouldn't" ($10–$12); *Roosevelt*—"Essex County Woman's League Pro Roosevelt," with FDR in red heart shape with white background, ⅞-inch ($135–$150); "I'm For Roosevelt And Wallace," ⅞-inch jugate ($65–$75), also in 1-inch version ($85–$100); FDR Official 1941 Inauguration Medal, Type 2, 1941, uncirculated ($300–$350).

## FORTIETH ELECTION—1944

*President:* Franklin D. Roosevelt (D)
*Vice President:* Harry Truman

*Defeated candidates:*
Thomas E. Dewey (R) and John Bricker

The 1944 election was the first wartime presidential contest since the Civil War. FDR appeared steadfast in wanting to remain at the helm. Opposition to 1940 running mate Henry Wallace was so intense that FDR would settle for "the new Missouri Compromise," Harry S. Truman. Thomas Dewey, Governor of New York, and J. W. Bricker, conservative Governor of Ohio, headed the Republican contingent. Though pollsters predicted a close election, the Democrats breezed in again, 432 electoral votes to 99. On April 12, 1945, only months after taking his oath of office as president for the fourth time, Franklin Roosevelt died of a cerebral hemorrhage, and Harry Truman became president.

Collector's choices: *Dewey*—"Dewey–Bricker" bluetone jugate with red and white background ($125–$135); "Dewey and Bricker for Prosperity," 6-inch centerpiece pinback, blue and white ($300–$325); Thomas Dewey cast-metal statue, 4-inch-high painted figural ($20–$25); *Roosevelt*—"Roosevelt–Truman," 1½-inch sepiatone jugate ($50–$75); "Dewey's All Wet," die-cut cardboard hanger in shape of pair of lady's bloomers ($20–$25); "Re-Elect Roosevelt" portrait in red, white, and blue shield ($50–$75); campaign poster, "Roosevelt–Truman For Lasting Peace. Security For All," jugate in red, white, and black ($125–$150).

## FORTY-FIRST ELECTION—1948

*President:* Harry S. Truman (D)
*Vice President:* Alben Barkley

*Defeated candidates:*
Thomas E. Dewey (R) and John Bricker
J. Strom Thurmond (STR) and Fielding Wright

Wits dismissed Harry Truman with the one-liner, "To err is Truman," but the interim president following FDR's death fooled them all by reviving an old FDR coalition of farmers, laborers, ethnics, and the South. Fifty of the nation's leading political writers picked Dewey as winner. The pollsters had Dewey ahead by a wide margin. Odds-makers called the Republican frontrunner a 15 to 1 favorite. But "Give 'em Hell Harry" (as one Democratic slogan button called him) received a plurality of over 2 million popular votes and won handily in the Electoral College, 303 to 189.

Collector's choices: *Truman*—anti-Truman pinback with HST's face superimposed on an eight-ball; the proverbial symbol of tough luck had been presented to Truman as a joke gift at a Los Angeles Press Club roast early in the campaign ($800–$850); "For President Harry S. Truman/For Vice President . . ." Truman–Barkley oval bluetone jugate ($135–$150); "Truman Crusaders" acrostic with letters inside red-bordered cross ($100–$125); "I'm Just Wild About Harry" musical scale, illustrated Inaugural pinback, 1949 ($75–$85); *Dewey*—"Keep Your Donkey (donkey head rebus) Off The White House Grass. It's All Dewey"; 1½-inch cartoon classic ($120–$130); "Two Many Jacks From Missouri"; small donkey heads encircle Capitol dome, 1¼-inch cartoon button ($115–$125); "Dewey–Warren" 9-inch red, white, and blue jugate centerpiece ($125–$150); "Dewey Defeats Truman," November 3, 1948, famous blooper edition of *Chicago Tribune* ($900–$950).

## FORTY-SECOND ELECTION—1952

*President:* Dwight D. Eisenhower (R)
*Vice President:* Richard Nixon

*Defeated candidates:*
Adlai Stevenson (D) and John Sparkman

The eloquent Adlai Stevenson, Governor of Illinois, talked himself into the leading candidate's role to test a seemingly unbeatable World War II war hero candidate, the enormously popular Dwight D. Eisenhower. Eisenhower's major bombshell came late in the campaign when he announced he would end the war in Korea if he became president. Ike's running mate, Richard Nixon, had just weathered a major crisis when the *New York Post* revealed that a group of wealthy Californians had set up a sizable "slush fund" of over $18,000 when Nixon was in the Senate. Nixon took his appeal to the nation via television with his impassioned "Checkers" speech; the nation bought it, and he remained on the ticket.

Eisenhower's plurality in November proved overwhelming—more than 6½ million votes; he carried 30 states, with 442 electoral votes to Stevenson's 89.

Eisenhower–Nixon jugate with eagle atop shield, red, white, blue, black, and gold 3-inch centerpiece ($35–$50); "Ike/Dick," 2½-inch vertical oval shape jugate with red-striped background ($200–$225); "Womanpower For Eisenhower," tiny elephant cartoon wearing skirt and lady's flowered hat against large V background ($60–$70); "Hooray For Adlai," double-line border bull's-eye bluetone portrait ($175–$200); "Stevenson–Humphrey Will Sweep The Country!" possible dream slate ($125–$150) produced by the Humphrey Minnesota delegation at the Democratic National Convention; "Vote Straight Democratic," silhouetted heads of Stevenson–Sparkman jugate centerpiece ($130–$150).

## FORTY-THIRD ELECTION—1956

*President:* Dwight D. Eisenhower
*Vice President:* Richard Nixon

*Defeated candidates:*
Adlai Stevenson (D) and Estes Kefauver

Stevenson sharply criticized Eisenhower's foreign policy in the 1956 race, pointing to the Republican's "liberation policy" that recklessly encouraged uprisings in the Middle East and Eastern Europe, but when they revolted the United States could do nothing to help the insurgents. Stevenson's attacks evoked little change in voter attitudes. Ike won the most smashing victory since FDR's rout of Landon in 1936, 457 electoral votes to Stevenson's 73. The election, hailed as a triumph for "Modern Republicanism," in reality was again Ike's personal triumph.

Collector's choices: *Eisenhower*—Eisenhower For the Deaf button, which shows only the hand signals for letters I-K-E ($35–$40); Eisenhower battery-operated GOP elephant toy by Linemar, which waves "I Like Ike" flag in trunk when activated ($85–$100); "Mothers For Mamie/Keep A Mother In The White House" (possibly alluding to Stevenson's divorced status); slogan appears in red in large white heart outline ($60–$75); *Stevenson*—"Adlai And Estes—The Bestest," four-leaf clover jugate cartoon pinback ($200–$225) "Dollars For Democrats" TV quiz show take-off, with Stevenson–Kefauver jugate portraits inside TV screen ($25–$30); crossed legs with hole in shoe cartoon, "For '56," one of many campaign items featuring Stevenson trademark ($15–$20).

## FORTY-FOURTH ELECTION—1960

*President:* John F. Kennedy (D)
*Vice President:* Lyndon Johnson

*Defeated candidates:*
Richard Nixon (R) and Henry C. Lodge

John F. Kennedy, a senator from Massachusetts, had narrowly missed being Stevenson's running mate in 1956 before Kefauver prevailed on the third ballot in an open convention. Hubert Humphrey of Minnesota provided the major opposition in the 1960s primaries, but he withdrew after JFK won 60 percent of the vote in pivotal West Virginia. Kennedy's closest rival at the Democratic Convention, Lyndon Johnson, was offered, and accepted, the second slot. For the Republicans, Richard Nixon, who had remained in Ike's shadow for eight years, was nominated on the first ballot, with Henry Cabot Lodge, chief U.S. representative to the UN for second place. Pivotal in 1960 was the first televised series of debates between major presidential contestants. JFK, who lacked the national exposure of Nixon, appeared to be switching roles, by starting out as the underdog and winding up upstaging Nixon, with more specific and vital information on the tip of his tongue. Toward the end of the campaign Eisenhower belatedly stepped in to lend his immense prestige to the Nixon candidacy. In the largest voter turnout in the nation's history, JFK emerged the winner, with 303 electoral votes versus Nixon's 219 and the closest popular vote since the 1888 Cleveland–Harrison contest.

Collector's choices: *Nixon*—"It's Time To Elect Nixon President," with words forming square clock face ($125–$150); "Nixon Lodge/Vote Republican" jugates in $\frac{7}{8}$-inch and $1\frac{1}{4}$-inch standards ($125–$150 each); "Match Him," silhouetted-head Nixon portrait ($225–$250); *Kennedy*—"Our Next President," Kennedy portrait against U.S. flag background ($65–$75); Kennedy "no name" bleed bust portrait, $3\frac{1}{2}$-inch centerpiece ($75–$100); "Shoe-workers For Kennedy" ($90–$100); "Jack Once More in '64" (post-election item anticipating second term [$150–$175]).

## FORTY-FIFTH ELECTION—1964

*President:* Lyndon B. Johnson (D)
*Vice President:* Hubert Humphrey

*Defeated candidates:*
Barry Goldwater (R) and William Miller

With John F. Kennedy's assassination on November 22, 1963, Lyndon B. Johnson assumed the mantle and the New Frontier segued to the Great Society. Little time was lost in securing the passage of the historic Civil Rights Act of 1964 and other legislation critical to LBJ's "War On Poverty." Extreme rightist Barry Goldwater, along with little-known upstate New York Congressman William Miller, were the Republicans' choice to end an eight-year Democratic reign. The 1964 campaign saw the Democrats constantly putting Goldwater on the defense as "he shot from the lip." Goldwater was never able to explain fully a phrase that came back to haunt him throughout the campaign: "Extremism in defense of liberty is no vice!"

The pollsters were never in doubt. As predicted, LBJ won handily, carrying 44 states. Goldwater was outnumbered 486 to 52 in the electoral count. It proved to be the most lopsided victory since FDR overwhelmed Landon in 1936.

Collector's choices: *Goldwater*—Anti-Johnson cartoon pinback, "A 'Page' From The Past," with LBJ grabbing Bobby Baker's arm, "My Strong Right Arm"; Baker was a former LBJ protege under indictment at the time for shady dealings ($100–$125); "Look Ahead With Goldwater," black, white, and orange 2¼-inch centerpiece item ($50–$60); "Man of Courage," Goldwater portrait, 3½-inch pinback in black, yellow, and red ($30–$35); "It Needs Goldwater For Good Roots/The Democratic Lyndon Tree," cartoon pinback, black on gold ($30–$35); "Colorado For Goldwater," portrait button in black and gold on white ($50–$60); Goldwater three-dimensional items: "Goldwater/The Right Drink For The Conservative Taste," gold can ($10–$15); "Goldwater AuH20/The Soap For Conservative People/4-Year Protection," soap bar ($10–$12); *Johnson*—"Ladies For Johnson–Humphrey" bull's-eye portrait on blue and white pinback ($40–$45); "Essex County Democrats For Johnson/New Jersey," portrait pinback, red, white, and blue ($50–$60); "Support Johnson and Civil Rights," portrait litho pinback ($125–$135); "Go With Goldwater," cartoon of an A-bomb mushroom cloud; black and white pinback ($8–$10); "Young Citizens For Johnson," red, white, and blue cartoon, Democratic donkey grinning ($12–$15); three-dimensional items: plastic dashboard figure, LBJ in Stetson hat ($12–$15); anti-Goldwater and Miller "Panic Button" novelty ($10–$12).

## FORTY-SIXTH ELECTION—1968

*President:* Richard M. Nixon (R)
*Vice President:* Spiro Agnew

*Defeated candidates:*
Hubert Humphrey (D) and Edmund Muskie
George Wallace (A) and Curtiss LeMay

Richard Nixon staged a remarkable comeback in 1968, after his defeat to JFK in 1960 and his failure to win the governorship of California in 1962. At the Republican Convention, he easily staved off challenges from two governors, Nelson Rockefeller of New York and California's Ronald Reagan. "Spiro Who?" Agnew of Maryland was picked in the second slot, no doubt appealing to the border states and the Deep South. LBJ took a lot of wind out of the Republicans' sails by announcing a reduction in American bombing in North Vietnam and launching peace talks, and at the same time removing himself from the race in 1968. In a Democratic Convention clearly divided between the Hawks and the Doves, LBJ's running mate, Hubert Humphrey, emerged as presidential nominee, with Edmund Muskie of Maine as vice-president. Nixon's stand on integration and law and order was so similar to the views of American Independence Party candidate George Wallace, they found themselves appealing to the same voters in the South. The police riot with anti-Vietnam War demonstrators at the Chicago Convention badly hurt Humphrey's cause. It was also soon obvious that being shackled with LBJ's Vietnam policy was turning off voters. It was not until late in September, when Humphrey finally took a stronger stand on de-escalating the war, that he received the support of fellow Democrats Edward Kennedy, Eugene McCarthy, and other Doves. It proved to be too little, too late, although the popular vote was close. Nixon's margin of victory was 43.3 percent versus 42.7 percent although the Republicans received 302 electoral votes to Humphrey's 191. Wallace made an impressive showing for a third-party candidate: 5 states and 46 electoral votes.

Collector's choices: *Humphrey*—"Peace Memorial Statue in St. Paul, Minnesota, City Hall" silver, blue, and black pinback with ribbon, "HHH" boldly overprinted over illustration of statue ($40–$50). "We're For Him," wiggle-eye cartoon pinback in blue, green, and white of young man and woman ($25–$30), "America Needs Humphrey–Muskie" jugate portraits inside map outline of United States, red, white, blue, and black ($55–$60). *Nixon*—many pinbacks for Nixon–Agnew in 1968 were produced for the collector market. With a few possible exceptions, any item from this candidacy is priced under $10. Among three-dimensional items, a "Nixon '68 Agnew" cast-iron elephant bank, 2¾ inches high, has potential ($25–$30). There is a

Humphrey–Muskie donkey bank match 4¼ inches high ($30–$35). Novelty Spiro Agnew ceramic soap bubble pipe (also Nixon match) ($25–$35). Spiro Agnew cartoon wrist watch surprisingly became a cult item when the vice president was forced to leave office ($25–$35).

## FORTY-SEVENTH ELECTION—1972

*President:* Richard M. Nixon (R)
*Vice President:* Spiro Agnew (replaced by Gerald Ford and Nelson Rockefeller)

*Defeated candidates:*
George McGovern (D) and Thomas Eagleton*
(replaced by R. Sargent Shriver)

Senator George McGovern from South Dakata, a dark horse for 1972, had emerged after 1971 as the leading spokesman for a variety of protest groups, including anti-Vietnam activists, ERA, and black civil rights workers. He headed the Democratic ticket with a call for immediate withdrawal of U.S. troops from Vietnam, plus amnesty for those who refused to serve their country in that war. Abolishing capital punishment, banning handgun sales, and advocating free choice as to life-styles and private habits were all major platform considerations. Missouri Senator Thomas Eagleton was McGovern's choice for vice-president. Nixon's renomination was not unlike a coronation. During the campaign he remained mostly aloof from the in-fighting, nurturing his image as world leader while sending Spiro Agnew and his staff members on the campaign trail. On election eve Republican National Committee Chairman Robert Dole stated, "We aren't saying we'll win all fifty states, but we aren't conceding anything." Dole's prediction came uncomfortably close. Nixon took 49 of the 50 states (Massachusetts being the lone dissenter) and *received* 521 electoral votes versus McGovern's 17.

Collector's choices: *McGovern*—"Come Home America" stylized outline map of United States with states appearing as trees ($10–$12); "George McGovern For President" photo portrait against U.S. flag background with pair of doves ($15–$17); "Grass Roots McGovern Volunteers" ($14–$16); anti-Nixon cartoon pinback featuring caricature by David Levine of Nixon, with pen drawing of Suez Canal area on stomach (à la LBJ with his abdominal scar) and holding finger to lips for secrecy ($7–$10); "Robin McGovern," McGovern in high feathered Robin Hood cap, with bow and quiver of

---

*Following the revelation that Eagleton had a past history of severe mental depression, heavy pressure from McGovern's advisers led him to ask Eagleton to withdraw. R. Sargent Shriver of Massachusetts, former Peace Corps director, replaced Eagleton on the ticket.

arrows ($15–$20); "McGovern 72" poster, multicolor, illustrated by Sanger ($15–$20); "Carole King, Barbra Streisand, James Taylor For McGovern" pinback ($35–$40). *Nixon*—"Nixon & Agnew" mixed media (folk art) "Nixon Now More Than Ever" suspenders ($10–$15); "Heritage Groups" Nixon/Agnew 1970s Republican National Convention Nationalities Division, large presidential seal at right ($15–$20); "Puerto Rican–Hispanic Young Republicans ($20–$25); "I'm A Friend Of Jimmy Hoffa/Nixon Free Hoffa," Teamsters Convention 1971 pinback ($20–$25); Liverpool-type Watergate ceramic pitcher; obverse shows portrait cluster of Nixon, John Mitchell, Haldeman, and other scandal-implicated White House staffers; opposite side is transfer of George Washington and inscription: "I Can't Tell A Lie"; beneath spout are transfers of an eagle and Judge John Sirica, intertwined magnetic tapes and reels line the base and rim.

Over three campaigns, more than 1,500 varieties of Nixon pinbacks were issued, most of which proved to be singularly unexciting.

## FORTY-EIGHTH ELECTION—1976

*President:* James E. Carter (D)
*Vice President:* Walter Mondale

*Defeated candidates:*
Gerald Ford (R) and Robert Dole

While McGovern had found it impossible to tap the support of mainstream American voters, Jimmy Carter, an outsider, a former governor of Georgia, and vastly inexperienced in political in-fighting on Capitol Hill, somehow found the magic formula. For two years prior to the election, Carter relentlessly criss-crossed the country shaking hands and declaring, "My name is Jimmy Carter and I'm running for president." Incumbent Gerry Ford, who inherited the presidency when Nixon stepped down after Watergate, faced a tough primary fight with the popular two-term governor of California, Ronald Reagan, before emerging victorious.

In the much ballyhooed TV debates of the bicentennial election, Ford's handling of a question on Soviet domination of Eastern Europe was so inept that he never fully recovered from his image as a mistake-prone, inept bumbler. Carter too had his cross to bear. His ill-advised *Playboy* interview and comment on "lust" became headline news and caused great merriment in the Ford camp. The slips of the tongue prompted this quip from Johnny Carson: "I have a late score from the newsroom. Jimmy Carter is ahead of Gerald Ford, two blunders to one." In November, the voters gave Carter 297 electoral votes, to Ford's 240, and a margin of victory of almost 1,700,000 votes.

## FORTY-NINTH ELECTION—1980

*President:* Ronald Reagan
*Vice President:* George Bush

*Defeated candidates:*
James E. Carter (D) and Walter Mondale
John Anderson (I) and Patrick Lucey

Reagan was able to turn the war-or-peace issue against Carter, charging that his vacillation, his weakness, his allowing our allies to no longer respect us posed "a far greater danger of unwanted inadvertent war." Reagan's stand was that America "build up its defense capability to the point that this country can keep the peace." The nation obviously endorsed this policy, as November saw Reagan swamping Carter at the polls with a popular plurality of almost 8,300,000 votes; 489 electoral votes to Carter's 49.

## FIFTIETH ELECTION—1984

*President:* Ronald Reagan
*Vice President:* George Bush

*Defeated candidates:*
Walter Mondale (D) and Geraldine Ferraro

The most significant fact about the 1984 race was that Geraldine Ferraro became the first woman to appear on the national ticket for a major political party. Reagan and Bush ran up the largest plurality of any campaign in history.

Neither 1980 nor 1984 offered much in the way of exciting memorabilia for collectors. Pinbacks from both parties are still readily available for $2 to $3.

# THE CANDIDATES

An alphabetical listing of the winners and losers in national elections, past and present. Under each candidate's name, collecting categories from A (as in Advertising) to T (as in Toys, Dolls, Games, Puzzles) also appear in ABC sequence.

# JOHN ADAMS TO WOODROW WILSON

## JOHN ADAMS

John Adams, Federalist from Massachusetts, was the first Vice-President of the U.S. serving under George Washington, 1789–97. The second President of the U.S., he served 1797–1801. Served earlier as U.S. diplomat in Europe. Attended Continental Congress as Massachusetts delegate. As Vice-President, Adams set a record of having cast 29 tie-breaking votes in the U.S. Senate, a record which still stands today. Also known by rather uncomplimentary nickname: "His Royal Rotundity."

## JOHN QUINCY ADAMS

John Q. Adams, son of President John Adams, was a Democrat/Republican from Massachusetts. He served in the U.S. Senate 1803–08 as a Federalist; in the House, 1831–48 as a Whig. Secretary of State 1817–25 under James Monroe. Elected sixth President of U.S. 1825–29. John Q. Adams was only man to win the presidency with both fewer electoral votes and fewer popular votes than his opponent (Andrew Jackson.)

                                                                    **Price Range**

*Sewing and Grooming Accessories*

☐ "Adams and Liberty," stenciled slogan and pair of flags design with roped border; hinged lid with ribbon supports; paper engraving of J. Q. Adams mounted under glass inside lid; 5"w x 3"l; rainbow colors ..................................... 1050.00  1150.00

☐ "Adams Forever," as above .................. 950.00  1000.00

☐ "Be Firm With Adams," same as above ........ 1000.00  1100.00

85

Price Range

☐ "People's Choice," variant of thread boxes above
but in hexagonal shape ...................... 1000.00    1100.00

☐ "Victory For Adams"; wreath above pair of flags
and entwined olive sprays enclose slogan (Hake
3007) 5"w x 3"l; rainbow colors .............. 950.00    1000.00

## SPIRO THEODORE AGNEW

When Spiro Agnew was picked by Richard Nixon as his choice for running mate in 1968, a *Washington Post* editor wrote that Agnew's candidacy was perhaps the most eccentric political appointment "since the Roman Emperor Caligula named his horse a consul." The redneck ex-Governor of Maryland became well known overnight for his insensitive rhetoric on the campaign trail. He accused rival Hubert Humphrey of "being squishy soft on Communism" and attacked the press corps as "nattering nabobs of negativism."

In 1973, an investigation into corruption in Baltimore County, Maryland, uncovered evidence that implicated Agnew of kickbacks, extortion and bribery. Faced with prospects of a prison sentence, Agnew pleaded *nolo contendere* and handed in his resignation on October 10, 1973 (see Richard Nixon).

## CHESTER ALLAN ARTHUR

In his entire career, Chester Arthur never won a public office on his own. A wealthy lawyer and gentleman boss of the Republican Party in New York City, he was actually born in Vermont. A supporter of a third term for Grant, he became a compromise candidate for second slot, when the Blaine forces nominated Garfield as President in 1880. Became 21st President upon Garfield's death a few months after the inauguration and finished one term (1885) (see James Garfield).

Since incumbent Chester A. Arthur merely filled out Garfield's unexpired term and was not nominated by the Republicans in 1884, campaign items aside from ties with Garfield, are virtually nonexistent. One of few commemorative relics is "An Artist's Fine Paint Box," with lithograph-on-wood portraits of Presidents Garfield and Arthur, $100–$110 (see color photograph). Another is a gutta percha collar box with embossed portrait, $110–$125.

## ALBEN WILLIAM BARKLEY

Alben Barkley, a Democrat from Kentucky, had served in the House and U.S. Senate for over 35 years (1913–1949) when, at the age of 70, he became Vice-President under Harry Truman in 1949. Known affectionately as "The Veep," he was highly respected by Harry Truman (although Justice William O. Douglas had been Truman's first choice for running mate). HST even went so far as to make Barkley a member of the Security Council. "The Veep" was said to have actively had a hand in such policy decisions as intervention in Korea and the recall of General Douglas MacArthur. In 1953, Barkley returned to his home state of Kentucky and made another successful run for the Senate (see Harry Truman).

## JOHN BELL

Former Speaker of the House John Bell, a Whig from Tennessee, ran for President under the Constitutional Union banner in 1860, with the single-minded purpose of preservation of the Union. Edward Everett of Massachusetts was nominated for the second slot. Bell finished a poor third in the four-party race in '60, carrying only three border states.

## JAMES GILLESPIE BLAINE

James Blaine, a Maine Republican, served in the House 1863–76; Senate 1876–81; Speaker 1869–75; Secretary of State, 1881 and again from 1889–92. Ran as Republican candidate for President in 1884, losing to Grover Cleveland.

Price Range

### Canes and Umbrellas

☐ "Blaine I.K.M.P." (meaning of initials obscure) effigy cane head; white metal; $2\frac{1}{2}$"h ............ 125.00    135.00

☐ "Blaine Plumed Knight" effigy cane head; hollow cast lead or metal; $2\frac{1}{2}$"h .................... 135.00    150.00

### Lapel Devices

☐ "Blaine & Logan Plumed Knight" shell; three flags atop each jugate circle portrait (Hake 3084; Warner 170) $2\frac{1}{4}$"h; gilt brass ....................... 400.00    425.00

James Blaine (D) candidate for president, 1884; flag banner ($600–$650).

| | Price Range | |
|---|---|---|
| ☐ Blaine die-stamped pine tree–shaped ferrotype; circular Blaine portrait encircled by star shape and flags above (pine tree is state tree of Blaine's home state of Maine) (Hake 3080) 2¼"; gilt brass shell | 225.00 | 250.00 |
| ☐ Blaine–Logan spectacles in brass with cardboard photos in each lens (Hake 3104) 3"w .......... | 225.00 | 250.00 |

*Toys, Games*

| | | |
|---|---|---|
| ☐ "Blaine Is In. How Can Harrison Get Him Out?" blocks of five administrations puzzle, 1884; 4" x 4"; red, white, blue wood ...................... | 50.00 | 75.00 |

## JOHN CABELL BRECKINRIDGE

Breckinridge was a Democrat from Kentucky who served in the House from 1851–55; in the Senate, 1861. Was nominated to run as President for the Southern Democrats in 1860. He finished second in four-man race with 39 electoral votes, but third in popular votes, carrying 11 slave states.

## WILLIAM JENNINGS BRYAN

Bryan, a Democrat from Nebraska, served in the House 1891–95. He was unsuccessful candidate for the highest office in 1896, 1900, and 1908, losing handily in all three campaigns. Noted for his spellbinding gift of oratory, his "Cross of Gold" speech delivered at the Democratic Convention in 1896, is considered the most impassioned in political annals. Was Secretary of State under Wilson, 1913–15. Bryan is one of the most popular presidential candidates among collectors, and several classics from his three races rank among the top ten in the hobby.

*Badges, Stickpins, Studs, Hangers*

| | Price Range | |
|---|---:|---:|
| ☐ Bicycle atop scrolled bar with ornate circular framed hanger; paper jugate portraits of Bryan–Sewall (Hake 3144) 2¼ "; brass; black, white | 135.00 | 150.00 |
| ☐ Bicycle badge, riderless; Bryan–Sewall insets in wheels (Hake 362; Warner 489) 1¼ "w; black, silver; McKinley match ...................... | 135.00 | 150.00 |
| ☐ Bicycle badge, die-cut, with Bryan–Sewall insets in wheels, pedaled by figure of man labeled "16 to 1"; "White House For 4 Years" along frame (Hake 361) 1"w; light blue, black, silver; McKinley match | 300.00 | 325.00 |
| ☐ Broom (base) stickpin with Bryan inset photo (Hake 384) 1"; gold, black .................. | 35.00 | 45.00 |
| ☐ Bryan–Sewall hanger from shield; "16 to 1" appears on die-cut shield; "Victory 1896" appears above black and white oval portrait insets (Hake 12) hanger 2"; 3¾ "w/shield; brown, silver, red with tan background. ........................... | 90.00 | 100.00 |
| ☐ Capitol, "A Sure Winner" metal badge (see McKinley) (Hake 302); transposes with Bryan when button is pressed; 1¼ " ........................ | 150.00 | 175.00 |
| ☐ Bryan–Stevenson jugate portraits on shield (Hake 23) 1¾ "; red, white, blue, black on silver; appears with hanger metal clicker (unlisted) 1½ "l ...... | 60.00 | 65.00 |
| ☐ Coal bucket, die-cut stickpin, "Empty" (Hake 367) 1"; black with embossed lettering ............ | 15.00 | 20.00 |
| ☐ Coal shovel and bucket dimensional pinback with embossing, "Bust The Trust" (Hake 368) 1"h; black ...................................... | 25.00 | 30.00 |

Price Range

☐ Eagle mechanical with gold bug in beak; paper photos of Bryan and Sewall in wings (Hake 305) 1½"; silvered brass, gilded bug; sepia photos . . . . . . . . .   225.00    250.00

☐ Eagle with oval hanger badge; Bryan portrait in filligreed oval frame hanger (Hake 380) 2¼"; brass, sepiatone . . . . . . . . . . . . . . . . . . . . . . . . . . . . . . . . .   30.00    35.00

☐ Eagle with shield-within-a-shield; stickpin; Bryan portrait encased in smaller framed shield (Hake 382) 1¼"h; gilded brass; black and white photo   30.00    35.00

☐ Eagle with watch face "16 to 1" hanger; black face with Roman numerals in silver (Hake 3159) 2¼"h; brass, black, silver . . . . . . . . . . . . . . . . . . . . . . . . . .   45.00    55.00

☐ Fireplace bellows stud embossed with Bryan bust profile and lettering "Bryan Blows Best" (Hake 3061) 1"; gilded brass . . . . . . . . . . . . . . . . . . . . . . .   15.00    20.00

☐ Flag with Bryan inset; enameled stickpin (Hake 351) 1"w; red, white, blue; numerous other Bryan flag variants . . . . . . . . . . . . . . . . . . . . . . . . . . . . . .   50.00    60.00

☐ Four-leaf clover enameled stickpin; initials: B (for Bryan), S (Stevenson), ampersand, and "16–1" appear on leaves (Hake 400) ¾"; red, purple, green, gold . . . . . . . . . . . . . . . . . . . . . . . . . . . . . . . . . . .   15.00    20.00

☐ "Free Silver" die-cut stickpin, embossed (Hake 389) ¾"w; silver . . . . . . . . . . . . . . . . . . . . . . . . . . . . .   15.00    20.00

☐ "Free Silver" stickpin; flexed arm wielding sword with circular portrait disk of Bryan below (Hake 383) 1¼"; gold, black . . . . . . . . . . . . . . . . . . . . . . .   35.00    45.00

☐ Gold and silver coins balance scale stickpin; larger gold coin on crossbar with smaller silver coin (Hake 336) 1"w; gold and silver finish . . . . . . . . . . . . . . .   30.00    35.00

☐ Gold bug stickpin with arrow piercing body (Hake 327) 1¼"h; gilded brass . . . . . . . . . . . . . . . . . . . . .   50.00    60.00

☐ Flag, hand-held mechanical badge; opens to Bryan and Sewall photos (Hake 347) 1¼"w; silver, black; McKinley match . . . . . . . . . . . . . . . . . . . . . . . . . . .   125.00    135.00

☐ Man in coffin mechanical; coffin has coin behind it; gold figure (McKinley?) in coffin (Hake 370) . . . .   200.00    225.00

Price Range

☐ "My Choice," Bryan–Kern jugate tin mechanical; scene of White House within die-cut shield border; candidates' portraits pop up from behind shield (Hale 349) 1¾"h x 2"w; red, white, blue, black; sepia photos . . . . . . . . . . . . . . . . . . . . . . . . . . . . . . . . 175.00    200.00

☐ "Never A Quitter" lapel stud mechanical; slogan on rolled fabric, pulls down from brass holder like window shade; small brass pull loop (Hake 374) 1¼"w; pale pink fabric, brass . . . . . . . . . . . . . . . . . . . . . . . . 50.00    60.00

☐ Pig with silver coin on tail; stickpin (Hake 342) 1¼"w; black with silver . . . . . . . . . . . . . . . . . . . . . 50.00    60.00

☐ Rooster badge with large coin processional hanger attached; coin has embossed Bryan profile; rooster and "Bryan–Stevenson" also embossed (Hake 3060) 5"; brass . . . . . . . . . . . . . . . . . . . . . . . . . . . . 150.00    160.00

☐ Rooster on bar with ribbon and star-shaped hanger; Bryan's portrait in star's center (Hake 3152) 3½" overall; red, white, blue ribbon; brass rooster; black and white paper portrait . . . . . . . . . . . . . . . . . . . . . 45.00    55.00

☐ Scrolled "Emancipated" embossed bar with eagle and shield; embossed bust of Bryan with lettering in shield . . . . . . . . . . . . . . . . . . . . . . . . . . . . . . . . . . . 235.00    250.00

☐ Silver bug mechanical with Bryan and Sewall paper photos in wings (Hake 307) ¾"; silvered brass; sepia photos . . . . . . . . . . . . . . . . . . . . . . . . . . . . . . . . 135.00    145.00

☐ Silver bug mechanical with Bryan photo inset in wing; symbols embossed in other wing (Hake 304) 1"h; silvered brass with sepia photo . . . . . . . . . . . 150.00    175.00

☐ Silver bug with Bryan head die-cut stickpin; embossing: "Bryan For President" (Hake 369) 1¾"; silver . . . . . . . . . . . . . . . . . . . . . . . . . . . . . . . . . . . . 50.00    60.00

☐ "16 to 1," scrolled bar with shield disk; "Free Silver" hanger with flag (Hake 3057) 2¼" aluminum; red, white, blue flag . . . . . . . . . . . . . . . . . . . . . . . . 30.00    35.00

☐ "16 to 1" silver ingot with paper photos of Bryan and Sewall badge (Hake 341) 1¾"; silver with sepia photos . . . . . . . . . . . . . . . . . . . . . . . . . . . . . . . . . . . 110.00    120.00

Price Range

☐ Skeleton stickpin, "Death To Trusts," with spring attached to skeleton; legend reversed from black on torso (Hake 328) $1\frac{1}{2}''$; gold, black; McKinley match . . . . . . . . . . . . . . . . . . . . . . . . . . . . . . . . . . . . . . . . . . 225.00    250.00

☐ "These Two and Prosperity," celluloid pinback with Bryan bust portrait and figural ear of corn hanger (Hake 3240) $3''$h; black and white image; silver ear of corn . . . . . . . . . . . . . . . . . . . . . . . . . . . . . . . 100.00    125.00

☐ Trident spearing gold bugs stickpin; "Bryan and Sewall" embossed on handle (Hake 329; Warner 213) $\frac{7}{8}''$ x $1\frac{1}{4}''$; white metal trident with gold bugs    115.00    125.00

☐ "True Bi-Metalism, No Straddle-Bug," octagonal metal hanger; cartoon of silver bug and gold bug strolling with arms around each other and carrying money pouches labeled "16" and "1" (Hake 302) $3\frac{1}{4}''$; silver, gold, black background . . . . . . . . . . . 65.00    75.00

☐ Unflattering caracature of man; mechanical stickpin (Bryan? McKinley? The Trusts?); mouth opens to reveal paper photo of Bryan (Hake 337) $\frac{3}{4}''$w; black metal . . . . . . . . . . . . . . . . . . . . . . . . . . . . . . . . . . 175.00    200.00

☐ Watch face with embossed hands and numerals; "16 to 1" theme (Hake 334) $1''$ dia.; gold, silver . . . . 45.00    55.00

☐ "W. J. Bryan. Our Choice" bar with star hanger; ornate scrolled bar with die-cut star hanger (Hake 360) $1\frac{3}{4}''$h; silver, brass . . . . . . . . . . . . . . . . . . . . . 25.00    30.00

☐ Workingman's stickpin mechanical; wears "crown of thorns"; push lever and crown rises from head; disk with Bryan portrait appears at left (Hake 3066) $1''$; brass; the elite among Bryan mechanicals . . . 550.00    600.00

☐ "You Can't Lose Him" pinback mechanical; Bryan's name, die-cut in gold, pops up from behind item (Hake 364) $1\frac{1}{2}''$h; white, black, gold . . . . . . 90.00    100.00

☐ Bryan flag stickpin; "Shall The People Rule? Or The Trusts Continue?" $1''$; bust portrait of Bryan in flag's center (Hake 3063; Warner 611); red, white, blue, black . . . . . . . . . . . . . . . . . . . . . . . . . . . . 100.00    110.00

## Cartoon/Pictorial Pinbacks

| | Price Range | |
|---|---|---|

☐ "A Clean Sweep," rooster with broom under wing (Hake 274) ⅞"; multicolor . . . . . . . . . . . . . . . . . . 15.00  20.00

☐ "Anti-Amalgamation" 16–1 and 8 Hours (unlisted) 1¼"; multicolor . . . . . . . . . . . . . . . . . . . . . . . . . . . 125.00  150.00

☐ "Anti-Imperialism" inscription in Latin on rim; seated Liberty figure holds globe with North America outline; wreath over Bryan's head (Hake 408; Warner 236) 1½"; multicolor . . . . . . . . . . . . . . . 700.00  750.00

☐ "Boy Orator" cartoon; Little Pinkies Advertising premium (unlisted) ⅞"; black on white . . . . . . . . 20.00  25.00

☐ Bryan and Uncle Sam offering constitutional government to Puerto Rico; large snake labeled "Trusts" is coiled to crush a crown-wearing McKinley, 1900 (Hake unlisted; Warner 526) 1¼"; sepiatone . . . . . . . . . . . . . . . . . . . . . . . . . . . . . . . . . 900.00  1000.00

Advertising pinback is takeoff on RCA Victor "His Master's Voice." Image in speaker horn changes from Republican Bryan to Democrat Taft when pin is turned ($1,000–$1,200).

Price Range

☐ Bryan racetrack caricature with Bryan in lead on back of donkey; Taft trails in distance; 1908 race (Hake 3221; Warner 599) 2¼"; black on white; Taft match ............................... 500.00    600.00

☐ Bryan vs. McKinley occupy White House mechanical; clever caricatures; as Bryan enters White House, McKinley watches from window; pull string and scene is reversed (Hake 3065; Warner 243) 1¾"; black on aluminum .................... 350.00    400.00

☐ Anti-Bryan: "Bray-on [Donkey rebus] and Sewell" (Unlisted) 1¼"; black on white .............. 50.00    60.00

☐ Clockface with small bust of Bryan inset at VI; hands point to XVI to I with gold and silver symbols on each hand; marvelous rebus (Hake unlisted; Warner 206) ⅞"; gold, silver, white, black ..... 400.00    425.00

☐ Clockface, as above (Hake unlisted; Warner 207), ⅞" ....................................... 175.00    200.00

☐ More uncommon version of (Hake 267) 16–1 clockface (Warner 212) ......................... 75.00    100.00

☐ Club rebus, "Bryan Kern 36 [picture of large club] Club" (Hake 429) ⅞"; red, blue on white ...... 45.00    50.00

☐ Democratic doctrines: "National Democratic Convention, Chicago, Ill., July 7, 1896"; photo insets of Bryan at top with three girls, representing "Reliable Money," "Equal Rights," "Monroe Doctrine" (Hake 262) 1¼"; black on white .............. 45.00    55.00

☐ Eagle with arched, spread wings forms top part of shield portrait insets of Bryan–Kern; large T-shape with shield background (Hake 3199; Warner 300) 1¾"; multicolor ............................ 525.00    550.00

☐ Eclipse: "Partial Eclipse Will Be Total in November"; Bryan image slanted; obscures most of McKinley portrait (Hake unlisted; Warner 239) 1¼"; dark brown, white ......................... 500.00    550.00

☐ Eclipse: "Total Eclipse Nov. 6"; gold sun with McKinley inset being obscured vertically by silvermoon Bryan image; sun's rays radiate across top half of pinback (Hake 415) 1¼"; black, silver, gold 500.00    550.00

Price Range

☐ Moon (or sun?) caricature "I Am A Silver Man"; (Hake 427) $\frac{7}{8}$"; silver, black ................. 35.00    40.00

☐ "My Billy" "For President. Wm. J. Bryan of Neb."; caricature of billygoat with Bryan head (unlisted; see Spring 1987 *Keynoter*) 1¼"; black on white 250.00    300.00

☐ "My Hobby. A Winner." Bryan riding a broom with ostrich head on handle (vague symbolism, *per*haps alluding to his hiding head in sand over critical issues?) (Hake 407) 2"; multicolor; one of the key pieces of 1900 race (see McKinley hobby horse match)...................................... 1500.00    2000.00

☐ "Nebraska For Bryan"; hand waving flag with native son slogan (Hake 428; Warner 319) $\frac{7}{8}$"; red, rose shade, yellow, green, blue background (Nebraska Bryan Volunteers item) ................ 55.00    65.00

☐ "No Cross Of Gold. No Crown Of Thorns"; illustration of cross with thorns (Hake 272) $\frac{7}{8}$"; rose, green on white ............................ 75.00    85.00

☐ "Newsboy" cartoon; Little Pinkies Advertising premium; carries newspaper, "N.I.T." (unlisted) $\frac{7}{8}$"; black on white ............................ 20.00    25.00

☐ "No Dinner Pail Lunch For Me. I Am For Bryan And A Square Meal"; sketch of large turkey on table with all the fixings and Champagne bottle (Hake 3224) 1¾"; multicolor; braided brass rim 500.00    550.00

☐ "No English Dictation 1776–1896, 16 to 1, We Demand The Money Of The Constitution"; eagle with shield and crossed flags (Hake 3237) 1½"; stud; red, white, blue ............................ 100.00    110.00

☐ Also $\frac{7}{8}$" (Hake 280) ........................ 40.00    50.00

☐ "No Twilight Zone. The Nation. The State"; caricature of "The Trusts" mugging "The People" under black pall beneath Bryan's bust image (Hake 3233; Warner 305) 1¾"; black, white .............. 350.00    400.00

☐ Ohio horseshoe, eagle and cornucopia; small Bryan inset inside horseshoe; 1908 (unlisted) 1¾"; multicolor ...................................... 1200.00    1400.00

Price Range

☐ "People's Airline"; Bryan bicycling on high wire in the clouds on his way to Washington (Hake 412) 1¼"; shades of blue on white ................ 900.00    1000.00

☐ Photograph in front of house of 16 silver bugs and one gold bug (Bryan is in foreground leaning on gate post); "Tomlinson Bros., Hannibal, Mo." (Hake 3235; Warner 240) 1½"; sepiatone; blue lettering—possibly a sample? ................... 250.00    275.00

☐ Presidential chair; Bryan in chair sitting atop sprawled-out McKinley; 1896 race (Hake 3279; Warner 208) ⅞"; multicolor; McKinley match. 300.00    350.00

☐ Scales of Justice: "Freedom And Justice" Anti-Imperialists 1900 (Hake 3346) ⅞"; black on white 60.00    70.00

☐ "Shall The People Rule?" Giant question mark superimposed over Bryan portrait (Hake unlisted; Warner 313) ¾"; blue, white, black ........... 225.00    250.00

☐ Steer's head rebus: "Down With The [Beef] Trust" (Hake 260) 1¼"; black on white .............. 20.00    25.00

☐ "The Bottom Of The Dinner Pail" "Vote For Bryan"; bottom is ripped out of pail in dramatic rebuttal to numerous McKinley dinnerpail pinback slogans (Hake 413) 1¼"; red, white, light blue .. 225.00    250.00

☐ "To The White House"; Bryan on bicycle, wearing beanie; "Silver" appears in each wheel hub (Hake 420) ⅞"; blue on white; McKinley match....... 250.00    300.00

☐ Shamrock; "Democracy Stands For People Not Trusts; Bimetalism Not Monometalism; Republic Not Empire"; words appear on all three leaf petals; "1900" (Hake 263) 1¼"; green, red, black on white 65.00    75.00

☐ "Tree of Life"; "Tree That Does Not Bear Good Fruit Shall Be Dug Out By The Roots And Cast Into The Fire" (Bryan's fundamentalist philosophy); square inset of seated Bryan flanked by illustration of dead tree being dug out and tree that is flourishing; 1908 race key item (Hake 3029; Warner 302) green, black, on buff .................... 600.00    650.00

☐ "United We Stand. Divided We Fall"; Bryan shaking hands with laborer; "Not Trusts" "16 to 1" "Labor Bryan" (Hake 264) 1¼"; sepiatone ..... 525.00    550.00

Price Range

☐ Same as above (Hake 265; Warner 234) except multicolor ...................................... 725.00    750.00

☐ U.S. map with circular portrait of Bryan inset; slogans around rim; 1900 race (Hake unlisted; Warner
52⑨) 1¼"; brown on cream .................. 650.00    750.00

## *Jugates*

### BRYAN–KERN—1908

☐ "Bryan and Kern" conjoining bust portrait; black
photo with flesh tones (Hake 110) ⅞"; pale blue
background (reproduced as celluloid button) .... 15.00    20.00

☐ "Bryan" and "Kern" in oval insets framed by gold
filigree and red, white, blue shield at top (Hake 78)
2"; red, blue, black, gold on white ............ 125.00    150.00

☐ Bryan–Kern kidney-shaped portrait insets (Hake
105) 1¼"; black and white photos; red, gold; white
background with brilliant aqua border ......... 120.00    130.00

☐ "Bryan and Kern," oval shaped with portraits
(Hake 91) 2¼" sepiatone .................... 125.00    150.00

☐ Bryan and Kern portraits divided by stylized mace
and scepter (Hake 90; Warner 307) 1¾"; red,
white, blue, black, gold; match to Taft (Warner
288) ...................................... 325.00    350.00

☐ "Clean Sweep For Democrats in 1908";
Bryan–Kern ovals are staggered and divided by
stylized broom (Hake 93) 1¼"; yellow, red, white;
black background; key item .................. 275.00    300.00

☐ "Democratic Candidates 1908"; "Bryan & Kern"
conjoining bust portraits; in filigree brass frame suspended from ribbon with "Vim, Vigor, Victory" in
gold over red (Hake 80) 1½"; black, red, white; 5"
overall .................................... 160.00    175.00

☐ Eagle with spread wings and crossed flags are background for Bryan–Kern oval insets (Hake 86) 1¼";
dark blue on buff (item has been reproduced) ... 145.00    155.00

☐ Entwined ovals of Bryan–Kern (Hake 88) 1½";
gold border; black, red on white .............. 225.00    250.00

|  | Price Range | |
|---|---|---|
| ☐ Filigree gold-framed Bryan–Kern insets in oval pinback (Hake 99) 1″w; black, gold; dark blue background ...................................... | 125.00 | 135.00 |
| ☐ Linked diamond-shaped insets of Bryan–Kern with upside-down stylized shield and circle dividing pair; very Art Deco in concept (Hake 96; Warner 308) 1¼″; multicolor ............................ | 175.00 | 200.00 |
| ☐ Miss Liberty presents oval insets of Bryan–Kern in folds of her red-white striped dress; her head is outlined against yellow sun (Hake 102) 1¼″; red, white, yellow; black and white portraits; blue background ...................................... | 225.00 | 250.00 |
| ☐ Slanted ovals in ornate framing with torch bearing Miss Liberty and Hera flanking shield; dark blue background with six stars at top (Hake 87) ..... | 350.00 | 375.00 |
| ☐ Statue of Liberty; beam from torch shines on oval insets of Bryan–Kern (Hake 3198) 1¾″; multicolor | 550.00 | 560.00 |
| ☐ Uncle Sam holding rectangular portraits of Bryan–Kern with laurel leaf and star (Hake 89) 1½″; orange, blue, tan, black, white; red background ...................................... | 375.00 | 400.00 |
| ☐ "Wm. J. Bryan" "John W. Kern"; eagle with spread wings tops ovals (Hake 95) 1¼″; black on white | 125.00 | 135.00 |
| ☐ Also red, white, blue version ................. | 110.00 | 125.00 |

## MISCELLANEOUS

| | | |
|---|---|---|
| ☐ "Bryan and Bennett. For President and Governor"; bust insets in large "B"; West Virginia jugate (Hake 247) 1¼″; red, sepia, buff ................... | 175.00 | 200.00 |
| ☐ "Our President" "Our Chairman"; bust portraits of Bryan and Democratic party chairman (unidentified), 1900 race (Hake 246) 1½″; black on white photo with red, white, blue rim ............... | 115.00 | 125.00 |

## BRYAN–SEWALL—1896

| | | |
|---|---|---|
| ☐ Bryan–Sewall "Victory 1896"; sepia portraits in ovals; stud (Hake 5) 1¼″; red, white, black, red background ................................. | 80.00 | 90.00 |

Price Range

☐ Clockface jugate of Bryan and Sewall; small insets of pair with hands set at "16 to 1" (Hake 405; Warner 205) ⅞"; black on white ................. 200.00   225.00

☐ "Free Silver"; appears above Bryan–Sewall bust portraits (Hake 10) 1¼"; black on white (button has been reproduced) ...................... 35.00   45.00

☐ "Our Choice" Bryan–Sewall portraits appear in window; enameled mechanical; item can be turned to reveal McKinley–Hobart (Hake 13) 1"; orange, green, yellow background .................... 160.00   175.00

☐ Bryan–Sewell in center of large rosette satin (corsage?) with bow and tassels (Hake 4) 1" button in dark brown on white; rosette in reds, pinks; brown bow and tassels; 5"h overall .................. 60.00   70.00

☐ Bryan–Sewall "16 to 1" stud (Hake 6) ⅞"; red, blue, black on white ...................... 55.00   65.00

☐ Bryan–Stevenson crossed-flags badge (Hake 348) ¾"; red, white, blue, black; gilded shell ........ 90.00   100.00

## BRYAN–STEVENSON—1900

☐ "Anti-Imperialist Club; Rock Island" [IL] "Stand By The Republic"; oval insets of Bryan–Stevenson appear across flag banner (Hake 39) 1¼"; red, blue, black; white background ..................... 200.00   225.00

☐ Similar version with "The Watchword" heading 200.00   210.00

☐ Bryan–Stevenson aluminum mechanical disk; portraits appear in circular windows; "Democrats—W. Jennings Bryan" appears in two slots; shows McKinley–Roosevelt when rotated (Hake 25) 1½"; aluminum black ........................... 200.00   225.00

☐ "Bryan–Stevenson" conjoining bust profiles (Hake 37) 1¼"; sepiatone ......................... 140.00   150.00

☐ Bryan–Stevenson conjoining portraits (Hake 20) 2"; sepiatone ............................... 40.00   50.00

☐ "Bryan & Stevenson" conjoining portraits within circle; draped flag at top (Hake 19) 2"; red, white, blue, black rose; pale blue background ......... 50.00   60.00

☐ "Bryan–Stevenson" "Free Silver" oval portrait insets (Hake 47) 1¼"; dark blue on white ....... 85.00   95.00

Price Range

☐ Bryan–Stevenson oval insets with flags, eagle, and musical notes framing them (Hake 35) 1¼"; red, white, blue; McKinley-Hobart match .......... 400.00    425.00

☐ Bryan–Stevenson oval portraits; eagle at top; cornucopia with "16 to 1" at bottom (Hake 21) 1½"; red, white, black; pale blue background ............ 250.00    260.00

☐ Also ⅞" .................................. 145.00    155.00

☐ "Bryan and Stevenson" oval portrait insets flanking Capitol building (Hake 36) 1¼"; sepiatone (see McKinley–Roosevelt match) .................... 200.00    225.00

☐ "Bryan and Stevenson, Tammany, 1900"; New York item (Hake unlisted; Warner 237) ⅞"; red border with lettering reversed in white, black ... 325.00    350.00

☐ Circular insets of Bryan–Stevenson against red, white, blue wide border (Hake 27) 1¼"; pale blue, black ...................................... 85.00    95.00

☐ "Bryan and Stevenson" oval insets against Capitol dome backdrop (Hake 63) ⅞"; sepiatone (one of most prized Bryan jugates in this size) ......... 85.00    95.00

☐ "Choice Of The People"; "Bryan and Stevenson" (Hake 76) ⅞"; black on buff ................. 65.00    75.00

☐ "Guards Of Chicago" conjoining portraits Bryan–Stevenson (Hake 22) 1½"; dark brown, white ...................................... 160.00    175.00

☐ "Read Bergen County Record" with paired Bryan–Stevenson conjoining portraits (Hake 41) 1¼"; sepiatone ............................. 100.00    125.00

☐ Red, white, blue flag background, conjoining Bryan–Stevenson bust portrait; names appear in Hebrew (Hake 58) 1¼" ..................... 135.00    150.00

☐ Shield with "Bryan–Stevenson" circular insets (Hake 23) 1½"; red, blue shield; with pale blue background ................................. 25.00    35.00

☐ Also appeared in 1¼" (as a litho, not a cello) ... 15.00    20.00

☐ T-shape motif with star at top divides Bryan–Stevenson portraits (Hake 49) .......... 80.00    100.00

| *Portrait Buttons* | Price Range | |
|---|---|---|
| ☐ Bryan bust portrait in clock face with hands at 16 (min.) to 1 (Hake 129) 1½″; multicolor with blue, red and yellow braided rim .................. | 225.00 | 250.00 |
| ☐ Also available in 1¼″ ...................... | 135.00 | 150.00 |
| ☐ Bryan image in rounded rectangle held by Miss Liberty, who has other arm draped around sword; laurel leaves frame her head and top of Bryan portrait (Hake 118; Warner 306) 1½″; multicolor, with gold rim ................................... | 275.00 | 300.00 |
| ☐ "Bryan League" 1908; Bryan in silver framed keystone (Hake 229) ⅞″; silver lettering against black background .............................. | 20.00 | 25.00 |
| ☐ Bryan portrait frames inverted wishbone; banner across middle (Hake 123) 1¼″; red, white, blue, black ....................................... | 65.00 | 75.00 |
| ☐ Bryan portrait oval inset in folds of flag held in large eagle's beak (Hake 120) 1½″; red, white, blue, gold, black; pale green background ................. | 200.00 | 225.00 |
| ☐ "Commoner" safe; guarantee of bank deposits; Bryan image on door of floor safe (Hake 171) 1¼″; portrait in blue tone; safe-light blue; red, white, blue rim; key item ............................. | 150.00 | 175.00 |
| ☐ Crossed flags; superimposed Bryan photo (Hake 208) ⅞″; black, red, white, blue; gold background | 30.00 | 40.00 |
| ☐ Daisy; small circular bust inset of Bryan in center of flower; slogan "Free Silver 16 to 1" appears almost subliminally in white petals (Hake 187) ⅞″; white, red, pale blue; black background ........ | 50.00 | 60.00 |
| ☐ "Democratic National Convention, Kansas City, 1900" Bryan portrait in center of sunflower (Hake 148) 1¼″; red petals; sepia portrait; white lettering on black background ........................ | 90.00 | 110.00 |
| ☐ "Facing The Future. Let The Majority Rule" (Hake 216) ⅞″; black on white .................... | 45.00 | 55.00 |
| ☐ "For President" "William Jennings Bryan"; Bryan photo in circle inset; lettering in large, bold type (Hake 170) 1¼″ .......................... | 75.00 | 85.00 |

Price Range

☐ Horseshoe; Bryan portrait framed by inverted good luck piece (Hake 163) 1¾"; gold, red, white, blue, black ...................................... 35.00     45.00

☐ "I Am For Peace" legend appears under angel with spread wings; pair of doves with laurels in beaks frame oval Bryan inset (Hake 410) 1¼"; red, white blue border; dark blue background, green laurel    160.00     185.00

☐ Laurel-framed Bryan bust portrait with star-topped shield; eagle heads peering out from lower part of shield hold banner in beaks (Hake unlisted; Warner 314) 1¼"; yellow, white, blue, red, green ....... 225.00     250.00

☐ "No Crown Of Thorns, No Cross Of Gold"; slogan wraps around border (Hake 176) ⅞" stud; black on white, red rim .......................... 115.00     125.00

☐ "Nitrate Of Soda Helps The Farmer"; Bryan bust photo (Hake 198) ⅞"; black on white ........ 45.00     50.00

☐ "Our Standard Bearer. The Nation's Commoner"; Bryan portrait appears above husks of four ears of corn; celluloid oval-shaped pinback attached to flag suspended by bar that reads "Delegate"; overlaps on blue ribbon—"Official"—National Democratic Convention, Denver, 1908 (Hake 124; Warner 299) button, 2¼"h; gold, yellow, black, white; 6" overall    600.00     650.00

☐ "Smoke John Smith" Bryan bust; advertising premium (Hake 190) ⅞"; black on white ........ 20.00     25.00

☐ Stars; Bryan black and white portrait inset pops out of bright red star amid myriad smaller stars against black background (Hake 151) 1¼"; black, white, red, tan ..................................... 35.00     45.00

☐ "The Indianapolis News. The Great Hoosier Daily"; Bryan bust portrait in football-shaped inset (Hake 233) ⅞"; black, dark, blue; white stars; bright orange background .................... 125.00     135.00

☐ Young herald in kilts blowing horn draped with flag, Bryan bust portrait superimposed in circle inset; a superb Maxfield Parrish illustration; key item; various shades of blue, orange, red, brown, black with tan background (Hake 119; Warner 303) 1½"; matching Taft ........................ 300.00     350.00

| *Slogan Pinbacks, Studs* | Price Range | |
|---|---|---|
| ☐ "Are You A Gold Bug? I'm Not" (Hake 301) $7/8$"; green on white; High Admiral . . . . . . . . . . . . . . . . | 10.00 | 12.00 |
| ☐ "Europe Wants Gold. We Want Silver"; stud (Hake 290) $7/8$"; black on white . . . . . . . . . . . . . . . . . . . | 10.00 | 12.00 |
| ☐ "I'm Solid Silver" (Hake 3369) $7/8$"; black on silver | 10.00 | 12.00 |
| ☐ "I Will Carry Silver If It Breaks My Back"; stud (Hake 289) $7/8$"; blue on white . . . . . . . . . . . . . . . | 10.00 | 12.00 |
| ☐ "Our Candidate Voted For Bryan"; slogan in keystone outline; stud (Hake 432) $1\frac{1}{4}$"; black and white . . . . . . . . . . . . . . . . . . . . . . . . . . . . . . . . . . . . | 40.00 | 50.00 |
| ☐ "Our Platform 16 to 1 Will Sweep The Country"; stud (Hake 288) $7/8$"; black, white . . . . . . . . . . . . | 10.00 | 12.00 |
| ☐ "Silver Is Good Enough For Me"; stud (Hake 291) $7/8$"; black on white . . . . . . . . . . . . . . . . . . . . . . . . | 10.00 | 12.00 |
| ☐ "16 Bread. 1 Butter"; enameled stud, porcelain (Hake 3341) $7/8$"; brown on white . . . . . . . . . . . . | 60.00 | 65.00 |
| ☐ "16 Parts Beer. 1 Part Foam"; stud (Hake 282) $7/8$"; black on white . . . . . . . . . . . . . . . . . . . . . . . . . . . . | 14.00 | 16.00 |
| ☐ "The Banks Don't Want Free Silver. I Do. I Don't Own A Bank" (unlisted) $7/8$"; black on white . . . | 20.00 | 25.00 |
| ☐ "The Constitution Follows The Flag"; "Bryan" in center of stud (Hake 3393) $3/4$"; red, black . . . . . . | 12.00 | 15.00 |
| ☐ "The Money We Want" (Liberty-head coin) rebus; stud (Hake 3349) $7/8$"; bronze color on white . . . | 20.00 | 22.00 |
| ☐ "U.S." (Unlimited Silver) High Admiral cigarettes premium (Hake 295) $7/8$"; red on white (one of a series) . . . . . . . . . . . . . . . . . . . . . . . . . . . . . . . . . . . | 10.00 | 12.00 |
| ☐ "W.B.s O.K." (Hake 430) $1/2$"; black on white . . | 15.00 | 20.00 |
| ☐ "Will Little Willie Get It. If You Have Money Bet It"; stud (Hake 284) $7/8$"; white, blue . . . . . . . . . | 14.00 | 16.00 |
| ☐ "Equality—Justice—A New Deal"; Bryan shaking hands with Indian Chief, sunburst and view of teepees contrast with bustling city in background (Hake 3281) $1\frac{1}{4}$"; red, blue on white . . . . . . . . . | 200.00 | 250.00 |

Price Range

☐ "From Denver To Washington"; caricature of Bryan tipping hat from open roadster; broom projects from running board with banner "Clean Sweep For Democrats" (Hake 3279) 1¼"; black on white   350.00   400.00

☐ "From Lincoln To Washington. William Jennings Bryan For President. 1908"; full-length portrait of Bryan with small inset Washington and Lincoln images; also views of Bryan's Nebraska home and White House (Hake 3211) 2¼"; black on white   500.00   550.00

☐ Liberty-head coins (16) with coin in center (1) rebus; stacked coins form border (Hake 266) 1¼"; silver coins with bronze coin behind black background ...................................   50.00   75.00

☐ "We Need Relief From The Trust On Beef" (Hake 259) 1¼"; black on white ....................   20.00   25.00

### Trigates

☐ Anti-Bryan trigate—Bryan–Croaker [sic]–Aguinaldo—"Three Of A Kind"; Bryan is cast in company with two tyrants, Richard Croker (note deliberate misspelling on button), Tammany Hall kingpin, and Emilio Aguinaldo, a notorious Filipino leader (Hake 112; Warner 232) 2¼"; sepiatone   225.00   250.00

☐ Bryan, Stevenson, and unidentified coattail candidate (Hake 48) 1¼"; black on white ...........   115.00   125.00

☐ "Indiana's Choice" Bryan–Stevenson–Kern; oval insets (Hake 40) 1¼"; sepiatone .............   175.00   200.00

## JAMES BUCHANAN

Served in the House as Democrat from Pennsylvania in 1821–31; U.S. Senate 1834–45; Secretary of State under Polk, 1845–49. Became 15th President of U.S., 1857–61. Known affectionately as "Old Buck," he was our only bachelor president.

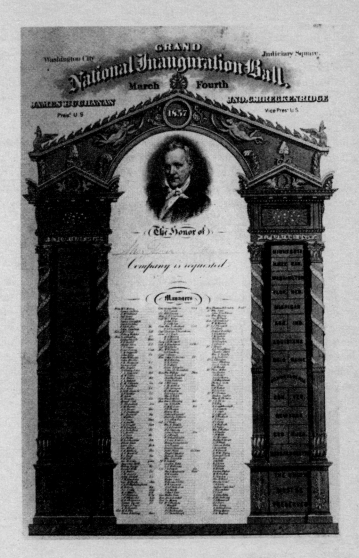

Invitation to Grand Inaugural Ball
for James Buchanan, 1857
($150–$175).

## AARON BURR

Aaron Burr, one of the most controversial of all who entered the political scene, is most famous for his 30–year vendetta with Federalist power broker Alexander Hamilton, which climaxed with a duel in which Hamilton was mortally wounded. The Democrat Republican from New York served in the U.S. Senate from 1791–97 and was judged one of the best officers that ever presided over a deliberative assembly. Burr and Jefferson each received 73 votes as winners in the 1800 election (although Burr had been slated for the second office). It took 36 ballots and seven days of mounting tension before the deadlock was broken in favor of Jefferson. Burr served as Vice-President from 1801–05, but the two lived under an uneasy truce. In 1806, he was arrested (and later acquitted) for treason. Burr's true intentions remain obscure, but it is believed he had ambitions to rule his own little empire by taking over a piece of territory in the West (see Jefferson).

## GEORGE HERBERT WALKER BUSH

Bush, a Massachusetts transplant who entered politics in Texas, served as Chairman of Republican National Committee in 1973–74; served two terms in the House as Houston's first-ever Republican in Washington. Ambassador to the United Nations, 1970–73. In the 1976 primaries, running against his eventual partner on the national ticket, Ronald Reagan, Bush coined the phrase, "voodoo economics" to describe Reagan's fiscal proposals. Acknowledged to have the inside track for the Republican presidential nomination in 1988 (see Ronald Reagan).

## BENJAMIN BUTLER

Butler was nominated for president by the Greenback Party in 1884; he inspired more fascinating three-dimensional items than all other third-party candidates combined.

**Price Range**

### Ceramic Novelties and Statuary

☐ "A Match For Everyone"; bisque china matchbox; high-relief outward-facing busts of Butler on all four sides; Civil War military cap is lid handle; "Contraband of War/Set Them To Work" (Butler's famed response when asked what to do with freed slaves), 1874; 5"h; white, lightly glazed ........     150.00     200.00

Price Range

☐ Caricature soap sculpture; Butler with bag in hand. Gen. Butler was accused of looting Southern estates following end of Civil War .................. 75.00 100.00

☐ Butler cast-lead paperweight; silhouetted profile bust; 3″h; gilt finish ......................... 25.00 35.00

☐ Butler bronze oval portrait plaque; 7½″l; bronze finish ....................................... 75.00 85.00

## Lapel Devices

☐ Butler–West shield-shaped shell with paper portraits; eagle perched on pole; two stars and tassels below; 1884; 1¾″h; gilt brass ................ 500.00 525.00

☐ Spoon-shaped clasp with suspended medal; "Workingmen's Friend" borders circular photo of Butler on cardboard; Circle of 23 stars encircle 1884 date on reverse; 1″h, white metal .................. 250.00 275.00

## Toys, Banks

☐ Gen. Benjamin Butler cast-iron still-bank caricature; portrayed as green-backed frog holding paper money in one hand; "For The Masses" embossed on left arm; "Bonds and Yachts For Me" on right (alludes to his ownership of famous yacht *America*) 6¼″h; yellow body; green arms, legs; made by J. & E. Stevens, 1878; one of ultimate rarities among still banks ................................... 1400.00 1500.00

☐ Gen. Butler walking clockwork toy; made by Ives, 1880s; 10″h; cast iron, wood; clothing: red pants, blue tunic ................................... 5000.00 6000.00

☐ "Magic Gen. Butler" jiggling figure toy (see illustration); 4″dia; green, blue, or brown wooden cup, glass enclosed (see illustration) ............... 600.00 700.00

A. A Davis catalog flyer for U. S. Grant and Ben Butler "Jiggler" novelty toys. (Flyer itself is highly collectible.) Toys valued at $600 to $700.

## JOHN CALDWELL CALHOUN

Calhoun, a Republican from South Carolina, served as Vice–President under both John Q. Adams and Andrew Jackson, 1825–32. He had also been Secretary of War under James Monroe. Calhoun had eyes only for the Presidency, but lacking support in 1824, Calhoun dropped from the race, labeling himself one of the "cantbees." A constant thorn in Jackson's side, Calhoun became the first Vice–President to resign from office in 1832 (preceding Spiro Agnew by over 140 years). The reason: he felt he had no forum for his views.

## JAMES EARL CARTER

Jimmy Carter, former peanut farmer, commander of a nuclear submarine, and one-term Governor of Georgia, won a narrow victory over incumbent Gerry Ford in 1976 to become the 39th President of the U.S. In 1980 Carter was swamped by Ronald Reagan, gaining the dubious distinction of experiencing the most stunning defeat for a presidential incumbent since Hoover lost to FDR a half century earlier.

**Price Range**

### Cartoon/Pictorial Pinbacks

☐ Alaska outline map, "Carter/Mondale" reversed out of black background (Hake 2308) 2"; black, white . . . . . . . . . . . . . . . . . . . . . . . . . . . . . . . . . . . . . .     40.00     50.00

☐ "Born Again Christians For Carter"; large cross (Hake 2505) 1"; black, white . . . . . . . . . . . . . . .     5.00     7.00

☐ Capitol dome atop peanut; " '76" superimposed on nut (Hake 2344) 2½"; brown, black, yellow . . . .     5.00     7.00

☐ "Carter Has It A To Z"; St. Louis Arch in center with "A To Z" at base (Hake 2378) 1½"; green, red, white . . . . . . . . . . . . . . . . . . . . . . . . . . . . . . . .     3.00     5.00

☐ Carter peanut taking bow wearing Uncle Sam outfit and top hat (Hake 2166) 3"; red, white, blue, black     4.00     6.00

☐ "Conservationists For Jimmy Carter/President"; cartoon of large eagle overseeing forests, lakes, farmlands; large sun in background (Hake 2254) 2½"; yellow, brown, black . . . . . . . . . . . . . . . . . .     8.00     10.00

☐ "Dairyland Democrats For Carter-Mondale"; cameo portraits against map of Wisconsin (Hake 2021) 1½"; red, black, white . . . . . . . . . . . . . . . .     12.00     15.00

☐ "I'm Nuts About Carter"; cartoon of Mr. Peanut in typical top hat (Hake 2249) 2½"; black, yellow     4.00     6.00

☐ "Mad About Carter," oblong Mayan image (Hake 2327) 2"; red, yellow . . . . . . . . . . . . . . . . . . . . . . .     7.00     9.00

☐ Peanut balancing on Democratic donkey's head; cartoon portraits of Carter–Mondale atop peanut (Hake 2023) 3"; brown, black, yellow . . . . . . . . .     7.00     9.00

☐ Playboy bunny symbol wearing famous Carter grin (Hake 2255) 2¼"; white reversed out of black . .     3.00     4.00

☐ "The Coming Of Carter"; Carter wearing farmer's outfit including straw hat (Hake 2278) 2½"; multi-color . . . . . . . . . . . . . . . . . . . . . . . . . . . . . . . . . . . .     3.00     4.00

☐ "The Grin Will Win. Jimmy Carter For President in '76."; large cartoon peanut with toothy grin (Hake 2386) 1½"; green, brown, white . . . . . . . .     2.00     3.00

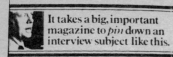

It takes a big, important magazine to *pin* down an interview subject like this. CARTER TALKS IN PLAYBOY

WHERE ELSE BUT IN PLAYBOY

"Carter talks in Playboy" promotional flyer. David Frent regards attached pinback as a truly significant item that influenced voter attitudes regarding Carter in 1976 race ($12–$15).

| | Price Range | |
|---|---|---|
| ☐ "Vote For Jimmy Carter—I am Just Working for Peanuts [rebus] Delegates" (Hake 2352) 1½ "; red, black, white | 35.00 | 40.00 |

### Inaugural Pinbacks—1977

| | | |
|---|---|---|
| ☐ 49th Inauguration, Jan. 20, 1977; oval insets of Jimmy and Rosalyn Carter, Walter and Joan Mondale with U.S. Capitol in background; presidential seal below: "Leaders For A Change" (Hake 2056) 4"; red, white, blue, black | 3.00 | 5.00 |
| ☐ "First President Inaugurated of the 3rd Centennial/The Spirit of '76. Jimmy Carter—Inaugurated Jan. 20, 1977"; illustrations of Washington and Carter (Hake 2059) 4"; black, white | 3.00 | 5.00 |
| ☐ "Inauguration Day, Jan. 20, 1977 . . ."; oval portraits of Carter–Mondale; draped flags in background (Hake 2058) 4"; red, white, blue | 3.00 | 5.00 |
| ☐ "Tennesseans/Inauguration Washington D.C. . . ."; conjoining Carter–Mondale portraits (Hake 2066) 4"; blue, black, white | 12.00 | 15.00 |
| ☐ "Welcome To Washington/Jan. 20, 1977"; Carter family portrait, including children, grandchildren; photograph full-length; White House and Capitol building in background (Hake 2062) 4"; black, white | 3.00 | 4.00 |

## *Jugate Pinbacks—1976* 

**Price Range**

☐ "America Needs A Change"; Carter–Mondale
bull's-eye design (Hake 2014) 3″; red, white, blue ............ 3.00 ...... 5.00

☐ "Californians For Carter–Mondale"; portraits
under pair of leaf fronds (Hake 2016) 3″; black,
green, yellow ............................... 5.00 ...... 7.00

☐ "Carter–Mondale. Vote Democratic"; portraits out
of U.S. map outline (Hake 2001) 6″; red, white,
blue, black ................................. 20.00 ...... 25.00

☐ "Carter Vs. Ford. The Great Debates of '76" (Hake
2017) 3″; red, white, blue, black (Ford and Carter
portraits with respective party symbols) ........ 2.00 ...... 3.00

☐ "First Ever In America/Vice Presidential De-
bate/Oct. 15th., 1976"; portraits: "Senator Walter
Mondale" and "Senator Robert Dole" (Hake 2018)
3″; red, white, blue, black ................... 2.00 ...... 3.00

☐ "Get America Moving Again/Carter–Mondale in
'76"; dominant campaign theme (Hake 2015) 3″;
red, white, blue ............................. 3.00 ...... 5.00

☐ "Iowans For Carter–Mondale/1976"; conjoining
oval portraits (Hake 2030) 2½″; dark blue, white ...... 5.00 ...... 7.00

**HOPEFULS**

☐ "Carter/Church '76"; silhouetted portraits of Carter and Frank Church, Idaho senator and possible
running mate prior to Democratic Convention
(Hake 2225) 2½″; black, white .............. 30.00 ...... 35.00

## *Multigate*

☐ "N.D.C. 1 Baltimore County"; four circle portraits:
Carter, Mondale, and two unidentified coattails
(Hake 2521) 2½″; black, white .............. 12.00 ...... 15.00

## *Portrait Pinbacks*

☐ "America Needs Carter/A Man Of The Soil"; full
figure of Carter kneeling with peanut plant in hands
(Hake 2154) 3″; red, white, blue, black ........ 2.00 ...... 3.00

Price Range

☐ "A New Vision/Jimmy Carter For America/Jimmy Carter"; flasher pinback (Hake 2189) 2½"; black, white .......................... 3.00     4.00

☐ "Get America Moving Again/Carter In '76"; Carter silhouette against map outline of U.S. in flag design (Hake 2139) 3½; red, white, blue, black ... 2.00     3.00

☐ "I Ask For Your Help. You Will Always Have Mine. Jimmy [facsimile signature]"; posturization of Carter; reversed out of dark blue (Hake 2186) 3½"; blue, white .......................... 3.00     4.00

☐ "Jimmy Carter For President in '76"; identical bull's-eye design and slogan applies to six different pinbacks, with only slight variations in photographic pose (Hake 2133) 3½"; red, white, blue, black ...................................... 2.00     3.00

☐ Also Hake 2133–38 ...................... 2.00     3.00

☐ "Jimmy Carter For President, 1976 Democratic Convention"; bull's-eye portrait (Hake 2220) 2½"; red, white, blue .......................... 3.00     4.00

☐ "My Name Is Jimmy Carter ... and I'm Running for President", bull's-eye photo of smiling Carter (Hake 2132) 3½"; red, white, blue, black ...... 2.00     3.00

☐ "Oregonian For Jimmy Carter [photo rebus] President"; map of Oregon outline (Hake 2279) 2"; black, white .............................. 18.00     20.00

☐ "Tennesseans For Jimmy Carter"; bull's-eye portrait (Hake 2270) 2"; red, white, black ......... 16.00     18.00

☐ "Vote For Jimmy Carter, Democrat For President"; oblong portrait (Hake 2280) 2"; black, white 16.00     18.00

### Trigates

☐ "For Kentucky's Future/United We Stand"; Carter–Mondale and unidentified coattail candidate (Hake 2520) 2½"; blue, white, black ...... 6.00     8.00

☐ "Every Good Man Needs A Good Woman In Congress"; small photo insets of Carter, Mondale, and Janet Meyner from New Jersey (Hake 2524) 2½"; black, green, white.......................... 5.00     7.00

## LEWIS CASS

Lewis Cass, a Democrat from Michigan, was a territorial governor for many years (1813–21). He served in the U.S. Senate from 1845–48 and was Secretary of State under Buchanan, 1857–60. In 1848, he became the first Democrat to run for President from the Old Northwest; coupled with General William Orlando Butler of Kentucky. Whigs portrayed Cass as a windbag (General Gass) in the 1848 race. Zachary Taylor defeated Cass by a narrow margin. Lewis Cass is one of those candidates who inspired very few campaign–related artifacts.

## HENRY CLAY

Henry Clay, of all the losers in the national arena, ranks among the most distinguished and able statesmen in our history. His career spanned almost half a century, beginning in the U.S. Senate in 1806–07 and ending in 1852. He served as Speaker of the House for four terms and was Secretary of State 1825–29 under John Quincy Adams. In a four–way race among Democrat Republicans, Clay ran against Adams, Andrew Jackson and William Crawford in 1824; when no candidate had pulled a majority, Clay awarded his votes to Adams, thus assuring the latter's victory. Clay ran with John Sergent against Jackson and Van Buren as a Whig in 1832 (the Kentuckian began his career as a Democrat Republican). In 1844 Clay and Frelinghuysen were defeated by James K. Polk and George Dallas. Nicknamed the "Gallant Harry of the West," Henry Clay is best remembered for his statement made long after his relentless quest for the highest office. In championing the controversial Compromise of 1850, Clay announced, "I would rather be right than President." Collectors of three–dimensional memorabilia and campaign ribbons find much to admire in the three candidacies of Henry Clay.

Price Range

### *Lapel Devices—Badges and Tokens*

☐ Clay bust profile, right facing, in classical toga brass
token; (Hake 3053); 1¾″; gilt brass. 1832 ...... 250.00 275.00

☐ "Our Flag/Trampled Upon"; Clay holding battered flag with right hand upraised. Brass token;
(Hake 3059) 1¾″; gilt brass; 1844 ............ 200.00 225.00

Clay–Frelinghuysen (Whig), Currier & Ives print, 1844, hand-tinted ($300–$359).

### Posters

☐ "Clear The Way For Old Kentucky/I'm That Same Old Coon." Cartoon of a raccoon (Clay's favorite nickname) sitting on a fence rail holding its tail; (Hake 3002), black on white . . . . . . . . . . . . . . . . .   700.00   750.00

☐ "Clay-Frelinghuysen Grand National Whig Banner" 1844; hand-tinted; Currier & Ives . . . . . . . . .   225.00   250.00

### Textiles

☐ "The Same Old Coon/Henry Clay and Frelinghuysen" flag banner; red, white, blue, brown sketch of raccoon . . . . . . . . . . . . . . . . . . . . . . . . . . . . . . . . . .   1500.00   1700.00

### Timepieces

☐ Mahogany mantle clock with reverse painting on glass of Henry Clay bust portrait (Hake 3014) . .   1700.00   1800.00

### Tobacco Accessories

☐ "Henry Clay/The American Statesman" leather cigar case. Name in scroll; bust portrait; eagle, shield; (Hake 3019) 5"l x 2⅞"w; full color painted images (several versions) . . . . . . . . . . . . . . . . . . . .   650.00   700.00

☐ Henry Clay effigy pipe, white meerschaum: Clay deep relief portrait on 3"h bowl (Hake 3020) . . .   125.00   150.00

☐ "Henry Clay" snuff box: papier-mâché, hand colored with black rim. Clay is seated at desk with document in hand (Hake 3011), 3¾"; multi-colored (at least three versions are known); see color photograph . . . . . . . . . . . . . . . . . . . . . . . . . . . . . . . . . .   550.00   600.00

## GROVER CLEVELAND

Born in New Jersey, Grover Cleveland was admitted to the bar and practiced law in New York. He quickly moved up the political ladder from the precinct level: Assistant District Attorney, Erie County, New York, 1863–65; Sheriff of Erie County for two years; Mayor of Buffalo, 1882; Governor of New York, 1883–84. He actually ran his campaign as Democratic presidential nominee from the Governor's office in Albany in 1884. Cleveland became the 22nd President of the U.S., 1885–89, but was defeated by Benjamin Harrison in 1888. In 1892, it was *his* turn to oust Harrison, thereby becoming the only U.S. President to serve non-concurrent terms. Cleveland once proposed that they erect a monument to him, "not for anything I have ever done, but for the foolishness I have put a stop to."

Hale & Kilburn Car Seats advertising trade card shows Grover Cleveland, Theodore Roosevelt, and Susan B. Anthony, along with Mark Twain, Thomas Edison, and other VIPs; red, black, and white ($35–$45). *(Kit Barry Collection)*

|  | Price Range | |
|---|---|---|

### *Lapel Devices*

☐ "Cleveland and Thurman" brass shell; figural crowing rooster; names in slanted sign on body (Hake 3178) 2½"; gilt brass with red crown . . . . . . . . . . 75.00   85.00

Advertising poster for Rushford Wagon features
Cleveland (D), James Blaine (R), and Ben Butler
(Greenback party) in 1884 race to White House
($100–$125).

|  | Price Range | |
|---|---|---|
| ☐ "I Know It" same figural design as above with post-election "crowing" (Hake 3180) . . . . . . . . . . . . . . | 40.00 | 45.00 |
| ☐ "National Association Democratic Clubs, 1888"; large circular jugate ambrotype in brass frame; ornate arched bar with die-stamped irregularly shaped shield, draped flags; suspended anchor and ribbon; impressive centerpiece (Hake 3181) 6"l overall; gilt brass; dark blue ribbon . . . . . . . . . . . . | 400.00 | 450.00 |
| ☐ Presidential chair mechanical shell; ambro portrait pops up from cushion (Hake 3198) . . . . . . . . . . . . | 150.00 | 175.00 |
| ☐ "White House Express" train engine brass shell with Cleveland photo in front; "1884" embossed above cowcatcher (Hake 3182) 2¾"h; gilt brass | 235.00 | 265.00 |

Grover Cleveland and Benjamin Harrison used unique checkerboard in Old Checker Whiskey poster from 1892 ($700–$800).

## *Lighting Devices*

|  | Price Range | |
|---|---|---|
| ☐ Kerosene lamp with etched glass portraits of Cleveland and Thurmond, 1888 . . . . . . . . . . . . . . . . . . | 125.00 | 135.00 |
| ☐ Railroad-type lantern; crossed U.S. flags on deep blue glass chimney marked Cleveland–Hendricks–1884 . . . . . . . . . . . . . . . . . . . . . . . . . . . | 150.00 | 175.00 |

## *Tobacco Accessories*

| | | |
|---|---|---|
| ☐ Match safe; brass figural Grover Cleveland bust; hinges at base to open for matches; matching examples for McKinley, Grant, Harrison; 2½″h; brass finish . . . . . . . . . . . . . . . . . . . . . . . . . . . . . . . . . . . . | 125.00 | 150.00 |
| ☐ Ceramic Grover Cleveland figural pipe; 1888 and 1892 campaigns; modeled likeness by Charles Kurth, Brooklyn, NY; Harrison match . . . . . . . . | 75.00 | 85.00 |

Kurz & Allison Art Publishers advertising lithograph promotes portraits of leading candidates prior to Republican and Democratic national conventions in 1884 ($150–$175). *(Photo courtesy of Rex Stark Auctions)*

Democratic candidates Cleveland–Thurman cotton bandanna, 1888 ($85–$100).

Cleveland–Harrison bisque figures on wooden balance scale, 1888 ($450–$500).

| *Toys and Banks* | Price Range | |
|---|---|---|
| ☐ Cleveland campaign egg; brass rooster marked "Cleveland" pops out of composition egg activated by spring mechanism; advertising giveaway; "I Crow for Cleveland" slogan . . . . . . . . . . . . . . . . . | 100.00 | 125.00 |
| ☐ Cleveland vs. Harrison balanced scale; bisque figures swathed in U.S. flags suspended from wooden balance bar; maker unknown; scale 5½"l; figure 2½"h; red, white, blue, black . . . . . . . . . . . . . . . | 600.00 | 700.00 |
| ☐ Grover Cleveland political euchre card game; 52-card deck with candidates caricatured as face cards (Hake 3043) . . . . . . . . . . . . . . . . . . . . . . . . . . . . . | 100.00 | 125.00 |
| ☐ Cleveland–Hendricks/Harrison–Morton checker-box game; litho paper on wood; maker unknown (checkers bear candidates portraits) . . . . . . . . . . . | 125.00 | 150.00 |

## GEORGE CLINTON

George Clinton was one of the first of the big city bosses. He controlled Democrat Republican politics in New York State from the American Revolution to the late 1820s. Clinton served six terms as Governor of New York and two terms in the House prior to his nomination as Thomas Jefferson's running mate in 1804 and Madison's in 1808. The 1804 election marked the first time the 12th Amendment was in effect, providing that separate ballots be held for President and Vice-President (the 1800 debacle, when Jefferson and Burr finished in a tie for the number one spot, precipitated this legislation). Clinton was a perfect beneficiary of the spoils system. His true aspirations were for the presidency and his relationship with both Jefferson and Madison was anything but cordial. Clinton even refused to attend his running mate Madison's inauguration in 1809, and in 1811 he broke a tie which defeated the renewal of the U.S. Bank, a bill Madison favored. Clinton died the following year, the first Vice-President to do so in office (see Jefferson and Madison).

## SCHUYLER COLFAX

Schuyler Colfax, a Republican from Indiana, served in the House, 1855–69; Speaker of the House, 1863–69. In 1868 he ran for high office with U.S. Grant of Illinois, marking the first slate in electoral history from contiguous states. The pair easily defeated Horatio Seymour and Francis P. Blair. Colfax served as Vice-President from 1869–73. He will be remembered as "The Smiler" and the "Joiner," the second monicker being not so complimentary, for he was known to use his power in high places to garner bribes.

## CALVIN COOLIDGE

If there ever was a politician who paid his dues to reach the highest office in the land, it was Calvin Coolidge, Republican from Vermont. From the precinct level up, Coolidge ran for public office on twenty different occasions, winning all but one of his races.

In the end, however, an element of luck led to his biggest break. In 1919, the first year Coolidge was governor of Massachusetts, the Boston police went out on strike and were fired. Union leader Samuel Gompers appealed to Governor Coolidge to reinstate them; the Governor denied the petition, stating, "there is no right to strike against the public safety, by anyone, anywhere, any time." He moved into the national spotlight, just as the Republicans were convening at their National Convention in 1920 and Coolidge was nominated by a landslide for the second slot behind Warren Harding. The Republicans won handily against Cox–Roosevelt; two years into the term, Harding died of a heart attack and "Silent Cal" became 30th President of the U.S. Under

Calvin Coolidge President match for "Ford For VP" ($100–$125).

Campaign poster—Republicans encouraged a ticket of Coolidge–Ford in 1924, but world's foremost businessman later pulled out of race ($125–$135).

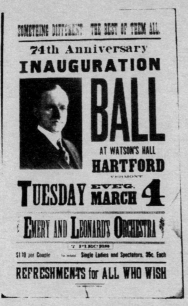

Calvin Coolidge Inauguration Ball poster, Hartford, Vermont, March 4, 1925 ($75–$100).

the slogan "Keep Cool With Coolidge," and with Charles Dawes of Illinois as his running mate, he was easily victorious against Democrat John Davis in 1924.

**Price Range**

### Automotive Accessories

LICENSE TAGS

☐ "Coolidge" 12"w x 2¼"h; black, white; "Coolidge For President"; 12"w; red, white . . . . . . . . . . . . . .  45.00  55.00

☐ "Vote For Coolidge" 12"w x 2¼"h; black, white painted tin . . . . . . . . . . . . . . . . . . . . . . . . . . . . . .  35.00  40.00

☐ "Keep Coolidge In" 12"w; black, white . . . . . . . .  30.00  35.00

RADIATOR ATTACHMENT

☐ "Voters Of The U.S.A. Keep Cool-Idge. Less Taxes. Larger Service. Balanced Bu$iness." 3½"-dia shield within circle; red, white, blue. . . . . . . .  200.00  225.00

SPARE TIRE COVER

☐ "Keep Cool With Coolidge"; black, white oilcloth cover . . . . . . . . . . . . . . . . . . . . . . . . . . . . . . . . . . . .  300.00  400.00

| | Price Range | |
|---|---|---|
| ***Banks*** | | |
| ☐ Calvin Coolidge Still Bank, maker unknown, 1924, pottery, brown-toned, slogan: "Do as Coolidge Does . . . Save," 4"h (Hake 2047) . . . . . . . . . . . . | 75.00 | 100.00 |
| ***Cartoon/Pictorial Pinbacks*** | | |
| ☐ "Coolidge–Dawes. Full [rebus] Dinner Pail" (Hake 59) ⅞" red, white, blue; reproduced . . . . . . . . . . . | 20.00 | 25.00 |
| ☐ "Coolidge & Dawes, National Republican Club"; stylized eagle (Hake 61) ½"; blue, white . . . . . . . | 20.00 | 25.00 |
| ☐ "Coolidge & Dawes" on elephant's blanket (Hake 52) ⅞"; red, white, blue . . . . . . . . . . . . . . . . . . . . | 10.00 | 15.00 |
| ☐ Also ½" size (Hake 87) . . . . . . . . . . . . . . . . . . . . | 15.00 | 20.00 |
| ☐ "Coolidge Fourth of July Club," picturing Liberty Bell (Hake 68) ⅞"; red, white, blue, gold . . . . . . | 75.00 | 100.00 |
| ☐ "On The Square"; schoolhouse pictured (Hake 67) ⅞"; red, white, blue . . . . . . . . . . . . . . . . . . . . . . . . | 150.00 | 175.00 |
| ☐ "Lincoln Tour. Coolidge & Dawes"; depicts map of U.S. showing campaign route (Hake 53) ⅞"; red, white, blue . . . . . . . . . . . . . . . . . . . . . . . . . . . . . . | 25.00 | 35.00 |
| ***Intaglio Ceramic Tiles*** | | |
| ☐ Calvin Coolidge bust profile ceramic tile; 4⅜"l; 2⅞"w; light blue glaze; Coolidge's facsimile signature barely discernible in white at lower left; made by Robertson Art Tile, Trenton, New Jersey . . . . | 65.00 | 75.00 |
| ☐ Calvin Coolidge bust profile ceramic tile; same dimensions and image as above; light green glaze . . | 65.00 | 75.00 |
| ***Jugate Pinbacks*** | | |
| ☐ "Coolidge and Dawes" conjoining portraits; (Hake 2) 1¼"; sepiatone . . . . . . . . . . . . . . . . . . . . . . . . | 400.00 | 450.00 |
| ☐ Also 1½" size . . . . . . . . . . . . . . . . . . . . . . . . . . . | 475.00 | 525.00 |
| ☐ "Coolidge Dawes Club. Albany County" conjoining portraits (Hake 3) ⅞"; black, sepia, white (has been reproduced as a cello) . . . . . . . . . . . . . . . . . | 150.00 | 175.00 |

**Price Range**

☐ "Coolidge and Dawes" slanted oval portraits; reversed out of black (Hake 5) $\frac{7}{8}$"; black, white; appeared in same size as stud (Hake 4) .......... | 75.00 | 100.00

☐ "Coolidge and Dawes", eagle tops oval portraits (Hake 8) $\frac{7}{8}$; red, white, blue, black lithograph .. | 125.00 | 150.00

☐ "Coolidge and Dawes" scepter separates oval portraits (Hake 9) $\frac{7}{8}$"; red, white, blue, black lithograph ...................................... | 175.00 | 200.00

☐ "Coolidge & Dawes. For The Nation's Cause"; shield tops oval insets, slanted (Hake 2001) $1\frac{1}{4}$"; red, white, black .......................... | 1100.00 | 1200.00

☐ "Coolidge and Dawes" slanting conjoining portraits (Hake 23) $1\frac{1}{4}$"; black, white ............ | 675.00 | 700.00

☐ "For President. For Vice President. Coolidge. Dawes"; interlinked ovals (Hake 6) $\frac{7}{8}$"; black, white (has been reproduced as both a litho *and* a cello) ...................................... | 20.00 | 25.00

☐ "Our Candidates"; four stars, striped shield atop canted ovals; "Coolidge and Dawes" and sunburst appear at bottom (Hake 2004) 6"; red, white, blue, black; wire easel backing; nice centerpiece item .. | 1400.00 | 1500.00

☐ "Republicans X"; unusual oval portraits of Coolidge–Dawes; Dawes has hair parted down middle (Hake 7) $\frac{7}{8}$"; red, white, blue bands; black portraits | 35.00 | 45.00

☐ "Vote For Coolidge–Dawes. The Republican Candidates For President & Vice President. 1924"; ornate oval frames (Hake 1; Warner 367) $1\frac{3}{4}$"; black, white, gold-braid rim ...................... | 375.00 | 400.00

☐ "Washington D.C. March 4, 1925" inaugural jugate; large oval portraits (Hake 2002; Warner 723) $1\frac{1}{4}$"; black, white; parade souvenir ........... | 450.00 | 475.00

### Mirrors

☐ Coolidge–Dawes jugate oval portraits separated by Capitol dome; eagles perch on top of ornate framed images (Hake 2005; Warner 366, pinback only) $2\frac{1}{8}$"; black white .......................... | 850.00 | 900.00

Price Range

☐ "Coolidge–Du Pont–Robinson" trigate oval insets; "The Lady On The Other Side is requested to vote for ..." (candidates names) (Hake 89) 2″; black, white ....................................... 150.00   175.00

### Portrait Pinbacks

☐ "Calvin Coolidge"; flag-bordered torso portrait floats in white background (Hake 11) 1½″; red, white, blue, black .......................... 125.00   150.00

☐ "Calvin Coolidge"; letters reversed out of black suit (Hake 16) ⅞″; black, white (not campaign, but part of presidential set) ......................... 15.00   20.00

☐ "Coolidge" in banner under portrait, which bleeds off collet (Hake 12) 1¼″; sepiatone ........... 100.00   125.00

☐ (Hake 13) 1½″; sepiatone .................... 95.00   120.00

☐ Coolidge portrait, oval pinback (Hake 88; Warner 370) 2⅜″; sepiatone ....................... 150.00   175.00

☐ Coolidge portrait by Harris & Ewing, Washington, DC photographer (Hake 34; Warner 725) ⅞″; white, black ............................... 50.00   75.00

☐ Coolidge portrait with thin black circle in border (Hake 37) ⅞″; black, white ................. 35.00   50.00

☐ "For President. Firm As The Rock of Ages. Keep Coolidge." (Hake 32) ⅞″; red, white, black ..... 100.00   125.00

☐ "For President. Calvin Coolidge"; circle inset (Hake 14) 1¼″; black, white border .......... 75.00   100.00

☐ "For President. Calvin Coolidge"; bleed image (Hake 15) 1¼″; black, white ................. 125.00   150.00

☐ "For President [Calvin Coolidge portrait] "Calvin Coolidge" (Hake 19) ⅞″; black, white ........ 35.00   45.00

☐ "Home Town Coolidge Club, Plymouth, Vermont" (Hake 1) ⅞″; red, white, blue, black (not to be confused with 1¼″, green-border souvenir edition for "Coolidge Centennial, July, 1972") ............ 25.00   35.00

☐ "Keep Coolidge" framed portrait in keystone design (Pennsylvanis item) (Hake 33) ⅞″″; reversed out of black ............................... 20.00   25.00

☐ Also issued in ½″ size (Hake 45) ............ 10.00   15.00

Price Range

☐ "Keep Coolidge" portrait (Hake 2019) 3½"; black,
white; nice centerpiece item; also in 2¼" size ... | 275.00 | 300.00

☐ "Keep Coolidge," reversed out of Coolidge's suit
(Hake 21) ⅞"; black, white .................. | 15.00 | 20.00

☐ "Keep Square Deal Coolidge"; words appear in
square around portrait (Hake 28; Warner 724) ⅞";
black, white; key item from 1924 race ......... | 200.00 | 225.00

☐ "Let Well Enough Alone"; Coolidge portrait (Hake
36) ⅞"; black, white ...................... | 75.00 | 100.00

☐ "National Coolidge College Club" reads in white
border around circle portrait (Hake 18) ⅞"; black,
white ..................................... | 50.00 | 75.00

☐ "Our President. Deeds Not Words." (Hake 25)
3¾"; browntone; centerpiece ................. | 400.00 | 450.00

☐ "Sane and Safe. Coolidge"; portrait; framed by lau-
rel branches (Hake 27) ⅞"; black, white ....... | 250.00 | 275.00

☐ "Support The Coolidge Administration"; also
comes with dated (1926) ribbon; Congressional
election item (Hake 10; Warner 369) 1⅝"; red,
white, blue, black, gold lettering and rim ....... | 200.00 | 225.00

☐ Smiling Coolidge; only portrait known to show
trace of smile on Cal's usually dour visage (Hake
2013) 1¼"; black, white .................... | 125.00 | 150.00

**MEMORIAL**

☐ "Calvin Coolidge Memorial, Plymouth, Vermont,
Aug. 3, 1934; small circular portrait (Hake 2017)
1¼"; black, white ......................... | 25.00 | 30.00

### Posters

☐ Calvin Coolidge Inauguration Ball, Hartford, Vermont, March 4, 1925; 22"h x 14"w; red, white
black; cardboard poster ..................... | 75.00 | 100.00

☐ "Calvin Coolidge For President" poster; 12"h x
10"w; sepiatone portrait .................... | 30.00 | 40.00

**128** *Political Memorabilia*

Price Range

☐ "Our President. Hon. Calvin Coolidge"; see illustration and description with Henry Ford companion poster .................................. 100.00 125.00

### Slogan/Name Pinbacks

☐ "Connecticut Coolidge Club" inside large "C" (Hake 69) ¾" oval; red, white, blue ........... 12.00 15.00

☐ "Coolidge" (Hake 2031) ¾"; red, white, blue (countless variants in various color combinations) 15.00 20.00

☐ "Coolidge Again" brass pinback (Hake 2030) ⅞"; raised letters on green background ............ 35.00 40.00

☐ Also as red, white, blue (Hake 2029) ⅞" ....... 20.00 25.00

☐ Same as above (Warner 727) 1¾" ............. 100.00 125.00

☐ "Coolidge And Dawes" numerous variants (Hake 54–57, 62, 64, 65, 2025); each ................ 5.00 10.00

☐ "Coolidge By 50,000" (Hake 78) ⅞"; blue out of white bands; blue background ................ 15.00 20.00

☐ "Coolidge Club Of Northampton" (Hake 82) ½"; red, white, blue ............................. 15.00 20.00

☐ "Coolidge And Courage" (Hake 31) ⅞"; red, white, blue ................................ 20.00 25.00

☐ "Grafton Coolidge Dawes Club" (Hake 63) ⅞"; teal blue, bronze ........................... 25.00 30.00

☐ "Keep Coolidge" (Hake 2026) ⅞"; brown, white lithograph .................................. 10.00 15.00

☐ Also several versions in stylized lettering (Hake 2033; 2034); each ........................... 30.00 35.00

☐ "Coolidge Of Course" (Hake 2028) ¾"; white, black ..................................... 35.00 40.00

☐ "Fanueil Hall Keep Cool With Coolidge Club" (Hake 29) ⅞"; black, white ................. 50.00 75.00

☐ "Keep Coolidge"; one of hobby's largest buttons (Hake 2011) 2½" red, white, blue ............. 75.00 85.00

☐ "Keep Cool With Coolidge" (Hake 2027) ⅞" black, white ............................... 50.00 75.00

☐ "Let's Go With Coolidge" (Hake 70) ⅞"; white reversed out of blue .......................... 15.00 20.00

Price Range

☐ "New Jersey Women's Coolidge Club" (Hake 86) blue, white .................................. 25.00  30.00

☐ "Safe With Cal" (Hake 74) ⅞"; black, white .... 30.00  35.00

## *Watch Fobs*

☐ "For President 1924, Calvin Coolidge"; celluloid watch fob with hole for leather strap (Hake 24; Warner 368) 1½"; blue, white ................ 250.00  275.00

☐ Irregular-die-cut, shaped brass fob with embossed Capitol dome, flag, eagle, with cello inset bust portrait; "For President. Calvin Coolidge"; 1¾" including tab; gilt finish; black, white portrait ..... 40.00  50.00

☐ "Ring For Coolidge," dimensional brass bell fob; letters incised; 1"h; brass finish ............... 20.00  25.00

☐ "Ring For Coolidge And Dawes," dimensional brass bell fob; letters incised; 1"h; brass finish ... 20.00  25.00

☐ Wreath-die-cut embossed brass; "For President. Calvin Coolidge"; 1¾" with tab; brass finish; Cox match ...................................... 50.00  75.00

☐ Wreath with eagle perched atop; wide tab appears across wing span; cello inset "Coolidge" under portrait; 1¾"; brass with black cast; black, white; portrait cello; Harding match ................... 75.00  100.00

## JAMES COX

A newspaper publisher and former Governor of New York, James Cox made an unsuccessful run for the Presidency in 1920, heading the Democratic ticket with Franklin D. Roosevelt. Cox is considered very collectible. Cox–Roosevelt jugates from 1920 are so uncommon as to place them in a class by themselves.

Price Range

### *Baggage Tag/Key Chain Fob*

☐ "Cox–Roosevelt" lettering with "Washington, 1920"; engraved oval eagle atop shield (Hake 2055) 2"w; chrome finish; hole for chain as baggage tag or key holder ............................... 40.00  50.00

| *Cartoon/Pictorial Pinbacks* | Price Range | |
|---|---|---|
| ☐ "Crow, Don't Croak"; rooster cartoon, obviously crowing (Hake 2039) $7/8$"; black on white; generally acknowledged as a Cox pinback .............. | 25.00 | 35.00 |
| ☐ "For President, James M. Cox"; bucking donkey with Cox portrait inset in animal's side (Hake 2017) $1\frac{1}{4}$"; black, brown, white .................... | 1000.00 | 1100.00 |
| ☐ "League of Nations"; group of Greek or Roman (?) goddesses in classical attire; attributed to Cox forces, as one of their pledges was to work for the League (unlisted) $7/8$"; multicolor ............. | 35.00 | 45.00 |

## *Clothing*

| | | |
|---|---|---|
| ☐ "Cox For President"; eagle atop flag/shield; cloth beanie; red, white, blue ...................... | 125.00 | 135.00 |

## *Cutlery*

| | | |
|---|---|---|
| ☐ Cox–Roosevelt jugate pocketknife.* (Hake unlisted; Warner 361) $3\frac{1}{4}$"; black, white; U.S. Capitol on reverse; Harding–Coolidge match ........... | 2000.00 | 2200.00 |
| ☐ Cox–Roosevelt jugate pocketknife; "Our Choice"; eagle and shield atop vertical portraits; Poses are identical to Cox–Roosevelt razor (Hake 2002); this one's unlisted .............................. | 2000.00 | 2300.00 |
| ☐ Cox–Roosevelt jugate razor; images and design identical to pocketknife above (Hake 2002) approximately 7"; black, white; made by Golden Rule, Chicago; reverse shows White House and Capitol ... | 1000.00 | 1200.00 |

---

*An anti-Cox/Roosevelt version of this jugate knife was issued which bore the inscription "Vote For Cox. He's a Hun, and One Hundred Percent Wilson" on the reverse; value range: indeterminate.

## Jugate Pinbacks—Cox–Roosevelt

Undisputedly the rarest, most fervently pursued jugates in the hobby, Cox–Roosevelt received perhaps more notoriety than deserved when a unique, 1¼″ black and white specimen set a record at $33,000 during the New England Rare Coin Auction of the Don Warner Collection of Political Americana in 1981.

Of the 10 or 12 (depending on whom you talk to) varieties known, there are but *five* 1¼″ Cox–Roosevelt jugate pinbacks that have surfaced publicly. Dave Frent, cataloger of the Warner collection, estimated that a total of only 70 of these elusive jugates have come to light.

|  | Price Range | |
|---|---|---|
| ☐ "Americanize America. Vote For Cox and Roosevelt"; (Hake 2011) ⅞″; black, white . . . . . . . . . . . | 4500.00 | 5000.00 |
| ☐ "Cox–Roosevelt Club"; conjoining portraits (Hake 1) 1″; bluetone, white; red lettering . . . . . . . . . . . . | 4000.00 | 4500.00 |
| ☐ Cox–Roosevelt conjoining portraits (Hake 2010; Warner 715) ⅞″; black, white; also exists in 1¼″; only three known . . . . . . . . . . . . . . . . . . . . . . . . . . . | 3000.00 | 4000.00 |
| ☐ Cox–Roosevelt conjoining portraits (Hake unlisted; Warner 198) 1¼″; black, white. | | |
| Quite possibly unique, this specimen brought $5,800 in a 1976 auction (APIC #CRJ3). Estimated at $10,000, it skyrocketed to $33,000 at the Warner auction in 1981. Present value indeterminate. | | |
| ☐ "Cox and Roosevelt" conjoining portraits; (Hake 2008) 1¼″; black, white . . . . . . . . . . . . . . . . . . . . . | 4000.00 | 4500.00 |
| ☐ "Sunburst Eagle"; eagle from which emanate an ever widening array of stripes, plus flag waving below; background for circular insets of Cox–Roosevelt (Hake 20009; Warner 359) ⅞″; black, white; also exists in 1¼″; only one known | 4000.00 | 5000.00 |

## Portrait Pinbacks

|  | | |
|---|---|---|
| ☐ Cox bust portrait; no lettering (Hake 2016) 1½″; black on white . . . . . . . . . . . . . . . . . . . . . . . . . . . . | 450.00 | 500.00 |
| ☐ Cox bust portrait; no lettering; slightly different viewing angle of Cox (Hake 2022) 1½″; black on white . . . . . . . . . . . . . . . . . . . . . . . . . . . . . . . . . . . | 450.00 | 500.00 |

Price Range

☐ "Cox For President"; large lettering borders portrait; extends from ear to ear (Hake 2) 1¼"; black on white .................................. 335.00 350.00

☐ Cox portrait outline extends through black, gray pinstriped circle (Hake 6) 1¼"; black, gray, white; "James M. Cox" appears just above lower arc of circle ........................................ 90.00 100.00

☐ Cox portrait with no lettering; appears in gray circle with wide white border (Hake 8) 1¼"; black, gray, white ...................................... 175.00 225.00

☐ Cox oval portrait pinback; dramatic photograph almost totally dominates image area (Hake 13; Warner 365) 2¾"h x 1⅞"w; black on white; only known Cox oval piece ...................... 300.00 325.00

☐ Cox raised-dome-design portrait inset against stars in blue field at top; stripes along sides of circle and below (unlisted) 1¾"; red, white, blue, black; previously unknown until 1982, when a matched set (see Harding) was offered in a Mark Jacobs Mail Auction; one other set is known .................. 1500.00 2000.00

☐ "For President, James M. Cox" (Hake 2012) 6"; red, white, blue; fanned stripes at sides of portrait; great centerpiece item ...................... 2000.00 2500.00

☐ "For President" reversed out of black; "Cox" appears just above head (Hake 11; Warner 363) ⅞"; black, white ............................... 150.00 160.00

☐ "For President. James M. Cox"; V-shaped caption banner just across lapels in Cox portrait (Hake 9) ⅞"; black, brown, white ..................... 350.00 375.00

☐ "For President. James M. Cox"; variant of Hake 4 with slight change in pose, minus gray circle background, and cream rather than white (Hake 5) 1¼"; black, cream .......................... 300.00 350.00

☐ "For President. James M. Cox"; wide border of white encircles gray inset with Cox portrait (Hake 4) 1¼"; black, gray, white ................... 300.00 325.00

☐ "James M. Cox"; lettering reversed out of suit in portrait (Hake 7) 1¼"; black, cream .......... 175.00 200.00

Price Range

☐ "Peace, Progress, Prosperity"; "For President" (Cox portrait rebus) (Hake 16) ½"; black, white; this item has been reproduced as a cello . . . . . . . .    95.00    115.00

☐ "James M. Cox" sepia portrait (Hake 2024; Warner 718) 1½"; sepiatone . . . . . . . . . . . . . . . . . . . . . . .    225.00    250.00

☐ "James M. Cox" in banner across necktie; brass rim (Hake 15) ⅞"; sepiatone, gilt brass . . . . . . . . . . . .    100.00    125.00

☐ Same as above (Hake 17) ½" . . . . . . . . . . . . . . . . .    75.00    110.00

☐ Stars and Stripes; Cox portrait in circle inset, bordered at top by blue field with 17 white stars; red, white stripes at midpoint to bottom (Hake 14) ⅞"; red, white, blue, black . . . . . . . . . . . . . . . . . . . . . . .    325.00    350.00

## CONGRESSIONAL PINBACKS

☐ "James M. Cox For Congress"; younger portrait, Cox without glasses (Hake 2014) 1¼"; black, gray, white . . . . . . . . . . . . . . . . . . . . . . . . . . . . . . . . . . . .    275.00    300.00

## GOVERNOR-RELATED PINBACKS

James Cox served as Governor of Ohio 1916–1920.

☐ "For Governor. James M. Cox"; portrait bleeds off image area (Hake 57) ½"; sepiatone . . . . . . . . . . .    125.00    150.00

☐ "Inauguration. James M. Cox, Governor of Ohio. 1917" (Hake 2033; Warner 716) 2⅛"; black, white    500.00    525.00

☐ "Notification Ceremonies For Gov. James M. Cox. Nominee For President, Dayton, Ohio, Aug. 7, 1920"; all lettering appeared on black, white ribbon; cello (Hake 20; Warner 360) 2¼"; black white . .    1500.00    2000.00

☐ "Notification Day. Franklin County, Dayton, Ohio. Aug. 7, 1920. Democratic Organization" (Hake 2025; Warner 365) 1¼"; black, white . . . . . . . . . .    400.00    425.00

☐ "Our Governor" Cox portrait (Hake 2027; Warner 717) 1¼"; black, white; possibly a Democratic National Convention item from San Francisco, 1917    225.00    250.00

## POSTERS

☐ "America First"; Cox–Roosevelt jugate oval portraits against furled flag background; eagle with banner in talons hovers above; brief biographical

Price Range

sketches of both candidates appear in lower right-
and left-hand corners (Hake 2006) 20"h x 16"w;
black, white, sepia .......................... 135.00    175.00

☐ Cox–Roosevelt jugate poster; portraits flank Capitol dome; oval portraits of Grover Cleveland,
Thomas Jefferson, and Woodrow Wilson appear
just below Capitol building in foreground (Hake
2004) 20"h x 16"w; black, white, sepia ........ 150.00    175.00

## Slogan/Name Pinbacks

☐ "Cox"; ornate curlicue typeface (Hake 18) 1¼";
red, white, blue ............................. 65.00    75.00

☐ "Cox and Cocktails" (Hake 19) ⅞"; white out of
black ...................................... 125.00    135.00

☐ "Cox" (Hake 56) ⅞"; red lettering on gold star
against four divided sections: red, blue, white, green    65.00    75.00

☐ "Cox–Roosevelt"; the latter appears diagonally
across large "Cox" letters; two versions; (Hake 28)
⅞"; white reversed out of blue with red background    20.00    25.00

☐ (Hake 29) ⅞"; white reversed out of red with blue
background ................................. 20.00    25.00

☐ "Cox-Sure" (Hake 32) ½"; dark blue and light blue;
Cox's running mate, FDR, hated this pinback ... 25.00    30.00

☐ "Cox"; white reversed out of red outline map of
Cox's home state of Ohio; blue background (Hake
40) ½" .................................... 40.00    50.00

☐ "Jim Cox" reversed out of red; also in blue/white
combination (Hake 34) ½" .................. 30.00    35.00

## Timepieces

☐ Cox–Roosevelt pocketwatch; oval portraits appear
just above dial stem (unlisted) approximately 2¼";
chrome, black, white ....................... 2000.00    2200.00

*Watch Fobs*                                          **Price Range**

☐ Donkey heads facing inward to Cox oval portrait against shield background; Cox name appears in rectangular box; lithographed tin fob and mirror on reverse; match for Harding–elephant fob (Hake 41); red, white, blue, gray, black ................. 1450.00   1500.00

☐ "For President, James M. Cox"; portrait inset cello in stitched seam leather holder with tab (Hake 43; same cello as Hake 9) $1\frac{3}{4}$"h; black, white; black leather ..................................... 350.00    375.00

☐ Shield and laurel leaves, embossed brass; sepiatone cello portrait "James M. Cox" inset (Hake 42) $1\frac{1}{2}$"h; brass finish ......................... 175.00    200.00

☐ Shield with portrait of Cox; irregular shape with brass filigree, laurel branch border; Harding match (Hake 45) $1\frac{3}{4}$"; gilt finish ................... 50.00     75.00

☐ Shield with wide tab; jugate bas-relief portraits; embossed, die-cut brass (Hake 2007) $1\frac{1}{2}$"; brass finish   50.00     75.00

☐ Shield with wide tab; laurel branches tied at lower point of elongated die-cut shield with ribbon; Cox portrait in bas relief (Hake 2047) 2"; gilt finish .. 75.00    100.00

☐ Winged eagle, "Our Choice," atop slanted oval embossed jugate portraits, Cox–Roosevelt; tab for watch strap. Harding–Coolidge match (Hake 44) $1\frac{1}{2}$"; in silver or gilt finish .................. 75.00    100.00

☐ Wreath die-cut embossed with eagle at top; tab for strap goes across eagle's wing span; brass with cello inset, "James M. Cox" (Hake 2046) 2"; black, white cello; brass finish .......................... 200.00    225.00

## CHARLES CURTIS

Charles Curtis, our 31st vice-president, served with Republican Herbert Hoover from 1928 to 1932. He was again a Hoover running mate in 1932; the pair was soundly defeated by FDR. The only vice-president to claim ancestry with the original natives, he was of the Kaw Indian tribe. Curtis was called by political pundit Oswald Villard, "the apotheosis of mediocrity." Curtis had his eye on the presidency at the 1928 Republican Convention but garnered only minimal support.

Price Range

*Miscellaneous*

☐ "For President, Charles Curtis"; bust portrait in black circle; wide border; (Hake 2035) 1¼"; black, white ...................................... 15.00 20.00

☐ "Boosting [bust line drawing, Curtis rebus] For Vice-President" (Hake 2036) 1"; black, white ... 75.00 100.00

☐ "Vice President Charles Curtis Notification, Topeka [Kansas] 1932"; smiling bust portrait (Hake 23) 2"; sepiatone; red rim border .............. 100.00 125.00

## GEORGE M. DALLAS

George Dallas, a Democrat from Pennsylvania, served in the U.S. Senate from 1831–33. He was elected Vice–President under James K. Polk, 1845–49. The Pennsylvanian may be remembered by the Democratic slogan, "Polk, Dallas and Texas"—not very catchy but it proved to be a winner.

## HENRY G. DAVIS

Henry Davis, a Democrat from West Virginia, an obscure millionaire and the oldest man (at 82) ever to run for national office, was added to the ticket with Alton B. Parker in 1904. Expected to make contributions to the party coffers and campaign vigorously against TR, he did neither (see Alton Parker).

## JEFFERSON DAVIS

Jefferson Davis of Mississippi was sworn in as president of the Confederate States of America in 1861, with Alexander Hamilton Stephens as vice-president. Along with a few souvenir medalets and ferrotypes and one Davis cameo, only two or three ribbons constitute the political trinketry of the CSA.

Price Range

*Miscellaneous*

☐ "Jeffy's Dream" cartoon; Jefferson Davis asleep on cotton bale dreaming of foreign ships in port, clamoring to support the Confederacy in order to obtain cotton; Black slaves are scaling ladder leading into the clouds; browntone; cartoonist unknown ..... 75.00 100.00

Price Range

☐ "The Right Man In The Right Place" inscribed around circular portrait of Davis inside blue silk rosette attached to silk ribbon, a miniature Confederate flag (may have been a handmade unique badge); red, white, blue ........................... 650.00  700.00

☐ "The Right Man In The Right Place. Jeff Davis/Our First President"; sepia ferrotype, bust portrait of J. Davis ........................ 110.00  125.00

☐ "The South Forever/Southern Confederacy/Jeff Davis President/A. H. Stephens, Vice President"; CSA flag flying in center of ribbon; red, white blue; circle in flag has seven white stars ............ 250.00  300.00

☐ A. H. Stephens ribbon; name only ............ 135.00  150.00

☐ Figural pipe—Jefferson Davis; red clay; curved shank and stem ........................... 175.00  200.00

☐ Attractive amber plate, 9¼" dia. with embossed portrait of Jeff Davis, produced by L. E. Smith Glass Co., Mount Pleasant, PA; also found in milk glass; but the plates are not of the period, having been produced in 1960 as a commemorative item 25.00  30.00

## JOHN W. DAVIS

John Davis, a New York lawyer from West Virginia who had once been ambassador to Great Britain and had served as Woodrow Wilson's Solicitor–General, was nominated by the Democrats in 1924 to unseat Calvin Coolidge. Davis failed to tar Coolidge with the brush of Teapot Dome and could not fight Republican prosperity. Democratic coffers were pretty bare in 1924, and elusive Davis–Bryan jugates, in particular, are eagerly sought by collectors.

Price Range

*Automotive Accessories*

☐ "Davis For President" 14"w x'2"h; white on orange; license tag attachment; painted tin ....... 50.00  75.00

☐ "Let Davis Do It"; 14"w x 2"h; black on white; license tag attachment; painted tin .............. 60.00  80.00

Davis–Bryan (D) message jugate, "Honest Government," 1924 race. Ribbon from Utah state Democratic convention carries key campaign slogan, "Better Days With Davis." A recent discovery for the hobby ($2,000 plus). *(Photo courtesy of APIC Keynoter)*

| *Badges, Medals, Stickpins, Studs* | Price Range | |
|---|---|---|
| ☐ "Davis," trailing star diamond-shaped metal badge (Hake 2022) 1"h; chrome finish . . . . . . . . . . . . . . | 35.00 | 50.00 |
| ☐ "Don't Forget [teapot rebus]" die-cut metal stickpin; words embossed on teapot (Hake 2026) 1"w; gilt finish . . . . . . . . . . . . . . . . . . . . . . . . . . . . . . . . . | 125.00 | 150.00 |
| ☐ "Notification" embossed bar, ribbon, badge: "John Davis, August 11, 1924, City of Clarksburg, West Virginia"; embossed log cabin in foreground, skyscrapers in background (Hake 2034) 1½" dia. hanger; 3¼" l overall; brass finish . . . . . . . . . . . . | 50.00 | 75.00 |

Price Range

☐ Watch token; John Davis bronze medal for pocket watch chain attachment in vest or possibly as lapel hanger; bas-relief bust portrait of Davis (Hake unlisted; Warner 382) 1"l; bronze finish .......... 100.00 125.00

## Cartoon/Pictorial Pinbacks

☐ "G.O.P. Your Waterloo" Teapot Dome symbol superimposed on Capitol dome (Hake 35) ½"; sepiatone ....................................... 200.00 225.00

☐ "Doom" reversed out of blue silhouette of teapot (Hake 31) ⅞"; blue, white lithograph .......... 135.00 150.00

☐ Teapot Dome cartoon, "Better Days With Davis (Hake 33) ⅞"; black, white ................. 325.00 350.00

☐ Teapot silhouetted against black background with Capitol Dome superimposed (Hake 2021) ½"; black, white ............................... 200.00 225.00

☐ Democratic rooster crowing, "1924"; cartoon; (Hake 22; Warner 381) ⅝"; red, white ........ 35.00 45.00

## Jugate Pinbacks

☐ "Davis And Bryan" (Charles) conjoined portraits (Hake 2002; Warner 371) 1¼"; black, white; key item rarity; mate to LaFollette–Coolidge jugates 4000.00 4200.00

☐ "Davis And Bryan" conjoining portraits. head-on view (Hake 2003) 1¼"; black, white .......... 3500.00 4000.00

☐ "Davis And Bryan Club. St. Joseph, Mo."; oval pinback; circular jugate portraits; (Hake 2004) 1¼"l x ¾"h; black, white ................... 3000.00 3500.00

☐ "Davis And Bryan—Nebraska"; oval pinback with circular jugate portraits (Hake 2005) 1¼"l x ¾"h; black, white ............................... 2700.00 2900.00

☐ "Davis And Bryan" sepiatone jugate (Hake 26) ⅞"; sepia and white .......................... 1000.00 1100.00

☐ "Davis–Bryan" canted portraits (Hake 1) ⅞"; black, white ............................... 600.00 650.00

Price Range

☐ "Honest Government"; Davis–Bryan jugate with ribbon, "Delegate Convention, Salt Lake City, August 27, 1924" and "Better Days With Davis" (unlisted) $1\frac{1}{4}"$ cello; black, white; only message jugate for Davis–Bryan, discovered as late as 1982 and only five known . . . . . . . . . . . . . . . . . . . . . . . . . . . .    4000.00    5000.00

☐ "President. John Davis. Vice-President Chas. Bryan" (Hake 2006) $\frac{7}{8}"$; black, white . . . . . . . . .    2500.00    2700.00

COATTAILS JUGATES
☐ "For President. Davis. For Governor. Nelson" (Hake 32) $\frac{7}{8}"$; black, white . . . . . . . . . . . . . . . . .    300.00    325.00

☐ "Work And Win. Davis And Stanley"; Augustus Stanley of Kentucky, who lost bid for reelection to U.S. Senate in 1924 (Hake 2016; Warner 734) $\frac{7}{8}"$; black, cream . . . . . . . . . . . . . . . . . . . . . . . . . . . . . .    275.00    300.00

## *Paper (Ephemera)*

☐ "A Vote For Davis Is A Vote Against Special Privilege. Remember Tea-Pot Dome"; die-cut cardboard window hanger in shape of giant teapot (Hake 2001) $7"$h x $8\frac{1}{2}"$w.; black on white . . . . . . . . . .    35.00    50.00

☐ "Davis and Bryan Campaign Fund Financed By The People"; paper badge soliciting contributions; $1\frac{1}{2}"$; red, white, blue . . . . . . . . . . . . . . . . . . . . . . .    50.00    75.00

☐ "Davis–Bryan Victory" paper tag; names run vertically so that third letter in each (V and Y) begin and end word "Victory" in H-shape design; $2"$sq; red, black, white; oval portraits of Davis–Bryan (also a pinback design) . . . . . . . . . . . . . . . . . . . . . .    75.00    85.00

☐ "John W. Davis. Help Make A Great West Virginian President"; Davis portrait-pledge card; $3\frac{1}{4}"$w x $5\frac{1}{2}"$h . . . . . . . . . . . . . . . . . . . . . . . . . . . . . . . . . .    25.00    30.00

## *Portrait Pinbacks*

☐ "Clarksburg, West Virginia, 1924. For President. Hon. John W. Davis"; cello attached to bar reading "John W. Davis. Notification. August 11"; portrait

**Price Range**

appears above "For President"; (Hake 2010) 2"
cello, black, white; 2¾" with bar-brass embossed   1300.00   1400.00

☐ "Davis" appears across necktie of portrait. (Hake
4); 1½"; black, white ........................   400.00   450.00

☐ Also ⅞" (Hake 9; Warner 733) ...............   250.00   275.00

☐ Also 1¼" (Hake 2011; Warner 374) ...........   375.00   400.00

☐ Davis—no lettering; portrait bleed off collet (Hake
2012), ⅞"; black, white .....................   150.00   175.00

☐ "For President. John W. Davis"; wording reversed
out of suit lapels in portrait; attached to short red,
white, blue ribbon and "Souvenir" bar (Hake 2028;
Warner 729) 4"; brown, white; also came with wire
easel bracket for self-standing; highly rare, desirable
centerpiece ................................   1200.00   1400.00

☐ "For President. John W. Davis"; large lettering in
border around circular portrait (Hake 3) 1½";
sepiatone ...................................   500.00   550.00

☐ "For President. John W. Davis"; three-quarters
profile, circular portrait. (Hake 6; Warner 375)
1¼"; black, white .........................   300.00   325.00

☐ "For President" above Davis bleed portrait; "John
William Davis" (Hake 5; Warner 731) only known
Davis pinback that spells out full name; 1¼";
black, white, gray; mates to LaFollette and Coolidge .....................................   335.00   375.00

☐ "For President. John W. Davis"; candidate appears
in pensive mood in this uncommon portrait cello
(Hake 2007; Warner 730) 2"; black, white; key
item; Also 1¼" size .......................   850.00   900.00

☐ "For President. John W. Davis" (Hake 30; Warner
732) ⅞"; black circle inset; lettering in white border   200.00   225.00

☐ "For President. John W. Davis"; lettering grouped
around head, reversed out of black inset portrait;
white border, thin black line set off as circles within
a circle; draped red, white, blue flag frames upper
two thirds of pinback (Hake 27) 1½"; red, white,
blue, black, gray; key item .................   1100.00   1200.00

Price Range

☐ "For President. John W. Davis"; flag-draped sepia circle inset portrait (Hake unlisted; Warner 372) $1\frac{3}{4}''$; red, white, blue, gold, sepia; possibly unique; only one to surface to date sold at Warner auction in 1981 .................................... 2000.00 plus

☐ "John W. Davis"; portrait and name reversed out of black (Hake 13) $\frac{7}{8}''$; white out of black ..... 100.00    125.00

☐ "Victory"; wishbone-framed portrait with red, white, blue banner across middle of button as background (Hake 8) $\frac{7}{8}''$; red, white, blue, gold, sepia 400.00    425.00

## GUBERNATORIAL PINBACKS

John Davis was a successful nominee for Congress from West Virgina in 1910 and 1912.

☐ "For Congress. John W. Davis"; portrait between letters (Hake 2014) $\frac{7}{8}''$; black, white .......... 200.00    225.00

☐ "John W. Davis For Congress"; a youthful portrait, minus the white hair (Hake 2013; Warner 735) $1''$ 250.00    275.00

### *Slogan/Name Pinbacks*

☐ "Back To Honesty With Davis" (Hake 2017) $\frac{7}{8}''$; black, white ............................... 125.00    150.00

☐ "Better Days With Davis" (Hake unlisted; Warner 736) $\frac{7}{8}''$; blue, white ........................ 200.00    250.00

☐ "Davis" (Hake 20; Warner 740) $\frac{7}{8}''$; red, white, blue ..................................... 50.00    60.00

☐ "Davis" (Hake 23; Warner 741) $\frac{5}{8}''$; white reversed out of black ............................... 35.00    45.00

☐ "Davis" (Hake 37) $\frac{3}{4}''$; white reversed out of blue, lithograph .................................. 75.00    85.00

☐ "Davis"; letters on white swath against black background (Hake 2020) $\frac{1}{2}''$; black, white ......... 50.00    60.00

☐ "Davis and Bryan" (Hake 14) $\frac{7}{8}''$; white reversed out of black ............................... 65.00    75.00

☐ "Davis and Bryan" in white band of three-section lithograph (Hake 15) $\frac{1}{2}''$; red, white, blue ...... 50.00    60.00

☐ Several variants, including (Hake 16, 17) lithos; the former has been reproduced; each ............ 44.00    55.00

Price Range

☐ "John W. Davis For President's Club" (Hake 2018)
⅞"; black, white; cello ...................... 75.00     100.00

☐ Also (Hake 18) ⅞"; red, blue; litho ........... 75.00     85.000

☐ "Davis–Smith" (Hake 24) ⅞"; black, white ..... 50.00     75.00

☐ "Davis–Smith" with star between names (Hake 25)
⅞"; blue, white ............................ 60.00     80.00

☐ "Victory," formed by running horizontally and picking up the third letters, V (from Davis) and Y (from Bryan), which run vertically on pinback (Hake 39) ⅞"; black, red lithograph; red stars .. 135.00     150.00

## CHARLES GATES DAWES

Charles Dawes, a wealthy Illinois businessman and former Budget Director, was nicknamed "Hell and Maria" for his volatile platform style. A crony of Mark Hanna, McKinley's campaign manager, Charles Dawes successfully led the Illinois contingent to put the 25th President over the top in 1896. In 1923 he headed a commission investigating Europe's economic recovery following World War I. The result was the Dawes Plan, which won him a Nobel Peace Prize in 1925. Dawes proved to be a "quiet" Vice-President, however. Herbert Hoover later appointed him Ambassador to Great Britain (see Calvin Coolidge).

## EUGENE VICTOR DEBS

Eugene Debs first came into prominence in 1894 during a Pullman railroad worker's strike. As president of the American Railway Union (ARU), Debs had helped organize the workers. President Cleveland called out Federal troops to crush the strike and 20 workers were killed. Debs was sent to prison for six months. In 1900 Debs ran for President under the Socialist Party of America banner and received 88,000 votes. He ran five times in all—in 1900, 1904, 1908, 1912 and 1920. Although Debs never picked up any electoral votes, he did manage almost a million votes in both the 1912 and 1920 races. In the dramatic 1920 campaign, he ran from his prison cell from the Atlanta Federal Penitentiary. President Wilson had sentenced him there for his anti-war speeches. Harding pardoned him in 1921. Eugene Debs is judged as one of the most popular of political candidates among collectors, rating number one among third-party entrants. Numerous artifacts picture him in his convict's uniform.

Price Range

## Lapel Devices

☐ "Social Democratic Party": no–name Debs–Harriman jugate; (Hake SOC 1) ⅞"; red, white, black. 1900 .............................. | 200.00 | 225.00

☐ "Labor Leaders/No Government by Injunction": Debs–Harriman jugate with large red bow; (Hake SOC 2) 1¼"; red, cream, black. 1900 .......... | 325.00 | 350.00

☐ "Debs–Harriman" jugate with oval portraits; (Hake SOC 3) 1¼"; red, gold, black, cream. 1900 | 200.00 | 210.00

☐ "Socialist Candidates/1904/Debs–Hanford"; farm and factory worker figures stand behind oval jugates. (Hake SOC 4) 1¼"; multicolor .......... | 220.00 | 230.00

☐ "Socialist Party/Workers Of The World Unite" Debs bull's-eye portrait. (Hake SOC 5) ⅞"; red, black, white. 1904 ......................... | 80.00 | 90.00

☐ "Debs–Hanford/1908" jugate with hand–held torch separating oval insets; (Hake SOC 6) ⅞"; red, black, white .............................. | 150.00 | 170.00

☐ "Eugene Debs–Ben Hanford" jugate ovals with clasped hands in circle inset and gold filigree; (Hake SOC 7) 1¼"; red, black, gold, white. 1908 ..... | 120.00 | 130.00

☐ "Gene Debs" Oval browntone portrait Debs; (Hake SOC 8) 1"h; browntone. 1912 ................ | 100.00 | 110.00

☐ "Socialist Party" Debs–Emil Seidel jugate; (Hake SOC 9) 1¼"; black, white, red rim. 1912 ....... | 235.00 | 250.00

☐ "Socialists Candidates/1912/Debs–Seidel" jugate; (Hake SOC 10) ⅞"; red, bluetone, white ....... | 100.00 | 110.00

☐ "Socialist Candidates . . ." (same lettering as Hake 10) jugates with fruit cluster atop ovals. (Hake 3084) 1¾"; red, black, white, gold ............ | 400.00 | 425.00

☐ "Convict No. 2253 For President": no–name Debs portrait; (Hake SOC 14) 1"; red, black, white, 1920 | 375.00 | 400.00

☐ "For President/Convict No. 9653": Debs bull's-eye portrait with cell bars in background (Hake SOC 15) ⅞"; black, red, white, 1920 .............. | 275.00 | 300.00

Price Range

☐ "Debs–Stedman" jugate with Statue of Liberty between oval insets. (Hake SOC 16) ⅞"; red, white, blue, black, 1920 ........................... 260.00    275.00

### Pennant

☐ "Eugene Debs Socialist Party" portrait pennant; red, gold, white, black ....................... 200.00    225.00

### Statuary

☐ Eugene Debs Convict bronze bust; 6½"h ....... 75.00    85.00

## THOMAS E. DEWEY

Thomas E. Dewey, a former racket–busting district Attorney and Governor of New York, ran for President in 1944 against Franklin Roosevelt and again in 1948 against Harry S. Truman. He was resoundingly defeated both times. Expected to win easily in 1948, he saw Truman run up a 2,000,000 popular vote plurality—one of history's great miscalculations.

Price Range

### Automobile License Attachments

☐ "Dewey/We Are Due For A Change" slogan (Hake 2100) ...................................... 25.00    30.00

☐ "Let's Go Places"; die-stamped elephant figural (Hake 2102) .............................. 15.00    20.00

☐ "Let's Go Places With Dewey/Warren" (portrait rebus); "Win With Dewey & Warren" (Hake 2008); red, white, blue ........................... 65.00    75.00

☐ "Pembroke Republican Association/Dewey/ Warren" (Hake 2101) ...................... 25.00    30.00

☐ "Pennsylvania 4 Dewey"; white reversed out of blue outline of state (Hake 2099); 11½"w x 6"h; blue, white ..................................... 20.00    25.00

☐ "Win With Dewey And Warren" (Hake 2001); black, blue ................................ 65.00    75.00

☐ "I'm For Dewey" (unlisted) ................. 35.00    40.00

## Banks

Price Range

☐ Thomas Dewey Metal Figure, maker unknown, 1944, cast metal, painted, name embossed on base, 4″ height (Hake 2004) ...................... 15.00    25.00

## Cartoon/Pictorial Pinbacks

☐ "Back To Independence, Missouri" appears on drawing of road sign (Hake 97) ¾″; red, white, blue; red rim .............................. 8.00    10.00

☐ "Clear Everything With Sidney" (Hake 48) 2¼″; red, white; alludes to influence of CIO Political Action Committee head, Sidney Hillman; in "calling the shots" for FDR ........................ 15.00    20.00

☐ "Dewey–Bricker N.Y. Young Republicans Club"; small elephant seated, makes big shadow silhouette (Hake 107) ¾″; blue, white .................. 5.00    8.00

☐ "Dewey" elephant acrostic; "Dewey" superimposed on cartoon can be read four ways (Hake 2016) 1¾″; black, white ..................... 35.00    45.00

☐ "Dewey–Warren" large elephant (Hake 61) 1¼″; black, white. ............................... 15.00    20.00

☐ "Get Your Donkey [donkey head rebus] Off The White House Grass. It's All Dewey"; White House in background (Hake 52) 1½″; red, white, blue border; green, black, white image area; key item for 1940 ...................................... 120.00    130.00

☐ "Keep The Ass [donkey rebus] Off The White House Grass/It's All Dewey" (Hake 66) 1¼″; blue, white ...................................... 100.00    110.00

☐ "National Convention"; GOP elephant marching with smile on face (Hake 47) 2″; blue, white; 1944 race ...................................... 8.00    10.00

☐ "Two Many Jacks From Missouri"; small donkey heads encircle Capitol dome (Hake 65) 1¼″; black, gray, white; key item from 1948 .............. 115.00    125.00

| *Jugate Pinbacks* | Price Range | |
|---|---|---|

**DEWEY–BRICKER—1944**

☐ "Dewey And Bricker" silhouetted portraits (Hake 2) ⅞"; black, white ........................... 70.00  80.00

☐ "Dewey And Bricker For Prosperity"; oval portraits within shield outline (Hake 127) 5½"; blue, white ....................................... 300.00  325.00

☐ "Dewey–Bricker"; silhouetted portraits in white band (Hake 1) 1¼"; red, white, bluetone; celluloid reproduction exists .......................... 125.00  135.00

☐ Also ⅞" (Hake 3) ........................... 25.00  30.00

**DEWEY–WARREN—1948**

☐ "Dewey And Warren" bull's-eye jugate (Hake 123; Warner 807) ⅞"; blue, white; error jugate with Bricker on left (pinback later was reissued with portraits in proper sequence) .................... 45.00  55.00

☐ "Dewey And Warren"; staggered oval portraits with large flag background (Hake 6) 1¼"; sepia, red, white, blue; has been reproduced in celluloid 20.00  25.00

☐ Also 3¼" (Hake 2005) ...................... 25.00  35.00

☐ "Dewey–Warren" conjoining portraits (Hake 2007) 3½"; black, white .......................... 15.00  20.00

☐ "For President/Thomas E. Dewey; For Vice President/Earl W. Warren"; small eagles top, bottom (Hake 7) 1¼"; black, white ................. 100.00  110.00

☐ "Tenth Anniversary Of National Federation of Women's Republican Clubs"; Dewey–Warren portraits (Hake unlisted; Warner 451) 1⅝" x 1⁷/₁₆"; actually a ribbon fob with tab; black, white, gold 150.00  175.00

☐ "Vote Republican For Dewey–Warren"; silhouetted heads (Hake 13) 3¼"; red, white, blue ..... 30.00  35.00

☐ Also 1¼" (Hake 2002) ...................... 170.00  190.00

☐ Also 9" (Warner 449) ....................... 125.00  135.00

*Portrait Pinbacks*

☐ Dewey "no–name" portrait (Hake 4) 2¼"; black, white with red, white, blue rim ............... 10.00  15.00

| | Price Range | |
|---|---|---|

☐ "Dewey's Due In '48" (Hake 39) $\frac{7}{8}$"; bluetone, white ........................................ 10.00   15.00

☐ "Dewey For President" (Hake 18) $1\frac{3}{4}$"; black, gray, white ................................. 50.00   60.00

☐ Also $\frac{7}{8}$" (Hake 22) ......................... 20.00   25.00

☐ "For President/Thomas E. Dewey"; small eagle profiles flank portrait (Hake 15) $2\frac{1}{4}$"; bluetone, white ........................................ 10.00   12.00

☐ Also $3\frac{1}{2}$" (Hake 2011) ...................... 10.00   15.00

☐ "God Bless America/Dewey/1944–48" (Hake 126) $1\frac{1}{2}$"; red, white, bluetone; lithograph .......... 10.00   12.00

☐ "Go Forth With Dewey"; numeral 4 overprinted on word "Forth" in red (Hake 34) $\frac{7}{8}$"; red, white, bluetone; lithograph ......................... 8.00   10.00

☐ "Our Next President/Thomas E. Dewey"; bull's-eye design with small eagles on sides (Hake 124) $1\frac{1}{4}$"; red, white, blue ...................... 15.00   20.00

☐ "Thomas E. Dewey" appears in scroll under bleed portrait (Hake 19) $1\frac{1}{2}$"; browntone ........... 8.00   10.00

☐ Also $\frac{7}{8}$" (Hake 20) ......................... 8.00   10.00

### Slogan/Name Pinbacks

☐ "All 48 In '48" (Hake 2032; Warner 808) $3\frac{1}{2}$"; red, white, blue; slogan also used by Truman forces .. 25.00   30.00

☐ "Campaign Committee/Thomas E. Dewey For District Attorney"; 1937 (Warner 451) $2\frac{1}{4}$"; blue, white; Dewey's record as racket-busting D.A. earned him a New York state governorship in 1942   100.00   110.00

☐ "Dewey Or Don't We" (Hake 72) $1\frac{1}{4}$"; red, white, blue, red rim ............................... 10.00   12.00

☐ "Dewey The Racket Buster/New Deal Buster" (Hake 71) $1\frac{1}{4}$"; black, white ................. 10.00   12.00

Price Range

☐ "4H/Help Hurry Harry Home" (Hake 98) ⅞"; green, white .............................. 8.00 10.00

☐ "4H/Help Hustle Harry Home" (Hake 99) ⅞"; red, white, blue ........................... 15.00 20.00

☐ "I'm On The Team/Dewey Volunteer" (Hake 49) 2"; red, white, blue ........................ 10.00 15.00

☐ "Mothers/Sisters/Wives/Sweethearts/Dewey–Bricker" (Hake 58) 1¼"; red, white, blue lithograph ..... 20.00 25.00

☐ "Our Dewey Special Is Due" (Hake 56) 1½"; blue, white ...................................... 15.00 20.00

☐ "Start Packing Harry/The Deweys Are Coming" (Hake 69) 1¼"; blue, white .................. 20.00 25.00

☐ "Stop Tammany Jrs./Draft Dewey" (Hake 2043) 1¼"; black, blue ........................... 25.00 30.00

☐ "The Issue Is Truman's Record/Nothing Else!" (Hake 131) 1½"; blue, white ................ 45.00 55.00

☐ "Truman For Ex-President" (Hake 54) 2"; red, white, blue ............................... 20.00 25.00

☐ "Truman Screwy To Build A Porch For Dewey" (Hake 64) 1¼"; blue, white lithograph; refers to alterations on White House during Truman's first term; item has been reproduced .............. 10.00 12.00

☐ "W" (very large letter) Do We/We Do/Win With Dewey & Bricker"; 1944 (Hake 125) ⅞"; blue, white ...................................... 50.00 60.00

☐ "Washington Could Not Tell A Lie/Roosevelt Could Not Tell The Truth/Truman Does Not Know The Difference" (unlisted) 2"; blue, yellow 55.00 65.00

## STEPHEN A. DOUGLAS

Stephen A. Douglas, a Democrat from Illinois, served in the House and U.S. Senate from 1843–61. Running as a Popular Sovereignty Democrat for president, he lost to Lincoln in 1860 (he refused to endorse a pro-slavery platform and delegates from eight southern states bolted the party). Douglas won only 29% of the popular vote and finished a poor fourth (even Breckinridge and Bell outpulled him) in electoral votes.

## DWIGHT DAVID EISENHOWER

Dwight Eisenhower, former Supreme Commander of the Allied Forces in Europe in World War II was elected the 34th U.S. President in 1952. Born in Kansas and raised in Texas, he declared his candidacy in New York, where he was President of Columbia University. As was the case with another West Point graduate, U. S. Grant, Eisenhower was without prior political experience. Grant and Eisenhower were also the only two Republicans to serve out two complete four-year terms. "Ike" undoubtedly could have been elected for a third term were it not for the limitations set by the 22nd Amendment.

Price Range

### *Automotive Accessories*

#### LICENSES
☐ "Inaugural" oval portraits of Eisenhower and Nixon; 12" x 6"; black, white ............... 45.00    55.00

☐ "In 1954 Give Ike a Republican Congress"; elephant in circle at left (Hake 2238) 12" x 6"; blue, black ...................................... 15.00    20.00

#### LICENSE ATTACHMENTS
☐ "I Like Ike"; arched letters above five stars in rectangle with upper sloped corners (Hake 2242) 12" x 6"; blue, white ........................... 10.00    15.00

Dwight Eisenhower Toby mug, ceramic, as general several years prior to becoming 34th president of the United States, ca. early 1950s ($65–$75).

A sampling of slogan pinbacks from the Coolidge, Eisenhower, and Willkie forces—all still priced under $10 each.

Nixon and Eisenhower carved wooden figures, ca. 1950s; made in Sweden ($45–$50 each).

| | Price Range | |
|---|---|---|
| ☐ "I Like Ike"; die-stamped semicircle with Capitol domes on each side; white, dark blue .......... | 15.00 | 20.00 |

Price Range

☐ "Our Next President"; die-stamped silhouette bust of Eisenhower above strip containing slogan; chrome finish ............................... 25.00 30.00

☐ "We Like Ike"; eagle with spread wings in die-stamped shield shape; 6"w; red, white, blue ..... 15.00 20.00

## Cartoon/Pictorial Pinbacks

☐ "Block Captain For Ike"; illustrated cartoon of block-shaped figure saluting (Hake 85) 1½"; black, yellow ..................................... 25.00 30.00

☐ "Don't Be Fooled By The New Look [cartoon of Democratic donkey with blanket that reads] On The Old Ass/Vote Republican" (Hake 89) 3¼"; red, white, blue ........................... 15.00 20.00

☐ "Don't Let This Happen To You. Vote For Ike"; cartoon of large shoe with hole in it, popularized by Stevenson forces (Hake 81) 2¾"; red, white, blue ....................................... 10.00 15.00

☐ Also ⅞" (Hake 101) ........................ 6.00 8.00

☐ "Eisenhower/Guard My Future"; bull's-eye photograph of small baby (Hake 173; Warner 814) ⅞"; red, white, blue; alludes to Korean War ........ 85.00 95.00

☐ "Eisenhower in '56"; large parading elephant (Hake 2068) 1½"; black, white .................... 8.00 10.00

☐ "If You Like Ike [on large banner held in elephant's tusks] Vote Republican," emblazoned on elephant's blanket (Hake 86) 3¾"; red, white, blue ....... 20.00 25.00

☐ "Ike" name appears only via hand signals for deaf and dumb; illustration of three hands conveying each letter (Hake 117) 1¼"; red, white, blue; a graphics classic ........................... 35.00 40.00

☐ "Press/Ike/Dick 1956/Intelligence"; words work around large pair of open scissors (Hake 95; Warner 459) 2"; red, white, blue .................... 35.00 40.00

☐ "Southerners For Eisenhower"; crossed U.S. and Confederate flags (Hake 2116) 1½"; red, white, blue, black ................................. 55.00 65.00

Price Range

☐ "Time For A Change"; baby in diapers, crawling; "I Like Ike" appears on diapers (Hake 108) 1¼"; black, white; appealing litho .................. 20.00    25.00

☐ "We Need A Change"; enraged GOP elephant bearing placard (Hake 2121) 1½"; black, white    8.00    10.00

☐ "Womanpower for V [large letter] For Eisenhower"; tiny elephant wearing daisy hat and skirt carrying "G.O.P." pennant (Hake 84; Warner 812) 1½"; red, white, blue ....................... 60.00    75.00

## *Inaugural Pinbacks*

### JUGATES

☐ "43rd Inauguration/Consent Of The Governed"; Mamie, Ike, Dick, Pat bust silhouettes (Hake 27) 3½"; sepiatone, blue, buff .................... 35.00    40.00

☐ "Inauguration Day/Eisenhower/Nixon/Jan. 20, 1957/I Like Ike & Dick"; oval portraits with Capitol dome in background (Hake 24) 3⅛"; red, white, blue ....................................... 20.00    25.00

☐ "Inauguration Day/Pennsylvania/January 20th/ 1953"; predominantly blue background vs. red for 1957 pinback (Hake 18; Warner 820) 3⅛"; red, white, blue ............................... 45.00    55.00

### SINGLE PORTRAITS—EISENHOWER

☐ "Dwight David Eisenhower/Inauguration/ January 20, 1957"; red, blue stars flank bull's-eye portrait (Hake 19) 1½" red, white, blue ........ 8.00    10.00

☐ "Eisenhower" in scroll beneath DDE portrait superimposed on Capitol building; "Inauguration 1953 ..." (Hake 15) 1½"; black, white ........ 10.00    12.00

☐ "Inauguration Jan. 20. 1957/Eisenhower/ Washington D.C."; slight variation in portrait and angle of Capitol view (Hake 20) 1½"; black, white 10.00    12.00

## *Jugate Pinbacks—1953–1957*

☐ "Eisenhower/Nixon" conjoining portraits (Hake 2001) 4"; black, white ...................... 35.00    40.00

Price Range

☐ "Eisenhower/Nixon" conjoining portraits flanked by red, blue elephants (Hake 8) 3"; red, white, blue | 25.00 | 30.00

☐ "Eisenhower/Nixon"; tapered lettering of name at top; portraits in middle band (Hake 2018; Warner 810) 3½"; red, white, blue; 1952 race .......... | 65.00 | 75.00

☐ Also 1¼" (Hake 6) ......................... | 190.00 | 215.00

☐ "Eisenhower/Nixon" written in script (Hake 2008) 3"; red, white, blue, black ................... | 35.00 | 40.00

☐ "Ike & Dick/Sure To Click/For President/For Vice President"; oval portraits (Hake 2021) 1½"; red, white, blue ............................ | 15.00 | 20.00

☐ Same slogan with slight design variation (Hake 4) 2½" ...................................... | 25.00 | 30.00

☐ "Ike/Dick"; circle insets in oval-shaped pinback; red, white stripes background (Hake 11) 2½"h x 1½"w; red, white, blue, black ............... | 185.00 | 200.00

☐ "Ike/Dick/Don't Change The Team In The Middle Of The Stream" (unlisted) 2"; red, white, blue; 1956 | 55.00 | 65.00

☐ "I Like Ike/Vote Republican"; jugate portraits in middle of three patriotic bars (Hake 2023) 1½"; red, white, blue ............................ | 25.00 | 30.00

☐ "Junior Ike and Dick Club"; silhouetted heads (Hake 2) 2"; red, white, blue lithograph ........ | 20.00 | 25.00

☐ "Let's Back Ike & Dick"; conjoining portraits (Hake 7) 1¼"; red, white, blue lithograph ...... | 10.00 | 15.00

☐ Also 1¼" celluloid (Hake 2006) .............. | 65.00 | 75.00

☐ "President/Vice President"; shield atop two ovals enclosed by laurel branch border (Hake 2004; Warner 452) 1¾"; red, white, blue, black; key item for 1956 race and scarcest of the Eisenhower jugates;* sold at $577 at 1981 Warner Auction .......... | 300.00 | 350.00

☐ "President/Vice President. Eisenhower/Nixon"; oval portrait in shield outline topped by winged eagle (Hake 1)* 2¾"; red, white, blue, silver .... | 30.00 | 35.00

☐ Also 3" (Hake 2011) ........................ | 60.00 | 75.00

*Smaller example did not appear until 1960 and may be a reproduction.

Price Range

☐ "They're For You—Ike/Dick"; conjoining portraits (Hake 3) 2¾"; yellow, brown, red, buff, flesh-tones ...................................... 20.00 25.00

☐ Also 1¼" (Hake 5) ......................... 10.00 12.00

☐ "Vote For A Better Future. Eisenhower/Nixon"; oval portraits (Hake 9) 2½"; red, white, blue, black 15.00 20.00

☐ "Vote Republican. Pull 1st. Lever For Eisenhower/Nixon" (Hake 2019) 1½"; red, white, blue, black ...................................... 35.00 40.00

## Mirrors

☐ "I'm For Ike" slogan pocket mirror (Hake 2212) 2"; black, white ............................... 15.00 20.00

☐ "Re-Elect Eisenhower/Nixon/Peace/Progress/Prosperity" jugate pocket mirror (Hake 2003; Warner 454) 3½"; red, white, blue, black .......... 50.00 60.00

## Portrait Pinbacks

☐ "Eisenhower In '48"; hopeful item; when both parties were attempting to draft Ike (Hake 25) 1¼"; bluetone .................................. 12.00 15.00

☐ "For The Love Of Ike/Vote Republican" (Hake 67) ⅞"; black, white ........................... 10.00 15.00

☐ Also 2" (Hake 216) ......................... 10.00 12.00

☐ "Give Ike A Republican Congress"; "Ike" with portrait in shield outline (Hake 35) 2¼"; red, white, blue ............................... 10.00 12.00

☐ "I Like Ike"; line-drawing flasher pinback (Hake 2088) 2¼"; black, white .................... 8.00 10.00

☐ "I Like Ike" silhouette portrait (Hake 31) 2"; bluetone ....................................... 8.00 10.00

☐ "I Like Ike" silhouette line sketch (Hake 2039) 3½"; black, white ......................... 20.00 25.00

☐ "I Like Ike"; silhouette of Ike head in large shield outline (Hake 2014) 4"; red, white, blue, black .. 15.00 20.00

☐ Also 9" (unlisted) ......................... 20.00 25.00

Price Range

☐ "I Still Like Ike. He's Good Enough For Me"; portrait with Uncle Sam in background (Hake 2041) 1¼"; red, white, blue ...................... 10.00 15.00

☐ "My Friend Ike"; clasped hands under portrait—one white, one brown (Hake 51) 1¼"; black, brown, white lithograph .................... 12.00 15.00

☐ No–name Eisenhower portrait; wears general's uniform (Hake 29) 2¼"; multicolor .............. 8.00 10.00

☐ "O.K. Ike Club" Eisenhower in uniform (superimposed on sunflower) portrait; "Sunflower Ordinance Works"; die-cut shield shape (Hake 2218; Warner 819) 1¼" x 1⅛"; multicolor .......... 40.00 45.00

☐ "The Man Of The Hour/Eisenhower" (Hake 2027) 1½"; red, white, blue ...................... 12.00 15.00

☐ "We Like Ike" endorsement by *Long Island Newsday* with edition of paper behind portrait (Hake 2109; Warner 456) 1¾" black, white; key item from Ike's 1952 campaign ........................ 50.00 60.00

## Slogan/Name Pinbacks

☐ "Adlai Likes Ike Too" (Hake 111) 1¼"; yellow, blue ......................................... 10.00 15.00

☐ "All For Ike Club/Ike For All" (unlisted) 1¼"; black, white .............................. 15.00 20.00

☐ "Better A Part Time President Than A Full Time Phoney"; (Hake 82) 2¼"; red, white, blue ...... 10.00 15.00

☐ "Dem-Ike-crats For Eisenhower" (Hake 110) 1¼"; blue, yellow .............................. 10.00 12.00

☐ "Draft Eisenhower For President/The People's Choice" (early 1950s item; Ike had not as yet declared) (Hake 121) 1¼"; red, white, blue ....... 20.00 25.00

☐ "Eisenhower For Nixon Day"; probably 1960 item (unlisted) 1¼"; blue, white ................. 12.00 15.00

☐ "Eisenhower/With Peace & Prosperity" (Hake 88) 1½"; blue, white ........................... 15.00 20.00

**Price Range**

☐ "Get Well Ike/America Needs Your Heart"; refers to Ike's heart attack in 1955 (unlisted); ⅞"; black, white . . . . . . . . . . . . . . . . . . . . . . . . . . . . . . . . . . . . .  15.00  20.00

☐ "If Ever We Needed Him We Need Him Now" accompanied by small musical notes illustration (Hake 102) 1¼"; orange, black . . . . . . . . . . . . . .  12.00  15.00

☐ "I'm For Ike"; big letters, entirely in script (Hake 103; Warner 462) 1¼"; red, white, blue; 1952 race  12.00  15.00

☐ "I Like Ike"; partially in script; the most vibrant of numerous slogan pinback variants. (Hake 94) 2"; red, black . . . . . . . . . . . . . . . . . . . . . . . . . . . . . . . .  8.00  10.00

☐ "I Like Ike" (Hake unlisted; Warner 816) oval shape; 2¾"w x 1¾"h; red, white, blue . . . . . . . .  35.00  40.00

☐ "I'm Wit Choo Ike" (Hake 172) ⅞"; red, white, blue . . . . . . . . . . . . . . . . . . . . . . . . . . . . . . . . . . . . .  8.00  10.00

☐ "Let's Clean House With Ike & Dick" (Hake 91) 2"; red, white, blue . . . . . . . . . . . . . . . . . . . . . . . . .  8.00  10.00

☐ Also 1" (Hake 93) . . . . . . . . . . . . . . . . . . . . . . . . .  7.00  9.00

☐ "Make The White House The Dwight House" (Hake 112) 1¼"; yellow, black . . . . . . . . . . . . . . .  8.00  10.00

☐ "Me For Milt"; following uncertainty in 1956 as to Ike running again, some Republicans seemed ready to back his brother Milton (unlisted) ⅞"; black, white . . . . . . . . . . . . . . . . . . . . . . . . . . . . . . . . . . . . .  8.00  10.00

☐ "Monongahela Railroad Employees Will Spike For Ike" (last four words in large letters inside swirl pattern) (Hake 2128; Warner 461) 1¼"; red, white, blue . . . . . . . . . . . . . . . . . . . . . . . . . . . . . . . . . . . .  35.00  40.00

☐ "New York State Citizens For Eisenhower/Nixon Election Night/Nov. 6, 1956"; Republican headquarters victory celebration (Hake unlisted; Warner 460) 2¼"; red, white, blue . . . . . . . . . . . . . .  25.00  30.00

☐ "Remember 1912. Win With Ike"; hint to Robert Taft supporters in primary that split between Teddy Roosevelt and William Howard Taft cost Republicans the 1912 election; 1952 race (Hake 2062; Warner 452) 3½"; red, white, blue . . . . . . . . . . . . . .  30.00  35.00

| *Textiles* | Price Range | |
|---|---|---|

PENNANTS

☐ "I Like Ike" bust portrait on left; large tapered lettering; red, white .......................... 10.00  15.00

☐ "Your Best Bet In 52. Gen. D. Eisenhower/Pres./Richard Nixon/V. Pres."; line illustration of standing elephant, candidates, and Capitol dome; white, blue ................................ 12.00  15.00

☐ "Second Inauguration 1957" bust profiles; blue, white ...................................... 12.00  15.00

RIBBONS

☐ "Good Government"; white ribbon with blue lettering attached to "Eisenhower" name celluloid pinback ...................................... 20.00  25.00

☐ "Hawthorne Proudly Endorses Eisenhower–Nixon/1956"; line illustration of Ike; "Hawthorne County Republican League ............ 15.00  20.00

☐ "Men Of The Year/1956"; Eisenhower and Stevenson portraits; advertising piece for Century Woven Label Co., N.Y.C.; First Annual Exposition, New York Coliseum ............................ 10.00  12.00

☐ "Welcome Mr. President/November 1st. 1956/ Philadelphia, Pa."; Ike bust portrait; ribbon hangs from blank bar; Liberty Bell metal hanger inserted at end of ribbon ............................ 20.00  25.00

## CHARLES FAIRBANKS

Charles Fairbanks, one of the early conservative Republicans, was a Senator from Indiana who became Theodore Roosevelt's running mate in 1904. Fairbanks, a protege of Mark Hanna, McKinley's campaign manager, had been suggested by Hanna for the number two spot (Hanna despised "that damned cowboy," Roosevelt).

Fairbanks, however, had his own aspirations for the presidency. As TR's Vice-President, he attempted to thwart Roosevelt's Square Deal reform measures. When TR backed Taft for the Republican nomination for president in 1908, Fairbanks later retaliated by working to help undo the Bull Moose party and their leader in 1912. Fairbanks accepted the second spot on the Republican ticket in 1916, which saw them lose by a narrow margin. He died a few years later, in 1918 (see Teddy Roosevelt and Charles Hughes).

## MILLARD FILLMORE

Millard Fillmore, a Whig from New York, served in the House 1833–35 and 1837–43. He became Vice–President in 1849 under Zachary Taylor and assumed the Presidency one year later when Taylor died in office (1850–53). The 13th U.S. President was passed over for the nomination by the Whigs in 1852 in favor of another Mexican War hero, General Winfield Scott. Fillmore made another try for the Presidency with the American Whig ("Know Nothing") Party in 1856, running with Andrew J. Donelson of Tennessee under the slogan "Americans Must Rule America." Fillmore finished a poor third to Fremont and the winner Buchanan, managing to win only eight electoral votes (see Zachary Taylor).

|  | Price Range | |
|---|---|---|
| *Badges, Medals—1856* | | |
| ☐ Bust token, Fillmore facing right; largest, best designed of handful of Fillmore tokens; detailed biographical data on reverse (DeWitt MF 1856–1; Warner 72) 39mm; white metal . . . . . . . . . . . . . . | 110.00 | 120.00 |
| ☐ Bust token, Fillmore facing left; name encloses bust; H. Miller, Louisville, KY, engraver; "Americans Shall Rule America" enclosed by olive branches (DeWitt MF 1856–6) 28mm; white metal . . . . . . . | 75.00 | 85.00 |
| ☐ Brass shell; scroll inscribed "Mil'd Fillmore," reverse intaglio (DeWitt MF 1856–8) 26 x 20mm; brass finish . . . . . . . . . . . . . . . . . . . . . . . . . . . . . . . | 350.00 | 400.00 |
| *Ceramics and Glassware* | | |
| ☐ Glass paperweight, "Millard Fillmore/President Of The United States/1850"; frosted intaglio bust profile of Fillmore; hexagonal shape; $3\frac{1}{2}''$h x $1''$h; made by New England Glass Co., East Cambridge, MA . . . . . . . . . . . . . . . . . . . . . . . . . . . . . . . . . . . . . | 325.00 | 350.00 |
| *Lighting Devices* | | |
| ☐ Parade pierced-tin lantern with "Fillmore/ Donelson" inscribed on door, names divided by pair of stars; approx. $9''$h; black or plain tin finish | 1400.00 | 1500.00 |

*Lithographed Paper Under Glass with Pewter Frame—1848\**

Price Range

☐ Colored lithographed bust, "Millard Fillmore," facing quarter right (Hake ZT 3003; DeWitt ZT–1848–45); Zachary Taylor is on obverse; 65 mm ....................................... 1100.00   1200.00

☐ Similar to above except that Fillmore faces quarter left (Hake 3005; DeWitt ZT–1848–47) ......... 1100.00   1200.00

*Lithographed Paper Badge*

☐ "The Union/Our Whole Country/Fillmore & Donelson"; circle die-cut with top of shield projecting; portraits enclosed by stripes, bordered by stars (Warner 73) $3\frac{1}{2}$"; red, white, blue, black ....... 400.00   450.00

*Prints, Posters*

1848 CAMPAIGN

☐ "Millard Fillmore/Whig Candidate For Vice President of the United States"; from a Plumbe daguerreotype; Currier & Ives .................. 115.00   125.00

1856

☐ Millard Fillmore–Andrew Donelson jugate; olive leaves encircle ovals, topped by shield and eagle (Hake 3001) Currier & Ives .................. 250.00   275.00

1857

☐ "Millard Fillmore/Thirteenth President of the United States/And National American Candidate For the Fifteenth President of the United States," from a photograph by Mathew B. Brady; vignette to left of Fillmore image; Currier & Ives ....... 275.00   300.00

---

*Millard Fillmore was running mate to Zachary Taylor on the victorious Whig ticket, serving as vice-president 1848–1850. On Taylor's death in 1850, Fillmore succeeded as president.

Price Range

## Textiles

### BANNERS

☐ "No 11/Fillmore & Donelson/No North/No East/No South/No West"; directions appear in each corner; silk; gold, green; 61½"w x 47"h; 1856    1400.00    1500.00

☐ "Put None But Americans On Guard"; paper litho with portraits of Washington, Jackson on obverse; "Fillmore and Donelson/For Peace, Harmony and the Union" on reverse; 41"w x 39"h; red, white, blue, black; red fringe ......................    1300.00    1400.00

### RIBBONS

☐ "Fillmore–Donelson/National Union" conjoining-portrait jugate enclosed by laurel branches (Hake 3010; DeWitt MF-1) black, white ............    900.00    950.00

☐ "For President/Millard Fillmore; For Vice President/Andrew J. Donelson" below simulated draped flag; portrait of Fillmore in field (upper right) surrounded by stars (Hake 3011; DeWitt MF-5) red, white, blue, black ................    375.00    400.00

☐ "Fillmore Club"; portrait of Fillmore with facsimile signature (Warner 74); name of town usually appeared at very top; example sold at Warner auction marked "Stamford"; example in DeWitt (MF-6) listed as Boston ...........................    250.00    275.00

## GERALD RUDOLPH FORD

Gerald Ford was born in Nebraska but began his political career in Michigan. He served in the House from 1949–73 and was Minority Leader for a number of terms. In 1973 he was appointed Vice–President to replace Spiro Agnew. In 1974 he replaced Richard Nixon, when Nixon stepped down following the Watergate scandal. The 38th U.S. President lost in his bid for re–nomination to Jimmy Carter in 1976.

Price Range

## Cartoon/Pictorial Pinbacks

☐ "Back To The Peanut Farm" Capitol dome atop elephant's head (Hake 2024) 3"; blue, gray, black, white ........................................    3.00    5.00

Price Range

☐ "Ford [Model T rebus] For President" (Hake 2009) 2¾"; red, white, blue, black . . . . . . . . . . . . . . . . . .    4.00      6.00

☐ "Don't Settle For Peanuts"; GOP elephant crushing large peanut with trunk (Hake 2039) 1¾"  . .    2.00      3.00

☐ "Is There A Ford In Your Future?" cartoon of Ford standing in open convertible (unlisted) 3"; black, white . . . . . . . . . . . . . . . . . . . . . . . . . . . .    3.00      5.00

☐ "Jerry Baby/Lean As A Hound's Tooth"; cartoon profile (unlisted) 2¾"; black, white . . . . . . . . . . . .    5.00      7.00

☐ "Peanut Crunch"; elephant's foot stomping on peanut (Hake 2036) 2"; black, white . . . . . . . . . . . . .    2.00      3.00

☐ "Shoot Out at Kansas City. I Was There. Republican National Convention"; Ford and Reagan in cowboy outfits; Ford wears white hat; Reagan, black (Hake 2016) 2¼; red, white, black . . . . . . .    3.00      5.00

☐ "Wouldn't You Rather Have A Ford . . . A Ford"; cartoon of Ford with small football and Ford auto (unlisted) 2¾"; black, green, white . . . . . . . . . . .    3.00      5.00

## *Jugate Pinbacks—1976*

☐ "Confidence–Peace–Prosperity/Ford–Dole in '76"; buckeye design (Hake 2003) 1¾"; red, white, blue, black . . . . . . . . . . . . . . . . . . . . . . . . . . . . . . . . . .    2.00      3.00

☐ "Ford–Dole in '76" conjoining silhouetted portraits (Hake 2002) 4"; black, white . . . . . . . . . . . . . . . .    3.00      5.00

☐ "Ford–Dole in '76"; portraits similar to above but at lower angle (Hake 2004) 1¾" black, blue . . . .    3.00      5.00

☐ "Ford–Dole '76. America's Choice"; elephant head with candidates' portraits on each side; cartoon (Hake 2007) 2¾"; black, white . . . . . . . . . . . . . .    3.00      5.00

☐ "Ford–Dole"; vertical insets on top and bottom of pinback with names in middle (Hake 2006) 2"; green, black, white . . . . . . . . . . . . . . . . . . . . . . . .    2.00      4.00

☐ "Prosperity, Peace and Public Trust/Ford–Dole"; conjoining portraits with both candidates smiling (Hake 2005) 2¼"; black, red, white . . . . . . . . . . .    8.00      10.00

## *Portrait Pinbacks*

### FORD FOR U.S. REPRESENTATIVE

Gerald R. Ford first ran for a seat in the U.S. House of Representatives from Michigan in 1949 and remained there until 1973. When Richard Nixon named him vice-president in 1973, Ford was Speaker of the House.

|  | Price Range | |
|---|---|---|
| ☐ "Jerry," full-length portrait of Ford carrying briefcase; name runs vertically from shoulder to coat-tails (from late 1960s run for House seat) (Hake 2123) $1\,2/3''$; black, white lithograph .......... | 20.00 | 25.00 |

### FORD FOR PRESIDENT

| | | |
|---|---|---|
| ☐ "Experience Counts/Elect Gerald R. Ford in '76"; bull's-eye portrait, quarter profile (Hake 2022) $3\frac{1}{2}''$; red, white, blue, black ................. | 3.00 | 5.00 |
| ☐ Also 2" (Hake 2026) ....................... | 2.00 | 3.00 |
| ☐ And $1\frac{3}{4}''$ (Hake 2038) ..................... | 2.00 | 3.00 |
| ☐ "Ford in '76"; partial Ford portrait (bleeds off pin at right) (Hake 2040) $1\frac{3}{4}''$; red, white, black .... | 3.00 | 5.00 |
| ☐ "He's #1 [large numeral] with me. Kansas City, August 1976"; circular inset portrait under numeral (Hake 2018) $2\frac{1}{4}''$; black, green, white .... | 4.00 | 6.00 |
| ☐ Oval portrait (no-name) inside oval shape (Hake 2008) $1\frac{3}{4}''$; black, white .................... | 5.00 | 7.00 |

## THEODORE FRELINGHUYSEN

Frelinghuysen served in the U.S. Senate from New Jersey 1829–35, and later entered politics in New York to run as Vice–President under Henry Clay in 1844. He helped inspire the slogan "The country's risin'/for Clay and Frelinghuysen" (see Henry Clay).

## JOHN C. FREMONT

The first presidential candidate from the newly organized Republican Party, John Fremont of California was a noted army officer and explorer of the West. He served in the U.S. Senate from 1850–51, prior to his presidential nomination in 1856. His anti-slavery views proved unpopular in 1856 and he was defeated by Buchanan. Despite a split with Millard Fillmore and the Know–Nothings, the Republicans showed considerable "muscle" for a new political party.

## JAMES A. GARFIELD

Garfield, an Ohio Republican, served in the House, 1863–80. Known as "Boatman Jim" from his early work on the Ohio canal, Garfield emerged as a dark horse in 1880 and swept to a stunning victory over Hancock. Only a few months after his inauguration, the 20th U.S. President was assassinated by a disappointed office seeker.

**Price Range**

### *Badges, Medals, Stickpins—1880*

JUGATES

☐ Garfield–Arthur eagle; crossed cannons bar linked to wreath-shaped hanger with laurel branches, shield; sepia cardboard photographs in shell frame (Hake 3042) 1¾"l; gilt finish ................ 360.00     370.00

☐ "Garfield–Arthur"; eagle clasp; cardboard photos in pearled oval frames in irregularly shaped shell with embossed star, rays, shield; ribbon attached (Hake 3041) 1½"; bronzed shell ............. 340.00     350.00

"Hurrah For Garfield–Arthur," cotton banner, 1880 ($650–$700).

Price Range

☐ Eagle clasp variant of Hake 3041, with subtle differences in configuration of eagle and hanger (Hake 3040) gilt brass; red, white, blue ribbon ........     375.00     400.00

☐ "Garfield–Arthur" ferrotypes with names above busts in oblong pearled frames; ornate shield-shaped shell with row of 17 rosette ornaments atop shield; tassels below (Sullivan JG 1880–19) 1¼"; gilt brass ...................................     475.00     500.00

☐ "Garfield–Arthur" ferro, similar to above, with eagle and crossbar atop (Hake 3029) 1¾"; gilt finish ........................................     510.00     535.00

## PORTRAIT BADGES

☐ Garfield winged-eagle clasp; ferrotype in circular mount with nine points on star background; quarter-right portrait (Hake 3030) 1¾"; brass finish ........................................     235.00     250.00

☐ Garfield winged eagle atop beaded circular frame with Garfield ferrotype; pair of furled flags on each side of frame (Hake 3034) 1½"; gilt brass ......     235.00     250.00

☐ Garfield shield-clasp ring linking nine-point star hanger with quarter-right ferrotypes; red, white, blue ribbon attached (Hake 3033; Sullivan JG 1880–25) 2½"; brass finish ...................     250.00     275.00

☐ Garfield with wreath of roses frame around ferrotype on circular background with heart-shaped filigree (Hake 3037; Sullivan JG-1880-28) 1"; gilt brass ........................................     200.00     225.00

☐ Garfield stud with small profile ferrotype set in brass rim (Hake 3038) 1"; brass finish .........     165.00     175.00

## JOHN NANCE GARNER

John Nance Garner was the first of FDR's three vice-presidents, serving two terms—1932, 1936. A native of Texas, he won a seat in that state's legislature in 1898. He came to the House of Representatives in 1902 and remained for 30 years, as Minority Leader and then Speaker of the House. Twice Garner challenged FDR for the presidency—in 1932 and in 1940.

Price Range

### *Automotive Accessories*

☐ "Garner For President"; word "Four" bisects Capitol dome illustration; 11"w; blue, ivory ......... 50.00     60.00

### *Portrait Pinbacks*

☐ "Garner For President"; bull's-eye portrait; 1¼"; black, white ................................ 50.00     60.00

☐ Also versions in 2½" and ⅞" sizes; at least six are black/white reverses out of black; each ........ 20.00     25.00

☐ "John Garner For President"; essentially same pose as above with first name added; ⅞"; black, white; three known versions, each ................... 20.00     25.00

☐ "John Nance Garner/Speaker Of The House" black/white portrait reversed out of black; ribbon attached. "Garner For President" in gilt lettering reading vertically; 2½"; gilt, blue ribbon; approximately 5" ................................... 75.00     100.00

☐ "John N. Garner For Congress, 15th District"; size and color undetermined; early 1900s ........... 50.00     60.00

## ELBRIDGE GERRY

The "Gentleman Democrat" from Massachusetts was a signer of the Declaration of Independence. His background was a shipper and sometime privateer. President Adams appointed Gerry as one of three commissioners in the famous XYZ Affair. He returned from his peace mission in France and served two terms as Massachusetts governor. Elected Vice-President under Madison, he died two years later in 1814. By proposing a redistricting plan in his home state that would assure a healthy majority for his party (the area in question was shaped like a salamander), the pundits combined the two and added the term "gerrymander" to the political lexicon (see James Madison).

## BARRY MORRIS GOLDWATER

Barry Goldwater, a cult hero to the American conservative community since the early 1960s, has served as a U.S. Senator from Arizona since 1953, upsetting LBJ's predecessor as majority leader, Ernest McFarland. In 1961, a master plan was set into motion, as one of the textbook cases of how to win a nomination. Clinton White of the Young Republicans put together a nucleus of what would eventually become the Draft Goldwater Committee. Despite opposition from party leaders Dwight Eisenhower, Nelson Rockefeller, Governors George Romney and William Scranton, all of whom chose a more moderate course, Barry Goldwater easily won the presidential nomination at the Republican National Convention, with another "go for the jugular" conservative such as himself, William Miller of New York, as running mate. Goldwater will always be remembered for a quote from his acceptance speech, "Extremism in the defense of liberty is no vice. Moderation in the pursuit of justice is no virtue." This extremist image, of a would-be dangerous warmonger, who posed a threat to reinstate Jim Crowism and destroy Social Security, cost Goldwater dearly. LBJ's popular plurality in overwhelming Goldwater, was 16,000,000 votes, the largest up to that time.

**Price Range**

### Cartoon/Pictorial Pinbacks

| | | |
|---|---|---|
| ☐ "All The Way With L.B.J."; A-bomb mushroom cloud cartoon sketch (Hake 2165) 1½"; black, white | 3.00 | 5.00 |
| ☐ "A Page From The Past. My Strong Right Arm"; cartoon of Bobby Baker and LBJ (Baker was a former Senate page who became LBJ's protege and later was investigated by the Senate for shady dealings; the Republicans constantly attacked LBJ for his association with devious companions, e.g., Baker, Billy Sol Estes, and Matt McCloskey) (Hake unlisted; Warner 838) 3"; blue, white, black | 75.00 | 85.00 |
| ☐ "Au H20 '64"; illustration of large glass of water with chemical symbol overprinted (Hake 2134) 2"; white, black, yellow | 15.00 | 17.00 |
| ☐ "Democrats For Goldwater"; donkey with horn-rimmed glasses (Hake 53) 1¼"; orange, black | 3.00 | 5.00 |
| ☐ "Don't Be An Ass. Vote Republican"; donkey cartoon (Hake 35) 1½"; black, white | 4.00 | 6.00 |
| ☐ "Goldwater in '64"; illustration of Air Force jet. (Goldwater piloted jets in the Air Force Reserve) (Hake 52) 1¼"; black, white, gold | 6.00 | 8.00 |
| ☐ "If I Were 21, I'd Vote For Barry Goldwater"; cartoon of large GOP elephant (Hake 2016) 6"; black, white | 12.00 | 15.00 |

Price Range

☐ "It Needs Goldwater For Good Roots . . ."; cartoon of Democratic Lyndon Tree with roots that have died out (labeled "Viet Nam," "Racial Violence," "Cuba," etc.) (Hake 34) 3¼"; black on gold . . . .    30.00    35.00

☐ "Join The Fighting Irish/Vote Miller V.P."; large shamrock (Hake 45) 1¼"; white, gold, green . . .    3.00    5.00

☐ "King Lyndon The First"; caricature of LBJ as king (Hake 2140) 1½"; black, gold, white . . . . . . . . . .    6.00    8.00

☐ "L.B.J. For Ex-President. Hi-Fi Political Record?"; pinback simulates LP record with hole in center and grooves (Hake 2119) 2¼"; black, white . . . .    15.00    17.00

☐ "Start Packing"; cartoon of LBJ and Ladybird with suitcases and dog, Ladybird astride donkey; flasher pinback; "The Goldwaters Are Coming"; Barry and Peggy Goldwater are riding on GOP elephant's head and trunk with load of suitcases (Hake 2085) 3½"; multicolor; one of the choice cartoon flashers    10.00    12.00

☐ "That Same Old Coon"; Goldwater and raccoon cartoon; small type reads: "Republican National Emblem 1844" (a nose-thumbing raccoon was used by Henry Clay forces in the 1844 campaign) (Hake 2049) 3½"; black, white . . . . . . . . . . . . . . . . . . . . .    12.00    15.00

☐ "The L.B.J. Cocktail. America On The Rocks"; sketch of cocktail glass (Hake 2164) 1½"; black, white . . . . . . . . . . . . . . . . . . . . . . . . . . . . . . . . . . .    6.00    8.00

☐ "Turn Out Light Bulb Johnson"; large caricature of LBJ shaped like light bulb (alludes to Johnson's austerity announcement about turning out lights in White House to save utility costs) (Hake 16) 1½"; black, red . . . . . . . . . . . . . . . . . . . . . . . . . . . . . . .    5.00    7.00

### Jugate Pinbacks—1964

☐ "A Choice For A Change/Goldwater/Miller" (Hake 2) 1¼; bluetone portraits; red, white . . . . .    3.00    5.00

☐ "A Choice Not An Echo. Goldwater-Miller" (Hake 7) 1½"; red, white, blue, black . . . . . . . . . . . . . .    3.00    5.00

Price Range

☐ "America Needs Goldwater & Miller"; silhouetted portraits on U.S. map outline (LBJ mate); oval shape (Hake 2002) 3¼"; red, white, blue, black ... 8.00 ... 10.00

☐ "Choice Not Change" bull's-eye portraits (Hake 2026) 3½"; red, white, blue, black (interesting in that in a way it contradicts 1964 Republicans' "A Choice For A Change" slogan) ............... 5.00 ... 7.00

☐ "Goldwater And Miller"; silhouetted bust portraits top large names (Hake 2028) 3½"; red, white, blue, black ..................................... 4.00 ... 6.00

☐ "G.O.Party 1964" appears in circular emblem, "Barry/Bill" under silhouetted heads (Hake 2031) 3½" black, white, gold ...................... 10.00 ... 12.00

☐ "For America. Goldwater '64/Miller"; staggered, silhouetted profiles, conjoining; illustration (Hake 2010) 6"; black, white ...................... 35.00 ... 40.00

## Portrait Pinbacks

☐ "AuH20 [Goldwater portrait rebus] "1964 Our Next President" (Hake 2079) 1¼" blue, white .. 8.00 ... 10.00

☐ "Barry Goldwater Our Next President"; bull's-eye portrait (Hake 2042) 3½"; red, white, blue, black ... 5.00 ... 7.00

☐ "Coloradans For Goldwater"; bull's-eye portrait (Hake 12) 1½"; black, gold, white ............ 50.00 ... 60.00

☐ "Extremism In The Defense Of Liberty ... Goldwater in '64"; portrait above quote (Hake 10) 2¼"; black, white, blue lettering on rim ............. 12.00 ... 15.00

☐ "Goldwater Booster" (Hake unlisted; Warner 842) 2⅛; black, red ............................. 15.00 ... 20.00

☐ "Goldwater–Miller"; circular insets against large eagle background (LBJ mate); rectangular pinback (Hake 2004) 2¾"w x 1¾"h; red, white, blue, black, gold ...................................... 3.00 ... 5.00

☐ Goldwater "no name"; small "B64" (Barry for '64) monogram appears to left of portrait; patriotic ribbon cascades from top of button, around portrait to bottom (Hake 2014) 6"; red, white, black .... 10.00 ... 12.00

| | Price Range | |
|---|---|---|
| ☐ Goldwater "no name" portrait with stylized sun outline (Hake 2015) 6″; red, blue, white, black .. | 30.00 | 35.00 |
| ☐ "In Your Heart You Know He's Right" (Hake 2041) $3\frac{1}{2}$″; red, white, blue, black ............ | 8.00 | 10.00 |
| ☐ "Look Ahead/Barry Goldwater" (Hake 11; Warner 839) $2\frac{1}{4}$″; black, white, orange ............ | 45.00 | 50.00 |
| ☐ "Man Of Courage." photo under slogan (Hake 2033; Warner 837) $3\frac{1}{2}$″; black, red, cream, yellow | 30.00 | 35.00 |
| ☐ "Peninsula Citizens For Goldwater" (Hake 31; Warner 840) 1″; bluetone; California item ...... | 20.00 | 25.00 |
| ☐ "The Nation Needs Goldwater"; profile with stars in border (Hake 2018) 6″; red, white, blue, black | 10.00 | 12.00 |
| ☐ "Save America/Vote Republican"; oval portraits against waving-flag background (Hake 2029) $3\frac{1}{2}$″; red, white, blue, black ...................... | 12.00 | 15.00 |
| ☐ "The Best Men For The Job. Goldwater/Johnson" (Hake 2027) $3\frac{1}{2}$″; red, white, blue, black ...... | 5.00 | 7.00 |

### Slogan/Name Pinbacks

| | | |
|---|---|---|
| ☐ "All The Way With L.B.J. But Don't Go Near The Y.M.C.A." (Hake 2022) $1\frac{1}{2}$″; black, white ..... | 12.00 | 15.00 |
| ☐ "Au H20 1964" (Hake 70) $\frac{7}{8}$″; blue lettering on white background with red rim .............. | 10.00 | 12.00 |
| ☐ "Americans For Goldwater" (Hake 2089) 3″; blue, white ...................................... | 10.00 | 12.00 |
| ☐ "Goldwater and Miller Are The Men in '64" (Hake 58) $\frac{7}{8}$″; white reversed out of red ............ | 5.00 | 7.00 |
| ☐ "Greeks For Goldwater"; Greek alphabet completely borders pin (Hake 50) $1\frac{1}{3}$″; dark blue on green ...................................... | 5.00 | 7.00 |
| ☐ "I'm A Beatle Fan. In Case Of Emergency Place My Vote For Barry" (Hake 2063) $3\frac{1}{2}$″; black, white ...................................... | 12.00 | 15.00 |
| ☐ "L.B.J. Will Be Home On The Range When Goldwater Gets Done" (Hake 2061) $3\frac{1}{2}$″; blue, white | 15.00 | 17.00 |

*Trigate* **Price Range**

☐ "Original Emblem of The Republican Party When
Party Was Founded In Pittsburgh—1855"; eagle
with shield and sunburst illustration; small cameo
portraits of Goldwater, Miller, Scott; Pennsylvania
coattail (Hake 9) 2¼"; blue, white ........... 12.00 15.00

## WILLIAM ALEXANDER GRAHAM

William Graham, a Whig from North Carolina, ran for Vice-President
in 1852 with General Winfield Scott. At the time, he was Secretary of Navy
under Millard Fillmore. He served as a Senator from 1840–43 and as Governor of North Carolina, 1845–49 (see Winfield Scott).

## ULYSSES SIMPSON GRANT

U. S. Grant, an Ohio Republican elected from Illinois, was Commander
of the Union forces in the Civil War. He became the 18th U.S. President and
served from 1869–77. His two terms were marred by scandals of bribery and
corruption, and he is generally accorded low marks for his presidency.

**Price Range**

*Ceramics*

☐ Ceramic mug; transfer of "Maj. Gen. Ulysses S.
Grant" on obverse, Maj. Gen. Gillmore on reverse;
bordered with blue bands, top, bottom; white background .................................... 275.00 300.00

☐ Plate with border of embossed alphabet letters;
transfer portrait of "Maj. Gen. Ulysses S. Grant"
in center; made in Staffordshire; probably 1872
campaign item; milk glass ................... 100.00 125.00

☐ Plate, hand-painted commemorative, with bust portraits of Lincoln, Gen. Sherman, Gen. Grant; ca.
1863; eagle with shield and flag in center; 7"dia;
multicolor with gold rim; milk glass ........... 1000.00 1100.00

NOVELTIES

☐ Trinket box, ceramic; bust portrait of Grant amid
flags, guns, other military symbols; ornate scrolled
base; 5½"h; white ......................... 300.00 325.00

Invitation to Grant–Colfax Inaugural, March 4, 1869, enhanced by being addressed to noted photographer Mathew Brady and wife ($150–$200).

|  | Price Range | |
|---|---|---|
| ☐ Bust, Parianware; pedestal bust with "U.S. Grant"; approximately 8″h; English | 325.00 | 350.00 |
| ☐ Bust, Parianware, similar to above but minus pedestal; "U.S. Grant" on base: 7″h | 175.00 | 200.00 |

## Glassware

| | | |
|---|---|---|
| ☐ Goblet, Grant–Wilson, hand-blown clear crystal glass; 1872 race; medallion profiles of U.S. Grant and Henry Wilson on opposite sides; 6½″h (Lindsey #286) | 400.00 | 450.00 |

### MEMORIAL GLASSWARE

| | | |
|---|---|---|
| ☐ Bread tray, glass, square with intaglio image of Grant in general's uniform; pattern design on background; inscribed "Patriot and Soldier"; 9½″sq with 1½″h raised sides; made by Bryce Higbee & Co., Pittsburgh, in 1885 | 35.00 | 45.00 |

Interest in U. S. Grant items has intensified during recent years. Albumen photograph of 18th president as lieutenant general was signed under portrait ($800–$900).

|  | Price Range | |
|---|---|---|
| ☐ Plate, clear glass in center with frosted glass border decoration of overlapping maple leaves; "Let Us Have Peace. U.S. Grant" in large letters encircle border; 10⅜"; clear glass edition .............. | 35.00 | 45.00 |
| ☐ Blue glass edition ........................... | 45.00 | 55.00 |

## HORACE GREELEY

Influential, often controversial editor of the *New York Tribune,* Greeley was involved in such notable causes as temperance, women's rights, abolition of slavery, organizing labor, and protective tariffs. He ran for president on the Liberal Democratic ticket against Grant in 1872.

**Price Range**

### *Ephemera (Paper Memorabilia)*

☐ "Go West! Go West! Go West!" Anti-Greeley campaign card talks about boat ride down "Salt River" (a term symbolizing political oblivion) via

Tammany Bank, manufactured in the early 1870s during U. S. Grant's administration, when corruption and scandals were rampant. Manufactured by J. & E. Stevens Co. of Cromwell, Connecticut ($135–$150).

|  | Price Range | |
|---|---|---|
| Underground Railroad with Greeley as commander-in-chief; $4\frac{1}{2}$"w x $3\frac{3}{4}$"h; illustration of train with passengers, plus several small military figures; black, white .......................... | 65.00 | 75.00 |

### Lapel Devices

| | | |
|---|---|---|
| ☐ Jugate ferrotype of Greeley–Brown with names above; encircled in stippled gilt frame (Warner 135) $1\frac{1}{4}$"; gilt brass; black, white ferro ............. | 400.00 | 425.00 |
| ☐ Quill pen ferrotype with circle portrait of Greeley in feather; "The Pen Is Mightier Than The Sword" inscribed along spine (Hake 3003; DeWitt HG 1872-13) $3\frac{1}{4}$; gilt brass ...................... | 1100.00 | 1200.00 |
| ☐ "Quaker Hat" figural suspended from die-stamped bas-relief clasped-hands bar (DeWitt HG 1872-15) $1\frac{1}{2}$"l; tin shell .............................. | 1000.00 | 1100.00 |

Horace Greeley (Greenback party) cardboard fan, 1872. Anti-Greeley cartoon appears on reverse ($150–$175).

Horace Greeley–Benjamin Gratz Brown jugate ferrotype. The pair ran on the Liberal Democratic ticket in 1872 ($650–$750).

**KEY CHAIN OR LAPEL CHARMS**                    **Price Range**
☐ Stanhope's Anti-Greeley pot-metal pig; Greeley's
  portrait viewed through pig's backside ¾"1 . . . . .    150.00    175.00

Price Range

☐ Stanhope telescope, made of ivory with Greeley's
image; 1"l .................................. 175.00     200.00

*Novelties*

☐ Fan-die-cut silhouette of Greeley's head; cardboard, with wool tufts of hair around ears and chin
to simulate whiskers; reverse gives sharply satirical
anti-Greeley caricatures; "Patd. applied for,
McLoughlin Bros. N.Y."; round wooden handle;
black on buff .............................. 175.00     200.00

*Textiles*

☐ Greeley, B. Gratz Brown ribbon listing presidential
electors and candidates (no illustrations) (Warner
143) 9"l; black, white ....................... 75.00     100.00

*Tobacco Accessories*

☐ Cast-iron figural Horace Greeley match safe; Greeley wears Quaker hat; 6"l; natural finish; has been
reproduced ................................. 125.00     135.00

## HANNIBAL HAMLIN

Hannibal Hamlin, a Maine Republican who had originally been a Democrat, served as Vice-President under Lincoln in 1861–65. Hamlin's views on
Reconstruction in the ante-bellum South were considered too severe by Lincoln, who turned to Andrew Johnson as his running mate in the 1864 campaign (see Abraham Lincoln).

## WINFIELD SCOTT HANCOCK

Hancock, a Civil War general and hero of the Battle of Gettysburg, was
appointed military governor of Texas and Louisiana in 1868. In 1880, the
Democrats selected him as their presidential choice to run against James Garfield. Hancock lost by a narrow popular margin to Garfield in an impressive
turnout of 78.4 percent of the eligible voters.

## WARREN GAMALIEL HARDING

Warren Harding, an Ohio Republican, was editor-publisher of the *Marion Star*. He served in the Ohio Senate from 1900–04; Lt. Governor, 1904–06; from 1915–20, the U.S. Senate. In 1921, with Calvin Coolidge as running mate, Harding became the 29th President of the U.S.

In the midst of investigations concerning bribery and conspiracy in the Veterans' Bureau and oil field manipulations, including the Teapot Dome scandal, Harding died from what may have been a heart attack (there was a great deal of speculation that he may have been poisoned to prevent his testifying against party cronies). Harding is ranked as one of the least memorable presidents; collectors, however, still eagerly seek out Harding-Coolidge jugates from 1920, as they are very hard to come by.

**Price Range**

### *Badges, Stickpins, Studs, Medals*

| | | |
|---|---|---|
| ☐ "G.O.P" elephant, enameled stickpin; "Harding and Coolidge" on blanket (Hake 77) 1″w; white, gold, black; also appeared in blue, red, black . . . . | 35.00 | 45.00 |
| ☐ "Don't Throw Your Vote Away. Put It In This Trunk"; celluloid hanger on stickpin; elephant with round ball inset with Harding photograph coiled in trunk (Hake 75) 1¼″h; red, white, blue, black . . | 45.00 | 55.00 |
| ☐ "Harding" cello-covered paper in brass bar; red, white, blue ribbon with buckeye (Ohio symbol) attached to ring (Hake 87) 3¼″ overall; actual buckeye . . . . . . . . . . . . . . . . . . . . . . . . . . . . . . . . . . . . . . . . | 25.00 | 35.00 |
| ☐ Harding portrait stickpin with brass rim (Hake 3032) ½″; black, white . . . . . . . . . . . . . . . . . . . . . . . | 25.00 | 30.00 |
| ☐ Harding portrait cuff links (Hake 2037) ½″; black, white . . . . . . . . . . . . . . . . . . . . . . . . . . . . . . . . . . . . . | 25.00 | 35.00 |
| ☐ "Warren G. Harding" medal; bust of Harding in profile (Hake 70) 1¼″; brass finish . . . . . . . . . . . | 25.00 | 30.00 |
| ☐ "Member" appears on brass-framed celluloid-layered paper in bar; short ribbon with "Harding Club"; hanger with three-quarters portrait of Harding (Hake unlisted; Warner 355) hanger; black, white, brass rim; ribbon, blue with gold lettering; approximately 3½″l . . . . . . . . . . . . . . . . . . . . . . . | 150.00 | 175.00 |

Price Range

☐ "McKinley's Neighbors And Friends of Stark County Greet Our Next President," appears on ribbon; hanger celluloid pinback attached (Hake 2001 with ribbon; Warner 713) hanger, black, white; ribbon, white with gilt lettering; 3″ overall; Ohio local item ...................................... 350.00   400.00

☐ "Warren G. Harding For Governor" bar with paper flag ribbon; paper portrait hanger with Harding in rare profile (Hake 2012) 2″l; red, white, blue, black ................................ 100.00   110.00

☐ "Warren G. Harding For President" bar with short cloth ribbon; rectangular paper portrait hanger of Harding (Hake 2013) 2″l; black, white ......... 100.00   110.00

☐ Harding oval portrait within long arrow-like design; bookmark (Hake 2033) approximately 4″l; black, white; celluloid ............................. 35.00   45.00

☐ Flag bow badge with celluloid hanger, "Member Harding–Coolidge Republican Club of Jay County" (Hake 2019) 2″ overall .............. 90.00   100.00

☐ "Nose Thumber" mechanical badge; top-hatted man in tails; forked devil's tail is lever; when pressed sends arm to nose (Hake 74) 1½″; gilt brass   50.00   60.00

☐ "Win With Harding" embossed enamel stud, shield shape (Hake 81) ½″; red, white, blue, brass finish   15.00   20.00

## Banks

☐ Warren Harding Still Bank, maker unknown, 1920s, cast metal in bronze finish, 4½″h (many savings banks began issuing still banks in likenesses of presidents, beginning in the 1920s; most often, they were of cast metal with bronze finish and featured advertising from the local money lender) ....... 35.00   50.00

## Cartoon Pinbacks

☐ "For President. G.O.P. Warren G. Harding"; cartoon elephant with circle inset photo of Harding (Hake 2015) 1¼″; black, white, gray .......... 800.00   850.00

Price Range

☐ "For President. Warren G. Harding," variant of Hake 2015 in size and white vs. gray elephant (Hake 2016) 1¼"; black, white ............... 900.00    1000.00

☐ "G.O.P. On Top"; elephant balancing on globe with U.S. flag waving in trunk (Hake 2017) 1¼"; black, white ........................................ 50.00    65.00

☐ "G.O.P. Harding–Coolidge On T.O.P."; elephant balancing on globe; "1920" on scroll below (Hake 2018) ⅞"; black on white .................... 150.00    175.00

☐ "Harding–Coolidge G.O.P."; elephant against keystone background (Hake 47) ⅞"; gold, black ... 10.00    15.00

☐ "Harding–Coolidge Victory"; elephant head profile (Hake 50; Warner 356) ⅞"; red, white, blue, brown; issued by Republican League of Massachusetts ........................................ 25.00    35.00

## Cutlery

☐ Eagle atop furled flag over oval Harding portrait, "President, U.S.A." (Hake 2035) silver finish on white metal; commemorative rather than campaign-oriented ......................... 50.00    60.00

☐ Harding bust oval portrait with names of all previous presidents through Harding embossed on a slant vertically on knife; silver finish, white metal; German made; versions were also known for Wilson and TR .............................. 35.00    45.00

☐ Harding–Coolidge jugate knife; black and white portraits under celluloid (Hake unlisted; Warner 354) 3¼"l; match to Cox–Roosevelt jugate knife 350.00    400.00

## Jugate Pinbacks

☐ Harding–Coolidge conjoining portraits (Hake 27; Warner 707) ⅞"; gray, white ................. 450.00    500.00

☐ Also 1¼" size ............................ 500.00    600.00

Price Range

☐ Overlapping staggered oval insets, Harding–Coolidge (Hake 26; Warner 708) $7/8''$; brown, white (also issued in black, white); considered the more common among prized jugates from this campaign, which marked the phasing out of celluloid in favor of lithographed pinbacks ............. 400.00 450.00

☐ "Warren G. Harding & Calvin Coolidge. President & Vice-President"; oval insets over spread-wing eagle and shield (mostly obscured) (Hake 1; Warner 352) $1¾''$; gray, white ........................ 1100.00 1300.00

☐ "Harding—For President; Coolidge—For Vice-President" in elaborate scrolls under oval portraits (Hake 2009; Warner 353) $7/8''$; one of the most graphically appealing of the $7/8''$ jugates; brown, white ..................................... 575.00 625.00

☐ Harding–Coolidge conjoining portraits; no lettering (Hake 2) $1¼''$; sepiatone .................... 575.00 600.00

☐ "Harding–Coolidge" portraits (Hake 3) $7/8''$; black, white ..................................... 500.00 550.00

☐ Harding–Coolidge (minor variant from Hake 2) $7/8''$; black, white .......................... 450.00 500.00

☐ "Harding & Coolidge Junior Booster. America First"; portraits with four stars reversed out of blue and red, white stripes surrounding (Hake 28) $¾''$; red, white, blue, black, white lettering reversed out of red border .............................. 1500.00 1700.00

## Trigate Pinbacks

☐ Harding, Coolidge, and unidentified coattail candidate, "Republican Candidates"; "1920," and draped U.S. flags below (Hake 25) $1¼''$; red, white, blue, black ................................. 1300.00 1500.00

☐ Harding, Fremont, Lincoln portraits with years they ran for president, 1920, 1856, 1860, respectively (Hake 2007) $2¼''$; black, white .......... 225.00 250.00

## Memorial Pinbacks

Warren G. Harding died in office on August 2, 1923, only the third president (the others being William Henry Harrison and FDR) to die of natural causes while serving as president.

| | Price Range | |
|---|---|---|
| ☐ "In Memoriam"; bust portrait of Harding, with solid black border (Hake 86) 1"; black, gray, white | 10.00 | 15.00 |
| ☐ Filigreed black border with Harding portrait; no lettering (Hake 84) ¾"; black, white . . . . . . . . . | 15.00 | 20.00 |
| ☐ "In Memoriam. Warren G. Harding" reversed out of black suit in Harding photograph (Hake 85) 1¼"; black, white; black rim . . . . . . . . . . . . . . . | 20.00 | 25.00 |
| ☐ "In Memoriam. Warren G. Harding" bust portrait of Harding (Hake 83) ⅞"; black, white . . . . . . . . | 10.00 | 15.00 |

## Mirrors

| | | |
|---|---|---|
| ☐ Elephant heads abut Harding oval portrait from both sides; inset appears in large flag shield (Hake 30) 1½"; red, white, blue, black, gray . . . . . . . . . | 1100.00 | 1200.00 |
| ☐ Elephant heads; same image as above but with advertising message: "Best Ever. Schoenberg Clothes Makers. Chicago"; lettered outer rim; tag for use as fob (Hake 2038) 1¾" with tag; red, white, blue, black, gray* . . . . . . . . . . . . . . . . . . . . . . . . . . . . . . | 1300.00 | 1400.00 |

## Miscellaneous Novelties

| | | |
|---|---|---|
| ☐ Harding embossed-leather change purse; laurel-bordered portrait with pair of draped flags on each side; snap catch; commemorative item; approximately 5" wide . . . . . . . . . . . . . . . . . . . . . . . . . . . . . | 35.00 | 45.00 |
| ☐ Smaller size, same as above but 4" wide, is more elusive . . . . . . . . . . . . . . . . . . . . . . . . . . . . . . . . . . . | 45.00 | 55.00 |

*Sold at Warner Auction as pinback with hanger removed (Warner 351) at $1705.00.

| *Name, Slogan Pinbacks* | Price Range | |
|---|---|---|
| ☐ "Harding, Coolidge, Cox" (Hake 35; Warner 357) ¾"; red, white, blue (not to be confused with Harding's opponent, Gov. James Cox of Ohio; this is Channing Cox, candidate for governor of Massachusetts | 25.00 | 30.00 |
| ☐ "America First. Harding and Kendall Club, Des Moines, Iowa" (Hake 2025) 1"; black, white | 15.00 | 20.00 |
| ☐ "Harding and Coolidge, Smile, 1920" (Hake 53) ⅞"; red, white, blue | 25.00 | 30.00 |
| ☐ "Prosperity, Protection, Willis And Harding" (Hake 46) ¾"; black, white | 15.00 | 20.00 |
| ☐ "Harding And Prosperity" (Hake 62) ⅞"; black, white | 15.00 | 20.00 |
| ☐ "I Am A Harding Booster" (Hake 38) ⅞"; red, white | 35.00 | 40.00 |
| ☐ "Harding And Prosperity" lettering straight across vs. arched as in Hake 62 (Hake 2028) ⅞"; black, white | 40.00 | 50.00 |
| ☐ "Ex-Servicemen's Harding Club"; star in black circle (Hake 64) ⅞"; red, black, white | 30.00 | 35.00 |
| ☐ "Think Of Harding. America First" (Hake 42) 1¼"; red, black, white | 50.00 | 60.00 |
| ☐ "Harding and Coolidge" 13-star border (Hake 40; Warner 714) 1¼"; red, white, blue | 40.00 | 50.00 |
| ☐ "Under The 19th Amendment. I Cast My First Vote Nov. 2nd, 1920" (Hake 72) 1¾"; black, orange (complete item includes yellow "Harding–Coolidge" name ribbon) | 40.00 | 50.00 |
| ☐ "Harding For Governor" (Ohio) (Hake 2030) ⅞"; black, white | 35.00 | 40.00 |

## *Portrait Pinbacks*

| | | |
|---|---|---|
| ☐ "For President. Warren G. Harding"; bust portrait (Hake 6) 1¼"; white reversed out of black | 125.00 | 150.00 |
| ☐ "For President. Warren G. Harding"; portrait in circle; type in white outer border (Hake 7) 1¼"; black, white | 135.00 | 155.00 |

Price Range

☐ "For President. Warren G. Harding"; lettering runs along both sides of portrait (Hake 2010) 1¾"; black, white .............................. 235.00 255.00

☐ "For President. Warren G. Harding"; portrait in center (Hake 14, 15, 16) ⅞"; red, white or blue border; each ................................. 5.00 10.00

    *Note:* These three pinbacks have been reproduced, the red and blue versions in both lithograph and celluloid issues.

☐ "For President"; letters are staggered to left of portrait; "Warren G. Harding" staggered to right of image (Hake 19) ⅞"; white reversed out of black; also sepia variant .......................... 35.00 50.00

☐ "Harding For President"; lettering wraps around smiling Harding portrait (Hake 5) 1¼"; black, white; similar to Warner 709 ................. 200.00 225.00

☐ "For President" tiny lettering; facsimile signature (Hake 29) 1¼"; white reversed out of black .... 200.00 225.00

☐ Also a ⅞" gray, white variant ................ 75.00 100.00

☐ Harding bust portrait, wearing bow tie; no lettering (Hake 8) 1¼"; white out of black ............. 100.00 110.00

☐ "I'm For Harding"; bust portrait (Hake 23) ⅞"; white out of black ......................... 20.00 25.00

☐ Harding portrait amid star field and stripes border (Hake 18; Warner 710) ⅞"; red, white, blue .... 75.00 100.00

☐ "Member First Harding Club"; stars and stripes border (Hake 34; Warner 711) ⅞"; red, white, blue, black; club was organized in Harding's home town of Marion, Ohio .......................... 75.00 100.00

☐ Oval bust portrait; no lettering (Hake 71; Warner 358) 2¾"l; 1⅞"w; sepiatone; Cox match in black, white ..................................... 135.00 150.00

☐ Harding bust portrait; no lettering (similar to Hake 8; Warner 706) 3½"; black, white; nice centerpiece item ..................................... 125.00 150.00

☐ "Warren Harding" in scroll border under portrait; gold brass rim (Hake 2014; Warner 712) 1¼"; sepiatone ................................. 100.00 110.00

Price Range

☐ "Warren G. Harding" in scroll under portrait (Hake 9) browntone ......................... 75.00 100.00

☐ "Warren G. Harding" portrait; brass rim (Hake 10) 1¼"; black, white, gilt; celluloid reproduction is known ..................................... 75.00 85.00

☐ "Warren G. Harding" reversed out of black in coat; image bleeds off lower curl (Hake 11) 1¼"; black, cream ..................................... 25.00 30.00

☐ "Warren G. Harding"; name blocked out just below collar; portrait floats (Hake 12) 1¼"; black, white 125.00 150.00

☐ "Souvenir, President Harding's Pacific Coast Tour"; portrait framed by pair of draped flags (Hake 39) 1¼"; red, white, blue, black ........ 50.00 65.00

## Posters

☐ Harding–Coolidge jugate poster with winged eagle topping oval portraits; blue field of U.S. flag visible just above each oval; stylized shield between images; facsimile signatures below; 21"l x 16"h; red, white, blue, gold, black ...................... 65.00 75.00

☐ "Our Choice" jugate window decal; Harding–Coolidge "America First. Back To Normal. Law & Order"; 5"h x 7"w; red, white, blue, black, gold 60.00 65.00

☐ "Harding" name decal; approximately 3" sq; white reversed out of dark blue .................... 25.00 35.00

☐ "America First" campaign card; trigate oval portraits of Harding, Coolidge, and DuBois Penrose, a state senator candidate, Pennsylvania; Capitol dome looms at top along with spread eagle, crossed flags; six stars; "Election Tuesday, November 2, 1920"; 5¼"h x 3¼"w; multicolor ............ 20.00 30.00

☐ "America First. Warren Gamaliel Harding and Calvin Coolidge" oval jugate poster; biographical descriptions in each corner; eagle and crossed flags atop portraits; 1920; 24"h x 18"w; sepiatone .... 100.00 125.00

## *Statuary*

Price Range

☐ Bronze statue of Laddie Boy, Harding's well-known pet wire-hair terrier; dog holds copy of *Marion Star* (Ohio) newspaper in mouth .................. 75.00 | 100.00

☐ Souvenir penny with embossed Harding profile portrait; Kansas City, ca. early 1920s; 3"dia.; bronze finish ...................................... 20.00 | 25.00

## *Tobacco Accessories*

☐ "America's First—Our First Americans. 1795–1920"; complimentary trio of Garcia Vega cigars celebrating 125th anniversary of *New York* Commercial, "The National Business Newspaper," May 23, 1921; pack is 5½"l; black, gold, white 45.00 | 55.00

☐ Harding jumbo cigar with band in gold and black and featuring Harding portrait; 8"l ............ 25.00 | 35.00

## *Watch Fobs*

☐ "For President, Warren G. Harding" surrounds Harding portrait on white cello inset in stitched leather cutout with tab for strap (Hake 36) 1½"; black on white; black leather ................. 350.00 | 400.00

☐ "Harding & Coolidge" die-cut brass shaped as shield with laurel branches; two rows of stars embossed just below tab; bas-relief portraits (Hake 68) 1¾"; brass finish .......................... 75.00 | 85.00

☐ "Warren G. Harding" die-cut brass shield with bas-relief portrait, Harding; filigree around shield (Hake 69) 1¾"; brass finish ................. 40.00 | 50.00

☐ Winged eagle atop slanting jugate ovals, Harding–Coolidge; laurel branches border lower end of exaggerated oval with tab (Hake unlisted) match to Roosevelt–Cox (Hake 44); gilt finish on brass ... 75.00 | 85.00

Advertising trade card shows Grover Cleveland and Benjamin Harrison pedaling to White House in 1888 race, won by Harrison. By giving card a small, quick, circular motion, viewer gets feeling of motion ($20–$25).

## BENJAMIN HARRISON

Benjamin Harrison, a Republican originally from Ohio, established his political reputation as a U.S. Senator from Indiana, serving from 1881–87. Harrison was an ex-Civil War General who had distinguished himself leading infantry charges with the 70th Indiana Volunteers. His illustrious grandfather was William Henry Harrison, the ninth U.S. President. An all-out protectionist, Harrison was hand picked by James Blaine as the Republican standard-bearer in 1888 to oppose Grover Cleveland.

"Little Ben," so called because he was only 5 feet 6 inches tall, waged a highly successful "front porch" campaign from his home in Indianapolis, by building up a war chest of over three million dollars, the largest funding up to that time. Harrison bested Cleveland by 233 to 168 electoral votes, despite polling approximately 100,000 fewer popular votes, to become the 23rd President of the U.S. He lost his bid for re-election in 1892 to Grover Cleveland, largely because voters were dissatisfied with high prices brought on by the McKinley Tariff Act and the incursion of the new Populist party who picked up a number of previously Republican western states.

Collectors avidly seek Harrison material that strongly identified with his grandfather's era, i.e., the famed beaver hat recreated in crystal, milk glass, figural tin torches, badges and even macerated currency. The log cabin and cider barrel, 1840 redux, decorated canes, bandannas, watch fobs and delegates badges. The 1892 campaign featured some of the most ingenius of all lapel devices, the mechanical badge, which died out with the advent of the celluloid pinback in 1896.

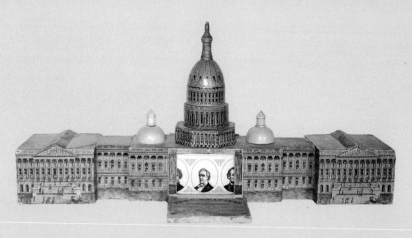

U.S. Capitol Building, "A Historioscope," W.S. Reed Toy Co., patented 1884, $1500–$1700. *(Photo by Madaline Friz)*

Notched William McKinley-Bryan, "My Hobby—A Winner," pinbacks, 2″ cartoon multicolors, c. 1900, $1000–$1200. *(Photo by Madaline Friz)*

McKinley–Bryan "Partial Eclipse Will Be Total" browntone pinback is one of the most desirable of a dozen "Eclipse" buttons from the 1900 campaign, $500–$550. *(Photo courtesy of Robert A. Fratkin)*

Taft–Sherman "Elephant Ears" jugate usually ranks among the top ten in the hobby, $850–$900. This classic from the '08 race has topped $1000 in several recent mail auctions.

Parker–Davis "Shure Mike" pinback, multicolor, 1904, $120–$130, classic piece.

Many rate this Wilson–Marshall 1912 rebus entry as the ultimate political pinback for powerful graphics and a great punch line, $2500 plus. *(Photo courtesy of Robert A. Fratkin)*

Theodore Roosevelt–Booker T. Washington "Equality" browntone pinback proved to be one of the most volatile attention-getters of any campaign in history. The 1904 classic brought $900 at the '81 Warner Auction and has been climbing ever since. *(Photo by Madaline Friz)*

Hughes–Fairbanks "no-name" jugate spelled the end of the Golden Era, but what a way to go! This superb multicolor from 1916 belongs in the top ten according to most knowledgeable collectors, $2000 plus. *(Photo courtesy of Robert A. Fratkin)*

Political fan, c. 1844, portrays the first eleven presidents in hand-tinted lithographs in oval cartouches. James K. Polk is indicated as the President Elect, $2500–$3000. *(Photo by Madaline Friz)*

Bryan clock classic from 1900 shows dial set at "16 to 1," an imaginative allusion to Free Silver issue, $135–$150.

Henry Clay snuff box. This is probably from the 1844 campaign when Clay headed the Whig ticket, $600–$700. From the Bruce DeMay Collection. *(Photo by Madaline Friz)*

Vibrantly colored, three-part, fold-out trade card shows Cleveland and Harrison and "dark horses," Fisk and Streater, in the 1892 race, $50–$75. *(Photo courtesy of Rich Maxson)*

Biscuit box, $22'' \times 12'' \times 4''$, paper label on wooden box, American Biscuit Mfg. Co., New York. Full-color view of the White House, with eight cameo black-and-white portraits of leading candidates from the 1896 campaign, $500–$600.

Cleveland–Stevenson Tammany Hall inaugural ribbon, March 4, 1893, 11″ length, multicolor, $125–$135. *(Photo by Madaline Friz)*

McKinley tile cribbage board, c. 1900s, approximately 12″ length, 3½″ width, multicolor, $250–$300.

Teddy Roosevelt canvas banner, 1904, $350–$400. *(Photo by Madaline Friz)*

Artist's paint box. Lithographed paper on wood depicts Presidents Garfield and Arthur, c. 1880s, $125–$150. *(Photo by Madaline Friz)*

Debs–Hanford Socialist Party cardboard poster, 1908, 20″ × 17″, $1000–$1100. *(Photo courtesy of Rex Stark)*

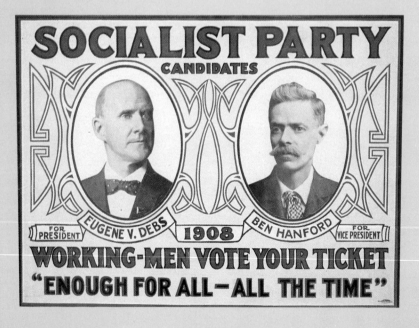

SOCIALIST PARTY
CANDIDATES
EUGENE V. DEBS
FOR PRESIDENT
1908
BEN HANFORD
FOR VICE PRESIDENT
WORKING-MEN VOTE YOUR TICKET
"ENOUGH FOR ALL — ALL THE TIME"

Theodore Roosevelt–Charles Fairbanks 1904 rebus shows a field of roses (Roseveldt) and lush banks along a meandering stream (Fair-Banks); perhaps the hobby's premier visual pun. There is only one copy known, and the likelihood of it appearing on the market precludes pricing. *(Photo courtesy of Frederick Jorgensen)*

"Calvin Coolidge For Vice-President" 1920 campaign, 1¼″, adds a dash of color to the generally lackluster era of political pinbacks, $750–$850. *(Photo by Madaline Friz)*

Theodore Roosevelt and Uncle Sam "At the Gate" 1904 pinback, multicolor, graphically endorses pro-equality theme, $1500–$2000. *(Photo courtesy of Robert A. Fratkin)*

Campaign (1896, 1900) celluloid gems from the dawning of the Golden Era. Especially choice—matched "Musical Notes" jugates for McKinley-Roosevelt, Bryan–Stevenson 1900 race, $400–$500 each. Clever cartoon multicolor (3rd from left, 2nd row) finds McKinley in presidential chair atop Bryan, $200–$225. Matched pinback, with Bryan at the advantage, goes slightly higher. Just below, McKinley pedals bicycle to the White House, $200–$225.

Harrison–Morton "Protection" bandanna, 1888
($75–$100).

**Price Range**

### Advertising

☐ Benjamin Harrison–Levi Morton jugate portraits;
Cracker Cakes wooden display box, 1888, C. Stol-
zenbach & Sons, Cracker Cakes, Zanesville, Ohio;
multicolor ................................. 350.00    400.00

### Jugate Badges

HARRISON–MORTON—1888

☐ Eagle with drooping wings atop oblong frame with
cardboard circular photographs, tinted; three stars
and names above busts; surmounted by red, white,
blue scroll (Hake 3201) 1½"w; white metal ..... 100.00    125.00

☐ Eagle flying with talons carrying arrows; clasp;
ribbon hanger with cardboard photographs of
Harrison–Morton vertically (Hake 3210) 3½"
overall; gilt metal ........................... 100.00    125.00

Harrison–Morton 1888 cotton bandanna; portraits derived from engraving by H. B. Hall's Sons ($75–$85).

|  | Price Range | |
|---|---|---|
| ☐ Eagle with olive branch, arrows in talons, mechanical; small catch spring below moves wings, reveals cardboard photographs; July 10, 1888 patent date on reverse (Hake 3206; Sullivan BH 1888-38) $1\frac{3}{4}$"; gilt brass | 300.00 | 325.00 |
| ☐ Horseshoe hanger with oval openings bearing cardboard photos; suspended from shield clasp with draped flags; mounted against red, white, blue ribbon (Hake 3216; Sullivan BH 1888-40) $2\frac{1}{4}$"; gilt brass | 115.00 | 125.00 |
| ☐ Maltese cross hanger with cardboard photos in oblong openings; shield atop, anchor, crossed axe and scythe below; suspended from shield and starred scrolled banner clasp (Hake 3217; Sullivan BH 1888-39) $1\frac{3}{4}$"; brass finish | 120.00 | 130.00 |

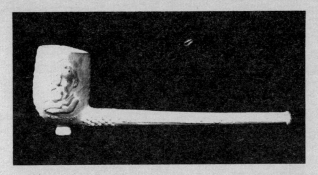

"Protection For American Labor," Benjamin Harrison figural clay pipe with embossed eagle and shield on opposite side of bowl ($65–$75).

"I Crow For Harrison," campaign egg, 1888. Brass rooster pops out of composition egg with spring mechanism; advertising giveaway ($250–$300). *(Bruce DeMay Collection)*

| | Price Range | |
|---|---|---|
| ☐ "Our Champions/1888/Protection For Home Industries" octagonal metal shell framing cardboard shield design in red, white, blue; linked to displayed eagle clasp (Hake 3200; Sullivan BH 1888-31) 2¾"; gilt brass | 225.00 | 250.00 |

Price Range

☐ Paired die-stamped ovals with cardboard portraits; scallop shell atop, shield, laurel branches below (Sullivan BH 1888-35) same as Hake 3214 without winged eagle clasp and attached ribbon ........  110.00  125.00

☐ Shell; winged eagle atop flag-draped circular frame with conjoining cardboard portrait (Hake 3218) 1¾" gilt brass ............................  100.00  120.00

☐ Shield-shaped with broom straws running vertically; rectangular jugate cardboard portrait on shield; handle below (Hake 3208; Sullivan BH 1888-41) 2½"h; red, white, blue straws; pebbled, gilt brass shield ...........................  140.00  150.00

☐ Shield-shapes back-to-back running horizontally with oval portraits within (Hake 3211; Sullivan BH 1888-32 with ribbon) 2¾"w; gilt brass; red, white, blue flag ribbon ............................  120.00  130.00

☐ Statue of Liberty die-stamped shell with Harrison–Morton portraits in scrolled frames flanking base of statue (Hake 3207) 1¾"; gilt brass ..........  210.00  225.00

☐ Wreath of heart shapes framing conjoined Harrison–Morton portrait figures in cardboard (Hake 3222) 1"; gilt brass ...................  100.00  110.00

☐ Wide scroll with mounted cardboard photos of Harrison–Morton; eagle with shield on breast atop (Hake 3221; Sullivan BH 1888-43) 1½"h; gilt brass  115.00  125.00

## HARRISON–MORTON JEWELRY BADGES
☐ Conjoined busts in moonstone against furled slanted flag, red, white, blue (Hake 3132; Sullivan BH 1888-55) 1¼"; enameled brass ............  200.00  225.00

☐ Eagle atop enameled red, white, blue shield mounted with conjoined moonstone silhouette-shape busts (Hake 3131) enameled brass .......  200.00  225.00

☐ Sepia photographs in oblong panels framed in ornate frond setting; winged eagle, crossed flags atop, shield below (Sullivan BH 1888-108) 1¾"; gilt brass .......................................  110.00  125.00

HARRISON–REID—1892                          **Price Range**

☐ Harrison–Reid images on pair of planchets; Harrison bust embossed; Reid paper photograph mounted; suspended from eagle clasp (Hake 3224) 2″; gilt brass .............................. 100.00    110.00

☐ Irregular ten-sided shape shell with oblong Harrison–Reid cardboard portraits; eagle atop (Hake 3226) 1½″; gilt brass ................. 140.00    150.00

☐ Harrison–Morton match (Hake 3220) .......... 110.00    120.00

☐ Harrison–Reid oval portraits topped by winged eagle; crossed flags, shield below (Hake 3228; Sullivan BH 1892-20) 1¼″; gilt brass .............. 140.00    150.00

☐ Variant with outfacing portraits (Hake 3229) .... 140.00    150.00

☐ Harrison–Reid oval portraits with braided frames atop shield (Hake 3230; Sullivan BH 1892-21) 1½″; gilt brass .................................. 135.00    150.00

*Noisemakers*

HORNS

☐ "Harrison Reid" tin parade horn; 36″l; red, white, blue; names stenciled in black ............... 225.00    250.00

☐ "Protection, Patriotism, Prosperity" campaign tin horn; 4″l; aslant with distinct bend in middle; tin finish ..................................... 75.00    85.00

RATCHETS

☐ "One Good Term Deserves Another" hardwood ratchet, one end shaped as beaver hat; Harrison portrait appears in multicolor label; Whitelaw Reid portrait on opposite side; 16½″l; Cleveland match 150.00    175.00
    *Note:* Ratchets from late 19th century featured a polished hardwood handle. Toothed wheel and pawl engages when frame is rotated creating *ack-ack* noise.

WHISTLES

☐ "Campaign Bugle. Harrison and Morton" wooden whistle with jugate paper label; 6″h; red, white, blue, black .................................. 125.00    135.00

W. H. Harrison ceramic cup with black
transfer of log cabin campaign symbol. Sign
on door reads: "To Let in 1841" ($350–$400).

## WILLIAM HENRY HARRISON

William Henry Harrison, a Whig from Virginia, first won national fame
in 1811 when he led his territorial militia in defeating a large scale attack
by Shawnee Indians at the Battle of Tippecanoe. In the War of 1812 he was
commissioned Brigadeer General and commanded the Northwest frontier.
Later he emerged as a U.S. Senator from Ohio (owning a spacious farm in
North Bend). In 1840, to oust Martin Van Buren from the White House, the
Whigs passed up Henry Clay and picked Harrison, who became the first candidate ever to "take to the stump" and actually wage a full-fledged campaign.
The slogan "Tippecanoe and Tyler Too" was ever so brilliantly merchandized
with log-cabin and hard cider barrel songbooks, badges, handkerchiefs, a
newspaper (Horace Greeley's *The Log Cabin*), Log Cabin Whiskey and even
a Tippecanoe shaving soap. Van Buren, meanwhile, was pictured as an effete
aristocrat, popularized by Thurlow Weed's epithet, "Sweet Sandy Whiskers."
Harrison rolled to an electoral triumph over incumbent Van Buren, 234 votes
to 60. John Quincy Adams in his diary wrote: "Harrison came in upon a hur-
ricane; God grant he may not go out upon a wreck." The words proved pro-
phetic. Harrison died within a month after the inauguration of pneumonia
and John Tyler emerged as the first "accidental President." Of all the pre-
Lincoln Presidents, William H. Harrison offers the greatest wealth of campaign memorabilia. Particularly collectible are the sulfide brooches that hark

William Henry Harrison bandanna, 1840, shows battle
scenes at Tippecanoe and Thames, log house at North
Bend, and other vignettes ($150–$200).

back almost exclusively to the 1840 race. Figural flasks, cup plates and all
manner of lusterware and ceramic novelties are a legacy of what the *Daily
Advertiser* called the "buffoonery of 1840."

**Price Range**

### Brooch Pins, Brass Shell

☐ Embossed brass log cabin, side view with cider barrel in foreground (Hake 3110) 1¼"sq; brass finish     250.00     260.00

☐ "Harrison & Reform" log cabin front view with flag flying from pole to left; cider barrel at right with mug atop (Hake 3111) 1"w x ¾"h . . . . . . . . . . .     225.00     250.00

☐ Log cabin three-quarters facing; cider barrel at left; a tree on each side of cabin (Hake 3112) 1"w x ¾"h; brass finish . . . . . . . . . . . . . . . . . . . . . . . . . . . . . . .     200.00     210.00

## Grooming Accessories

Price Range

HAIRBRUSH

☐ Painted brush with W. H. Harrison portrait amid floral pattern; wood; approx. 9"l; green, orange, red enamel with white bristles; black transfer portrait     1000.00     1100.00

TRINKET BOX

☐ Similar to thread boxes but larger; reverse painting on glass portrait of Harrison; inscribed above "Gen. Wm. H. Harrison"; 9"w x 6"h; red, white (stripes behind oval image); brown, black . . . . . . . . . . . .     1000.00 plus

## Scenes Under Glass—Brass-Framed, Hand-Colored

☐ Log cabin with large tree and fence at left; cider barrel, tree branch right (Hake 3100) 1¼"w x 1"h; green, white, black; brass frame . . . . . . . . . . . . . . .     375.00     400.00

☐ Same as above but more crudely executed and smaller (Hake 3101) 1"w x ¾"h; green, white black; brass frame . . . . . . . . . . . . . . . . . . . . . . . . . .     360.00     385.00

☐ Log cabin front view, "Harrison & Reform" above roofline (Hake 3102) (vertical) 1"h x ¾"w; black, white . . . . . . . . . . . . . . . . . . . . . . . . . . . . . . . . . . . .     425.00     450.00

## Sulfides

☐ "Maj. Gen. W. H. Harrison/Born Feb. 9, 1773" raised enamel under glass bust; on reverse, fort with flag atop, trees; "The Hero Of Tippecanoe"; in metal frame; 1¾"h x 1½"w (Hake 3103) white enamel on black field . . . . . . . . . . . . . . . . . . . . . . .     775.00     800.00

☐ "Harrison & Reform" log cabin with flag pole to left; tree, cider barrel, and mug at right; white enamel on black field; brass frame; 1"w x ¾"h . .     375.00     400.00

☐ "Harrison & Reform," similar to above with log cabin minus flag; cider barrel and mug on left; white enamel on black field; brass frame; 1"w x ¾"h . .     400.00     425.00

☐ "Harrison & Reform" log cabin with flag atop; tree on each side; white raised enamel on pink field; ornate metal frame; 1"w x ¾"h . . . . . . . . . . . . . . . .     400.00     425.00

See James Monroe "Ceramics" listing for doorknob with portraits of Monroe and Harrison.

Price Range

## *Tobacco Accessories*

☐ Pewter snuffbox; Harrison log cabin surrounded by trees; cider barrel, fencing incised on lid (Hake 3047) 3¼"w x 2"h; metal finish .............. 375.00     400.00

☐ Papier-mâché snuffbox; "W. H. Harrison/Ninth President of the United States"; torso portrait of Harrison; black transfer against pale orange or tan background ................................. 850.00     900.00

# RUTHERFORD B. HAYES

Hayes, an Ohio Republican, served in the House from 1865–67; was Ohio Governor, 1868–72 and 1876–77. He was elected the 19th President of the U.S. in 1877 and served one term ending in 1881.

Price Range

## *Ceramics and Glassware*

☐ "Hayes–Wheeler" redware mug; 4½"h; dark brown glaze ............................... 250.00     300.00

☐ Liberty Bell glass mug; 1876 Centennial item with embossed bell and Hayes–Wheeler names; 2"h; clear glass ................................. 75.00     100.00

## *Lapel Devices*

☐ "Centennial Candidates For 1876"; Hayes–Wheeler die-stamped shield shape with jugate portraits; 2"h; gilt brass; Tilden–Hendricks match .. 350.00     375.00

☐ E. D. Smith & Sons presidential campaign badges, salesman's sample card, with seven varieties of shell badges including two Centennial examples; sold for $2,200 at Warner Auction in 1981 ............ 2500.00     3000.00

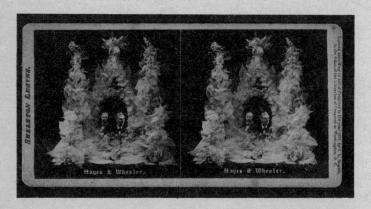

Hayes–Wheeler stereograph card, 1876 ($12–$15).

Rutherford and Lucy Hayes endorse Enterprise Sad Iron in advertising trade card ($25–$30).

Grand National banner, Currier & Ives
hand-tinted jugate print of Hayes–Wheeler,
1876 ($250–$300).

| *Toys, Banks* | Price Range |
|---|---|

☐ Rutherford B. Hayes mechanical bank by J. & E.
Stevens, 1875; cast iron painted black, white, natural; 8″h; only one known; possibly a prototype, although patent papers do exist ................ 3000.00 plus

## THOMAS HENDRICKS

Hendricks, a former Democratic Governor of Indiana, was a Vice-Presidential running mate to Grover Cleveland, serving from 1885–1887. Hendricks and Cleveland never saw eye to eye, because the former strongly favored the patronage system. Hendricks died nine months after taking office (see Grover Cleveland).

## GARRET AUGUSTUS HOBART

Garret Hobart, a New Jersey Republican, was a director of a number of corporations and banks and president of the Passaic Water Company when nominated to run with William McKinley for national office in 1896. Despite limited political experience, Hobart gained considerable respect and prestige as Vice-President. He was called "Assistant President" due to his effectiveness as a liason with the Senate and adviser to McKinley. Only two years into the administration, however, Hobart died of heart failure (see William McKinley).

## HERBERT C. HOOVER

Herbert Hoover, a mining engineer from Iowa, had served as U.S. Food Administrator for Wilson in World War I and was Secretary of Commerce under Harding and Coolidge. He was elected 31st President of the U.S. in 1929 but after the start of the Depression, was soundly defeated by Franklin Roosevelt in 1932.

**Price Range**

### *Automotive Accessories*

☐ "Herbert C. Hoover For President" (Hake 139; Warner 757) 3½"; blue, black, white; Dave Frent, cataloger for the Warner Auction in 1981, classifies this as license attachment .................... 150.00     175.00

☐ "Herbert Hoover" bust portrait inside bright red circle; chevron border in red, olive, tan (Hake 121) 3¼" with double tabs; red, tan, olive, black .... 25.00     50.00

☐ "Herbert Hoover. For President. Charles Curtis 1928"; Capitol dome; draped flag bunting with oval portraits superimposed (Hake 17) 3½"; red, white, blue, browntone; license attachment ........... 325.00     350.00

"Hoo Hoo Hoover," figural plaster statuette, 1932 ($75–$85). *(Frank Corbeil Collection)*

|  | Price Range | |
|---|---|---|
| ☐ "Hoover" name light reflecting license attachment (Hake 2120) 8"l; blue, white | 35.00 | 50.00 |
| ☐ "Hoover" name license attachment; 12"w; red, white, blue; raised letters | 25.00 | 35.00 |
| ☐ "Hoover"; Capitol dome at top; die-cast aluminum; $12\frac{1}{2}$"w x $5\frac{1}{2}$"h; silver finish | 30.00 | 35.00 |
| ☐ "Hoover For President" 12" x $4\frac{1}{4}$"; blue, black; Smith–Roosevelt match | 30.00 | 35.00 |
| ☐ Republican elephant license attachment; approximately $4\frac{3}{4}$"h; blue, white, brown; FDR–Democratic donkey match | 20.00 | 25.00 |
| ☐ "Hoover" oval license attachment; $5\frac{1}{4}$"w; painted blue and white lettering on orange background; 1928 campaign | 12.00 | 15.00 |
| ☐ "Hoover For President"; variant of above; $5\frac{1}{4}$"; painted blue and white on tin | 15.00 | 20.00 |
| ☐ "Safe and Sane With Hoover" (Hake 2014) 8"w; black on white tin | 25.00 | 35.00 |

Price Range

☐ "Vote For Herbert Hoover"; line drawing, very stylized, of Hoover bust (Hake 2128) 4"; black, white license attachment ..................... 50.00    75.00

☐ "Who But Hoover"; repeat of pinback slogan; 10¼"; blue on white ........................ 25.00    35.00

SPARE TIRE COVER
☐ "Have Confidence In Hoover. Re-elect Him"; black and white Hoover bust portrait; wire enforced oil-cloth ....................................... 150.00    175.00

## *Badges, Medals, Stickpins, Studs*

☐ "Bring Back Prosperity With A Republican Vote"; mechanical pinback; pull string and elephant boots donkey (Hake 122) 2"; black, white, aqua ...... 35.00    50.00

☐ Elephant, three-dimensional stickpin; celluloid (Hake 129) ¾"; dark gray ................... 10.00    15.00

☐ Elephant, die-cut head with curled trunk and ribbon bow, brass badge; "Hoover & Curtis, 1928" (Hake 126) 1¼"h; black finish; black ribbon .... 20.00    25.00

☐ Elephant, full-figure die-cut metal badge; "Hoover" in script across body (Hake 127) 1¾"w; chrome finish ....................................... 15.00    20.00

☐ Key stickpin, die cut, with "Hoover" incised across shank (Hake 128) 1"w; gilt-finish brass ........ 10.00    15.00

☐ "Hoover and Curtis" enameled elephant stickpin (Hake 119) 1"; black; red trim and lettering .... 15.00    20.00

INAUGURAL MEDAL, 1929
☐ "Inaugural/March 4, 1929"; Hoover bust profile (Hake 2129) 2¾"; bronze medal .............. 900.00    950.00

☐ Simulated celluloid "Hoover" swallowtail ribbon stickpin with long oval Hoover portrait (Hake 125) 4"l; red, white, blue, black ................... 50.00    60.00

☐ "Stick To Hoover" medalet hanger looped on stickpin; "No One Could Have Done Better"; embossed elephant (Hake 131) ¾" dia; copper finish ..... 10.00    15.00

☐ "Who, Who Hoover"; white enamel owl stickpin (Hake 120) ½"; white; gilt lettering .......... 15.00    20.00

**Price Range**

☐ Woman's brooch; oval Portrait in black/white celluloid (unlisted) 1⅝" x 1⅜"; in ornate white metal
frame; 2"l overall; Smith match . . . . . . . . . . . . . . . 75.00 100.00

☐ "Vote For Hoover" bar with die-cut bust head of
Hoover; pin attached with chain (Hake 2094) ¾"h;
gilt white metal . . . . . . . . . . . . . . . . . . . . . . . . . . . . . 35.00 45.00

## Banks and Games

☐ Herbert Hoover Elephant Still Bank, maker unknown, 1932, white with Hoover and Curtis embossed in black trim on side, 4¾"h, 7"w (Hake
2127) . . . . . . . . . . . . . . . . . . . . . . . . . . . . . . . . . . . . . 100.00 150.00

☐ "Herbert Hoover, Wins, Prove It!" puzzle, Cahoes
Novelty Co., Cahoes, New York, 1928, cardboard
with wood tiles, 5½" square . . . . . . . . . . . . . . . . . 50.00 75.00

## Cartoon/Pictorial Pinbacks

☐ "Hoover/A Clean Sweep For President"; oval
shape with illustration of Hoover upright vacuum
sweeper (unlisted) 1⅝"; orange, white, blue; made
by Seattle, WA, manufacturer; key item and crowd-
ing the top ten for best celluloid in modern era . . 3500.00 4000.00

☐ "Hoover" castle insignia of Army Engineering with
name superimposed (Hake 91) ⅞"; brown, white 25.00 30.00

☐ "It's An Elephant's Job." GOP elephant pushing
convoy truck while Democratic donkey flees scene
(Hake 2033) ⅞"; black, white lithograph from a
cartoon by C. L. Robinson © 1932 . . . . . . . . . . . 45.00 55.00

☐ Also 1¼" celluloid . . . . . . . . . . . . . . . . . . . . . . . . . 65.00 75.00

## Jugate Pinbacks

☐ Capitol dome jugate; portraits against flag draped
in each corner (Hake 17; Warner 396) 4"; red,
white, blue, browntone; centerpiece item, 1928 race 325.00 350.00

Price Range

☐ "For All Of U.S."; canted jugate portraits topped by winged eagle (Hake 3; Warner 398) 1¼": red, white, blue, gold ........................... | 150.00 | 175.00

☐ "Hoover and Curtis" above canted oval inset portraits; words reversed out of black (Hake 7) ⅞"; black, white; reproduction cello has been made .. | 75.00 | 100.00

☐ "Hoover and Curtis" reverse out of red at top and blue bottom (Hake 14) ⅞"; red, white, blue, black | 275.00 | 300.00

☐ Hoover–Curtis canted, conjoining no-name portraits (Hake 5; Warner 399) 1¼"; black, white .. | 125.00 | 150.00

☐ "Hoover–Curtis" conjoining portraits (Hake 8) ⅞"; black, white ........................... | 50.00 | 75.00

☐ Hoover–Curtis circular insets topped by part of eagle, tops of torches; shield, flag bunting below (Hake 1) 1¼"; red, white, blue, black ......... | 600.00 | 625.00

☐ "Hoover–Curtis. For President. Vice-President" (Hake 6) ⅞"; black, white lithograph .......... | 100.00 | 125.00

☐ "Hoover–Curtis" large shield with scepter, laurel branches, eagle at top (Hake unlisted; Warner 395) 1¼"; red, white, blue, key item .............. | 2500.00 | 3000.00

☐ "Hoover–Curtis" oval portrait insets in black circle background; wide border of flag bunting (Hake 4; Warner 755) 1¼"; red, white, blue, black ...... | 200.00 | 225.00

## Portrait Pinbacks

☐ "A Democrat For Hoover" bluetone portrait (Hake 33) 1" x 1"; blue, white ..................... | 50.00 | 75.00

☐ "For President Herbert C. Hoover"; portrait within black circle (Hake 27; Warner 760) 1¼"; black, white ...................................... | 25.00 | 35.00

☐ "For President. Herbert Hoover" (Hake 2015; Warner 754) 4"; browntone; centerpiece item ....... | 300.00 | 325.00

☐ "Herbert C. Hoover For President" (Hake 139; Warner 757) 3½"; blue, black, white; may originally have been intended as license tag attachment (see Hoover—Automotive Accessories) ......... | 150.00 | 175.00

Price Range

☐ "Hoo But Hoover" portrait with head appears in center of carnation (Hake 32) ⅞"; red, green, black, white ....................................... 25.00     35.00

☐ "Hoover" bleed portrait; large lettering (Hake 46) ⅞"; black, white ........................... 25.00     50.00

☐ Hoover no-name, circular black and white portrait against flag-draped backdrop (Hake 11) 2"; red, white, blue, black .......................... 100.00     125.00

☐ Hoover no-name oval bust drawing (Hake 145; Warner 403) 3¼" x 2⅜"; gray, white ......... 175.00     200.00

☐ Hoover no-name photographs (Hake 2019-2022) 2" sizes; black, white; slight variations in poses; each 100.00     200.00

☐ Hoover, no-name charcoal sketch portrait (Hake 2016) 4"; black, gray, white .................. 200.00     250.00

☐ "Hoover–Curtis" oval portraits; black background with spiraling striped patriotic bunting border (Hake 4; Warner 755) 1¼"; red, white, blue, black 175.00     200.00

☐ "Hoover–Curtis" portraits, conjoining (unusual images of both, who appear very gaunt) ⅞"; black, white ...................................... 175.00     200.00

☐ "Hoover For President" (Hake 2045; Warner 758) $15/16$"; red, white, blue, black; Smith match ..... 35.00     50.00

☐ "Make Hoover President" appears above portrait (Hake 38) ⅞"; red, black, white; black rim ..... 25.00     35.00

☐ Also black, white (Hake 2048) ............... 50.00     60.00

☐ "O.K. America. Play Safe With Hoover"; partly in script, wrapping around top of small circular portrait (Hake 24; Warner 400) 1¼"; red, white, blue, black; key item classic ...................... 300.00     325.00

☐ "Put Hoover On"; "Hoover" wraps under his chin in portrait (Hake 39) ⅞"; red, black, white; black rim ...................................... 25.00     30.00

☐ "Regular Republican Candidates"; small x's between words (Hake 12; Warner 402) 1¾"; red, white, blue; an election day, 1928, item often found with ribbon attachment ...................... 150.00     175.00

Price Range

☐ "Texas For Hoover"; tiny bust image (Hake 65) ½"; browntone (these smaller versions were intended for women's wear) .....................    35.00    45.00

☐ "Who But Hoover," above Hoover portrait (Hake 37) ⅞"; red, black, white, black rim; litho reproduction exists ..............................    25.00    35.00

## *Pocket Mirrors*

☐ "Field For Senator. Turner For Governor. Hoover For President. Vote Straight Republican Ticket"; 2"; black and white; staggered oval portraits of Hoover–Curtis .............................    150.00    175.00

☐ "Hoover. Curtis"; staggered oval portraits of candidates for 1928 Republican ticket; 2"; sepia photographs on orange background ................    400.00    450.00

☐ "Hoover For President"; Hoover bust portrait; 4"w x 2½"h; bluetone ......................    75.00    100.00

☐ "It's An Elephant's Job. No Time For Monkey Business"; cartoon of GOP elephant pushing truck marked "U.S. & Co." while Democratic donkey flees the scene; also featured as litho button; 2"; black on white (see also Hoover poster version)    50.00    75.00

☐ "The Lady On The Other Side Is Requested To Vote For Hoover, Kean, Larson"; 2"; black on white ........................................    200.00    225.00

☐ "The Lady On The Other Side . . ."; same wording as above but no pictures and only Hoover's name as candidate; 2"; red, black, white .............    75.00    100.00

## CHARLES EVANS HUGHES

Charles Evans Hughes, Republican from New York, was a former Governor of New York and Supreme Court Justice. A moderate Progressive, he ran for president in 1916 against Wilson. Hughes, after building up a sizable early lead, lost the entire West and solid South as Wilson edged him 277 electoral votes to 254.

**Price Range**

## Badges, Stickpins, Studs, Medals

☐ Cameo-type badge with gilt filigree frame, jugate portraits; Hughes–Fairbanks (Hake 1) $1\frac{1}{2}''$h; sepiatone, white, gilt; Wilson–Marshall match ... 175.00 200.00

☐ Eagle badge with oval, filigree brass frame hanger; Hughes bust portrait in oval (Hake 3007) $2\frac{1}{2}''$l overall; black on white photo; gilt eagle and frame 75.00 100.00

☐ "Executive Committee," brass-framed, celluloid covered bar; "Hughes And Fairbanks, Nov. 4, 1916" ribbon; cello with diagonal flag background with Hughes's portrait superimposed; $1\frac{3}{4}''$ dia; $6\frac{1}{2}''$ overall; black lettering on white ribbon; red, white, blue, black cello ..................... 400.00 450.00

☐ Flag pennant cello stickpin with draped U.S. flag behind circular portrait of Hughes (Hake 7) $1''$w; multicolor .................................. 85.00 100.00

☐ Flag pennant cello stickpin; Wheelman's emblem between oval portraits of Hughes–Fairbanks (Hake 6) $1''$w; bright burst of orange behind symbol and insets at top; blue, yellow, orange, black, white .. 150.00 175.00

☐ "Hughes Alliance Hanger"; Hughes portrait; rope twist frame with loop for hanging (Hake 3025) $1\frac{1}{4}''$l; black on white, gilt ................... 50.00 60.00

☐ "Republican Reception" bar-ribbon-hanger; doughnut cello around Hughes portrait, on brass embossed disk (Hake 3054) $1\frac{1}{4}''$ hanger; $4\frac{3}{4}''$ overall; gold lettering on white ribbon; red, white, blue, black cello ................................ 75.00 100.00

☐ "For President" brass with celluloid over paper bar; flag ribbon with die-cut profile of Hughes in ring hanger (Hake 3056) $1''$-dia hanger, brass finish; red, white, blue ribbon; gilt bar with black on white lettering ...................................... 35.00 50.00

☐ Shield badge with Hughes portrait, sepia paper photo (Hake 3006) $2''$l; sepiatone, gilt; possibly a gubernatorial item ......................... 150.00 175.00

☐ Shield, lithograph tin; "Our Choice"; Hughes portrait (Hake 74) $1\frac{1}{2}''$; black on pale orange ..... 75.00 100.00

206　*Political Memorabilia*

Price Range

☐ "Take A Peek At A Winning Card" cello stickpin; playing card design on obverse; flip card and Hughes portrait, "Hughes For President," and patent date shown on reverse (Hake 3041) 1½"l; black, red, white .................................. 100.00　110.00

## Gubernatorial Pinbacks—1908, New York State

☐ "Hughes Notification Meeting, Sept. 1908," flag bunting at top; tiny portrait inset (Hake 62; Warner 350) 1¾"; red, white, blue, gold, black (notification of nomination for governor of New York) ...... 150.00　175.00

☐ "For Governor. Charles E. Hughes"; full-face portrait; lettering in border encircling image (Hake 3062) 1¾"; black on white .................. 25.00　30.00

☐ Hughes bust portrait; no imprinting (Hake 3063) 1¾"; black on white ........................ 60.00　75.00

☐ Hearst–Hughes cockfight cartoon; New York state gubernatorial candidates' names appear on opposite sides of button (Hake 3060) 1¾"; red on white 225.00　250.00

☐ "For Governor. Charles E. Hughes" three-quarters bust portrait; lettering in circular border (Hake 3069) 1¼"; black on white .................. 20.00　25.00

☐ "Hughes Democracy" three-quarters bust portrait (Hake 3077) ⅞"; black on white; numerous variants ........................................ 15.00　20.00

☐ "Governor's Day, Aug. 28, '08, The Big Fair, Trumansburg, NY" (Hake 3074) 1¼"; black on white 50.00　75.00

☐ Horseshoe-framed Hughes portrait with bow at bottom; name appears in reverse on coat, just below collar (Hake 3067) 1¼"; red, white, blue, black 125.00　150.00

## Jugates

☐ Hughes–Fairbanks canted ovals (Hake unlisted; Warner 655) 1¼"; black on white; usually found in badly foxed condition; as with *all* Hughes–Fairbanks jugates, this item is in extremely short supply ................................ 600.00　700.00

**Price Range**

☐ Hughes–Fairbanks framed by flag and laurel branches (Hake 61; Warner 654) $\frac{7}{8}$"; red, white, blue, black, gold ........................... 300.00 350.00

☐ Hughes–Fairbanks conjoining bust portraits (Hake 58; Warner 347) $1\frac{3}{4}$"; gray on white; great centerpiece item ................................. 350.00 400.00

☐ Hughes–Fairbanks oval portraits flanking flag in center, with propeller mechanical spinner (Hake 59) $1\frac{1}{4}$"; red, white, blue, black, gold; key item from the 1916 Republican slate (Note: Many feel that the propeller was added at a later date) .... 1500.00 1600.00

☐ Hughes–Fairbanks "Republican Candidates—1916"; same pose as Hake 59 (see above) with difference in wording and scroll design below; $1\frac{3}{4}$"; black on white ............................. 500.00 600.00

☐ "Hughes–Fairbanks" oval portraits over stylized shield (Hake 3002) $1\frac{3}{4}$"; red, white, blue, black 1500.00 1600.00

☐ "Hughes–Fairbanks" conjoining portraits against flag background that slants across button; beadlike border (Hake 3003) $1\frac{1}{2}$"; red, white, blue, black, gold ...................................... 600.00 650.00

☐ "Hughes–Fairbanks" scroll under oval portraits; eagle with wings spread frames portraits at top (Hake 3004) $1\frac{1}{2}$"; red, white, blue, black ...... 900.00 1000.00

☐ "Hughes–Fairbanks" conjoining portraits (Hake 3005) $1\frac{1}{4}$"; black on white ................... 400.00 450.00

☐ Hughes–Fairbanks conjoining portraits (no legend) (Hake 3) $\frac{7}{8}$"; black on white* ................ 35.00 40.00

☐ Eagle with wing wraparound of oval Hughes–Fairbanks insets (Hake 64) $\frac{7}{8}$"; red, white, blue, black, gold, green ........................... 300.00 325.00

## COATTAIL JUGATES

☐ "Hughes And Bruce" conjoining portraits (Hughes was candidate for governor of New York, Bruce for lieutenant-governor?) (Hake 32) $1\frac{1}{4}$"; black on white; also $1\frac{3}{4}$" size ....................... 30.00 40.00

*Several minor $\frac{7}{8}$" variants of this button were issued, including several that carried the candidate's names reversed out of black; same value range as above.

MISCELLANEOUS JUGATES       **Price Range**

☐ "Lincoln–Hughes Club 1860-64; 1916" (Hake 63) 1¾"; black on white ........................    300.00    325.00

## Mirrors

☐ Hughes–Hearst cockfight cartoon mirror; New York State Governor item (see also Hake 3060 pinback) (unlisted) 1¼"; red, white .............    500.00    550.00

## Multigate

☐ "Good Luck. Good Times. Vote The Republican Ticket"; Hughes, Fairbanks, and two unidentified candidates in each of four insets in shamrock (Hake 2) 1"; green, black on white .................    75.00    85.00

## Portrait Pinbacks

☐ "Dutchess County Republican Clambake"; same familiar full view bust portrait (Hake 3008) 1¾"; black on white ............................    200.00    225.00

☐ "For President," winged eagle atop shield with oval portrait inset (Hake 3014) 1¼"; red, white, blue, gold, sepia ................................    300.00    350.00

☐ Hughes portrait view to just below winged collar; in limbo (Hake 3011) 1½"; black on white .....    125.00    150.00

☐ "Our Choice For President," three-quarters bust portrait (Hake 3009) 1½"; black on white ......    175.00    200.00

☐ Also 1" size ...............................    125.00    150.00

    The above pinbacks all show Hughes as a much younger man, as in the governor issues, with a full black beard. Other versions show Hughes with considerable gray in the beard, and it is parted in the middle.

☐ "Charles E. Hughes"; full-face view portraying a more gray-bearded candidate (Hake 3010) 1½"; black on white ............................    100.00    125.00

**Price Range**

☐ "Republican Candidate For President"; name and slogan encircle bust portrait; outer border features small eagle at top and flag streamers along sides (Hake 3015; Warner 349) 1¼"; white, blue, gold, black, red .................................. 175.00 200.00

☐ "Charles E. Hughes"; bust view includes part of torso; Hughes appears to be in his judicial robes; filigree and flag background (Hake 3016; Warner 656) red, white, blue, gold, black .............. 250.00 300.00

☐ "San Diego Exposition. Hughes Day"; bust portrait (Hake 3024) 1¼"; sepiatone .................. 125.00 150.00

☐ Vertical flag background with Hughes portrait; multistriped rim (Hake 67; Warner 348) 1¼"; red, white, blue, sepia (a "busy" button, with stripes running in all directions) .................... 200.00 250.00

☐ "For President. Charles E. Hughes" (Hake 19) ⅞"; browntone; gold rim ........................ 20.00 30.00

☐ "Chas. E. Hughes For President"; blue field at top with five stars. Stripes swirl around portrait inset (Hake 15) ⅞" ............................. 30.00 35.00

☐ Hughes facing right to left (unusual departure; closer details of subject's face) (Hake 9) 1½"; black, white, gold; rope-braid rim ................... 45.00 55.00

☐ Hughes bust portrait inside what appears to be stylized *O* (Hake 29) ⅞"; red, white, blue (rim); black portrait ................................... 50.00 60.00

☐ Shield, very tiny, on pewter blue with gold-trim rim; bluetone portrait (Hake 70) ⅞"; red, white, blue, gold ...................................... 50.00 60.00

☐ "My First Vote For President"; white lettering reversed out of red border; small bluetone bust portrait inset of Hughes, with name and "1916" reversed out of blue (Hake 68) 1¼"; red, white, blue 300.00 325.00

☐ "For President"; Hughes portrait in white decal design against red border (Hake 65) 1¼"; red, black, white ..................................... 175.00 200.00

Price Range

☐ "Our Next President. Hughes"; reversed out of black; bust portrait (different Hughes portrait; fuller face, to break the monotony!) (Hake 20) $\frac{7}{8}$"; black, white ............................... 40.00   50.00

☐ "For President. Chas. E. Hughes"; black portrait inset with "life preserver" border design (Hake 14) $\frac{7}{8}$"; red, white, blue, black ................... 25.00   30.00

☐ "Our Member For President" Hughes bust portrait (the younger version familiar in gubernatorial issues) (Hake 12) $1\frac{1}{4}$"; black on white .......... 90.00   100.00

## Posters

☐ Hughes–Fairbanks jugate poster; uses same stylized shield motif as Hake 3002 pinback; red, white, blue with sepiatone oval images; approximately 18"w x 12"h ...................................... 125.00   150.00

☐ "Preparedness–Protection–Prosperity" Republican Candidates Election, Tuesday, November 7, 1916" multigate poster; Pennsylvania slate; Hughes–Fairbanks and seven coattail candidates for state and local office; keystone seal in center; black on white; approximately 18"h x 12"w ............ 100.00   125.00

## Slogan/Name Pinbacks

☐ "Hughes Alliance 1916" embossed collar button (Hake 3045) $\frac{1}{2}$"; brass finish ................. 25.00   30.00

☐ "Hughes Day. Be Sure To Vote Nov. 7-1916" (Hake 3024) $1\frac{1}{4}$"; black on white ............. 65.00   75.00

☐ "Hughes And Fairbanks"; white swath across flag banner (Hake 38) $\frac{7}{8}$"; red, white, blue ......... 10.00   15.00

☐ "Massachusetts Hughes Alliance" (Hake 41) $\frac{7}{8}$"; red, white, blue sections .................... 10.00   15.00

☐ "Pennsylvania Hughes Alliance" (Hake 50) $\frac{1}{2}$"; red, white, blue ........................... 5.00   10.00

☐ "Hughes Workers For Law And Liberty" (Hake 43) $\frac{7}{8}$"; black on white ..................... 25.00   30.00

Price Range

☐ "Hughes"; Large $U$ and $S$ envelope entire pinback (Hake 39) ⅞"; red, blue on white; blue rim .... | 15.00 | 20.00

☐ "Hughes First Voters League" (Hake 73) ⅞"; three sections: red, white, blue ..................... | 20.00 | 25.00

☐ "Hughes And Direct Nominations"; oval (Hake 75) 1"h; white reversed out of red ............... | 75.00 | 100.00

☐ "Hughes For President; Willis For Governor; Herrick For U.S. Senator" (Hake 35) ⅞"; three sections: red, white, blue ...................... | 20.00 | 25.00

### Trigates

☐ "Hughes, Willis, Herrick" Ohio locals item (Hake 33) ⅞"; gray on white; trio was also featured on ribbon and poster .......................... | 20.00 | 25.00

☐ Hughes, TR, Taft; "Security, Harmony, Justice" appears over heads; "Hughes For President" (Hake 3017) 1¼"; black on white ................... | 550.00 | 600.00

### Watch Fobs

☐ Horseshoe die-cut brass fob with cello inset, "Charles E. Hughes"; 1½"l; brass finish; black-on-white portrait ............................. | 55.00 | 75.00

☐ Leather fob backing with cello inset (same image as above) 1¾"l; black, buff, fleshtones ............ | 60.00 | 70.00

☐ "Hughes For President—1916" embossed die-cut brass fob; portrait of Hughes in profile; draped flags on each side of oval; eagle with olive branch below; 1½"; brass finish .......................... | 30.00 | 40.00

## HUBERT HORATIO HUMPHREY

Hubert Humphrey, Democrat from Minnesota; served in U.S. Senate from 1949–64; 1971–78; Vice-President under Lyndon Johnson 1965–69. Ran unsuccessfully in 1968 for Presidency, losing to Richard Nixon. His verbosity earned him the nickname, "Minnesota Chats," and once prompted his mentor, LBJ, to sigh, "If I could just breed him to Calvin Coolidge" (see Lyndon Johnson).

Price Range

## Cartoon/Pictorial Pinbacks

☐ "Citizens For Humphrey," illustrated heads of various nationalities (Hake 14) 2⅛"; red, brown, black, buff ........................................ 8.00 10.00

☐ "Era Of Progress/Vote Democratic"; cartoon of Democratic donkey with star superimposed and mortar and pestle inside star (Hake 2036) 1¾"; black, tan, white .......................... 4.00 6.00

☐ "HHH"; cartoon of Humphrey working with flasks and beakers; "Fills the Prescription" (Humphrey was an ex-pharmacist); (Hake 9) 1⅓"; blue, black, buff ........................................ 6.00 8.00

☐ "HHH Capitol City St. Paul-itans For Humphrey & Muskie"; statue of classical figure on pedestal (Hake 2026) 2¼"; black, blue, gold; (also a silver variant) ................................... 40.00 45.00

☐ "HHH"; donkey caricature with flyer in teeth that has "HHH" written on it; wiggle-eye pinback (eyes jiggle when you shake pin); (Hake 2024) 3½"; tan, blue, black, white.......................... 30.00 35.00

☐ "Humphrey/Muskie"; stylized hand holding flower (Hake 2053) 3½"; pink, tan, black, green, white ...................................... 3.00 5.00

☐ "I'm a Humphtey Muskie-teer"; cartoon of man in Tyrolean hat with feather (Hake 17) 1½"; red, black ..................................... 6.00 8.00

☐ "McCarthy Committee For Humphrey Now"; words superimposed on stylized daisy (Hake 2055) 1¼"; brown, white litho .................... 6.00 8.00

☐ "My Man Humphrey"; cartoon of top part of HHH's head with wiggle eyes (Hake 2021) 3¼"; red, black, blue .......................... 30.00 35.00

☐ "1968 Action/Humphrey Muskie" (in streamlined lettering) "Not 1868 Reaction" (in Old English script); wiggle eyes under "1968 Action" (Hake 2023) 3¼"; red, white, blue ................. 35.00 40.00

☐ "The Humph Is Tops"; cartoon profile bust of HHH (Hake 2034) 1¾"; blue, white .......... 5.00 7.00

Price Range

☐ "We're For Him/HHH"; cartoon of man and woman with wiggle eyes (Hake 13) 3"; green, white, blue ........................................ 20.00 25.00

## Jugates

☐ "America Needs Humphrey–Muskie," silhouetted heads in U.S. map outline; "Minnesota United Democrats For Humphrey" in small letters border lower rim (Hake 2001) 3"; red, white, blue, black 55.00 65.00

☐ "Humphrey/Muskie," silhouetted heads between names (Hake 2002) 2¼"; black, red, white ..... 12.00 15.00

☐ "Humphrey/Muskie" staggered portraits against stylized flag banner background (Hake 3) 1½"; red, white, blue, black ........................... 3.00 5.00

☐ "Humphrey/1968/And Muskie" conjoining bust portraits; bull's-eye (Hake 2005) 3½"; red, white, blue, black ................................. 5.00 7.00

☐ "Humphrey–Muskie/Vote Democratic"; oblong portraits in bull's-eye (Hake 2013) 2¼"; red, white, blue, black ................................. 4.00 6.00

☐ Also 1¾" (Hake 2009) ..................... 3.00 5.00

☐ Also 1¼" (Hake 2008) ..................... 3.00 5.00

☐ "Public Service/Integrity/Dedication"; circle inset of Democratic donkey tops portraits (Hake 2007) 2"; red, white, blue, black lithograph .......... 12.00 15.00

☐ "Now Power. Humphrey/Muskie"; circle inset portraits; starburst under $W$ in "Power" (Hake 5) 3"; red, blue, black, white .................. 20.00 25.00

☐ "Responsible Leadership/Humphrey–Muskie"; bull's-eye portraits (Hake 2010) 3½"; red, white, blue, black ................................. 3.00 5.00

☐ Also 1½" (Hake 2006) ..................... 3.00 5.00

## Portrait Pinbacks

### PRESIDENTIAL

☐ "For President/Hubert Humphrey" bull's-eye portrait (Hake 6) 1½"; red, white, blue, black ..... 2.00 4.00

Price Range

☐ "For A New Day/Elect Humphrey"; sunburst at top; waist-high silhouette of HHH in lower left corner (Hake 2018) 2"; red, white, blue, black lithograph ...................................... 8.00    10.00

☐ "Humphrey For President/Unity/Responsible Leadership" (Hake 2027) 3½"; red, white, blue, black ..................................... 4.00    6.00

☐ Also 1¾" (Hake 2035) ..................... 4.00    6.00

☐ "Humphrey For President"; name arches over portrait; stripes, field of blue with stars frame left bottom of pin (Hake 10) 1½"; red, white, blue, black    2.00    4.00

☐ Also 3½" (Hake 2045) ..................... 3.00    5.00

☐ "Humphrey For President" bull's-eye portrait; patriotic striped border (Hake 11) 1½"; red, white, blue, black ................................. 2.00    4.00

**U.S. SENATE**

☐ "Humphrey For Senator"; portrait with flag background (Hake unlisted; Warner 844) 2¼"; red, white, blue; 1948 item; first of five successful elections to U.S. Senate from Minnesota ........... 20.00    25.00

*Slogan/Name Pinbacks*

☐ "Alaskans For HHH" oval shape (Hake 2089) 1¼" x ¾"; red, white, blue ..................... 12.00    15.00

☐ "Arriba Humphrey/Muskie"; slogan inside starburst (Hake 18) 1⅔"; red, black ............. 5.00    7.00

☐ "Here We Grow Again/Humphrey/Muskie" (Hake 2040) 1¾"; black, red, white .......... 6.00    8.00

☐ "Hubie Baby" (Hake 2039) 1¾"; white reversed out of black ............................... 4.00    6.00

☐ "Humphrey/Muskie" names repeated alternately and often overprinted on each other to form complete wheel (Hake 2051) 3"; red, white, blue, black    15.00    20.00

☐ "Little People For Humphrey" (Hake 2047) 1¾"; white reversed out of black ................. 5.00    7.00

☐ "Muskie/McCarthy/HHH" (Hake 2037) 1¾"; white, yellow, black ........................ 7.00    9.00

Price Range

☐ "Nixon's The One. Are You Kidding?" (Hake 2074) 1¼"; blue, white ...................... 3.00 5.00

☐ "Nix! On Nixon" (Hake 2077) 1¼"; red, white .. 3.00 5.00

☐ "Nixon + Spiro=0" (Hake 22) 1²/₃"; red, black 3.00 5.00

☐ "RX. Vote For A Better World. Humphrey & Muskie '68. Democratic ......................... 3.00 5.00

☐ "Viva!HHH/Muskie" (Hake 2058) 1²/₃"; red, black, yellow .............................. 5.00 7.00

### *Trigates*

☐ "Muskie–Guy–Humphrey"; circle insets inside shield (Hake 12) 2¼"; red, white, blue; issued for collector market ........................... 5.00 7.00

## ANDREW JACKSON

Andrew Jackson, Democrat from Tennessee, was General in War of 1812 and hero of decisive Battle of New Orleans. Served in House and Senate 1796–98 and 1823–25; Governor Florida Territory, 1821; served as seventh President of the U.S., 1829–37. Helped revive two-party politics in America, playing crucial role in developing the Democratic Party in 1825 to oppose John Q. Adams. He was nicknamed "Old Hickory."

Price Range

### *Badges, Tokens*

COLLAR BUTTONS

☐ "American Standard/Jackson Victory" (Hake 3029) 19mm; brass collar button .............. 225.00 250.00

☐ "Andrew Jackson/March 4/1829" Inaugural collar button (Hake 3027) 21mm; brass .............. 250.00 275.00

☐ "Andrew Jackson/President 1829" Inaugural collar button (Hake 3028) 18mm; brass ........... 210.00 235.00

TOKENS

☐ "Andrew Jackson" equestrian token (Hake 3025; Warner 9) 38mm; white metal ................ 450.00 475.00

☐ "Andrew Jackson/President Of The United States," left profile bust; 1829 (Hake 3024) 38mm; brass token ................................. 475.00 500.00

Price Range

☐ "General Jackson/The Gallant & Successful Defender Of New Orleans ..." 1828 (Hake 3021) 38mm; white metal ........................ 480.00    500.00

## Ceramics and Glassware

### CREAMERS

☐ "General Jackson/The Hero of New Orleans"; copper luster creamer; transfer bust image of Jackson; variations in border of image go from distorted oval to oval to oblong, in progressive sizes; 4¾"h .... 1300.00    1350.00

☐ Also 5¼"h ................................ 1350.00    1400.00

☐ Also 7½"h ................................ 1400.00    1450.00

☐ Liverpool creamer, "Gen'l Jackson, Hero of America"; circular black transfer bust portrait enclosed by olive sprays; eagle at top (actually, portrait is said to be of a young Lafayette; English makers were known for misspellings and misattribution) 700.00    800.00

### GLASSWARE

☐ Amber pint flask; A. J. profile facing left in general's attire with Jackson quote above bust; George Washington portrait, right-facing profile, on reverse ... 250.00    300.00

### PLATES

☐ "General Jackson/The Hero of New Orleans" (same portrait as on luster creamers) black transfer; 7¼"; black portrait; rimmed in brown enamel .. 600.00    625.00

☐ "General Jackson," younger portrait of Jackson in blue transfer; scalloped border; 8½"; blue, white 625.00    650.00

## Lithos Under Glass

☐ "Jackson"; engraved paper portrait under glass in plain pewter frame; portrait of Jackson with coat collar up and wide open (Hake 3001) black, white portrait; hanging loop ...................... 1150.00    1200.00

| *Prints, Posters* | Price Range | |
|---|---|---|
| ☐ "Andrew Jackson/Seventh President of the United States"; Jackson three-quarter-length portrait; green curtain backdrop; 12" x 9"; Currier & Ives | 300.00 | 350.00 |
| ☐ "Bloody Deeds of Gen. Jackson"; famous anti-Jackson coffin broadside; shows coffin silhouettes in stark black; a small vignette has Jackson running a man through with sword cane following a street quarrel in Nashville; 25"h x 17"w; black, white | 425.00 | 450.00 |
| ☐ "Genl. Andrew Jackson/The Union must and shall be preserved"; vignette equestrian portrait, vertical view; troops in background; Currier & Ives . . . . . | 250.00 | 300.00 |
| ☐ "Gen. Andrew Jackson/The Hero of New Orleans"; horse at left; Jackson's head at right; 12" x 9"; Currier & Ives . . . . . . . . . . . . . . . . . . . . . . . . . . | 250.00 | 300.00 |
| ☐ "King Andrew The First/Born To Command/Shall He reign Over Us, Or Shall The PEOPLE RULE!" Anti-Jackson broadside; black, white; 1832 . . . . . . . . . . . . . . . . . . . . . . . . . . . . . . . . | 600.00 | 650.00 |
| ☐ "The Pedlar and His Pack—Desperate Effort—An Overbalance"; cartoon print; satiric response to Anti-Jackson coffin broadside; also shows Henry Clay and J. Q. Adams; 11" x 15"w; hand-colored; 1828 . . . . . . . . . . . . . . . . . . . . . . . . . . . . . . . . . . . . | 200.00 | 225.00 |
| ☐ "Jackson Ticket"; oval Jackson woodcut portrait enclosed by four draped flags; eagle atop; "Honor and gratitude to the man who has filled the measure of his country's glory"—Jefferson quote; also lists two candidates for the Assembly below; black, white; 1828; earliest known presidential poster in support of a candidate . . . . . . . . . . . . . . . . . . . . . . | 550.00 | 600.00 |
| ☐ "Sacred to the Memory of the Mother Of John Woods"; anti-Jackson poster; holds Jackson responsible not only for death of a soldier in combat but also of his mother, who died of grief; lettering is enclosed in large coffin outline, with symbolic urns and angels' wings in each corner; issued July 4, 1828; black on white . . . . . . . . . . . . . . . . . . . . . . | 450.00 | 500.00 |

## Sewing and Grooming Accessories

Price Range

### THREAD BOXES

☐ "Jackson And No Corruption"; rainbow-colored pasteboard with gilt paper edging; inside lid is glass-enclosed portrait of Jackson; outside lid bears velvet pincushion with slogan; 5"w x 3"h x 1½" deep; multicolors; French import . . . . . . . . . . . . . . . . . .    950.00    1000.00

☐ "Jackson Triumphant"; same as above with slogan variation . . . . . . . . . . . . . . . . . . . . . . . . . . . . . . . . .    950.00    1000.00

☐ "Old Hickory Forever"; same as above with slogan variation . . . . . . . . . . . . . . . . . . . . . . . . . . . . . . . . .    950.00    1000.00

### TRINKET BOXES/PATCH BOXES

☐ "Gen. Andrew Jackson" trinket box; Jackson military bust with eagle and crossed olive branches below; 5"w x 3¼"h x 2" deep; hand-colored lithograph; inscription below in French; Paris import    1200.00    1300.00

☐ "Jackson" patch box; portrait of Jackson under glass on hinged lid; mirror inside; 2"h x 1½"w; black, white portrait; made like small book; ca. 1845; probably a memorial item and part of a set that sought to commemorate all presidents up to that time . . . . . . . . . . . . . . . . . . . . . . . . . . . . . . . . .    325.00    350.00

## Textiles

### BANDANNAS

☐ "Glorious Victory of New Orleans/Jackson Leading Troops To Victory"; small oval Washington at top; detailed battle scenes in foreground; historical vignettes on all four corners (Hake 3007) 24"w x 21½"l; brown, white . . . . . . . . . . . . . . . . . . . . . . . .    1600.00    1700.00

☐ "The Gallant Genl. Jackson Animating His Troops"; detailed scene of Battle of New Orleans; naval skirmishes depicted in vignettes on all four corners (Hake 3006) 25"w x 20½"h; brown, white    1200.00    1300.00

☐ Silk bandanna, "President's Proclamation Addressed to the People of South Carolina. 1832"; Jackson portrait under arched lettering: "Procla-

Price Range

mation"; four columns of verbiage (Collins 82) 23½"h x 18¼"w; black, white; printed by M. Fithian, Philadelphia, 1833 ................... | 850.00 | 900.00

RIBBONS

☐ "Gen. Andrew Jackson The Hero Of New Orleans"; soaring eagle with neck craned downward; runs horizontally (Warner 10) 9"w x 3¾"h; black on white ................................... | 475.00 | 500.00

☐ "President Jackson/Our Welcome Guest"; scrolled lettering; torso portrait of Jackson (Hake 3011; De-Witt AJ-3) black on white; decal edging ........ | 750.00 | 800.00

Campaign Jackson ribbons are very scarce. Scores of Jackson memorial ribbons were issued in 1845 and bring substantially lower prices.

## *Tobacco Accessories*

SNUFFBOXES

☐ "Major General Andrew Jackson/Battle of New Orleans/8th. June 1815"; Jackson military bust portrait, full face; 2¼"; black transfer, pumpkin-yellow papier-mâché; portrait in cloud background | 775.00 | 825.00

☐ "Major Genl. Andrew Jackson"; larger bust portrait than above minus cloud background; 2"; black transfer, orange background; papier-mâché ..... | 750.00 | 800.00

☐ Jackson no-name (on obverse) snuffbox; large, handsome bust portrait of Jackson in ruffled shirt, black coat; eagle on reverse with banner in beak inscribed; "Genl. Andrew Jackson Jan. 8 [probably an inaugural item] We love the gallant Chieftain who flung proud defiance to the furious foe ..."; 4"; black, white enameled papier-mâché ........ | 1750.00 | 1800.00

☐ Jackson also pictured on an 1844 snuffbox, which also features likenesses of Van Buren, Clay, and Webster ................................... | 650.00 | 700.00

## THOMAS JEFFERSON

Thomas Jefferson, author of Declaration of Independence; Governor of Virginia, 1779–81; U.S. Diplomatic Minister to France, 1785–89; Secretary of State under George Washington; Vice-President under John Adams, 1797–1801; third President of U.S., 1801–09; founder and first rector of University of Virginia, 1816–25; and all-round genius.

Price Range

### *Ceramics and Glassware*

☐ "Thomas Jefferson/President of the United States of America"; Liverpool mug with black and white transfer torso image (Hake 3002) .............    1600.00    1700.00

☐ Liverpool mug with same lettering as above; different Jefferson image; stars and scrolls added with names of 13 original states, enclosing oval portrait (Hake 3003) ...............................    1800.00    1900.00

☐ Liverpool creamware pitcher with same legend and image as Hake 3002, enclosed by oval of olive sprays; reverse has poem "Liberty thou Godde is heav'nly bright . . ." with border of stars and roll call of states, common on many Liverpool jugs (Hake 3004) ............................    1700.00    1800:00

☐ "We Are All Republicans/All Federalists/Thomas Jefferson . . ."; oval portrait of Jefferson, much more traditional in concept than above images; star and floral design border with names of states in entwined scrolls .............................    1800.00    1900.00

### *Lapel Devices*

☐ "Th. Jefferson" clothing button; bust to left, name above; "R. Martin" (Philadelphia button maker) and shank on reverse; letters PL punched over name (DeWitt TJ 1800-2) 21mm; silvered copper                1000.00 plus

☐ "Th. Jefferson, President Of The U.S. 4 March 1801"; Jefferson bust profile left; "JR" (engraver) appears on truncation; Liberty with liberty pole and scroll inscribed "Declaration of Independence" stands at rock; swooping eagle bears olive wreath;

**Price Range**

"Under His Wing Is Protection" borders top of coin
(Hake 3001; DeWitt TJ 1800-1) 45mm; issued in
bronze, silver, white metal ................... 1800.00     1900.00

## Textiles

### BANDANNA

☐ "Mr. Jefferson's Last Letter"; letter from Jefferson
to mayor of Washington, DC, declining to attend
a celebration; reproduced as memorial at Jefferson's
death July 4, 1826; black velvet border (Collins 68)
$9\frac{1}{2}$"l x $5\frac{1}{4}$"w; black on white; silk ........... 600.00     700.00

### FLAG BANNER

☐ "T. Jefferson/President of the United States/John
Adams/No More"; eagle above Jefferson bust portrait in starred oval; hand-painted banner; may be
unique (Hake 3005; Collins 32) 37"w x 30"h; red,
white, blue linen .......................... 4000.00     4500.00

Andrew Johnson "The
People's Choice" poster, a
promotional item from
Gaylord Watson, Map,
Chart and Book Publishers,
1860s ($375–$400).

## ANDREW JOHNSON

Andrew Johnson, Republican from Tennessee; served in the House and Senate, 1843–62; Vice-President under Lincoln, March 4 to April 15, 1865; 17th President of the U.S. following Lincoln's assassination, 1865–69. He missed impeachment by one vote, and was the only President to return to Congress, serving as senator from Tennessee from 1874–75.

## HIRAM W. JOHNSON

After Johnson's defeat in 1912 as TR's Progressive Party Vice-Presidential running mate, he ran successfully in California for governor and senator. In 1920 he made a futile bid for the presidency. Harding asked him to be his running mate, but he refused, due to a difference in ideologies. The following campaign items were from the 1920 race (see T. Roosevelt).

**Price Range**

### *Miscellaneous*

| | | |
|---|---|---|
| ☐ "America First" slogan pinback (unlisted) $\frac{1}{2}$"; black on white . . . . . . . . . . . . . . . . . . . . . . . . . . . . | 20.00 | 25.00 |
| ☐ "America First. Johnson For President" (unlisted) portrait; $2^3/16$"; blue on white; several $\frac{7}{8}$" variants were also issued . . . . . . . . . . . . . . . . . . . . . . . . . | 25.00 | 30.00 |
| ☐ "Back To Honesty" slogan pinback (unlisted) $\frac{7}{8}$"; blue on white . . . . . . . . . . . . . . . . . . . . . . . . . . . | 15.00 | 20.00 |
| ☐ "For President. Johnson"; bust portrait (Hake unlisted; Warner 653) $2^3/16$"; blue on white . . . . . . . | 50.00 | 60.00 |
| ☐ "I'm For Back To Honesty" slogan pinback (unlisted) red, white . . . . . . . . . . . . . . . . . . . . . . . . . | 20.00 | 25.00 |
| ☐ "I'm For Hiram" slogan pinback (unlisted) $\frac{7}{8}$"; red, white, blue; many variants in $\frac{7}{8}$" . . . . . . . . | 15.00 | 20.00 |
| ☐ "We're with you Hiram" "To Honor California's Own." "Sen. Johnson's Tour" ribbons . . . . . . . . . | 30.00 | 35.00 |

## LYNDON BAINES JOHNSON

Lyndon Johnson, Democrat from Texas, served in the House and Senate 1937–61. Vice-President under John F. Kennedy, 1961–63. Served as 36th President of U.S. 1963–69, assuming office when Kennedy was assassinated. Known as "Great Wheeler Dealer," Johnson rated high marks for "The

Great Society" domestic programs, including anti-poverty and a new civil rights bill. The escalation of the Vietnam war and intervention in Latin America (he sent Marines into Dominican Republic) doomed him politically and contributed to his surprise decision in 1967 not to seek another term.

**Price Range**

## Cartoon/Pictorial Pinbacks

☐ "Barry Is The Living End"; anti-Goldwater cartoon of rear end of GOP elephant (Hake 2099) 3½"; black, white .............................. 8.00 10.00

☐ "Cock-A-Doodle-Doo!" (cartoon of crowing rooster) "Johnson and Humphrey Too"; small circular inset illustration of rooster states, "The Democratic Party's First National Emblem" (Hake 50) 3"; red, white, blue ........................ 12.00 14.00

☐ "Dr. Strangewater; anti-Goldwater cartoon skull with atomic ring symbol encircling it; white reversed out of black (Hake 2169) 1¼"; black, white 15.00 17.00

Selection of cartoon pinbacks. Top, left to right: anti-LBJ; TR; anti–Hubert Humphrey; TR; Hoover; Adlai Stevenson; anti-Goldwater. All sell for under $10.

Price Range

☐ "Go With Goldwater" line drawing of large mushroom-shaped A-bomb cloud (Hake 2170) $1\frac{1}{4}$"; black, white; number of variants ......... 6.00 8.00

☐ "If I Were 21 I'd Vote For L.B.J."; small child in highchair (Hake 56) $1\frac{1}{4}$"; red, white, blue ...... 4.00 6.00

☐ "If I Were 21 I'd Vote For L.B.J."; thin-line border around Democratic donkey balancing on platform (Hake 2020) 6"; black, red ................... 15.00 20.00

☐ "It's Not Luck That Rules The Nation. It's The Man Vote"; horseshoe illustration (Hake 2093) $3\frac{1}{2}$"; red, white, blue ....................... 10.00 12.00

☐ "I Used To Be A Republican. Vote L.B.J."; jumbo elephant carrying umbrella and carpetbag over shoulder (Hake 24) $3\frac{1}{4}$"; red, white, black ..... 10.00 12.00

☐ "Keep A Firm Grip On The Reins/L.B.J."; illustration of star-studded leather rein (Hake 2025) 4"; red, white, blue lithograph ................... 10.00 12.00

☐ Also $\frac{7}{8}$" (Hake 73) ......................... 3.00 5.00

☐ "Ladies For Lyndon"; large Stetson hat and pair of spurs (Hake 2087; Warner 836) $3\frac{1}{2}$"; black, yellow 25.00 30.00

☐ "Rural American/Johnson-Humphrey"; names appear on rural mail box (Hake 46) red, white, blue lithograph .................................. 6.00 8.00

☐ "Think. Miller Could Be President" (anti-Goldwater) small photograph of Republican vice-presidential nominee William Miller (Hake 67) $1\frac{1}{4}$"; blue, white; vendor item, not campaign ... 3.00 5.00

☐ "What—Me Worry?" (anti-Goldwater) photo of Barry Goldwater inset in large mushroom A-bomb (Hake 2125) $2\frac{1}{4}$"; black, red, white ........... 25.00 30.00

☐ "Young Citizens For Johnson"; patriotic striped Democratic donkey cartoon (Hake 51) 2"; red, white, blue ................................. 18.00 20.00

## *Inaugural Pinbacks*

**Price Range**

☐ "45th Inauguration—Let Us Continue"; trigate of Lyndon Johnson, John Kennedy, and Hubert Humphrey; presidential seal and "The Great Society" appear under portraits (Hake 2021) 4"; red, white, blue .................................... 12.00    15.00

☐ "Inauguration Day. Washington D.C./January 20th/1965"; keystone symbols appear in scroll; portraits of LBJ and HHH set up to appear as if they were in reviewing box festooned with patriotic bunting; Pennsylvania item (Hake 21) 3¼"; red, white, blue, black .......................... 6.00    8.00

☐ "Inauguration Day. Washington D.C. ... The Great Society"; small portraits of LBJ and HHH (Hake 2002) 1¼"; red, white, blue ............ 4.00    6.00

☐ "Inauguration Jan. 20th, 1965"; single portrait of LBJ smiling; Capitol dome on right; "Lyndon B. Johnson, President" (Hake 2061) 3½"; red, white, blue, black ................................. 4.00    6.00

## *Jugate Pinbacks*

**JOHNSON–HUMPHREY**

☐ "AFL-CIO COPE For L.B.J. & H.H.H."; conjoining silhouetted heads; bluetone portraits (Hake 4) ⅞"; bluetone, red, white .................... 3.00    5.00

☐ "A Great Day For The U.S.A."; silhouetted heads (Hake 2004) 4"; red, white, blue ............. 15.00    20.00

☐ "A Winning Team For The People"; silhouetted portraits on shield background; "Democrats" appears below (Hake 14) 2"; red, white, blue ..... 3.00    5.00

☐ "Citizens For Johnson & Humphrey"; bull's-eye portraits (Hake 8) 1½"; red, white, blue (this item has been reproduced) ...................... 3.00    5.00

☐ "College Young Democrats For Johnson/ Humphrey"; open book with portraits on facing pages; "The Choice Is Clear" (Hake 9) 1½"; red, white, blue ................................. 3.00    5.00

Price Range

☐ "Democrats Are We For Johnson & Humphrey" (Hake 16) 2¾"; red, white, bluetone portraits; lithograph .................................... 5.00    7.00

☐ "Democrats Winning Key/Johnson & Humphrey"; key illustration, white reversed out of blue; silhouetted head portraits (Hake 13) 2¾"w x 2"h; red, white, blue lithograph ....................... 10.00    15.00

☐ "Johnson–Humphrey. Vote Democratic"; portraits in U.S. map outline (Hake 2012) 6"; red, white, blue, black ................................. 10.00    12.00

☐ "Win With Johnson–Humphrey in '64"; bluetone silhouetted portraits (Hake 17) 2¾"; red, white, blue ......................................... 6.00    8.00

## JOHNSON–KENNEDY

☐ "Let Us Continue"; large silhouetted bust of LBJ with screened portrait of John Kennedy in background (Hake 2057) 3½"; red, white, blue, black    10.00    15.00

☐ "Let Us Continue. Vote Democratic"; large star with mortar and pestle in center flanked by small portraits of JFK and LBJ (Hake 2056) 3½"; red, white, blue, black ........................... 15.00    20.00

## JOHNSON–HOPEFULS

Unaccountably, Lyndon Johnson's portrait appears with any number of Democratic aspirants or possible running mates prior to the National Convention. A standard design was used, with "Johnson" appearing in arc at top, potential running mate at bottom. A lone star appeared atop silhouetted portrait bull's-eye. Colors are red, white, blue, black; all pinbacks 3½".

☐ "Johnson–Brown" (Pat Brown, California governor) (Hake 2047) .......................... 12.00    15.00

☐ "Johnson–Kennedy" (Robert Kennedy, New York senator) (Hake 2048) ....................... 20.00    25.00

☐ "Johnson–Humphrey" (incumbent vice president) (Hake 2046) ............................... 10.00    12.00

☐ "Johnson–McCarthy" (Eugene McCarthy, Minnesota senator; presidential hopeful in 1968) (Hake 2049) ....................................... 15.00    20.00

☐ "Johnson–Ribicoff" (Abe Ribicoff, Connecticut senator) (Hake 2051) ....................... 12.00    15.00

Price Range

☐ "Johnson–Shriver" (R. Sargent Shriver, Democratic vice-presidential nominee in 1972) (Hake 2052) .................................... 12.00   15.00

☐ "Johnson–McNamara" (John McNamara, secretary of defense in JFK, LBJ administrations (Hake 2050) ..................................... 10.00   12.00

☐ "Johnson–Stevenson" (Adlai Stevenson, loser to Eisenhower in 1952 and 1956 (Hake 2053) ....... 15.00   20.00

☐ "Johnson–Wagner" (Robert Wagner, former mayor of New York) (Hake 2054) ............ 10.00   12.00

## Portrait Pinbacks

☐ "Alaska Needs Johnson" (Hake unlisted; Warner 835) 1½"; red, white, blue; very desirable state-related pinback; 1964 ....................... 65.00   70.00

☐ "All The Way With L.B.J." (Hake 2024) 4"; red, white, blue, black; key slogan appeared on numerous variants .............................. 10.00   12.00

☐ "L.B.J. Heart Of The U.S.A."; portrait inside heart outline (Hake 22) 2½"; red, white, blue ........ 20.00   25.00

☐ "L.B. Johnson"; smiling LBJ wearing Stetson. (Hake 28) 1½"; black, white ................. 4.00   6.00

☐ "Johnson The Man For The Job"; silhouetted bust against full flag background (Hake 2076) 3½"; red, white blue, black .......................... 10.00   12.00

☐ "Johnson U.S.A."; portrait in large shield (Hake 2071) 3½"; red, white, blue ................. 12.00   14.00

☐ "Our Next President, The Bartender's Friend" (Hake 2011) 1¼"; black, white; salesman's sample 8.00   10.00

☐ "Peace and Prosperity/Vote L.B.J. in '64"; portrait against bold vertical stripes (Hake 2013) 6"; red, white, blue ............................... 10.00   12.00

☐ "Prosper More/Vote L.B.J. in '64"; profile of LBJ against bold stripes (Hake 2014) 6"; red, white, blue, black ............................... 30.00   35.00

☐ "Re-Elect Johnson For President"; large silhouetted bust portrait (Hake 2073) 3½"; black, white 10.00   12.00

Price Range

☐ "Vote Democratic All The Way"; LBJ flasher pin-back; Hart, Staebler, Michigan coattails on reverse (Hake 2008) 2½"; black, white .............. 8.00    10.00

☐ "Vote Democratic/Pull 2nd Lever" (Hake 2078) 3½"; red, white, blue, black ................. 25.00    30.00

☐ "Win With Johnson"; Johnson with draped U.S. and presidential flags (Hake 2081) 3½"; red, white, blue ...................................... 4.00    6.00

## Slogan/Name Pinbacks—1964

☐ "All The Way With L.B.J." (Hake 62) 1¼"; red, white, blue lithograph ...................... 2.00    4.00

☐ Also ⅞" (Hake 77) ........................ 3.00    5.00

☐ "Ban The Bomb And Barry" (Hake 2174) 1¼"; black, white .............................. 8.00    10.00

☐ "Bury Barry" (Hake 2175) 1¼"; black, white ... 5.00    7.00

☐ "C5H4N403 On AuH20" (chemical symbols for uric acid and gold water) (Hake 2178) 1¼"; black, white ...................................... 8.00    10.00

☐ "Goldwater For Fuhrer" (Hake 2177) 1½"; blue, yellow ...................................... 10.00    12.00

☐ "Goldwater For Halloween" (Hake 2176) 1¼"; black, orange ............................. 5.00    7.00

☐ "Hari-Kari With Barry" (Hake 2199) 1"; blue, yellow ...................................... 10.00    12.00

☐ "In Your Guts You Know He's Nuts" (anti-Goldwater) (Hake 2100) 1½"; red, yellow ...... 8.00    10.00

☐ "Love That Lyndon" (Hake 2158) 1¼"; black, white ...................................... 10.00    12.00

☐ "My Only Vice Is Moderation" (Hake 2153) 1½"; yellow, black ............................. 5.00    7.00

☐ "Part Of The Way With L.B.J." (listed under Johnson in Hake 2190) but obviously anti-LBJ; 1"; black, white ............................. 5.00    7.00

☐ "Republicans, Independents For Johnson" (Hake 2167) 1¼"; black, white; one of many variants .. 5.00    7.00

**Price Range**

☐ "Scientists, Engineers, Physicians For Johnson"
  (Hake 2195) ⅞"; red, white, blue . . . . . . . . . . . .       10.00      12.00

## RICHARD MENTOR JOHNSON

Johnson was Vice-President under Martin Van Buren from 1837–41, the first to achieve that office from a western state. The colonial from Kentucky's chief claim to fame was that he had personally killed the legendary Indian Chief Tecumseh during the Battle of the Thames in October 1813. A Democratic ditty went: "Rumpsey dumpsey, rumpsey dumpsey/Colonel Johnson killed Tecumsee" (see Martin Van Buren).

## JOHN FITZGERALD KENNEDY

John F. Kennedy, Democrat from Massachusetts; served in the House, 1947–53; Senate, 1953–60. Elected 35th U.S. President 1961–63. Assassinated in Dallas, Texas, November 22, 1963. First Roman Catholic to become President, and youngest man ever elected President (Teddy Roosevelt was 43 when he succeeded McKinley, but 46 when first elected in 1904). Kennedy's plurality of only 0.2 percent was also smallest in history. His short-lived administration launched "The New Frontier."

Democratic Convention John F. Kennedy boater from 1950 race (missing label on top) ($15–$20).

Price Range

## Cartoon/Pictorial Pinbacks

☐ "Keep Up With The Kennedys"; words in shamrock (unlisted) $1\frac{1}{2}$"; green, white .............     30.00     35.00

☐ "Let's Back Jack"; caricature bust of JFK (Hake 29) $2\frac{3}{4}$"; blue, red, white; lithograph ..........     20.00     25.00

☐ "Member *Sons Of B*usiness Society"; anti-JFK pinback prompted by his remark that businessmen were SOBs; 1962; shows mournful-looking basset hound in doghouse (Hake 131) $1\frac{3}{4}$"; black, white     15.00     20.00

☐ "What Would You Like To Be Son?" "President, Dad." "I Mean When You Grow Up"; caricature of very toothy JFK in small boy's sailor suit and hat (unlisted) $4\frac{1}{2}$"; black, white; anti-JFK .....     375.00     400.00

☐ "Viva Kennedy"; large Mexican sombrero with lettering reading vertically on crown and horizontally on brim (Hake 77) $1\frac{1}{4}$"; red, yellow ...........     15.00     20.00

☐ Also dark blue, white (Hake 78) ..............     12.00     15.00

## Inaugural Pinbacks

### JUGATES

☐ "44th Inauguration 1961/John F. Kennedy/Lyndon Johnson/The New Frontier"; silhouetted portraits; small Capitol dome and eagle seal (Hake 14) 3"; red, white, blue, black, green, gold     20.00     25.00

☐ "44th Inauguration" (White House illustration); "John F. Kennedy/Lyndon B. Johnson/1961/The New Frontier" (Hake 15) $1\frac{1}{2}$"; red, white, bluetone     10.00     15.00

☐ Also $3\frac{1}{2}$" (Hake 2009) ......................     15.00     20.00

### PORTRAIT

☐ "Inauguration Day/January 20, 1961/Man Of The '60s"; fascimile signature; Capitol Building in background (Hake 17) $3\frac{1}{4}$"; red, white, blue, black ..     8.00     10.00

☐ "Inauguration Day/January 20, 1961/John F. Kennedy/35th President"; pair of Capitol dome illustrations on each side of JFK portrait (Hake 2041) $3\frac{1}{2}$"; red, white, blue, black ............     8.00     10.00

☐ $1\frac{3}{4}$" variant (Hake 13) ......................     5.00     7.00

Price Range

☐ "Inauguration ..." (wording identical to above); bust of Kennedy at left; Capitol building, center concourse (Hake 16) 1½"; red, white, blue ..... 5.00 8.00

☐ "Inauguration ..." (wording identical to above); JFK portrait superimposed on Capitol building (Hake 19) 1½"; black, white ................. 10.00 15.00

## *Jugate Pinbacks*

☐ "America's Men For The '60s"; canted silhouette portraits of Kennedy–Johnson (Hake 2007) 4"; red, white, blue ................................. 20.00 25.00

☐ "America Needs Kennedy–Johnson" (Hake 4) 2"; red, white, blue ............................ 8.00 10.00

☐ Also 3¼"; (Hake 5) ....................... 10.00 12.00

☐ "For America. For President. Pull That First Lever. Vote Straight Democratic"; conjoining portraits (Hake 6; Warner 828) 3½"; white, bluetone, black, red; Philadelphia item ................. 80.00 90.00

☐ "For America. For President. Vote Straight Democratic"; conjoining portraits, as above (Hake 2008) 3¾"; red, white, blue ....................... 35.00 45.00

☐ "For Experienced Leadership. Kennedy and Johnson"; silhouetted busts (Hake 12) 3¼"; red, white, blue, black ................................. 15.00 20.00

☐ "Kennedy/Johnson"; silhouetted bust portraits (Hake 3) ⅞"; red, black, white .............. 55.00 65.00

☐ "Kennedy/Johnson"; rectangular shape; circular portraits under winged eagle; starred border (Hake 2001) 2¾"w x 1¾"h; red, white, blue, black, silver 175.00 200.00

☐ "Kennedy/Johnson/Vote Democratic"; conjoining portraits; laurel branches (Hake 8) 3½"; black, red, blue, green, white ......................... 20.00 25.00

☐ "Leadership For The '60s/Kennedy/Johnson"; rectangle; silhouetted busts; stars (Hake 2) 3"w x 2"h; red, white, blue, black ................. 20.00 25.00

☐ "Leaders Of Our Country/Kennedy/Johnson/And A Friendly World"; small donkey above silhouetted heads (Hake 11) 3½"; red, white, blue, black ... 12.00 15.00

Price Range

☐ "My Choice For '60/Kennedy/Johnson"; graytone circular portraits (Hake 7) 2½"; red, white, blue, black . . . . . . . . . . . . . . . . . . . . . . . . . . . . . . . . . . . . . . . 8.00 10.00

☐ "Straight Democratic/Kennedy/Johnson"; silhouetted heads (Hake 2004) 4"; red, white, blue, black 200.00 225.00

MISCELLANEOUS

☐ "Kennedy For President/Vanden Heuvel For Congress" (Hake 62; Warner 469) 1¾"; red, white, blue, black; Vanden Heuvel ran in the 17th Congressional District of New York . . . . . . . . . . . . . . 65.00 75.00

☐ Also 3½" (Hake 2079) . . . . . . . . . . . . . . . . . . . . . . 85.00 95.00

## *Portrait Pinbacks*

☐ "America Needs Kennedy"; bull's-eye portrait (Hake 2047) 4"; red, white, blue, black . . . . . . . . 100.00 120.00

☐ "All The Way With J.F.K./Kennedy For President"; silhouette head portrait (Hake 41) 1¼"; red, black, blue, white . . . . . . . . . . . . . . . . . . . . . . . . . . . 100.00 110.00

☐ "Best For You/Best In View" (silhouette profile) "Kennedy" (Hake 36) 1½"; red, blue, black, white 5.00 7.00

☐ "Democracy For J.F.K."; bust portrait (unlisted) 3"; black, white . . . . . . . . . . . . . . . . . . . . . . . . . . . 1000.00 1100.00

☐ "Elect Kennedy President" (Hake 21) 2"; black, white . . . . . . . . . . . . . . . . . . . . . . . . . . . . . . . . . . . . 75.00 85.00

☐ "For President/John F. Kennedy"; bull's-eye portrait (Hake 2022) 3½"; red, white, blue, black; also in 5" and 6" sizes . . . . . . . . . . . . . . . . . . . . . . . . . . 10.00 12.00

☐ "For The Leadership We Need/Kennedy For President" (Hake 2025) 3½"; red, white, blue, black 5.00 7.00

☐ "Give The Key To Kennedy"; bust portrait (unlisted) 3"; black, white . . . . . . . . . . . . . . . . . . . . . . 1000.00 1100.00

☐ "It Seems To Me It's Kennedy"; portrait against flag background (Hake 2057) 1½"; black, white 215.00 225.00

☐ "Jack Once More in '64"; small silhouetted JFK at top (Hake 2035) 2½"; black, white . . . . . . . . . . . . 140.00 150.00

Price Range

☐ Kennedy flasher with LBJ on reverse; "JFK & LBJ" (unlisted) 3"; red, white, blue, black; considered rarest of the flashers .................... 75.00 100.00

☐ "Kennedy Is Best For Me"; bust silhouette (Hake 2038) 2½"; red, bluetone, white .............. 10.00 12.00

☐ Kennedy no-name portrait pinback; large bust portrait encompasses most of image area (Hake 20) 3"; red, white stripes; black, white photograph ..... 75.00 85.00

☐ Kennedy no-name profile portrait (Hake 39) 1¼"; black, white ................................ 30.00 35.00

☐ "Let's Back Jack"; JFK caricature (Hake 29) 2¾"; red, white, blue; lithograph .................. 15.00 20.00

☐ "On The Right Track With Jack"; bull's-eye JFK portrait (unlisted) 1¾"; red, white, blue ........ 15.00 20.00

☐ "Our Next President/John F. Kennedy"; profile portrait with stylized stars and stripes border (Hake 26) 3¼"; red, white, blue, black .............. 8.00 10.00

☐ "Our Next President"; silhouetted JFK head against furled flag background (Hake 32) 1½"; red, white, bluetone; red rim .................... 60.00 70.00

☐ "Progress For All/Forward With Kennedy"; JFK silhouette against shield background (Hake 28) 2"; red, white, blue, black ...................... 8.00 10.00

☐ "Support Our President/Vote Democratic"; bull's-eye portrait (Hake 33) 2¾"; bluetone .......... 50.00 60.00

☐ "Youth For John F. Kennedy"; bull's-eye portrait (unlisted) 3½"; red, white, blue, black ......... 100.00 125.00

☐ "Youth For Kennedy"; portrait identical to 1956 Kennedy vice-presidential pinbacks (Hake 2051) 2¼"; red, white, blue ....................... 160.00 170.00

### Slogan/Name Pinbacks

☐ "All The Way With J.F.K ... O.K!" (unlisted) 1¾"; red, white ............................ 15.00 25.00

☐ "Back Jack" (unlisted) 1½"; black, white ...... 35.00 45.00

| | Price Range | |
|---|---|---|
| ☐ "High Office Demands High Principle. Elect Kennedy President" (Hake 2052) 2½"; red, white, blue | 60.00 | 70.00 |
| ☐ "I Don't Want Nixon" (Hake 2069) 1¼"; black, white | 8.00 | 10.00 |
| ☐ "If I Were 21 I'd Vote For Kennedy" (Hake 2031) 4"; black, white; one of many slogan pinbacks in various sizes | 6.00 | 8.00 |
| ☐ "I'm For Jack" (unlisted) 1½"; red, white | 15.00 | 20.00 |
| ☐ "I Miss Ike . . . Hell, I Even Miss Harry" (Hake 132) 2½"w x 1¾"h; red, white; noncampaign; probably 1962 | 10.00 | 15.00 |
| ☐ "It Seems To Me It's Kennedy" Democratic slogan (Hake 2056) 1¾"; black, white | 30.00 | 35.00 |
| ☐ "*Jobs For Kinfolk*"; anti-JFK, 1962 (Hake 133) 1⅜"; red, white | 30.00 | 35.00 |
| ☐ "Join The New Frontier With Me" (unlisted) 1¼"; red, white, blue | 25.00 | 35.00 |
| ☐ "Kennedy The Best Man" (Hake 2034) 3½"; blue, white | 35.00 | 40.00 |
| ☐ "Kennedettes Girls For Kennedy And Johnson" (unlisted) 3½"; red, white, blue | 20.00 | 25.00 |
| ☐ "Kennedy Is The Remedy" (unlisted) 3½"; black, orange | 25.00 | 35.00 |
| ☐ "Kennedy Press Staff"; two rows of three stars (Hake 2033) 1¾"; black, white | 90.00 | 100.00 |
| ☐ "Kennedy T.V. 1960" (unlisted) black, white | 35.00 | 45.00 |
| ☐ "Khruschev Does Not Want Kennedy & Johnson. I Do" (Hake 71) 1¾"; red, white, blue | 15.00 | 20.00 |
| ☐ "Labor For Kennedy For Labor" (Hake 2068) 1¼"; blue, white | 12.00 | 15.00 |
| ☐ "Mamie Start Packing. The Kennedys Are Coming" (Hake 2032) 3¾"; blue, white | 10.00 | 12.00 |
| ☐ "Member Kennedy For President Club" (Hake 2075) ⅞"; red, black, white | 20.00 | 25.00 |
| ☐ Also as lithograph with slight lettering difference (Hake 2074) | 18.00 | 20.00 |

| | Price Range | |
|---|---|---|
| ☐ "*O*regon For *K*ennedy" Large *O* and *K* (Hake 2070) 1¼"; black, white .......................... | 12.00 | 15.00 |
| ☐ "Prostitutes Vote For Nixon Or Kennedy. We Don't Care Who Gets In!" (Hake 2014) 2½; yellow, black ................................. | 35.00 | 50.00 |
| ☐ Also in red, white (Hake 68) ................. | 40.00 | 50.00 |
| ☐ "Vote Kennedy Congress" (unlisted) 2¼"; red, white, blue ................................ | 85.00 | 90.00 |
| ☐ "Welcome Back Jack" (Hake 2061) 3¼"; red, white, blue ................................ | 35.00 | 40.00 |

### *Vice-Presidential Portrait Pinbacks*

John Kennedy served as U.S. senator from Massachusetts 1953–60. He was a leading contender for vice-president on the Stevenson ticket in 1956 but lost out in open convention to Estes Kefauver on the third ballot.

| | | |
|---|---|---|
| ☐ "A Profile In Courage/Elect U.S. Senator John F. Kennedy Vice-President"; 1956; bust portrait (Hake 2049) 2"; black, white ................. | 150.00 | 160.00 |
| ☐ "Elect John F. Kennedy Vice-President"; bust portrait (Hake 2050) 2"; black, white lithograph ... | 150.00 | 165.00 |

## WILLIAM RUFUS DeVANE KING

William King will be best remembered as the Vice-President who never served. Seriously ill with tuberculosis when nominated, he died before taking office. King, an Alabama Democrat, served in the U.S. Senate for nearly thirty years, and was appointed Ambassador to France under Presidents Tyler and Polk. In 1852, he was picked as Vice-Presidential nominee to balance the ticket with Franklin Pierce. The rather effete King effected a wig, long after they were out of fashion. Andrew Jackson frequently referred to him as "Miss Nancy." King's death created a Vice-Presidential vacancy that lasted until 1857 (see Franklin Pierce).

## FRANK KNOX

"Colonial" Frank Knox was publisher of the *Chicago Daily News;* he ran on the Republican ticket as Vice-Presidential candidate with Alf Landon in 1936. A former Bull Mooser and arch-conservative, as was his running mate Landon, he proved to be a Red-baiter. The strategy backfired (see Alf Landon).

## ROBERT LaFOLLETTE

"Fighting Bob" LaFollette ran as presidential candidate under the newly formed Republican Progressive Party in 1924, with Burton K. Wheeler as Vice-President. LaFollette was a member of the House from Wisconsin, 1885–91; the U.S. Senate, 1906–25. He was also Governor of Wisconsin, 1901–06. In the 1924 race, LaFollette proposed government ownership of railroads and water power resources, freedom for farmers and workers to organize, and collective bargaining. His party received almost a third as many votes as the winner, Calvin Coolidge, and became the first third-party candidate in this century to win electoral votes (13).

THE PEOPLE'S CHOICE
FOR PRESIDENT

Robert LaFollette, Progressive candidate for president, 1924 ($35–$45).

**Price Range**

## *Lapel Devices*

### JUGATES

☐ "LaFollette and Wheeler" conjoining portraits; (Hake LAF 1) 1¼"; black and white .......... 210.00 225.00

☐ "LaFollette-Wheeler" jugate, with feather plume atop ovals; (Hake LAF 3) ⅞"; browntone ...... 120.00 125.00

☐ "People's Choice" bull's-eye jugate (Hake LAF 2) sepiatone .................................. 200.00 210.00

### PORTRAIT PINBACKS

☐ LaFollette (picture in square inset) or Teapot Dome (picture of teapot) rebus. "C'mon BOB, Let's Go!"; (Hake LAF 7) 1"; browntone on cream ....... 425.00 450.00

☐ "I Gave My Dollar/Did You?" bullseye portrait. (Hake LAF 8) 1¼"; black, tan, cream ........ 100.00 110.00

### SLOGAN BUTTONS

☐ "Dollars For My Party": Liberty Bell illustration; "LaFollette-Wheeler Campaign"; (Hake LAF 14) 25.00 30.00

## *Political Campaign Posters*

☐ "LaFollette-Wheeler" jugate poster; sepiatone ... 125.00 150.00

☐ "Robert M. LaFollette/The People's Choice For President" 14"h x 10"w; sepiatone ............ 55.00 65.00

## *Statuary*

☐ Robert LaFollette bronze wall plaque; oval; 12"h 100.00 125.00

## ALFRED M. LANDON

Alfred Landon, Republican from Kansas, a former Bull Mooser and fiscal conservative, was Governor of Kansas prior to his nomination in 1936 for President, running against FDR. The "Kansas Lincoln," as he was called, lost to FDR 523 electoral votes to 8, the biggest landslide since Monroe's in 1820.

"The Depression Ass. Get Up. Let The Dollar Work." Eagle bites the Democratic donkey on the tail; bronze statuette, possibly a Landon anti-FDR item ($75–$85).

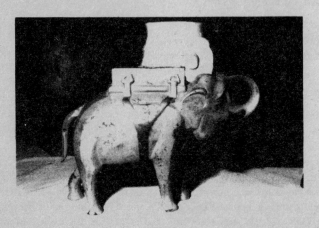

"Landon–Knox" cast-iron elephant cigarette dispenser. Push tail lever and cigarette comes out of mouth ($115–$125).

Price Range

## Automotive Accessories

☐ "Landon & Knox"; name license plate attachment; 4½"w x 3½"h; black, white; raised letters ..... 20.00 25.00

☐ "Landon, Barrows, White"; local name license plate attachment; black, white; raised lettering .. 20.00 25.00

☐ "Landon–Knox"; names appear in petals of sunflowers; 3½" dia; black, white; tab for attaching 20.00 25.00

☐ "Landon–Knox"; reflecting license attachment; names across petals of sunflower; silver-plastic layered reflecting area behind brown, yellow, black; 3½" dia plus tab for attaching ............... 25.00 30.00

☐ "Landon And Knox"; large circle enclosing sunflower at left, with GOP elephant in center of flower; 10¼"l; brown, yellow, black, white ..... 30.00 35.00

☐ "Landon And Knox"; conjoining jugate portraits in center of sunflower; 3½" dia; lettering appears in flange below; 6½"h overall ................ 35.00 40.00

☐ "Landon–Knox" appears on elephant's side; his two legs balance on barrel-tab section; black, white 30.00 35.00

☐ "Landon For President"; slogan in white reversed out of black; 3½"l rectangle with tab .......... 15.00 20.00

☐ "Landon For President" Landon portrait in die-cut oval with pair of sunflowers in background; brown, white, black .............................. 25.00 35.00

☐ "Landon" in large oval with elephant silhouettes top and bottom; 4"l; black, white ............. 20.00 25.00

☐ "Landon For President" in die-stamped aluminum ("For President" part embossed, along with a sunflower rosette); pair of tabs for attachment; silver finish ...................................... 25.00 30.00

☐ "Man Of The People. Landon For President"; die-stamped silhouette of bust of Landon; black, brown, buff ....................................... 35.00 40.00

☐ "Landon–Knox" in center of die-stamped sunflower with double tabs; yellow, brown, white ... 45.00 55.00

☐ "Leave It To Landon"; slogan reversed out of black in red reflecting circular die-stamped attachment 15.00 20.00

**Price Range**

☐ "The Spirit Of '76 in '36. Save America. Vote Republican"; shield at right with familiar fife, drummer, and flag bearer in line drawing; $11\frac{1}{2}"1$ ....    30.00    35.00

☐ "Let's Make It A Landon Landslide" slogan license attachment (Hake 2106) $11\frac{1}{2}"$; red, white, blue    40.00    50.00

☐ "Off The Rocks With Landon & Knox" slogan license attachment (Hake 2107) $11\frac{1}{2}"1$; blue, white    40.00    50.00

☐ "Restore Landon Americanism" (Hake 2103) $11\frac{1}{2}"$; red, white, blue .....................    35.00    40.00

## Banks

☐ Alf Landon Elephant Still Bank, maker unknown, 1936, gray with red blanket and gold letters "Land On Roosevelt, 1936," $5"h$ (Hake 2121) .........    100.00    150.00

## Canes, Umbrellas, Whips

☐ "Landon And Knox" wooden cane with attached retractable U.S. flag; names imprinted on side of cane in black; $35"1$.........................    50.00    65.00

## Cartoon/Pictorial Pinbacks

Landon–Knox GOP elephant—there are at least 30 different variants of this design, most of which are mired in the $5–$10 value range. The following comprise a few exceptions:

☐ (Hake 2017) $2"$; black, white, yellow; elephant appears inside sunflower outline ................    75.00    100.00

☐ (Hake 2023) $4"$; black, brown, yellow; elephant inside double row of sunflower petals ...........    35.00    50.00

☐ (Hake 2024) $1\frac{3}{4}"$; elephant sans sunflower; black, white .....................................    150.00    160.00

☐ (Hake 69) $1\frac{1}{4}$; white reversed out of electric blue, to at least break the monotony! ..............    15.00    20.00

☐ "Land-On The New Deal"; GOP elephant stomps on hapless Democratic donkey cartoon (Hake 2033; Warner 432) $1\frac{1}{4}"$; blue, black, white; one of the outstanding cartoon pinbacks in the hobby .....    350.00    400.00

**Price Range**

☐ "Land-On Washington"; caricature of Landon as pilot of twin engine aircraft flying over Capitol dome (Hake 24; Warner 433); $1\frac{1}{4}''$; red, white, (blueprint) blue; key item for Landon campaign, often ranked among top ten in the hobby . . . . . . .   300.00   350.00

Landon sunflower-design pinbacks—there are at least 50 variants of pinbacks adopting the Kansas sunflower symbol. Again, as with the GOP elephant designs, $5–$10 is the normal value range; with the following exceptions:

☐ "Landon For President" brackets large sunflower; (Hake 133) $2''$; yellow, brown, black, ivory . . . . .   50.00   60.00

☐ "Landon President" superimposed on sunflower petals (Hake 58) $1\frac{1}{4}''$; red lettering; yellow, brown, white . . . . . . . . . . . . . . . . . . . . . . . . . . . . . . . . . . . . .   45.00   55.00

☐ Also $2\frac{1}{4}''$ size (Hake unlisted; Warner 791) . . . . .   125.00   150.00

☐ "Republican State Convention. Landon. Huntington W. Va. August 13, 1936" (Hake 2011) $2''$; black, white ("Landon" in large letters superimposed across entire sunflower) . . . . . . . . . . . . . . . .   100.00   125.00

*Note:* For additional outstanding examples of use of sunflower motif, see Portrait Pinbacks listing.

### Jugate Pinbacks

☐ "Landon-Knox. G.O.P."; connecting circle inset portraits (line drawings) with famed sunflower symbol above; GOP elephant below; design featured in ten variants:

☐ (Hake 2) $1\frac{1}{2}''$; black, white, yellow/orange . . . . .   20.00   25.00

☐ (Hake 3) $1\frac{1}{4}''$; as above . . . . . . . . . . . . . . . . . . . . .   15.00   `20.00

☐ (Hake 4) $\frac{3}{4}''$; as above . . . . . . . . . . . . . . . . . . . . . .   10.00   15.00

☐ (Hake 5) $1\frac{1}{2}''$–$\frac{3}{4}''$ pinback with cloth petals . . . .   10.00   15.00

☐ (Hake 6) $\frac{3}{4}''$; inset in fob . . . . . . . . . . . . . . . . . . . .   15.00   25.00

☐ (Hake 7) $\frac{3}{4}''$; inset in badge . . . . . . . . . . . . . . . . . .   15.00   25.00

☐ (Hake 9) $1\frac{1}{4}''$; black, white only . . . . . . . . . . . . . .   50.00   65.00

☐ (Hake 10) $\frac{7}{8}''$; as above . . . . . . . . . . . . . . . . . . . . .   50.00   60.00

Price Range

☐ (Hake 11) ¾"; as above .................... 40.00    50.00

☐ (Hake 2002) 1¾"; as above ................. 60.00    70.00

☐ "Landon Knox Out Roosevelt"; clever wordplay with conjoining portraits (Hake 129) ⅞"; brown, yellow ...................................... 625.00    650.00

☐ "Landon–Knox" oval portraits in center of large Kansas sunflower (Hake 128; Warner 787) 1¼"; yellow, brown ............................... 600.00    625.00

☐ "Landon–Knox" silhouetted portraits (Hake 2001; Warner 430) 1¼"; cream, tan ................ 350.00    375.00

☐ "Landon–Knox" staggered portraits inside large sunflower (Hake unlisted; Warner 429) 1"; red, yellow, black, white; key item for Landon in 1936; only four known jugates; manufactured by Cruver ...    2000.00 plus

☐ Landon–Knox no-name jugate; flag bunting border (Hake 8) 1¼"; red, white, blue, black ......... 40.00    50.00

☐ Also appears in center of oilcloth sunflower (Warner 431) with red, white, blue ribbon and tiny plastic elephant ................................. 75.00    85.00

☐ "Landon–Knox" conjoining portraits bleed off pinback (Hake 2001) 1¼"; black, white .......... 360.00    385.00

☐ "Landon–Knox. For President. For Vice-President"; bluetone and white ovals; lettering reverses out of dark blue (Hake 17) ⅞"; bluetone, white, dark blue; lithograph ................. 75.00    100.00

☐ (Hake 13) black, white; lithograph ............ 75.00    100.00

☐ (Hake 14) sepiatone; lithograph ............... 85.00    110.00

☐ (Hake 16) bluetone, white background; lithograph    85.00    110.00

## Pocket Mirrors

☐ "The New Deal Is Spending $15,000.00 Every Minute, Night and Day. Turn this over and see who pays the bill. Vote For Landon and Knox and end this extravagance" (Hake 140) 2¾"w x 2"h; brown on buff ..................................... 35.00    45.00

| *Portrait Pinbacks* | Price Range | |
|---|---|---|
| ☐ "Alf M. Landon" gray background portrait; black border (Hake 2028) $1\frac{1}{4}$"; black, gray, white .... | 65.00 | 75.00 |
| ☐ "Alf M. Landon" gray background portrait; white border (Hake 2027) $1\frac{1}{4}$"; black, gray, white .... | 65.00 | 75.00 |
| ☐ "Alf M. Landon Notification. Topeka, July 23, 1936"; Landon portrait inside pinback with cloth sunflower petals (Hake 2003; Warner 434) $2\frac{3}{8}$; 5" with petals; yellow, olive, brown .............. | 175.00 | 200.00 |
| ☐ "Alfred M. Landon" silhouetted portrait; (Hake 34) $\frac{7}{8}$"; black, white ...................... | 20.00 | 25.00 |
| ☐ "Alfred M. Landon For President"; lettering in large scroll under portrait (Hake 35) $\frac{7}{8}$"; black, white ..................................... | 20.00 | 25.00 |
| ☐ "For President. Alfred M. Landon"; name wraps around under bust portrait (Hake 2010; Warner 789) $3\frac{1}{2}$"; red, white, blue, black ............. | 175.00 | 200.00 |
| ☐ "For President. Alfred M. Landon"; lettering and portrait reversed out of black (Hake 43) $\frac{7}{8}$"; black, white ..................................... | 15.00 | 20.00 |
| ☐ "Landon"; name appears just above head in portrait; inside sunflower (Hake 32) $\frac{7}{8}$"; black, white, brown, yellow .............................. | 100.00 | 110.00 |
| ☐ "Landon For President Club"; portrait reversed out of black; letters reversed out of red border (Hake 36) $\frac{7}{8}$"; red, black, white ................... | 15.00 | 20.00 |
| ☐ "Landon For President"; letters overprint on sunflower petals; portrait in center (Hake 48) $\frac{7}{8}$"; yellow, black, white .......................... | 30.00 | 35.00 |
| ☐ "Landon Knox Out Roosevelt" wordplay reversed out of blue border; bluetone Landon portrait (Hake 132) $\frac{1}{2}$"; blue, white ....................... | 90.00 | 100.00 |
| ☐ Landon no-name black-rim portrait (Hake 2030) 1"; black, white ........................... | 35.00 | 45.00 |
| ☐ Landon no-name bleed portrait (Hake 25) $1\frac{1}{4}$"; black, green, white, fleshtones ............... | 45.00 | 55.00 |
| ☐ Landon no-name oval pinback (Hake 20) $1\frac{1}{2}$"l; $1\frac{1}{4}$"w; sepiatone .......................... | 30.00 | 35.00 |

Price Range

☐ Landon no-name mini-oval Landon portrait amid clusters of photographed sunflowers (Hake 40) ¾"; sepiatone; black rim ........................ 65.00 75.00

☐ ½" variant of above in black, brown, blue green, yellow (Hake 42) .......................... 95.00 105.00

☐ "Notification Day. Topeka, Kansas. Kansas City, Missouri Will Win With Landon. July 23, 1936" (Hake unlisted; Warner 788) 4"; blue, white, black (compliments of the Union League Club of Kansas City) ...................................... 400.00 425.00

☐ "Sunflower Chain Club"; lettering in scroll across lower petals; portrait in center (Hake 33) ⅞"; black, brown, yellow, white .................. 80.00 110.00

## Slogan/Name Pinbacks

☐ "A Kansan For Landon" (Hake 139) ⅞"; black, white ...................................... 30.00 35.00

☐ "Americans Cannot Be Bought" slogan across sunflower (Hake 106) ⅞"; black, white, yellow ..... 10.00 12.00

☐ "American Democrat For Landon" (Hake 115) ½"; black, yellow lithograph; numerous variants 10.00 12.00

☐ "Climb On The Landon Bandwagon" (Hake unlisted; Warner 792) 2¼; red, white ............ 100.00 125.00

☐ "First Voters League. Start Right. Landon [numeral] 1" (Hake 111) ⅞"; black, yellow ....... 12.00 15.00

☐ "Landon And The Constitution" (Hake 107) ⅞"; red, white, blue .......................... 12.00 15.00

☐ "Landon, Deeds Not Deficits" (Hake 112) ⅞"; blue, white; lithograph ...................... 8.00 10.00

☐ "For An All American Landon Deal" (Hake 141) ⅞"; red, white, blue ....................... 20.00 25.00

☐ "Landon & Knox. I Bought A Dollar Certificate" (Hake 74) ⅞"; blue, brown, yellow, white ...... 10.00 15.00

☐ "Let Landon Lead U.S." (Hake 2057) ⅞"; black, red, white .................................. 20.00 25.00

☐ "Off The Rocks With Landon & Knox" (Hake 72) blue, white, red rim (a number of variants) ..... 30.00 35.00

Price Range

☐ "Ring It Again With Landon (illustration of Liberty Bell) (Hake 2056) ⅞"; blue, white ........ 20.00 25.00

☐ "Save America" (Hake 117) ½"; blue, white; lithograph ..................................... 5.00 7.00

☐ "Volunteers Save America" (Hake 116) ½"; blue, white; lithograph ........................... 5.00 7.00

## ABRAHAM LINCOLN

Abraham Lincoln, a Republican from Illinois, was a lawyer prior to his election to Congress, 1847–49. Elected 16th President of the U.S., 1861–65, he had just been re-elected before his assassination on April 15, 1865. Known as "Honest Abe" and "The Great Emancipator," he is acknowledged by many leading authorities as the greatest of all U.S. Presidents.

### Badges, Medals, Tokens

Abraham Lincoln has had more medals struck in his honor than any other president. His two campaigns (1860, 1864) plus his untimely assassination precipitated a rash of copies when political medalets were in their zenith. Space precludes going into detail here. For very detailed listings please refer to Hake's *Political Buttons, Book III,* and Edmund Sullivan's *American Political Badges & Medalets.*

Price Range

☐ 1860 Lincoln-bust rubber token; high relief; made of light brown hard rubber; uncirculated (DeWitt AL 1860-48; Warner 78) .................... 150.00 175.00

☐ Gilded-brass-frame ambrotype Lincoln portrait pin; yellow cardboard on reverse: "For President/Hon.Abraham Lincoln/Manufactured by/ Geo. Clark Jr., and Co., Abrotype Artists" 1½"h (Hake 3044; Warner 81) 2½"h x 2⅛"w; gilt brass rim ....................................... 1400.00 1500.00

### Folk Art

It would be difficult to put a dollar value on the following outstanding examples of Lincolniana in folk art as they are unique and seldom appear on the market. Suffice it to say, they would command prices of well up into four figures.

This prize daguerreotype, one of only a handful known for Lincoln, ca. 1860, sold at $17,600 at Winter Gallery in 1984, the 175th anniversary of his birth.

Lincoln memorial fan shows cameos of Union generals, vignettes of battle between *Monitor* and *Merrimac,* Lincoln being shot by Booth. Fan has pierced ivory ribs with gilt decoration ($1200–$1500).

Abraham Lincoln Staffordshire figurine; rare image of Abe on horseback ($1200–$1300).

Newspaper ad for Lincoln–Johnson and McClellan–Pendleton campaign badges. Priced at 11 cents in 1864, the Lincoln–Johnson jugate now brings $5,000 plus.

Lincoln ferrotype, 1864 ($800–$900).

Mathew Brady portrait ribbon of Lincoln, with facsimile signature, 1860. It reached a record-breaking $6,750 in a 1986 Rex Stark mail auction.

Abraham Lincoln cased daguerreotype and wooden parade axe, 1860; axe, $850–$900; daguerreotype $2,000 plus.

AN HEIR TO THE THRONE,
OR THE NEXT REPUBLICAN CANDIDATE

Satirical Currier & Ives cartoon features Lincoln and Horace Greeley ($200–$250).

# LINCOLN, HAMLIN,
## AND
# CURTIN!

LINCOLN & HAMLIN.

# W Butler & J Smith Futhey
### WILL ADDRESS A REPUBLICAN MEETING AT
# MILLTOWN,
## Tuesday Evening, Sept. 25th,
8 o'clock. The West Chester, Willistown, & Brandywine
# WIDE-AWAKE CLUBS
Will join in a Torch-Light Procession.    Come one, come all!

Broadside announcing "Wide Awake" Club's torchlight
procession; Lincoln–Hamlin slate, 1860 ($450–$500).

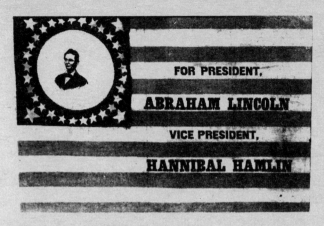

Lincoln–Hamlin flag banner from 1860 ($2,000 plus). *(Photo courtesy of Riba-Mobley)*

Lincoln pedestal bust ($450–$500).

Price Range

☐ Abraham Lincoln, Orator; carved wooden figure, approximately 8"h, polychromed; Lincoln holds rolled document in right hand; left hand is on closed Bible on small table; artist unknown; ca. 1880 . . .

☐ Ship's figurehead, carved polychromed wood from ship *Abraham Lincoln,* 1861; appears in National Gallery of Art, Washington, DC . . . . . . . . . . . . .

☐ Hooked and embroidered rug; Lincoln bust with pair of anchors that loop over head; stars in both upper corners; multicolors; ca. 1865 . . . . . . . . . . .

## Lighting Devices

☐ Ruby overlay, "Lincoln–Hamlin" parade lantern; crimped tin top; embossed filagreed tin bottom; carried by Sandwich Wide-Awakes in 1860 campaign; approx. 12"h; ruby glass; black tin; made by Boston & Sandwich Glass Factory, Sandwich, MA . . . . .    2000.00    2200.00

## Textiles

☐ 1860 Lincoln and Hamlin Brady jugate; many deem this the most elusive and desirable of Lincoln ribbons (see illustration of Lincoln single portrait by Brady) (Hake unlisted; Warner 82) 7¼"l; black, white . . . . . . . . . . . . . . . . . . . . . . . . . . . . . . . . . . . . . .    5000.00 plus

☐ "Lincoln, Hamlin and Liberty/Protection to American Industry" (contains noted backward *n* in Lincoln name; jugate circular portraits against scores of furled flags in background (Warner 83) 5¾"; black, white . . . . . . . . . . . . . . . . . . . . . . . . . . . . . . .    1000.00    1200.00

☐ "Lincoln, Johnson, The Union And Victory!" Lincoln bust portrait; ornate type (Warner 92) 6½"l; black on mustard; 1864 campaign . . . . . . . . . . . . .    450.00    500.00

☐ Lincoln electoral ticket silk ribbon; lists California presidential electors and Donal McRuer for Congress; illustration of sinking of Confederate ship *Alabama;* 1864 (Warner 96) 7"l; light red, white; possibly an artist's proof . . . . . . . . . . . . . . . . . . . . . . . .    275.00    300.00

*Toys*  **Price Range**

☐ Lincoln hurdy-gurdy automated sand toy; sand trickles down on wheel to activate figure of top-hatted Lincoln grinding hurdy-gurdy while monkey, with face of Gideon Welles, dances on table and plays violin to delight of youngsters; (Welles served as Lincoln's Secretary of Navy and was a loyal supporter); multicolor lithograph on cardboard, glass-enclosed; made by Cargani, Hartford, CT; 10"h x 8"w x 2¾"deep ................. 2,000.00 plus

## BELVA ANN LOCKWOOD

The first woman ever to practice law before the Supreme Court, Lockwood ran for president under National Equal Rights banner in 1884 and 1888.

Belva Ann Lockwood, leading suffragette and candidate for president in 1884, and Ben Butler, who championed equal rights, are lampooned in mechanical card with paper skirt that lifts up ($100–$125). *(Frank Corbeil Collection)*

Price Range

*Ephemera*

☐ *Equal Rights* tabloid newspapers published in 1880s
sought to debate issues with major political party
candidates; published by National Equal Rights
Party; per copy ........................... 35.00 50.00

☐ "National Equal Rights Party" campaign card; pictures Lockwood and running mate Marietta Stow 45.00 65.00

*Textiles*

☐ "For President/1888" rebus ribbon; illustration of
hand bell; "V"; illustrations of padlock and log
(Bell-V-Lock-Wood); black, white; gold tassels .. 150.00 175.00

## JOHN A. LOGAN

John Logan, Republican from Illinois, served in Congress from 1859–62;
1867–71; in the Senate 1871–77; 1879–86, and ran as Vice-President with
James Blaine on the Republican slate in 1884. A Civil War General, he was
known as "Black Eagle" and his chief claim to fame was founding the Grand
Army of the Republic (GAR) veterans organization. Many GAR artifacts
bear his name and image, particularly souvenir canteens inscribed, "We
Drank From The Same Canteen."

## JAMES MADISON

James Madison, Democrat Republican from Virginia, served in the House,
1789–97; Continental Congress 1780–83; 1786–88. He was Secretary of State
under Jefferson 1801–09, and signer of Declaration of Independence. Fourth
President of the U.S., 1809–17. Last of the Founding Fathers to serve as President, Madison's legacy had already been established with his role in drafting
the Constitution and Bill of Rights.

Price Range

*Ceramics*

☐ "James Madison/President Of The United States
Of America" in scroll at top; Liverpool creamware
pitcher with black transfer portrait, copied from

Price Range

John Vanderlyn; reverse has Madison portrait with
verse beginning "The rights of man shall be our
boast ..." ................................... 2000.00 plus

## *Lapel Devices*

The concept of manufactured lapel devices to influence choice of candidates had not as yet been developed by Madison's administration.

## *Textiles*

A small number of crudely conceived ribbon designs are known but seldom, if ever, surface on the market.

☐ "Liberty & Independence Our Country's Pride &
Boast"; medallion portraits of Madison as well as
Washington and War of 1812 battle scenes, including Gen. Jackson at New Orleans (Collins 42; Hake
3001) 33"l x 24"w; brown and yellow cotton; imported from Scotland ...................... 1100.00 1200.00

☐ Cotton bandanna, ca. 1815, "A Geographical view
of all the Post Towns ..." bears medallion likeness
of Madison, Adams, Jefferson, Washington (Collins
47) 26"w x 20½"h; blue on white; Scotch ...... 1200.00 1300.00

## THOMAS RILEY MARSHALL

Thomas Marshall, a two-term Indiana governor, proved to be a blunt and
often witty Vice-President under Woodrow Wilson (from 1913–21). Not
overly awed by the job when appointed a member of the Smithsonian, he
quipped that he looked forward to the "opportunity to compare my fossilized
life with the fossils of all ages." Marshall is best known, however, for his
rather enigmatic statement, "What this country needs is a good five-cent
cigar!" (see Woodrow Wilson).

Price Range

## *Pinbacks*

☐ "Marshall Moose Day. Hot Springs Arkansas, July
5, 1915"; Marshall bust portrait (Hake 3203) 1¼";
black, white ............................... 65.00 75.00

Price Range

☐ Marshall portrait badge with pair of ribbons attached (Hake 3119) 4"; black, white . . . . . . . . . . .    100.00    125.00

☐ "Tom Marshall For Me"; oval portrait pinback (Hake 3276) 1"l; black, white, gold . . . . . . . . . . .    10.00    15.00

☐ "Tom Marshall For Me" slogan pinback (Hake 3275) ⅞"; red, white, blue . . . . . . . . . . . . . . . . .    10.00    15.00

☐ "Vice President Notification Day. Indianapolis, Indiana, Aug. 20, 1912" (Hake 3121) 4"; red, white, blue, black; attached ribbon: gilt lettering on dark blue . . . . . . . . . . . . . . . . . . . . . . . . . . . . . . . . . . . .    75.00    100.00

☐ "Woodrow's Right Guard"; Marshall portrait (Hake 3202) 1¼"; black, white . . . . . . . . . . . . . . .    65.00    75.00

## GEORGE B. McCLELLAN

George McClellan, Democrat from New York, served as a General in the Union forces in the Civil War; promoted to Commander-in-Chief, he was later dismissed by Lincoln (1862). McClellan ran against Lincoln in 1864 and was heavily favored until a string of victories by Generals Grant, Sherman and Sheridan transformed the political picture. McClellan went down to a decisive defeat.

## GEORGE McGOVERN

George McGovern, a Democrat from South Dakota, was a former history professor who served as a minor official in John F. Kennedy's administration. He entered the U.S. Senate in 1968 and was a two-term incumbent when he emerged as a dark horse presidential candidate in 1972. He was considered the leading spokesman for all the fringe dissidents, the anti-Vietnam War activists, ERA, and social justice seekers. McGovern's overriding campaign pledge was to call for the immediate withdrawal of U.S. troops from Vietnam with amnesty for all those who had refused to enter military service, which eventually led to a split between McGovern and the Democratic party regulars. This, plus the Eagleton crisis (Eagleton, his running mate, was exposed as having a record of severe mental depression and was dropped and replaced by R. Sargent Shriver), precipitated an overwhelming Nixon victory.

Price Range

## Cartoon/Pictorial Pinbacks

☐ "Kiss Me/I'm For McGovern"; photo of pair of lips; flasher pin (Hake 2030) 3"; red, black, white         4.00         6.00

☐ "Let George Do It"; cartoon of tree with limbs outstretched like arms and bearing likeness of Richard Nixon; an axe appears at foot of tree (Hake 2056) 2¼"; black, white . . . . . . . . . . . . . . . . . . . . . . . . .         8.00         10.00

☐ "Let Me Make Myself Perfectly Clear. We Did Not Do Anything"; photograph of Nixon with arms raised in victory salute; tiny inset shots of pandas with word "Tzechers" under each (Hake 2037) 1¼; black, white . . . . . . . . . . . . . . . . . . . . . . . . . . . . .         15.00         20.00

☐ "Make America Happen Again . . . McGovern"; posturization of mountains, trees, stream (Hake 26) 2"; blue, green, white; has serial number printed below . . . . . . . . . . . . . . . . . . . . . . . . . . . . . . . . . . . . .         10.00         12.00

☐ Also 2¼" (Hake 2041) without serial number . . .         12.00         15.00

☐ "Make America McGovernable"; stylized illustration of dove with olive branch against U.S. flag background (Hake 2241) 1¼"; black, white . . . . .         10.00         12.00

☐ "McGovern" (inside map of U.S.) "Come Home America"; cartoon of Uncle Sam shaking hands with McGovern (Hake unlisted) 2¼"; black, white         10.00         12.00

☐ "McGovern [name appears across musical chart] Use the Power/18/Register and Vote"; silhouettes of pop singing stars Carole King, Barbara Streisand, James Taylor (Hake 2004) 3½"; black, white; also 3" size . . . . . . . . . . . . . . . . . . . . . . . . . . . . . . . .         35.00         40.00

☐ "McGovern/For Peace"; full figure of McGovern holding dove; "McGovern '72"; stylized dove with olive branch in beak (Hake 34) 1¼"; green, gold, white . . . . . . . . . . . . . . . . . . . . . . . . . . . . . . . . . . . .         2.00         4.00

☐ "McGovern '72"; posturization of dove in flight with olive branch in beak (Hake 2025) 3"; blue, pink, gold . . . . . . . . . . . . . . . . . . . . . . . . . . . . . . . .         6.00         8.00

Price Range

☐ Nixon no-name caricature with pen drawing an outline of Suez Canal area on stomach, one finger on lips, by cartoonist David Levine (Hake 2066) 1¾"; black, white; one of series of four Levine cartoons lampooning Nixon (Hake 2066–2069); each ..... 7.00    10.00

☐ "Poor Richard"; cartoon of Nixon dressed like Franklin and flying a kite marked " '72" (Hake 2031) 3"; black, white ....................... 6.00    8.00

☐ "POW!"; cloudlike shape; "McGovern/Shriver" (Hake 12) 1½"; red, white, blue ............. 4.00    6.00

☐ "Robin McGovern"; McGovern wearing high feathered hat; has bow and quiver of arrows (Hake 16) 3¾"; green, black, white ................. 15.00    20.00

## *Jugate Pinbacks*

☐ "Come Home America/McGovern/Shriver," conjoining portraits (Hake 2) 3⅛"; red, white, blue, black ...................................... 3.00    5.00

☐ Also 1¾" (Hake 2001) ..................... 3.00    5.00

☐ "McGovern/Shriver" portraits atop T-shape design with striped base, bordered by stars (Hake 2002) 3"; red, white, blue, black ............. 5.00    7.00

☐ McGovern/Shriver no-name pinback with oval portraits against flag background (Hake 10) 1½"; red, white, blue, black ...................... 3.00    5.00

☐ "Schenectady/McGovern/Shriver 1972" bluetone oval portraits with names in scroll below (Hake 11) 1½"; red, white, bluetone; New York item ..... 15.00    17.00

☐ "Vote For McGovern/Shriver"; silhouetted portraits (Hake 2003) 3¾"; blue, black, white ..... 4.00    6.00

## *Portrait Pinbacks*

CONGRESS

George McGovern from South Dakota served in the House from 1957–61; the Senate, from 1963–81.

Price Range

☐ "McGovern For Congress"; star and portrait just
above name (Hake 2284) 1¾"; red, white, blue;
1957 ...................................... 35.00     40.00

☐ "McGovern For Senator"; same design as above
with slight variation in portrait (Hake 2285) 1¾";
red, white, blue; 1963 ....................... 25.00     30.00

PRESIDENT

☐ "Come Home America/Elect McGovern in '72";
bull's-eye portrait (Hake 2011) 3½"; red, white,
blue, black ................................. 4.00     6.00

☐ Also 1¾" (Hake 2059) ...................... 3.00     5.00

☐ "George McGovern for President"; silhouetted
head between two stars (Hake 2019) 3"; red, white,
blue, black ................................. 3.00     5.00

☐ Also 1¾" (Hake 2064) ...................... 4.00     6.00

☐ "McGovern," left profile bleed off pin (Hake 2063)
1¾"; black, white .......................... 3.00     5.00

☐ Also 3½" (Hake 2014) ...................... 4.00     6.00

☐ "McGovern"; illustration of McGovern in quarter
profile (Hake 2058) 2¾"; white, brown, fleshtones,
gold ........................................ 4.00     6.00

### Slogan/Name Pinbacks

☐ "A President For The People/George McGov-
ern/Oklahoma" (Hake 2024) 3"; blue, white; Oklahoma item ................................. 6.00     8.00

☐ "Architects For McGovern," one of series of pinbacks that cited backing from every professional
and special interest group from "Advertising People" to "Wall St."; the manufacturer reran entire
set after the election, rendering pinbacks practically
valueless (Hake 2106) 1¾"; black, white ....... 1.00     2.00

☐ "Grass Roots McGovern Volunteers" (Hake 2079)
1¾"; blue, yellow .......................... 14.00     16.00

☐ "I Luv McGov," slogan inside starred heart shape
(Hake 2090) 1¾"; red, white, dark blue ........ 4.00     6.00

Price Range

☐ "Labor For McGovern/'72"; slogan inside large machine cog outline (Hake 2133) 1½"; yellow, black lithograph .......................... 3.00     5.00

☐ "McGovern" (Hake 2145) 1½"; white reversed out of black; one of scores of name pinbacks in which the *o* in "McGovern" is the peace symbol ...... 2.00     3.00

☐ "Let's Help Nixon *Out*" (Hake 2085) 1¾"; black, white, red ................................ 4.00     6.00

☐ "Texans For McGovern/Shriver"; white lettering against slanting red, blue stripes (Hake 2139) 1½"; red, white, blue .......................... 7.00     9.00

☐ " 'Those who have had a chance for four years and would not produce peace, should not be given another chance'—Richard Nixon, Oct. 9, 1968" (reminder of a broken campaign promise (Hake 23) 3"; black, white ........................... 4.00     6.00

## WILLIAM McKINLEY

William McKinley, Republican from Ohio, served in the House from 1877–84; 1885–91; Governor of Ohio, 1892–96. Elected 25th President of the U.S. in 1896 and 1901. He was assassinated in Buffalo in 1901 and succeeded by Teddy Roosevelt. McKinley's two campaigns ushered in the Golden Age of celluloid pinbacks. It also marked the first time posters, pennants, and novelties promoting a candidacy were mass produced. The popular slogan, "McKinley and the Full Dinner Pail," came to signify Republican prosperity.

Price Range

### *Advertising*

☐ Oval tray, 16" x 13"; horizontal, tin, full color; McKinley and Roosevelt jugate images surrounded by draped U.S. flag suspended at top of tray design by eagle's beak; also small view of White House in background. With advertising on surrounding panels ........................................ 250.00     300.00

☐ Without advertising; panels blank ............. 125.00     150.00

☐ Oval tray, 16" x 13"; vertical, tin, full color; bust portrait of McKinley; with advertising ......... 75.00     125.00

Matched white metal effigy cane heads of McKinley and Bryan, 1896 ($95–$110 each). Cleveland and Harrison, 1888, run $110–$125 each.

McKinley in Napoleon regalia with hand tucked into tunic; Toby mug ($175–$200). *(Frank Corbeil Collection)*

McKinley "Full Dinner Pail," glass pail with wire handle, tin cup/cap ($110–$125).

Three clever figural parade torches: McKinley dinner pail ($200–$250); W. H. Harrison log cabin ($250–$300); Benjamin Harrison hat ($150–$175).

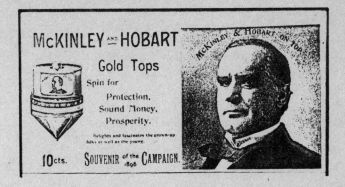

Advertisement for McKinley–Hobart Gibbs spinning top
($250–$275).

Advertisement for presidential
figural safes. McKinley (pictured)
is said to be scarcest of group of
six. Coin bank ($700–$800).

Price Range

☐ Rectangular tray with rounded corners; approx. 17″ x 14″; full-color cameo portraits of all presidents, from Washington through McKinley, with biographical data on top and bottom flanges; features advertising for W. S. Beamer Up-To-Date Shoes ...................................... 75.00  100.00

☐ Without advertising ......................... 50.00  75.00

☐ Coffee tin with paper label; approximately 2′ high; "McKinley Blend Coffee" by the O'Donohue Co.; 1900s; bust photo of McKinley inside filigree, surrounded by four stars in each corner of label; full color ...................................... 150.00  175.00

☐ Paper poster, 21″ x 29″; full color; Honest Long Cut Tobacco, "Presidential Possibilities," 1890; cameo bust portrait of McKinley appears in lower right-hand corner (one of 14 cameos of leading candidates from both parties); large chair appears in center of poster with package of Honest Long Cut on seat ....................................... 350.00  450.00

☐ Paper baggage tag, approx. 2½″ x 5″; McKinley bust portrait in field of simulated flag; "Compliments of the *Warren Daily Mirror*" appears in type between stripes; souvenir of Warren and Forest County, Pennsylvania, Republican excursion to McKinley's home in Canton, Ohio ............ 20.00  25.00

☐ Shell badge hanger, 5″ dia; bronze finish; portrait of McKinley in bas relief suspended from hanger of eagle with legend "Honest Dollar"; promotional giveaway .................................. 35.00  50.00

☐ Advertising pinback, ⅞″; black and white; bust portrait of McKinley; "Our Choice Roseberry Cigar" ................................... 55.00  65.00

☐ Advertising pinback, 1¼″ dia; Yellow Kid (Outcault cartoon character from *New York Journal*) peering through telescope; slogan "Looking For Better Times"; High Admiral cigarettes advertising giveaway; "N.I.T." (Not In Trust) appears on yellow nightshirt .............................. 15.00  20.00

**Price Range**

☐ Advertising pinback, 1¼″ dia; Yellow Kid appearing in Chinese regalia; slogan "Ain't I A Hot Idol. N.I.T."; High Admiral cigarettes giveaway .....    15.00     20.00

☐ Advertising ribbon, approx. 6″ x 2″; cloth; Sound Money Parade, *Frank Leslie's Popular Monthly,* New York City; 1896 giveaway ..............    35.00     45.00

☐ Advertising paper hanger, approx. 8″ dia; "Men Of The Hour," compliments of the Crane Ice Cream Co., McKinley bust portrait appears in circle at center of star, surrounded by 6 portraits of military heroes of the Spanish American War ..........    25.00     35.00

### Association and Club Items

During McKinley's "Front Porch" campaign in 1896, Republican national chairman Mark Hanna arranged for hundreds of delegations, representing farmers, workers, doctors, lawyers, trade associations, unions, and special interest groups, to visit the Canton, Ohio, homestead. Scores of buttons were issued to amass contributions and commemorate these visits. Similar buttons also appeared in the 1900 race.

PINBACKS

☐ R.R. Men's Sound Money Ass'n; Rochester, N.Y., 1900; photo of locomotive and tender (Hake 145) 1¼″; black on white .......................    50.00     65.00

☐ McKinley & Hobart Businessmen's National Campaign Committee; American flag pictured (Hake 147) ⅞″; red, white, blue, black .............    8.00     10.00

☐ Republican College League bust portrait of McKinley (Hake 3241) 1¼″; black, gold ............    20.00     25.00

☐ Wholesale Dry Goods Republican Club; McKinley bust portrait (Hake 3280) ⅞″; blue, black on white    25.00     30.00

☐ Woman's Republican Association of the U.S.; McKinley bust portrait (Hake 3281) ⅞″; black, red, white .......................................    45.00     55.00

☐ Wyoming Co. McKinley Club (Hake 3292) ⅞″; black on white ............................    20.00     25.00

☐ McKinley line drawing profile bust; porcelain disk (unlisted) 1¾″; multicolor ...................    110.00     125.00

Price Range

☐ McKinley "Rough Rider" (in uniform) (unlisted)
⅞"; multicolor .............................. 50.00 60.00

☐ McKinley–Hobart "Hide & Leather Sound Money
Association" (Hake 3344) (a similar button exists
for McKinley–TR; Hake 3345; Warner 330) ⅞";
brown, black on white ...................... 20.00 25.00

☐ McKinley Cudahy Packing Company Trans Mississippi Exposition premium; Uncle Sam and Miss
Liberty dancing; McKinley, flags above (unlisted)
2⅛"; multicolor ........................... 65.00 75.00

☐ National Steel Co., Ohio Works; bust portrait of
McKinley; 1900 (Hake 3225) 2"; black and white,
red, blue ................................... 45.00 55.00

## Autographs

☐ Land Grant, autographed document, McKinley,
Rutland, Vermont, January, 1898 ............ 150.00 200.00

☐ Cabinet photo, autographed in lower margin; Ward
Photographer, Mt. Vernon, Ohio, ca. 1895 ...... 250.00 300.00

## Canes, Umbrellas

CANES

Except where noted, all canes are approx. 33" long.

☐ McKinley bust on pedestal cane head; reads "Protection" and "Prosperity"; facsimile signature on
base; 3"; pewter; effigy image; Bryan match ..... 75.00 100.00

☐ McKinley bust with embossed name around neck;
3"; white metal; effigy image ................. 75.00 100.00

☐ McKinley flag cane; appears to be ordinary bamboo
cane, but a 15" pole with 9" x 16" glazed muslin
flag pulls out when tip is removed; Stars and stripes
with "McKinley-Hobart" running vertically at end
of flag; red, white, blue; black lettering; 38" long 350.00 400.00

☐ McKinley–Roosevelt bas-relief portraits on opposite sides of round cane head; approx. 2½"; white
metal ...................................... 100.00 125.00

Price Range

☐ Paper enameled cane with McKinley–Hobart portraits appearing vertically amid stars, stripes, and field of stars; bluetone photos with red, white, blue; wood part is also painted in patriotic colors, with round red knob at top; Bryan–Stevenson match — 75.00 — 100.00

☐ Tin noisemaker cane; "Patriotism, Prosperity Protection"; noisemaker attached to tin can horizontally at top to form handle; unpainted ......... — 100.00 — 110.00

☐ Torchlight cane; McKinley portrait lithographed on paper on tin; round knob at top of cane unscrews to reveal wick and fuel reservoir; blue, red, black — 150.00 — 200.00

**UMBRELLAS**

☐ McKinley–Hobart umbrella with images imprinted twice (four panels in all) with candidates' names above and slogans—"Protection, Sound Money" —below portraits; black, blue, red, white; cotton, metal, wooden handles ...................... — 250.00 — 300.00

☐ McKinley–Roosevelt umbrella similar to above, except that American flag is imprinted on remaining two panels and only candidates' names appear below portraits; red, white, blue, black ......... — 275.00 — 325.00

### *Cartoon/Pictorial Pinbacks*

☐ Anti-Bryan bust caricature; "In God We Trust, For the other 47 cents" (Hake 150) $\frac{7}{8}$"; black on white — 45.00 — 55.00

☐ Anti-Bryan "soup" kettle with Bryan's head popping out of it (Hake 297) $\frac{7}{8}$"; black on white ... — 75.00 — 85.00

☐ Bicycle, McKinley riding, wearing beanie, "To The White House"; "Gold" and "Silver" appear on wheels (Hake 298; Warner 201) $\frac{7}{8}$"; black and white with gold trim ...................... — 300.00 — 350.00

☐ Bicycle, tandem, with McKinley and Hobart riding; "Gold Didn't Get There July 7th. But Watch Us Take It There Nov. 3" (Hake 8; Warner 485) $1\frac{1}{4}$"; teal blue on white .......................... — 900.00 — 1000.00 plus

Price Range

☐ Bicycle, tandem; "McKinley and Hobart To Victory" (left facing) (Hake 283) 1¼"; black on white with gold rim .............................. 350.00  375.00

☐ Boy thumbing nose, "NIT" (Hake 152) ⅞"; black with orange-cast background ................ 15.00  20.00

☐ Broom with McKinley bust portrait in oval inset (Hake 296) advertises "McKinley Sweeper Cigars" ⅞"; black on white ........................ 55.00  65.00

☐ Bowling ball and tenpins with small bust portrait inset; "Canton For Me. Known the World Over City" (McKinley's home town and campaign headquarters in 1896 contest) (Hake 3246) 1¼"; black on white ................................... 75.00  85.00

☐ Capitol building, mechanical with small circular disk and bust of McKinley that appears in Capitol doorway when button atop pin is pressed; "A Sure Winner" (Hake 302) 1¼"; black on white (Bryan portrait disk replaces McKinley's when button is pressed again .............................. 175.00  200.00

☐ Carnation: "We Will Bloom Again For McKinley–Roosevelt"; 1900 (Hake 143) 1¼"; multicolor ... 15.00  20.00

☐ Coffin with voter lying in state; "Too Much Politics" (Hake 151) ⅞"; red and black on white ... 20.00  25.00

☐ Coffin with skeleton rising; "Too Much Politics"; stud (Hake 164); ⅞"; black on white .......... 20.00  25.00

☐ Cow, Mrs. O'Leary's; "Chicago Day Sound Money Parade" (Hake 141) 1¼"; black on white ...... 65.00  75.00

☐ Dinner pail rebus "Count on me [picture of McKinley] for a full [picture of dinner pail]" (Hake 69) 1900; 1¼"; dark brown on tan (has been reproduced) ..................................... 45.00  55.00

☐ Dinner pail variant with cornucopias flanking inset portrait of McKinley (Hake 293) 1900; 1¼"; brown on white ................................... 125.00  150.00

☐ Dinner pail; "McKinley, Roosevelt and You and more of the full dinner pail" 1900 (Hake 144) 1¼"; tan pail against orange circle on white ......... 60.00  75.00

**Price Range**

☐ Dinner pail with factory inset; "Do You Smoke? Yes, Since 1896. That's what McKinley Promises" (Hake 139) unusual, large (2") multicolor ...... 375.00 400.00

☐ Dinner pail, McKinley–Roosevelt jugate, "Full Dinner Bucket. Prosperity—Sound Money—Good Markets" (Hake 39) 1¼"; portraits in tan oval, buff-tone bucket on blue* .................... 35.00 45.00

☐ Dinner pail, McKinley–Roosevelt jugate (Hake 40) with same slogan as above; 1¼"; brown tone on buff, black background* ..................... 35.00 45.00

☐ Dinner pail, McKinley–Roosevelt, "Four Years of a Full Dinner Pail" (Hake 41) 1¼"; brown tone sketch of vertical pail ...................... 250.00 275.00

☐ Dinner pail, McKinley–Roosevelt (Hake 287) color variant of Hake 41; 1¼"; sepiatone ........... 200.00 210.00

☐ Dinner pail, "Protection Fills The Dinner Pail"; drawing of horizontal pail (Hake 3349) stud; ⅞"; black on white ........................... 35.00 45.00

*Note:* Over a dozen designs feature the solar eclipse theme, and all are as rare as the phenomenon itself. See also Bryan versions with positions reversed.

☐ Eclipse; McKinley portrait is in position to overshadow similar inset of Bryan among billowing clouds (Hake 295) "Eclipse Will be Total Nov. 6th. 1900"; 1¼"; black, pale blue on white ......... 500.00 550.00

☐ Eclipse; McKinley again partially obscures Bryan's inset portrait; "Partial Eclipse Will Be Total Nov. 6th, 1900 (Hake 68) 1¼"; sepiatone ........... 450.00 500.00

☐ Eclipse; large bust portrait of McKinley against backdrop of sun with rays emanating to edge of curl; small inset circle picturing Bryan over left shoulder; "Imaginary Eclipse Visible Only at Kansas Cy. July 4" (Hake 3232; Warner 215) issued after total solar eclipse May 28, 1900; 1½"; multicolor ...................................... 1000.00 plus

*Note:* Hake 39 and 40 dinner pail pinbacks are being reproduced.

Price Range

☐ Eclipse; variant of Hake 68; differences in type face and stylized sun's rays fanning around overlapping circle portraits (Hake 3237) $1\frac{1}{4}$"; dark brown on white ........................................ 500.00    550.00

☐ "Expansion"; McKinley and TR prevent Bryan from taking down Old Glory over Philipines (Hake unlisted) $1\frac{1}{4}$"; multicolor (only a few known) ... 1000.00 plus

☐ "Pro-Expansion"; McKinley is seated while Miss Liberty and Justice as robed figures stand at his side (Hake 299; Warner 224) $1\frac{1}{2}$"; multicolor ...... 800.00    900.00

☐ Also $\frac{7}{8}$" (Warner 505) ...................... 500.00    600.00

☐ Factory; McKinley oval inset against background of factory with smoking stacks; Statue of Liberty in New York harbor; "Protection–Expansion–Prosperity" (Hake 65; Warner 255) $1\frac{1}{4}$"; multicolor ...................................... 75.00    100.00

☐ Factory; McKinley bust portrait in center of solar disk with rays extended over factory lined with smoking stacks; "McKinley Prosperity"; (Hake 64) $1\frac{1}{4}$"; multicolor ............................ 65.00    75.00

☐ Flag; draped flags border row of gravestones of Spanish American War dead; adjoining panel shows factory and references to Depression in Cleveland's administration; large graphic *P* ("patriotism and prosperity") (Hake 140; Warner 231) Indiana Republican State Committee item; $2\frac{1}{8}$; multicolor ...................................... 200.00    225.00

☐ Imperialism; McKinley and Uncle Sam defending the country against invasion of Orientals; "Is This Imperialism? No blow has been struck except for liberty, humanity and money" (Hake 3258) $1\frac{1}{4}$"; multicolor ................................. 800.00    850.00

☐ Goldbug (one of many variations); "I'm a little goldbug" (Hake 205) $\frac{7}{8}$"; gold on black ....... 25.00    30.00

☐ McKinley in presidential chair, sitting on Bryan (see also Bryan match) (Hake 3279; Warner 488) $\frac{7}{8}$"; black and orange on white .............. 150.00    175.00

Price Range

☐ McKinley "Homestead"; Mac sits on front porch of Canton, Ohio, homestead (similar to Hake 292 but unlisted) $\frac{7}{8}$"; black on white photo . . . . . . . .    75.00    85.00

☐ McKinley "Homestead"; front porch sitting (Hake 292) $1\frac{1}{4}$"; sepiatone . . . . . . . . . . . . . . . . . . . . . . . .    175.00    185.00

☐ McKinley bust portrait on cardboard framed in brass rim (Hake 56) $3\frac{1}{2}$"; multicolor . . . . . . . . . .    45.00    55.00

☐ McKinley bust portrait with draped flag and laurel motif (Hake 49) 3"; red, white, black gold . . . . . .    35.00    45.00

☐ McKinley in oval inset surrounded by "Republicanism, Protection, Reciprocity, Solidarity, Expansion" (unlisted) $1\frac{1}{4}$"; sepiatone . . . . . . . . . . . . . . .    225.00    250.00

☐ McKinley profile stud; "Pennsylvania Will Head The Column To Victory, Nov. 3, 1896" (Hake 3229) 2"; sepiatone, with red, white, blue ribbon streamers; brass rim frame . . . . . . . . . . . . . . . . . .    20.00    25.00

☐ "My Hobby"; McKinley in cocked hat astride hobby horse; "My Hobby. A Winner" (Hake 290) 2"; multicolor . . . . . . . . . . . . . . . . . . . . . . . . . . . . .    1000.00 plus

☐ McKinley sitting on Bryan (see also Bryan match) (Hake 3279; Warner 488) $\frac{7}{8}$"; black and orange on white . . . . . . . . . . . . . . . . . . . . . . . . . . . . . . . . . . . .    150.00    175.00

☐ McKinley–Bryan? (donkey illustration) "When Shall We 3 Meet Again? (Hake unlisted) $\frac{7}{8}$"; black on white . . . . . . . . . . . . . . . . . . . . . . . . . . . . . . . . .    75.00    85.00

☐ Ohio Glorification; colorful Ohio scenic views blend with scrolls of state's native sons who became president–Hayes, Garfield, McKinley, Grant, Harrison (Hake unlisted) $2\frac{1}{4}$"; multicolor; 1900? . . . . . . . .    125.00    150.00

☐ Rose; "One Good Term Deserves Another" (Hake 156) $1\frac{1}{4}$"; red rose, black lettering on white . . . .    10.00    15.00

☐ Rough Riders; McKinley and Roosevelt riding tandem on horse, which bears face of Bryan and long ears; "Rough Riders" (Hake 3158; Warner 216) $1\frac{1}{4}$"; black on white . . . . . . . . . . . . . . . . . . . . . . .    550.00    600.00

☐ Satchel; "Rochester For McKinley"; initials C.T. appear on satchel (Hake 303) $1\frac{1}{4}$"; sepiatone . . .    85.00    100.00

Price Range

☐ Trans-Mississippi Exposition; McKinley seated at entrance in presidential chair greeting visitors; "Trans-Mississippi Exposition, 1898" (Hake unlisted; Warner 204) 1¼"; red, white, blue ...... 125.00 150.00

☐ Yellow Kid; cartoon character peers through telescope; "Looking For Better Times"; signed by Outcault; advertising premium for High Admiral cigarettes; Kid wears nightshirt with NIT written across middle (Hake 3264) 1¼; black and yellow 15.00 20.00

☐ Yellow Kid, cartoon character by Outcault, attired in Chinese costume; "Ain't I A Hot Idol. NIT"; High Admiral cigarettes premium (one in a series) (Hake 3265) ................................ 15.00 20.00

## *Ceramics*

### MUGS
☐ Two-handled McKinley–Hobart campaign mug; 1896; transfer pictures on two sides; 6"h; black on white; Bryan match ........................ 45.00 55.00

☐ "For Gold And Our Country's Honor" March 4, 1897, Inaugural mug; eagle perched on shield in clouds; 6"h; blue, gold, white ................ 100.00 125.00

### PITCHERS
☐ McKinley in Napoleon attire, Toby pitcher (he even has hand tucked inside tunic); enameled colors and excellent detail; 7"h; black, brown, yellow, red, blue, white, black .......................... 175.00 200.00

☐ McKinley as Napoleon, Toby pitcher variant; similar pose but in glazed green; also has been found in brown; 7"h ............................ 150.00 175.00

☐ Seated McKinley (Napoleon) in presidential chair; "McKinley Bill.—Hon. William McKinley"; 7½"h; multicolor; many consider this the ultimate Toby in the hobby ......................... 225.00 250.00

☐ McKinley cream pitcher; multicolor transfer of McKinley; 6"; white porcelain with gilded rim and handle; American flag transfer appears on reverse 45.00 55.00

Price Range

☐ McKinley–Hobart 1896 campaign pitcher; black transfer portraits with facsimile signatures; 10"h; ornate handle; black on white background (see Hake 3054) ............................... 150.00   175.00

☐ McKinley–Roosevelt 1900 campaign pitcher; identical to McKinley–Hobart as to shape and coloring 200.00   250.00

☐ McKinley–Hobart campaign pitcher; same images but handle has a dip in it; also smaller, 7"h .... 150.00   175.00

**PLATES**

☐ William McKinley three-quarters-view bust portrait transfer-print plate; approx. 9"; multicolored portrait against white background; 2" border of dark blue with gold filigree and trim; made by Knowles, Taylor and Knowles, East Liverpool, Ohio ...................................... 35.00   45.00

☐ William McKinley, same transfer print as above, surrounded by arrangement of red carnations; approx. 7"; white background with gold border stripe; marked Sevres ............................. 45.00   55.00

☐ McKinley–Hobart, irregular round plate; with transfer portraits of winner of 1896 race and signatures beneath; 9"; black on white background with gold rim trim; marked "Semi-Vitreous"; crown-topped trademark ......................... 45.00   55.00

☐ "Patriotism, Protection, Prosperity," famous McKinley 1896 campaign slogan in script under transfer portrait of McKinley; black on white background; 9"; "E.L.P. Co., Waco, china" ........ 55.00   65.00

☐ Straw hat or boater pin tray; milk glass; McKinley face pictured inside hat; made by McKee & Brothers, Pittsburgh; approx. 5"; white with gold hatband; Bryan match ........................ 65.00   75.00

☐ McKinley raised-bust portrait plate; Weller Pottery, Zanesville, Ohio; 7½"; blue; Parker match 65.00   75.00

☐ McKinley bas-relief profile portrait of McKinley; milk glass ribbon plate with Gothic border, McKinley's likeness in gold; also gold ribbon that intertwines in inner border open-weave loops; symbolic of Republicans favoring gold vs. silver in 1896 cam-

Price Range

paign; 9″; gold on white background; designed by David Barker for Canton Glass Co., Marion, Indiana ........................................ 25.00 35.00

☐ McKinley modified-scallop round plate; bust transfer portrait with signature and "1896" beneath; 7½″; reddish brown portrait; flourishes of gold around border; white background; maker unknown 45.00 55.00

☐ McKinley–Roosevelt 1900 Republican-slate milk glass plate; 5¼″; reddish-brown transfer; decal rim edging in green with round and heart-shaped loops; maker unknown (often the images are indistinct; among chinaware collectors, border is known as a "one-O-one") .............................. 35.00 45.00

☐ Ida McKinley modified octagon-shaped china plate; transfer portrait of "Mrs. McKinley" in oval border; one of series of six honoring presidents' wives; 6″ x 6″; multicolor portrait; white background; bears "Imperial China" marking ....... 15.00 20.00

☐ McKinley heavy ceramic plate; transfer portrait surrounded by garlands of flowers; 9¼″; probably a memorial item........................... 65.00 75.00

☐ McKinley lacy milk glass plate with transfer portrait under round center layer of clear glass; oval portrait is framed in blue paint; ca. 1900; 8¼″; blue, white background; gold outer rim ............. 85.00 95.00

☐ Blue-printed souvenir plate, McKinley's home; small cameo inset of McKinley appears along roof line; border of rose garlands; 9″; deep blue on white 25.00 35.00

☐ "Our Martyred Heroes"; oval portraits of Lincoln, Garfield, and McKinley with flags flanking elaborate scrollwork; 9″; multicolor portraits against olive green background in center; blue, red border stripes on white; issued soon after McKinley's assassination ................................. 45.00 55.00

☐ William McKinley memorial plate; modified scallop outline; biographical data under transfer portrait; 9″; black on white ..................... 25.00 35.00

Price Range

☐ McKinley souvenir china pin tray; portrait appears above picture of birthplace and president's signature; 6"l x 2"w; black on white .............. 20.00 25.00

☐ Royal Vienna porcelain plate with full-color hand-painted portrait of McKinley; artist signed Ahne; 9¾"; textured border in red, gold, blue, salmon, white ...................................... 1000.00 1100.00

*Note:* Vienna art tin trays issued ca. 1905 were inspired by and copied from earlier Royal Vienna porcelain, deemed much too expensive for the general populace. One of the few known to adopt a historical theme; most of them featured pretty girls.

☐ Scalloped candy dish; full-color McKinley portrait in center; approx. 7"; white with gold-tipped scalloping; probably of German manufacture ....... 55.00 65.00

☐ "President McKinley" bust portrait over crossed flags, black transfer in center; three pink, gold, and white floral shapes against Wedgwood blue background; approx. 9"; maker unknown ........... 75.00 85.00

☐ McKinley–Roosevelt jugate portraits inset in draped flags, eagle at top with wings spread; irregular round shape, approx. 9"; multicolor images against white background ................... 85.00 100.00

TILES

☐ Intaglio tiles of William McKinley and Garret Hobart; paper label; biographical data on reverse; 2¼" sq; teal blue; manufactured in 1896 by American Encaustic Tiling Co., Ltd., Zanesville, Ohio; Bryan and Sewall matches:

☐ McKinley ................................. 25.00 35.00

☐ Hobart .................................. 30.00 40.00

☐ "Our Next President"; McKinley campaign tile; bust portrait of McKinley in bas-relief profile; 3½"; pale blue ................................. 45.00 55.00

☐ McKinley polychrome tile; familiar three-quarters view found on numerous pottery and porcelain items; 6" sq; multicolor...................... 35.00 45.00

*Ephemera*                                              Price Range

☐ Interchangeable cutouts; art supplement from *Boston Globe,* August 23, 1896; full-color portrait cutouts of William McKinley and William Jennings Bryan, and their respective running mates, Mr. Hobart and Mr. Sewall, assembled by certain combinations of lettered pieces; multicolored . . . . . . . . . .      35.00      40.00

☐ Gridiron Club menu; "Has The Gridiron Club A Pull? Well We Should Smile!"; cartoon of McKinley dressed as Napoleon on a howdah atop the GOP (white) elephant (Hake 3009); size? . . . . . . . . . . . .     35.00      45.00

☐ Paper hat; August 9, 1896, supplement to Philadelphia *Press;* "Republican Candidate For President, William McKinley of Ohio" (Hake 3012) red, white, blue, black . . . . . . . . . . . . . . . . . . . . . . . . . . .     45.00      55.00

☐ Pro-McKinley, anti-Bryan facsimile paper currency; Bryan bill reads: "Worth 53 cents only"; McKinley bill reads: "Worth 100 cents One Dollar In Gold" (Hake 3036) 6"w x 2½"h; black on white; each . . . . . . . . . . . . . . . . . . . . . . . . . . . . . . . . . . . . .     15.00      20.00

## *Golden Era Political Pinbacks*

The first celluloid pinback manufacturer was Whitehead & Hoag of Newark, New Jersey. The design of the button that changed the whole impetus of political collecting was simplicity itself; it embodied a thin metal disk covered with a paper picture with a thin layer of celluloid, both of which were curled around the rim of the disk and secured by a metal ring. This ring also held a spring wire pin for attaching the button to the lapel. The final patent was filed March 23, 1896, and issued just four months later—in time for the biggest deluge of campaign lapel devices in history.

By the end of the Golden Era, over two hundred companies were manufacturing political pinbacks. The following designs were featured over a number of campaigns beginning with McKinley-Bryan in 1896 and a few overlapped into the 1920s. Whitehead & Hoag, the Baltimore Badge Co. of Baltimore, Maryland, Bastian Brothers of Rochester, New York, and Scovill Mfg. Company of Waterbury, Connecticut, were producers of some of the most vibrant art deco designs pictured on the following pages. Note in many cases that the popularity of the candidates and their relative availability come into play here, leading to some surprising price fluctuations.

Pictorial design—patriotic bow.
*(Sketch by Barbara Smullin, Hancock, NH)*

|  | Price | Range |
|---|---:|---:|
| **1900** | | |
| ☐ McKinley–Roosevelt jugate (Hake 57) $7/8''$ ...... | 10.00 | 12.00 |
| ☐ Same as above (Hake 26) $1\frac{1}{4}''$ ............... | 15.00 | 20.00 |
| ☐ Same as above; $2''$ ......................... | 20.00 | 25.00 |
| ☐ Same as above; local trigate (Hake 132) $1\frac{1}{4}''$ .... | 40.00 | 50.00 |
| ☐ Bryan–Stevenson jugate (Hake 54) $1\frac{1}{4}''$ ........ | 20.00 | 25.00 |
| ☐ Same as above (pose variant) $1\frac{1}{4}''$ ............ | 20.00 | 25.00 |
| ☐ Same as above; $7/8''$ ........................ | 15.00 | 20.00 |
| **1904** | | |
| ☐ Roosevelt single portrait variant (ribbon completely encircles pinback (Hake 64) $2''$ ............... | 50.00 | 75.00 |
| ☐ Roosevelt single portrait cello fob variant; $1\frac{1}{2}''$ .. | 50.00 | 60.00 |
| ☐ Parker–Davis jugate (Hake 3017) $1\frac{1}{4}''$ ........ | 70.00 | 80.00 |
| **1928** | | |
| ☐ Smith–Robinson jugate (Hake 2) $7/8''$ .......... | 100.00 | 125.00 |
| ☐ Same as above (color variant: red, white, blue, gold) (Hake 3) $7/8''$ ............................. | 75.00 | 95.00 |

Pictorial design—draped flag–linked ovals. *(Sketch by Barbara Smullin, Hancock, NH)*

| 1904 | Price Range | |
|---|---|---|
| ☐ Parker–Davis jugate (Hake 17) 1¼" ........... | 50.00 | 60.00 |
| ☐ Same as above (Hake 8) 1½" ................. | 85.00 | 95.00 |
| ☐ Parker–White gas engine advertising jugate (Hake 3013) 1½" ............................... | 225.00 | 250.00 |
| ☐ Roosevelt–Fairbanks jugate (Hake 6) 1½" ...... | 70.00 | 80.00 |
| ☐ Same as above (Hake 27) 1¼" ................ | 35.00 | 45.00 |
| 1908 | | |
| ☐ Bryan–Kern jugate (Hake 79) 1½" ............ | 130.00 | 150.00 |
| ☐ Taft–Sherman jugate (Hake 2) 2" ............. | 185.00 | 200.00 |

Pictorial design—Miss Liberty with ovals within dress folds. *(Sketch by Barbara Smullin, Hancock, NH)*

| 1904 | Price Range | |
|---|---|---|
| ☐ Roosevelt–Fairbanks jugate (Hake 24) 1¼ " ..... | 50.00 | 65.00 |
| ☐ Same as above (Hake 7) 1½ " ................. | 150.00 | 175.00 |
| ☐ Same as above (Hake 3131) 2" ................. | 115.00 | 135.00 |
| ☐ Parker–Davis jugate (Hake 14) 1¼ " .......... | 60.00 | 70.00 |
| ☐ Same as above (advertising pinback for Fountain Beer & Billiard Parlor) (Hake 15) 1½ " ........ | 125.00 | 150.00 |
| **1908** | | |
| ☐ Bryan–Kern jugate (Hake 77) 2" .............. | 215.00 | 235.00 |
| ☐ Variant (Hake 102) 1¼ " ..................... | 225.00 | 250.00 |
| ☐ Taft–Sherman jugate (Hake 20) 1¼ " .......... | 125.00 | 150.00 |

Pictorial design—Miss Liberty bust figure with arms upraised. *(Sketch by Barbara Smullin, Hancock, NH)*

| 1904 | | |
|---|---|---|
| ☐ Roosevelt–Fairbanks jugate (Hake 45) ⅞ " ...... | 30.00 | 50.00 |
| ☐ Same as above (Hake 19) 1¼ " ................ | 50.00 | 60.00 |
| ☐ Same as above; Zig-Zag Candies advertising pinback (Hake 16) 1¼ " ........................ | 160.00 | 175.00 |
| ☐ Roosevelt–local jugate (Hake 188) 1¼ " ........ | 35.00 | 50.00 |
| ☐ Parker–Davis jugate (Hake 37) ⅞ " ............ | 30.00 | 35.00 |
| ☐ Same as above (Hake 26) 1¼ " ................ | 50.00 | 60.00 |
| **1908** | | |
| ☐ Taft–Sherman jugate (Hake 41) ⅞ " ........... | 45.00 | 55.00 |
| ☐ Same as above (Hake 3127) 1¼ " .............. | 85.00 | 100.00 |
| **1912** | | |
| ☐ Wilson–Marshall jugate (Hake 19) ⅞ " ........ | 80.00 | 95.00 |
| ☐ Same as above (Hake 3080) 1¼ " .............. | 185.00 | 200.00 |

Pictorial design—filigree-shield with ovals. *(Sketch by Barbara Smullin, Hancock, NH)*

| | Price Range | |
|---|---|---|
| **1904** | | |
| ☐ Roosevelt–Fairbanks jugate (Hake 22) 1¼" ..... | 35.00 | 45.00 |
| ☐ Same as above (Hake 8) 1½" ................ | 75.00 | 100.00 |
| ☐ Same as above (Hake 3137) 2" ............... | 80.00 | 90.00 |
| ☐ Parker–Davis jugate (Hake 3009) 2" .......... | 100.00 | 125.00 |
| ☐ Same as above (Hake 3016) 1¼" ............. | 50.00 | 75.00 |
| ☐ Watson–Tibbles (Peoples Party) jugate (Hake PGP3) ⅞" ................................. | 250.00 | 275.00 |
| **1912** | | |
| ☐ Roosevelt–Johnson jugate (Hake 59) ⅞" ....... | 450.00 | 475.00 |
| ☐ Taft–Sherman jugate (Hake 39) ⅞" ........... | 25.00 | 30.00 |
| ☐ Taft–Lincoln jugate (Hake 30) 1½" .......... | 85.00 | 100.00 |
| ☐ Wilson–Marshall jugate (Hake 14) ⅞" ........ | 20.00 | 25.00 |
| ☐ Same as above (Hake 4) 1¼" ................ | 175.00 | 200.00 |
| ☐ Bryan–Kern jugate (Hake 104) 1¼" .......... | 100.00 | 120.00 |
| ☐ Same as above (Hake 109) ⅞" ............... | 20.00 | 25.00 |
| ☐ Roosevelt–LaFollette jugate* (unlisted) 1¼" .... | 45.00 | 55.00 |

*Often attributed as a 1912 campaign item, but in all likelihood it was issued in 1904, when LaFollette was running on the Republican ticket for governor of Wisconsin.

## *Inaugural Pinbacks*

Price Range

☐ McKinley Inaugural brass badge with hanger; 1897; arched bar bears raised letters; "Solvent"; eagle atop hanger with scroll; "Inaugural"; bust portrait of McKinley appears in a diamond-shaped pattern (Hake unlisted) 3"l; brass finish . . . . . . . . . . . . . . .      25.00      35.00

☐ McKinley bust portrait outlined by gold filigree and cluster of ribbons against backdrop of large oval badge; "McKinley" and "Roosevelt" in gold letters on streamers (Hake 3220) 5" x 3"; multicolor; the most dramatic of all McKinley inaugurals . . . . . .      225.00     250.00

☐ McKinley brass field military hat; "March 4, 1901" (unlisted in Hake) approx 2"; brass finish . . . . . .      25.00      35.00

☐ McKinley portrait framed by laural leaves; "Inauguration 1897"; pictorial of parade moving down Pennsylvania Avenue to Capitol (Hake 3218) 1¾"; on bar with chain; multicolor . . . . . . . . . . . . . . . .      45.00      55.00

☐ McKinley bust portrait of president conjoined with Garrett Hobart profiled in bas relief as brass hanger attached to bar with red, white, blue ribbons; "Republican Victory Souvenir"; final electoral returns are printed on reverse cardboard insert; "March 4, 1897" stamped on metal bar (Hake 3129) 5" dia. hanger; brass finish . . . . . . . . . . . . . . . . . . . . . . . .      75.00      85.00

☐ McKinley–Hobart jugate Inauguration pinback; "March 4th, 1897" (Hake 284) ⅞"; black on white      10.00      15.00

## *Jugates*

McKINLEY–HOBART—1896

☐ Crossed furled flags flank American shield above classic oval settings for portraits of McKinley and Hobart (Hake 281; Warner 199); arguably the most stunningly graphic jugate from the 1896 contest; 1½"; red, white, blue, black, gray . . . . . . . . . . . . .      200.00     250.00

☐ "Daily News is for McKinley–Hobart. Are You?" (Hake 19); ⅞"; red, dark blue on white . . . . . . . .      30.00      35.00

☐ "Honest Money and Protection"; shield with disk hanger (2" dia) (Hake 3138); 4"l; red, white, blue, black . . . . . . . . . . . . . . . . . . . . . . . . . . . . . . . . . .      75.00      85.00

Price Range

☐ "Our Choice," McKinley–Hobart mechanical; push lever at top of disk to switch party allegiance to Bryan–Sewell (unlisted) $1\frac{1}{4}$″; sepia bust images on aluminum ............................... 85.00    100.00

☐ "Republican Phalanx," McKinley and Hobart (Hake 9) $1\frac{1}{4}$″; black on white ................ 45.00    55.00

☐ "Sound Money"; McKinley–Hobart with Minuteman image in lower half of button (Hake 3158) $1\frac{1}{4}$″; black on white ........................ 100.00    110.00

☐ "Sound Money and Protection"; brass pin with conjoining profiles in bas relief; slogan appears in raised letters (unlisted) $2\frac{1}{2}$″; brass finish ............. 20.00    25.00

☐ Star; McKinley–Hobart bust portraits on die-cut star-shaped cardboard pinback (unlisted); red, white, blue .................................. 25.00    35.00

☐ Wheelman's Club; bicycle wheel motif (Hake 282); small portrait cameos in black against spokes of wheel and flag design; one of the premier Wheelman specimens; $1\frac{1}{4}$″; red, white, blue, black .... 125.00    150.00

McKINLEY–ROOSEVELT—1900

☐ Capitol building forms backdrop for jugate portraits of McKinley and TR (Hake 289; Warner 219) $1\frac{1}{2}$″; sepiatone .................................... 300.00    325.00

☐ Eagle and Rough Rider with cameo photos of McKinley and Roosevelt (Hake 23); red, white, blue, black with gold rim and trim ................. 100.00    125.00

☐ Musical notes; scale of notes in goldenrod color are integral part of center of button that frames jugate portraits; draped flags appear at top and bottom (Hake unlisted; Warner 217) $1\frac{1}{2}$″; red, white, blue, black, goldenrod; companion to horizontal oval jugate featuring McKinley and TR (Warner 504) .. 600.00    650.00

☐ Musical notes, oval format (Warner 504) $1\frac{1}{2}$″ x 1″; same colors as above ........................ 400.00    450.00

☐ Republican Club of Princeton University jugates pop out of Princeton coat of arms (shield) (Hake 38; Warner 218) $1\frac{1}{4}$″; school colors of orange and black with white background behind portraits ... 350.00    400.00

**Price Range**

☐ Rough Rider; split images of McKinley and Roosevelt, the latter wearing familiar Rough Rider hat
(Hake 288) 1¼"; sepiatone .................. 100.00   110.00

☐ Shield with large images within outline; (unlisted)
1¾"; multicolor with black tassel ............. 65.00   75.00

☐ Tied Bow; red, white, and blue ribbon tied in large
bow above portraits (Hake 26) 1¼"; red, white,
blue, black against gold background ........... 10.00   12.00
    Also appeared in 2" size ($15–$20).* An interest-
ing variant, 4" dia ($20–$25) anchors many TR collections.

McKINLEY–LINCOLN
☐ "Maintain The Flag; For Lincoln. For McKinley";
oval portraits of both separated by furled flag (Hake
291) 1¼"; black on white..................... 100.00   110.00

## *Memorial Pinbacks*

William McKinley was assassinated while attending the opening of the
Pan-American Exposition in Buffalo, New York, on September 6, 1901. He
died on September 14.

☐ "I Have Contributed To The Memorial. Have
You?" (Hake 268) 1¼"; black and white ....... 10.00   12.00

☐ "In Memorium"; McKinley portrait against gold
background with black border (Hake 270) 1¼";
gold, black, white .......................... 8.00   10.00

☐ "God's Will Be Done"; Sept. 14, 1901 (Hake 274)
1¼"; black portrait on white; black ribbon attached   8.00   10.00

☐ "President McKinley Assassinated. It is God's
Way. His will be done"; oval portrait of the fallen
president inset in large buffalo; below are two views
of Temple of Music and Williams House at Pan-
American Exposition. "Souvenir of Pan American
Exposition" (obviously hastily converted to memo-
rial piece) (Hake 3224) 6"; multicolor with easel   100.00   125.00

*This size known to be reproduced.

|  | Price Range | |
|---|---|---|
| ☐ Lincoln, Garfield, McKinley trigate; "Our Martyrs"; oval portraits of three assassinated presidents (Hake 269) 2"; black on white | 20.00 | 25.00 |
| ☐ "Where Our President Fell"; view of Temple of Music; (Hake 279) 1¼"; black on white | 10.00 | 12.00 |

## Multigates

|  | | |
|---|---|---|
| ☐ McKinley–Hobart–Roscoe Conkling; New York item (unlisted) 1¼"; black on white | 125.00 | 135.00 |
| ☐ McKinley–Roosevelt–Van Sant; Minnesota State Republican League (Hake 126) 1¼"; red and black with white lettering | 35.00 | 45.00 |
| ☐ McKinley–Frink–Roosevelt (Hake 127) 1¼"; black with names reversed in white | 35.00 | 45.00 |
| ☐ McKinley–Roosevelt–Tanner (John Tanner was candidate for governor of Illinois (Hake 132) 1¼"; red, white, blue, black (variant of several bow-ribbon McKinley–Roosevelt jugates) | 40.00 | 50.00 |
| ☐ McKinley–Roosevelt–Van Sant–Morris; Minnesota State Republican League (Hake 128) 1¼"; red, white, blue, black with gold background | 80.00 | 90.00 |
| ☐ McKinley–Washington–Grant–Lincoln; "The Right Men In The Right Place" (unlisted) 2"; multicolor | 150.00 | 175.00 |
| ☐ McKinley and his cabinet; President McKinley in center surrounded by all seven members of his cabinet in 1900, including John Hay and Elihu Root (Hake 3211; Warner 514); a unique motif; 3"; red, white, cream | 100.00 | 125.00 |
| ☐ McKinley and military leaders from Spanish American War, 1898, Admiral Sampson, Major Generals Miles and Shafter; battleship, sabers, flags depicted (Hake 3262) multicolor | 45.00 | 55.00 |
| ☐ Souvenir multigate; Peace Jubilee, Oct. 18, 19, 1898, Chicago; McKinley, Roosevelt, Dewey, and two other war leaders; "We Did It" (Hake 3263) multicolor | 45.00 | 55.00 |

*Noisemakers* **Price Range**

☐ Parade horn; "Protection To American Industry";
papier-mâché figural bust at front of horn depicting
McKinley in cocked hat and rest of Napoleonic
garb; 9"h x 14"l; black, blue, white . . . . . . . . . . .    250.00    275.00

☐ Parade horn, tin; "Patriotism, Protection, Prosperity"; embossed; 4½"; tin finish; also appeared in
larger size . . . . . . . . . . . . . . . . . . . . . . . . . . . . . . .    45.00    55.00

*Posters*

☐ "No Lowering Of The Flag. Full Dinner Pails";
McKinley–Roosevelt jugate bust portraits divided
by dominant design of draped flag that goes full
length of poster and forms a symbolic U.S. in the
bottom fold; 28" x 18"; multicolor . . . . . . . . . . . .    175.00    200.00

☐ "McKinley Was Right. 1900 Prosperity. Prosperity
at Home. Prestige Abroad. Sound Money"; Mc-
Kinley and Roosevelt stand on platform beneath
flag that reads: "One Flag; One Country"; bleak
scene of 1896 poverty and Depression under Cleveland pictured in upper left; lower right shows populace clamoring to embrace McKinley's policies;
bright sun on the horizon is topped by "Prosperity"; one of the classic campaign posters of any era;
size variable; multicolor . . . . . . . . . . . . . . . . . . . .    250.00    300.00

☐ "The Administration's Policies Have Been Kept.
The American Flag Has Not been Planted In Foreign Soil. To Acquire More Territory But For Humanity's Sake"—McKinley, July 12, 1900; Liberty
cap above draped flags and jugate portraits of
McKinley–Roosevelt; contrasts hard times of 1896
under Cleveland (at left of poster) vs. prosperous
times under McKinley in 1900; size variable; multi-
color . . . . . . . . . . . . . . . . . . . . . . . . . . . . . . . . . . . . .    250.00    300.00

☐ "McKinley Was Right In 1896"; quote about opening mills to American labor vs. opening mills to foreign silver; shows McKinley welcoming workers to

Price Range

factory, while Bryan is off to side greeting foreigners dumping silver at the mint; 34" x 47"; black, white, red; 1900 race ............................. 550.00 600.00

☐ "The Foolish Calf. A Message To Labor"; cartoon of farmer standing in middle of road with a mother cow while her calf runs away with a bellowing steer (the moral being that the calf was steered away from the full dinner pail and will be sorry later when suppertime comes); a reminder to voters of the hard times of 1896 under Cleveland and the Democrats and how McKinley brought prosperity; 30" x 24"; black on white; 1900 campaign ...... 300.00 350.00

☐ "The Tariff Is An Issue"; circular portraits of McKinley–Hobart; cartoon of Miss Liberty clad in armor with sword and shield, labeled "Protection"; contrasts busy factories, shipping centers vs. idle mills and lines of unemployed workers; 36" x 27"; black on white ............................ 450.00 500.00

☐ "Prosperity At Home, Prestige Abroad"; American flag bleeds off poster; eagle-topped jugate portraits of McKinley–Roosevelt appear on slant in the stripes area just to right of blue field; multicolor 200.00 250.00

☐ "McKinley. Good Times Coming!"; rooster (obviously McKinley) crowing as it stands atop the mutilated Democratic losing rooster; brown on buff woodcut; size variable; probably 1896 race; also appeared as ribbon ........................... 350.00 400.00

☐ "My Friends We Shall Have Prosperity With Full Protection, Promise Me"; eagle and draped flags with shield that reads "Honest Money"; McKinley stands on platform, "The People's Champion," with crowds of supporters raising their arms proclaiming, "Our Choice"; sunrise appears to right of McKinley's shoulder; 22" x 33½"; red, white, blue, black, yellow; 1896 race; also issued as a textile 500.00 550.00

☐ "Yours Very Truly"; jugate poster of McKinley–Hobart, with facsimile autographs below; 18" x 25"; black on white ........................ 40.00 50.00

Price Range

☐ William and Edith McKinley; conjoining photographs facing each other in profile; 10" x 14"; black on white under glass; appeared as both poster and print ...................................... 100.00   125.00

### Sewing and Grooming Novelties

☐ Pair of scissors with embossed portraits of William & Edith McKinley; 7"h; brass finish (TR and wife match)................................... 45.00   55.00

☐ William McKinley napkin holder; cello-layered button portrait of McKinley on engraved metal, spring-loaded ring; "Pat. July 1900, J. Frame, Toledo, O" 2¼"; black and white portrait; silver finish 25.00   35.00

☐ "A Clean Sweep" comb and brush set; a metal comb pictures McKinley likeness with laurel leaves frame; reads: "Our Next President"; comb clips on hair brush; approx. 3½"h x 4"w ............. 45.00   55.00

☐ "Honest Money" pin cushion; 2¼" wood base topped by cushion; McKinley's likeness appears on one square of base; "For President. William McKinley of Ohio" ........................... 55.00   65.00

☐ McKinley pedestal bust soap effigy figure (see also McKinley soap babies under "Toys," 3½"h; tan to amber color ............................... 55.00   65.00

### Shell Badges and Hangers

☐ Elephant's head with curled trunk (Hake 226) 1¼"l; gilded brass .......................... 75.00   85.00

☐ Elephant stick pin with "G.O.P." embossed on side (Hake 225) 1¾"l; gilded brass ............... 15.00   20.00

☐ Elephant mechanical with paper portraits of McKinley–Hobart; blanket snaps open on hinges; clasp opens at girth (Hake 228) 1"l; gilded; black photos ................................... 50.00   75.00

☐ Elephant with McKinley riding atop, "G.O.P." on blanket (Hake 229) 1"w; gilded brass; black blanket with reverse lettering ....................... 45.00   55.00

Price Range

☐ Gold bug; gilded wire with black bust portrait of McKinley on body (Hake 186) 2½"h; gilded steel; black photo ............................... 40.00    45.00

☐ Gold bug; short-legged bug with bas-relief bust of McKinley embossed at top of body (Hake 187) 3"h; gilded brass ............................... 35.00    40.00

☐ Gold bug, finely detailed but without identification (Hake 188) 1½"h; gilded brass .............. 12.00    15.00

☐ Eagle with gold coin processional hanger; "Vote with the Rough Riders"; bas relief of Teddy Roosevelt Rough Rider on horseback at San Juan Hill; cardboard on reverse with advertisement from newspaper (Hake 301) 5"; gilded brass ......... 125.00    150.00

☐ Eagle with gold coin with bas relief of McKinley bust profile; "McKinley For Prosperity"; bar suspended from eagle reads: "Honest Dollar" (Hake 3221) 5"; gilded brass ...................... 50.00    60.00

☐ Elephant head metal disk, "Capital—Labor—G.O.P."; mechanical; opens to red and yellow disks, one with cartoon of TR riding broncho. "He never was thrown"; other disk has line drawing of McKinley; "His policy brings prosperity" (Hake 3122) 1¼"; die cut; gray; red, yellow, black .... 150.00    175.00

☐ Frying pan stickpin with McKinley bas-relief profile (unlisted) 1"; gilded brass ................ 25.00    35.00

☐ Flag, hand-held mechanical, dimensional; unfurls to reveal McKinley–Hobart portraits (Hake 3106) 1¾"w; red, white, blue, gold ................ 100.00    125.00

☐ Variant has flag without hand that, when flipped, reveals words: "Give Us Mack or Business Will Go To Hell" (unlisted) ........................ 110.00    125.00

☐ Bicycle, die-cut shell with circular hanger containing McKinley–Hobart paper photos; scroll bar (Hake 3105) ............................... 150.00    175.00

☐ Bicycle, die-cut, pedaled by "Hanna"; small inset bust portraits of McKinley and Hobart in wheels; "White House—4 Years" along crossbar (Hake 230) 1"; gray, blue, brass .................... 250.00    300.00

Price Range

☐ Bicycle, riderless, die-cut; McKinley and Hobart portraits in wheels (Hake 231) 1″; black, orange, brass trim .................................. 100.00 125.00

☐ Broom, die-cut with ambrotype portraits of McKinley, Hobart (Hake 233) 5″h; sepia portraits; brass 70.00 80.00

☐ Broom with "Gold You Say Bryan" slogan inscribed (Hake 222); 2″h; gilded brass .......... 25.00 35.00

☐ Dust pan stickpin with paper insert portrait of McKinley (Hake 215) ¾″w; gilded brass .......... 25.00 35.00

☐ Eagle, gold medal hanger on stickpin; mechanical (Hake 216) 1¼″ medal; copper-colored brass ... 30.00 35.00

☐ Eagle, mechanical with silver bug in beak; wings flutter and when open reveal candidate's paper portraits inside (Hake 224) 1½″h; gilded brass with sepia portraits ............................. 235.00 260.00

☐ Elephant carrying donkey in trunk (Hake 227) 1½″l; gilded brass; donkey, gray ............. 30.00 40.00

☐ Gold nugget—"Gold Basis" (Hake 239) ¾″; die-cut; gilded brass; black lettering ............. 10.00 15.00

☐ Hat; McKinley's familiar wide-brim military hat; dimensional (Hake 238) 1″w; gilded brass with red and white shield .......................... 10.00 15.00

☐ Hat attachment; McKinley–Hobart oval jugates on band (Hake 7) 5″w; gilded tin with black lettering and portraits .............................. 50.00 60.00

☐ Lunch pail with McKinley bas-relief bust portrait; embossed lettering: "Full Dinner Pail" (Hake 236) 1½″h; gilded brass ........................ 45.00 55.00

☐ Money bag; "$ Sound Money" with ribbon and small (ballot box?) hanger containing embossed lettering: "Protection Bills"; dimensional (Hake 221) 50.00 60.00

☐ Horseshoe; "He's All Right. Who?"; mechanical; opens to paper bust portrait of McKinley (Hake 3123); stickpin 1½″h; gilded brass ............ 60.00 70.00

☐ Cocked hat à la Napoleon; stud pin (Hake 3067) ⅜″; gilded brass; several variants, some of which bear imprinting: "Protection" ................. 15.00 20.00

Price Range

☐ Gold bug horse blanket pin (Hake 204) 6"h; copper-color brass .................................. 45.00   55.00

☐ Gold bug mechanical dimensional with wings that fold back into body; paper photos of McKinley–Hobart on wings (Hake 189) 1¼"l; gilded brass (there are any number of variants of nonmechanical gold bugs from McKinley's 1896 race (see Hake 190–212), including stick pins and lapel studs as well as shell pins ........................... 50.00   60.00

☐ Gold bug brooch (Hake 198) 1"; red, blue, white, gilt ......................................... 35.00   45.00

☐ Gold bug, celluloid picture (1¼") on back of dimensional beetle (Hake 3042) 3"l; gilded brass; black photo .............................. 85.00   95.00

☐ Gold bug on bicycle, stickpin (Hake unlisted) ¾"w; gilded brass .............................. 50.00   60.00

☐ Liberty head coin stickpin (Hake 234) 1"; copper   20.00   25.00

☐ Pig, "Sound Money"; gold coin attached to pig's tail (Hake 213) 1¼"w; copper; pig is silver (see Bryan match)....................................... 60.00   75.00

☐ Presidential chair; McKinley in chair atop Bryan (Hake 237) ¾"h; gilded brass stickpin ......... 50.00   75.00

☐ Rose; cloth brooch with McKinley–TR paper portraits in rose bud (Hake 3104) 5"h; red, white, black   65.00   75.00

☐ Shield, die-cut hanger; paper McKinley inset photo within embossed Capitol dome (unlisted) 1¼"; enameled brass; red, white, blue ............. 45.00   55.00

☐ Yellow Kid, die-cut enameled stud (Hake 3061) ½"h; black, yellow enamel .................. 75.00   85.00

☐ Skeleton, mechanical stick pin; "16 to 1" on shield, which flips to reveal McKinley paper photo; 1896 (Hake 232; Warner 202) 1½" x ¾"; white on gold metal; black and white photo (one of the most desirable of McKinley shell mechanicals) ........... 400.00   425.00

## Slogan Buttons and Studs

☐ "Democrat? NIT" (Hake 153) ⅞"; blue on white   6.00   8.00

☐ "Good Roads" (Hake 161) ⅞"; gold on black ...   6.00   8.00

Price Range

| | | |
|---|---:|---:|
| ☐ "Hello Central, Give Me McKinley" (Hake 3367) ⅞" orange | 12.00 | 15.00 |
| ☐ "I Am A Gold Bug. But No Humbug"; enameled stud (Hake 3062) ½"; white, black | 35.00 | 45.00 |
| ☐ "I Am For Gold" (Hake 177) ⅞"; black on white | 6.00 | 8.00 |
| ☐ "I Am A Democrat. But Will Vote For McKinley"; stud (Hake 178) ⅞"; black and white | 6.00 | 8.00 |
| ☐ "I Am For Sound Money. Are You?" (Hake 159) ⅞" black on white | 5.00 | 6.00 |
| ☐ "In McKinley We Trust, In Bryan We Bust" (Hake 142) 1¼"; black and white | 6.00 | 8.00 |
| ☐ "In McKinley We Trust, To Keep Our Machines Free Of Rust" (Hake 160) ⅞"; black on white | 6.00 | 8.00 |
| ☐ "McKinley Button. Made In The United States" (Hake 3348) stud; ⅞"; black on white | 12.00 | 15.00 |
| ☐ "McKinley Takes The Whole Shooting Match" (Hake 173) stud; ⅞"; black on orange | 6.00 | 8.00 |
| ☐ "M-C Kin-Ley Sis-Boom-Ah, Hobart"; High Admiral cigarette premium (Hake 148) ⅞"; black on white | 6.00 | 8.00 |
| ☐ "Me And McKinley Are In It; Chew Faultless Gum"; premium (Hake 3364) ⅞"; black on white | 10.00 | 12.00 |
| ☐ "Open Mills Not Mints" (Hake 169) stud; ⅞"; black on white | 10.00 | 12.00 |
| ☐ "Sound Money & Protection"; enameled stud; O'Hara Watch Dial Co. (Hake 182) ⅞"; black and white with gold rim | 15.00 | 20.00 |
| ☐ "16 To 1 Means 0 To 8" (Hake 3362) ⅞"; black and white | 12.00 | 15.00 |
| ☐ "Silver Is Good, But Gold Better" (Hake 3340); enameled stud; O'Hara Watch Dial Co.; ⅞"; black on white; gold rim | 55.00 | 65.00 |
| ☐ "The Money We Want" Liberty-head coin rebus; stud (Hake 174) ⅞"; gold on black | 12.00 | 15.00 |

Price Range

☐ "Well I Guess"; mechanical celluloid; die-cut name "McKinley" in gold, pops up at top of button (Hake 304) $1\frac{1}{4}$"; black on white; gold . . . . . . . . . . . . . . .　75.00　85.00

☐ "What's The Matter With McKinley? He's All Right" (Hake 171) stud; $\frac{7}{8}$"; black on white . . . .　6.00　8.00

## Statuary

☐ Bronze plaque of McKinley–Roosevelt, dated 1900; sculpted by Jonah Williams, New York City; $13\frac{1}{2}$"h x $10\frac{1}{2}$"w . . . . . . . . . . . . . . . . . . . . . . . . . . .　250.00　300.00

☐ McKinley pot-metal pedestal bust statuette, signed G. H. Tannier © 1896; 7"h; brass finish . . . . . . .　45.00　55.00

☐ "Wm. McKinley" marked heavy metal pedestal bust, ca. 1896; "G. B. Haines, Chicago" etched on reverse; 7"h; dark bronze finish . . . . . . . . . . . . . .　35.00　50.00

## Timepieces

☐ Cast-iron "Protection/Prosperity" mantel clock; dial shaped like coin and reads: "Sound Money. 1896"; clock topped by McKinley dimensional bust; deep-relief symbols of commerce—a ship and locomotive cast on sides; $14\frac{1}{2}$"h; black finish . . .　800.00　850.00

☐ McKinley–Roosevelt pocket watch; silvered face with black numerals in white circles; pair of sepia-tone oval portraits of candidates appear on each side of dial stem; $1\frac{3}{4}$" dia . . . . . . . . . . . . . . . . . . .　600.00　700.00

☐ McKinley pocket watch; 1896; portrait on face; silver-plate design; "William McKinley/The Nation's Choice" inscribed on reverse; $1\frac{3}{4}$" dia . . . .　350.00　400.00

## Tobacco Accessories

☐ Match safe; bas-relief McKinley bust profile; embossed filigree at all four corners; top lifts up to dispense matches; 3"h; brass finish . . . . . . . . . . . . . .　85.00　110.00

Price Range

☐ Match safe; three-dimensional bust profile of Mc-Kinley; push button in neck releases lid at base to dispense matches; 2½"h; brass finish .......... 150.00 200.00

☐ Match safe with oval photograph torso view of Mc-Kinley; opens from side like a compact; 2¼"h; brass finish ................................. 75.00 85.00

## Toys, Games, Dolls, Puzzles

☐ Cap bomb; figural pedestal bust of McKinley; cast iron; name appears in script at bottom of top half; loop cast on McKinley's head for string insert (cap is placed between two halves and bomb is dropped abruptly on pavement to cause explosion) 2½"h 175.00 200.00

☐ McKinley–Bryan puzzle; "Without New York 16 to 1"; sliding wooden blocks; multicolor octagon box cover with double jugates: McKinley–Roosevelt and Bryan–Stevenson; 1900 race ..... 175.00 200.00

☐ McKinley–Hobart spinning top; Gibbs Mfgr. Co., Canton, Ohio; 1896; wood and metal with gold paper band depicting both Republican candidates, slogan "On Top, Protection, Sound Money, Pros-perity" (Hake 3034) 2"h; red, white, blue paint on wood ...................................... 175.00 200.00

☐ "Presidential Muddle Puzzle"; patented 1894; text reads: "I am neither Democrat or Republican, but I am of the opinion that when both parties get tan-gled up, as shown in my several combinations, they ought to be separated"; 12" x 4" metal board, notched in center; 16 black, white checkers. U.S. flags border game title (not specifically McKinley, but a favorite diversion during the 1896 race); known as a sequential movement puzzle ........ 75.00 100.00

☐ McKinley soap baby with lithographed box; tag on doll reads: "My Papa will vote for McKinley, gold standard, protection, reciprocity, and good times"; 4½"l; gold or tan; these novelties invariably show up with at least one broken foot and are extremely fragile; manufactured by Monarch Soap Company, Lancaster, PA ............................. 25.00 35.00

Price Range

☐ Same figure and packaging but colored black ....    35.00    45.00
   *Note:* A Bryan soap baby was also issued but by
a different maker, Andrew Jergens & Company,
Cincinnati, Ohio.

## WILLIAM EDWARD MILLER

William Miller, Republican from New York, served in the House from
1951–65. He was Chairman of the Republican National Committee, 1961–64.
A surprise running mate with Barry Goldwater in 1964, he is best remembered for the quote, "I'm a Catholic and Barry's a Jew *and* a Protestant. Anyone who's against this ticket is a damned bigot" (see Barry Goldwater).

## WALTER MONDALE

Walter Mondale, a Minnesota Democrat, served in the U.S. Senate from
1964 to 1976. He served as vice-president under Jimmy Carter from 1977 to
1981. Mondale made an unsuccessful bid for the presidency in 1984 with running mate Geraldine Ferraro, who was the first woman to be nominated as
a major party candidate on the national ticket. She served as a congress-
woman from New York from 1979 to 1984 (see Jimmy Carter).

Price Range

### *Ferraro*

☐ "America's First Woman Vice President/Geraldine
   Ferraro"; bull's-eye portrait; 3½″; red, white, blue,
   black .......................................    2.00    3.00

☐ "Geraldine Ferraro For Vice President"; bull's-eye
   portrait (as above) 3½″; black, white ..........    2.00    3.00

☐ "Geraldine Ferraro/Congresswoman/New York/
   Vice President '84"; bull's-eye portrait; 3½″; black,
   white ......................................    2.00    3.00

☐ Geraldine Ferraro no-name oblong pictorial; waist-
   high photo of Ferraro waving; 3½″h; multicolor    3.00    4.00

☐ "Gerry Ferraro/Vice President"; name pinback
   2½″; red, white ............................    2.00    3.00

☐ "Now! 1984" Ferraro no-name pinback; bull's-eye
   portrait with stars bordering; 2½″; red, white, blue    2.00    3.00

Price Range

☐ "Leaders For The 80s"; Ferraro–Woods jugate; "Mondale For President" at top; "Rothman For Governor" at bottom; Missouri item (Woods was a female candidate for lieutenant-governor) 2½"; multicolor ................................... 3.00  5.00

## Mondale

☐ "America Needs A Change/Walter Mondale in '84"; portrait; 3½"; red, white, blue, black ..... 2.00  3.00

☐ "Democratic Integrity"; multigate of Jefferson, FDR, Truman, Jackson, Kennedy, and Mondale with flag background 3½"; red, white, blue, black 3.00  5.00

☐ "Democratic National Convention/San Francisco ... "; bull's-eye portrait surrounded by stars; 3½"; red, white, blue, black .................. 2.00  3.00

☐ "Democratic Unity" (National Democratic Convention) Mondale–Jesse Jackson–Gary Hart trigate; 3½"; black, green, white ................ 3.00  5.00

☐ "Iowa Supports Mondale Ferraro/1984"; bull's-eye jugate; 3½"; black, white ................... 3.00  5.00

☐ "Mondale–Ferraro" conjoining portraits; 3½"; black, white .............................. 2.00  5.00

☐ "Mondale–Ferraro" CWA (Communications Workers of America) jugate with Capitol building in background; 3½"; red, white, black ......... 3.00  5.00

☐ "Mondale–Ferraro For New Leadership"; bull's-eye jugate; 3½"; black, red, white ............. 2.00  3.00

☐ "Mondale–Ferraro"; jugate insets in map outline of Montana with large steer's skull illustration superimposed ................................... 20.00  25.00

☐ "Mondale–Ferraro" oval jugates flank White House; 1¾"w; blue, black, white ............. 3.00  5.00

☐ "Mondale–Ferraro" oval jugate with figure of Justice standing between insets; 1¾"w ........... 3.00  5.00

☐ "This Iowan's Ready For A Change"; conjoining portraits superimposed on map of Iowa; 2½"; black, blue, white .......................... 5.00  7.00

Price Range

☐ "Run Reagan Run/The Mondales Are Coming";
jugate portraits of Joan and Walter Mondale with
Capitol dome in background; 3½"; black, white     2.00     3.00

☐ "St. Louis For '84"; jugate portraits of Mondale–
Ferraro with arch and skyline in background; 2½";
black, white ...............................     2.00     3.00

☐ "Unity In '84" trigate; portraits of Jesse Jackson,
(top) Mondale, Ferraro; 2½"; red, white, black     3.00     5.00

## JAMES MONROE

James Monroe, a Democrat Republican from Virginia, served in the U.S. Senate 1790–94; Continental Congress, 1783–86; Governor of Virginia 1799–02; Secretary of State under Madison, 1811–17. Monroe became fifth President of the U.S., 1817–25. As a member of Congress, Monroe had helped write the Northeast Ordinance with Rufus King, whom he was to rout some 30 years later by an electoral vote margin of 183 to 34 in the 1816 presidential election. As a special envoy to France for Jefferson, he and Robert Livingston, regular U.S. Minister, helped negotiate the treaty for the Louisiana Purchase. The greatest of Monroe's presidential achievements was the proclamation of the Monroe Doctrine in 1823—a proclamation which still resounds today.

Price Range

### Badges and Tokens

☐ "James Munro" [*sic*] gaming token; name between
olive sprays; reverse has eagle with olive branch in
right talons, arrows in left; shield on breast encircled by 15 stars (DeWitt JMON 1816-1) 17mm;
brass; British; one of a series ................     1000.00 plus

### Ceramics and Glassware

☐ "Munroe" [*sic*] black transfer bust portrait atop oblong border with name enclosed; ceramic mug;
2½"h ....................................     2100.00     2200.00

☐ "Munroe" [*sic*] eagle atop floral bordered area for
reverse out of blue name; English import; 2½"h;
blue, white (also in maroon, white) ............     900.00     950.00

Price Range

☐ "Monroe"; another mug was issued with proper
spelling and even more ornate floral decoration
around name; blue on white; 2½"h; 1808 ...... 850.00 900.00

☐ White raised-enamel bust portraits of Monroe (left)
and Harrison (right) facing each other; sulfide doorknob; black background; possibly by Baccarat;
2¾" dia .................................. 2000.00 plus

## Textiles

Although James Monroe's image is conspicuously absent from most presidential memorabilia, a few crudely executed ribbons are known to exist but
appear on the market on rare occasions.

☐ Campaign chintz commemorating Jackson's first
inauguration in 1829 with portrait bust of Monroe,
as well as all previous presidents (Hake 3008) blue,
white .................................... 400.00 450.00

☐ Silk bandanna (Collins 85) ca. 1835, featuring full
text of Declaration of Independence, followed by
the death announcements of Monroe as well as
John Adams and Thomas Jefferson; 30"h x 20"w;
black, white .............................. 250.00 300.00

## LEVI PARSON MORTON

Levi Morton, a New York Republican, served in the House 1879–81. He
served as Ambassador to France for four years. A wealthy dry goods mer-
chant, he was a leading fund raiser for the Platt-Conkling Republican machine in New York City. In 1888 he was elected Vice-President with Benjamin
Harrison. Morton was deemed the "model presiding officer" in the Senate.
After his four-year term, he was elected Governor of New York, 1895–97
(see Benjamin Harrison).

## EDMUND SIXTUS MUSKIE

Edmund Muskie, Democrat from Maine, served in the U.S. Senate from 1959–80. He was Governor of Maine from 1955–59. He ran as an unsuccessful candidate for Vice-President under Hubert Humphrey in 1968. He was appointed Secretary of State under Jimmy Carter, 1980–81 (see Hubert Humphrey).

## RICHARD MILHAUS NIXON

Richard Nixon, Republican from California, served in the House 1947–50; U.S. Senate 1950–53. He was Vice-President under Dwight Eisenhower from 1953–61. He became 37th President of the U.S., in 1969. In his second term, pressures from the Watergate scandal forced his resignation to avoid impeachment. Nixon lost his first bid for the presidency to John F. Kennedy in 1960.

While President, Nixon negotiated "peace with honor" in Vietnam; he helped communist China gain membership in the UN; he signed agreements with the Soviet Union that provided the first limitation on production and deployment of atomic weapons, leading to a thaw in the Cold War. In spite of these achievements, he will always be remembered for his nickname, "Tricky Dick" (see Dwight Eisenhower).

|  | Price Range | |
|---|---|---|
| *Cartoon/Pictorial Pinbacks* | | |
| ☐ "California Republicans" rooster and bear on floating map of California (Hake 2020) 1¼"; black, white | 30.00 | 35.00 |
| ☐ Cartoon portrait of Nixon (Hake 15) 1¼"; black, white | 5.00 | 7.00 |
| ☐ "Don't Be A Jackass"; elephant head cartoon (Hake 30) 1¾"; red, white, blue | 7.00 | 9.00 |
| ☐ "Hubert Humphrey Is A Slithy Tove"; cartoon of an anteater-type creature (Hake 2040) 1½"; black, white | 12.00 | 15.00 |
| ☐ "I Bet On Nixon. But I Can Still Wish You A Merry Christmas"; Santa Claus wearing barrel with straps; noncampaign (Hake 2076) 1⅛"; black, white | 25.00 | 30.00 |
| ☐ "Nixon–Agnew"; eagle in flight with red, white, blue stripes (Hake 80) 1½"; red, white, blue | 3.00 | 5.00 |

Price Range

☐ "Nixon–Agnew"; rearing GOP elephant (Hake 77) 1¾"; red, white, blue lithograph .............. 3.00 5.00

☐ "Nixon in '60"; parading elephant (Hake 2018) 1¼"; black, white ......................... 5.00 8.00

☐ "Nixon For Peace"; dove in clouds (Hake 2018) 1¼"; blue, white .......................... 5.00 8.00

☐ "Nixon For President"; elephant on hind legs wearing boxing gloves (Hake 2103) 1¼"; black, white 25.00 30.00

☐ "Nixon In '72/Reelect The President"; large stylized GOP elephant symbol with three stars on back (Hake 2015) 1¼"; red, white, blue ............ 8.00 10.00

☐ "Not For Sale"; words on sign in front of White House lawn (photograph); "Elect Nixon" (Hake 2004) 4"; black, red ......................... 40.00 50.00

☐ "Over 60 For '60. I'm A Senior Republican"; elephant in hat running with cane, which has attached tag that reads "60" (Hake 31) 1²/₃"; red, white, blue 10.00 15.00

☐ Presidential Seal in circular inset; "Heritage Groups/Nixon–Agnew; 1970s/Republican National Committee Nationalities Division (Hake 2048) 2"; red, white, blue .................... 15.00 20.00

☐ "Puerto Rican Hispanic Young Republicans"; elephant in diapers that reads "Miami Beach '72" shaking maracas marked "Nixon" and "Agnew" (Hake 2004) 1¼"; black, white .............. 20.00 25.00

☐ "This Is No Yoke"; cartoon of Humphrey as Humpty Dumpty sitting on wall (Hake 2024) 1¼"; black, white .............................. 5.00 7.00

☐ "What A Ticket"; Santa driving convertible with back full of presents, gazing up at billboard featuring "Nixon-Lodge 1960" portraits (Hake 2091) 1¼"; black, white .......................... 75.00 85.00

## *Jugates*

NIXON–AGNEW, 1968, 1972

☐ "America Needs Nixon–Agnew"; bull's-eye pinback with conjoining portraits (Hake 93) 3¼"; red, white, blue ................................. 5.00 7.00

Price Range

☐ "Nixon/Agnew" conjoining portraits (Hake 64) $1^2/_3"$; multicolor .......................... | 3.00 | 5.00

☐ "Nixon/Agnew" staggered conjoining portraits (Hake 66) $1^1/_4"$; bluetone portraits; red, white stripes ...................................... | 3.00 | 5.00

☐ "Nixon/Agnew"; stars and stripes with oval insets (Hake 65) $1^1/_3"$; red, white, blue .............. | 3.00 | 5.00

☐ "Nixon/Agnew" staggered ovals with shield and ribbon coil; "1968" no-name jugate (Hake 67) $^7/_8"$, red, white, blue, black ....................... | 5.00 | 7.00

☐ "Nixon in '68/Agnew"; silhouetted portraits on shield background (Hake 68) $1^2/_3"$; red, white, blue | 3.00 | 5.00

☐ "Now More Than Ever"; Agnew on left, Nixon right, waving arms in victory (Hake 97) $2^3/_4"$; multicolor; 1972 race ........................... | 3.00 | 5.00

☐ "Inauguration Day. Forward Forever" oval portraits; flags, Capitol building, White House; "Washington D.C. January 20, 1969" (Hake 72) $1^1/_2"$; red, white, blue, black ........................... | 3.00 | 5.00

### NIXON–LODGE, 1960

☐ "Best Choice For '64/Nixon And Lodge"; silhouetted bust portraits (Hake 2006) $2^1/_2"$; red, white, blue ....................................... | 5.00 | 8.00

☐ Also $3^1/_2"$ (Hake 2022) ...................... | 10.00 | 12.00

☐ "Experience Counts/Nixon–Lodge" conjoining portraits (Hake 2023) $3^1/_2"$; red, white, blue .... | 65.00 | 75.00

☐ Also $4"$ (Hake 2014) ........................ | 35.00 | 45.00

☐ Also $1^3/_4"$ (Hake 6) ......................... | 5.00 | 7.00

☐ "Experience Counts/Nixon–Lodge"; draped ribbon with circular jugate portraits superimposed (Hake 2019) $3^1/_2"$; red, white, blue ............ | 10.00 | 15.00

☐ "Experience Counts/Vote Nixon–Lodge/For President/For Vice President/For A Better America" (Hake 5) $2^1/_4"$; red, white, blue .............. | 10.00 | 12.00

☐ "Nixon/Lodge" conjoining portraits (Hake 1); $^7/_8"$; red, white, blue; lithograph ................. | 5.00 | 7.00

☐ Slight variance (Hake 2) (item has been reproduced) | 6.00 | 8.00

Price Range

☐ "Nixon/Lodge"; eagle with circular insets (Hake 2008) 2¾"w x 1¾"h; red, white, blue ......... 35.00    45.00

☐ "Nixon/Lodge" oval pinback; circular jugate portraits running vertically against striped background (Hake 2007) 2¾"h x 1¾"w; red, white, blue ... 20.00    25.00

☐ "Nixon/Lodge/Vote Republican"; conjoining portraits inside shield (Hake 2001) 1¼"; red, white, blue, black ................................ 75.00    80.00

☐ (Warner 472; Warner 473) also ⅞" (Hake 4)* ... 50.00    60.00

☐ "Our Nation Needs Nixon/Lodge"; conjoining portraits inside outline of U.S. map; oval shape (Hake 2009) 3½"w x 2½"h; red, white, blue; lithograph ....................................... 8.00    10.00

☐ "Peace Experience Prosperity/Vote Republican" (Hake 2021) 3½"; red, white, blue ........... 5.00    7.00

☐ Variant with added line, "Pull 2nd Lever" (Hake 2020) ...................................... 4.00    6.00

## Portrait Pinbacks

☐ "For President/Richard M. Nixon" (Hake 73) 1⅔"; red, white, blue, black ................ 10.00    12.00

☐ "Give America Another Great President/Nixon in '68"; silhouetted Nixon portrait; smaller silhouettes of Lincoln, Washington, TR above head (Hake 70) 1¾"; red, white, blue, black ................. 8.00    10.00

☐ "He's Good Enough For Me In '68/Nixon"; Uncle Sam pointing, with Nixon at his shoulder (Hake 71) 2¾"; red, white, black, blue rim ............. 15.00    20.00

☐ "Inaugural Day/Jan. 20th, 1973/Richard M. Nixon 37th President"; silhouetted portrait against full flag background (Hake 99) 3¼" red, white, blue, gold, black .......................... 25.00    30.00

☐ "Keep Dick On The Job"; silhouetted portrait at right (Hake 2033) 3½"; black, red, white ...... 12.00    15.00

*Note:* The 1¼" and ⅞" (Hake 2001; Hake 4) are the only known jugates to appear in historically standard sizes; rated tops of the 1960 Nixon–Lodge jugates.

Price Range

☐ "Nixon For President"; bull's-eye portrait with stars, stripes border (Hake 96) 1½" red, white, blue, black ............................... 3.00   5.00

☐ "Now More Than Ever"; Nixon profile bleed off pinback (Hake 98) 2¾"; multicolor; 1972 ...... 3.00   5.00

☐ Oversize "N"[ixon] In November" (Hake 2011) 6"; black, red, white .......................... 35.00   40.00

☐ "Our Nation Needs Richard Nixon"; bull's-eye portrait (Hake 2029) 3½"; black, white ........ 15.00   20.00

☐ "Re-Elect Nixon In '72"; silhouetted head (Hake 94) 1½"; red, white, blue, black ............. 3.00   5.00

☐ "Richard Nixon"; small eagles flank silhouetted head (Hake 2017) 4"; black, white ............ 12.00   15.00

☐ "Vote For President Richard M. Nixon"; bull's-eye (Hake 2032) 3½"; red, white, blue, black ...... 10.00   12.00

☐ "Win With Nixon"; bull's-eye (Hake 2031) red, white, blue, black ........................... 5.00   7.00

☐ "Youth For [Nixon rebus portrait]" (Hake 95) ⅞"; red, white, blue, black ...................... 3.00   5.00

### Slogan/Name Pinbacks

☐ "America Needs Nixon & Lodge" (Hake 32) 1¼"; red, white, blue .......................... 5.00   7.00

☐ "Ask A Veteran. He Knows. Nixon & Lodge/ Experience Counts" (Hake 33) 1¼"; red, white, blue ...................................... 10.00   15.00

☐ "Click With Dick" (Hake 58) ⅞"; red, white, blue (a reproduced item) ........................ 3.00   5.00

☐ "Connecticut Volunteers. The Nation For Nixon" (Hake 2114; Warner 832) 1¾"; red, white, blue 30.00   35.00

☐ "Don't Be Taken For Granted. Re-elect the President" (Hake 100) 2"; white reversed out of black 3.00   5.00

☐ "G.O.P. Victory/Nixon in '60" (Hake 52) ⅞"; red, white, blue ............................... 8.00   10.00

☐ "Grass Rooters For Dick" (Hake 60) ⅞"; green, white; lithograph (a reproduced item) .......... 6.00   8.00

Price Range

☐ "Help Kennedy Stamp Out Private Enterprise" (Hake 2111) ¾"; black, white ................ 25.00 30.00

☐ "I'm A Nixon Girl/Nixon For President" (Hake 59) ⅞"; red, white, blue ..................... 3.00 5.00

☐ "I'm Voting For Nixon. No Give Aways! Remember Yalta? No Apologies! Remember The Summit? No Pie In The Sky! Remember it's YOUR Money Jack will play Poker with" (Hake 2013) 2"; black, white ...................................... 40.00 45.00

☐ "It's Not Just Jack's Money He'd Spend. It's Yours" (Hake 2050) 1¼"; black, white ........ 15.00 20.00

☐ "It's Time To Elect Nixon President" acrostic of name "Nixon" running four ways to form square clock face; dials in center; classic design. (Hake 2097) 1¼"; red, white, blue ................. 40.00 45.00

☐ Also 2¼" (Warner 831) ..................... 75.00 85.00

☐ "Monongahela Railroad Employees Are Affixin' To Vote For Nixon" (Hake 36) 1¼"; red, white, blue 20.00 25.00

☐ "My Pick Is Dick" (Hake 56) ⅞"; blue, orange 10.00 12.00

☐ "You Got The Bird in '64/Don't get HUMPHed in '68/Vote Republican" (Hake 2028) 1¼"; black, yellow ...................................... 5.00 7.00

☐ "Mamie Start Packing. The Nixons Are Coming" (Hake 2052) 1¼"; red, white, blue ........... 5.00 7.00

☐ "Nixon's The One!" (Hake 88) ⅞"; red, white .. 3.00 5.00

☐ "Right On Mr. President" (Hake 110) 1¼"; dark blue, yellow; lithograph ..................... 3.00 5.00

☐ "Senior Power For The President" (Hake 104) 1⅓"; red, white, blue ...................... 3.00 5.00

☐ "Serbians for President Nixon" (Hake 101) 2"; red, white, blue; part of a set ..................... 3.00 5.00

☐ "Sock It To 'Em Spiro" (Hake 119) 1¼"; red, black 3.00 5.00

☐ "Vet For Nixon" (Hake 62) ⅞"; red, white, blue 5.00 7.00

☐ "Stick With Dick" (Hake 53) ⅞"; red, white, blue 3.00 5.00

☐ "Vote NiXon" (large X for ballot) (Hake 37) 1¼"; red, white, blue ............................ 7.00 9.00

Price Range

☐ "Women For Nixon" (stylized 3-color large $N$ monogram) (Hake 82) 1¼"; red, white, blue; lithograph ....................................... 3.00   5.00

## *Trigate*

☐ "Nixon–Agnew–McCarney"; circular insets on shield (Hake 76) 2"; red, white, blue .......... 3.00   5.00

## ALTON B. PARKER

Alton Parker, a conservative Chief Justice of the New York Court of Appeals, in 1904, headed the Democratic national ticket as presidential nominee, with 82-year-old Henry G. Davis of West Virginia as his running mate. They lost by a landslide to Teddy Roosevelt and Charles Fairbanks. Parker staged a lackluster campaign, but some of the more fascinating and best designed pinbacks from the Golden Age come from his candidacy.

Price Range

### *Badges, Stickpins, Pinbacks, Hangers*

☐ Eagle brass badge with ribbon attachment device and paper photo inset with brass shell hanger; Parker bust portrait (Hake 122) 1½"; bronze, black, white ....................................... 50.00   60.00

☐ "For President"; Parker portrait pinback with celluloid Tammany star attached to ribbon. (Hake 3174) 1¼" (pinback only) black, cream; ribbon, blue with gold lettering ...................... 125.00   135.00

☐ "For President" printed on paper insert behind celluloid in brass bar; flag ribbon attached with Parker portrait hanger (Hake 67) 2¼"; multicolor ..... 85.00   100.00

☐ Figural balance scales badge with embossed portraits of Bryan–Davis (Hake 3012) ............ 110.00   115.00

☐ "Our Choice"; bar with ornate embossed brass hanger of eagle and flags with paper photo inset of Parker (Hake 3153) 2" overall; gold, red, blue; Parker embossed bust tin shell badge (Hake 3151) 1½"; gilded brass .......................... 20.00   25.00

Parker–Davis Business Men's Association ribbon with appliqued U.S. flags and sepia jugate pinback ($150–$160).

|  | Price Range | |
|---|---|---|
| ☐ Parker–Davis token hanger, pierced (Hake 3150) 1¼"; bronze | 25.00 | 30.00 |
| ☐ "We Will Chop Our Way To The White House In 1904"; celluloid pinback with crossed flags under inset sketch of Jefferson. "Father of Democracy" (Hake 3152) 1½"; red, white, blue, black (has pierced hole for small hatchet attachment but most often shows up as pinback only) | 175.00 | 200.00 |
| ☐ Wind vane stickpin with Parker portrait inset in center (Hake 123) 1¼"; black photo; red, white, blue vanes | 60.00 | 70.00 |

### Canes, Umbrellas

| | | |
|---|---|---|
| ☐ Alton Parker portrait cello-top cane head; 1½"; sepiatone | 135.00 | 150.00 |

Price Range

☐ Alton Parker–Henry Davis jugate, paper on wood cane; rectangular portraits appear vertically over names; red, white, blue ...................... 85.00 95.00

☐ Alton Parker–Henry Davis jugate umbrella; images appear twice; four panels in all; black, white .... 275.00 300.00

## Cartoon/Pictorial Pinbacks

☐ Balance scale with rooster crowing, "Judge We're It"; Capital dome with "Fairbanks" scale; Parker portrait on balance scale carries more weight than Teddy Roosevelt portrait; unusual to find opposing candidates on same button (Hake 3006) 1½"; black on white ................................... 1000.00 1200.00

☐ Bust portrait; Parker with figural ear of corn attachment; Parker photo is framed by ornate scrollwork (Hake 133) "B.F.T.W." reversed out of black; gold ear of corn ................................. 110.00 125.00

☐ Bust portrait of Parker amid figures of soldier on horseback and battleship (Hake 131) 1¼" multicolor (Hake 72 is almost identical) ............ 90.00 100.00

☐ Capitol dome outlined against flag; stars and stripes frames Parker bust inset (Hake 74) 1¼"; red, white, blue, flesh tones ............................ 35.00 45.00

☐ Good luck symbols surround Parker bust portrait: ribbon-tied shamrock, rabbit's foot, and wishbone (none of which helped) (Hake 87) 1¼"; black, green, yellow gold .......................... 40.00 50.00

☐ "Hoeing His Way To The White House" (Parker as farmer); "For President, Alton B. Parker" (Hake 3055) multicolor .......................... 950.00 1050.00

☐ Horseshoe against flag background frames Parker portrait (Hake 75) 1¼" red, white, blue ........ 50.00 60.00

☐ Horseshoe, inverted; "For President, Alton B. Parker"; portrait with striped bow (Hake 85) 1¼"; gold, deep blue, light blue, black, white, flesh tones 35.00 50.00

☐ Multiple flags with star overlay and Parker inset photo (Hake 65) 1¼"; red, blue, black, buff .... 100.00 110.00

Price Range

☐ Uncle Sam riding backward on eagle in flight; holds
oval framed Parker portrait (Hake 64; Warner 578)
1¼" multicolor .............................. 135.00     150.00

☐ "Uncle Sam's 'White Elephant.' It's Game. It Fin-
ishes"; elephant astride football fettered by banner
labeled "Protection"; elephant blanket reads:
"Grand Old Pirate"; (Hake 112) 1½"; red, brown,
black, white; a classic item (lithograph reproduction has appeared) .......................... 125.00     150.00

☐ "Victory" in shadow type with Parker circle portrait over draped flags (Hake 92) 1¼" red, white,
blue, black ................................. 35.00      45.00

☐ Wedding cake, "It's Up To You" "Take Your
Choice"; Parker and Roosevelt in circular insets
hover over wedding scenes; Parker—a handsome
Caucasian bride and groom couple; Roosevelt—a
black groom in top hat with white bride (Hake
3014) 1¼"; sepiatone ...................... 2000.00    2200.00

☐ White House view as flag bunting is pulled aside;
Parker inset portrait in bunting (Hake 73) 1¼";
multicolor ................................. 45.00      55.00

☐ Several ⅞" variants (Hake 3111, 3112); each .... 25.00      35.00


## Jugate Pinbacks

☐ Bow; patriotic bow separates figure-eight Bryan–
Davis images across middle (Hake 23) 1¼"; red,
white, blue, black .......................... 60.00      70.00

☐ Crossed flags with scepter; circular insets of Parker–
Davis (Hake 7) 1½"; red, white, blue, black; bronze
background ................................ 325.00     350.00

☐ "Democratic Candidates, 1904"; conjoining portraits, "Parker–Davis" (Hake 25) 1¼"; sepiatone 80.00      90.00

☐ Eagle with draped flag in beak; oval portraits in flag
(Hake 3) 1½"; red, white, blue, black ......... 150.00     160.00

☐ Eagle with flag background; paired portraits framed
by spread wings (Hake 18) 1¼"; red, white, blue,
black ..................................... 50.00      60.00

Price Range

☐ Eagle and flag with crossed arrows in talons frame upper boundaries of paired portraits (Hake 13) 1¼"; red, white, blue, black, bronze . . . . . . . . . . .    60.00     65.00

☐ Also ⅞" (Hake 39) . . . . . . . . . . . . . . . . . . . . . . . . .    30.00     35.00

☐ "E. Pluribus Unum" eagle and flag atop paired oval insets (Hake 30) 1¼"; sepiatone . . . . . . . . . . . . . .    80.00     90.00

☐ Eagle preparing to soar against sunburst backdrop tops Parker–Davis in circular inset portraits with crossed flags framing lower third (Hake unlisted; Warner 278) 2¼"; sepiatone; key item . . . . . . . . .   800.00   850.00

☐ Eagle/shield motif splits Parker–Davis oval portraits; ropelike brass rim (Hake 3005; Warner 573) 1½"; sepia, cream; holed at top; shown in Hake with striped ribbon with gold lettering. "Reception Committee, Oct. 10, 1984" . . . . . . . . . . . . . . . . . .   190.00   200.00

☐ Keystone motif with Brian–Davis portraits and ornate scrollwork (Hake 129) 1¼"; dark brown on white . . . . . . . . . . . . . . . . . . . . . . . . . . . . . . . . . . .   175.00   185.00

☐ Liberty cap with stars and stylized scroll outlines Parker–Davis portraits (Hake 19) 1¼"; red, white, blue, black . . . . . . . . . . . . . . . . . . . . . . . . . . . . . . . .   100.00   110.00

☐ Miss Liberty, full-standing, displays ribbon-draped Parker–Davis oval portraits (Hake 14) 1¼"; red, white, blue, green gold, with braided brass rim . .    60.00     70.00

☐ Miss Liberty, identical image to Hake 14, minus brass rim and advertising "The Fountain Beer and Billiard Hall, San Francisco" (Hake 15) 1¼"; multicolored, as above . . . . . . . . . . . . . . . . . . . . . . . . .   125.00   150.00

☐ Miss Liberty, head and shoulders frames lower section of oval Parker–Davis portraits; 13 stars appear at top (Hake 28) 1¼"; red, white, blue, black; gold background . . . . . . . . . . . . . . . . . . . . . . . . . . . . . . .    60.00     75.00

☐ Miss Liberty (torso) with upraised arms framing interlinked oval portraits; rays emanate from top of insets to curl of button (Hake 26) 1¼"; red, white, blue, black on bronze . . . . . . . . . . . . . . . . . . . . . .    50.00     60.00

☐ Also ⅞" (Hake 37) . . . . . . . . . . . . . . . . . . . . . . . . .    30.00     35.00

Price Range

☐ "New York National Editorial Conference, Sept. 7th. 1904. Esopus, Sept. 8, 1904"; large quill pen divides staggered portraits (Hake 5; Warner 572) 1½"; sepia, cream .......................... 200.00 220.00

☐ "Our Choice"; conjoining figures in central portrait framed by looped ribbon (Hake 22) 1¼"; red, blue, black on white ............................. 100.00 110.00

☐ Oval shape, horizontal; conjoining Parker–Davis figures (Hake 6) 1"w; dark brown tone ......... 35.00 45.00

☐ "Shure Mike"; rooster in patriotic flag costume flanked by oval jugate insets; key item from 1904 Democratic slate (Hake 12) 1¼"; multicolor .... 125.00 150.00

☐ Stars from flag field and rope coiled around paired inset Parker–Davis portraits (Hake 20) 1¼"; red, white, blue, gold ........................... 100.00 110.00

☐ Tammany star topped Parker–Davis portraits framed by entwined laurels and ribbon ties (Hake unlisted; Warner 574) 1¼"; multicolor ......... 200.00 210.00

## Multigate Pinback

☐ Stylized shamrock outline reverses from black with portraits of Washington, Parker, Jefferson, Davis (reading clockwise) 2"; black and white ........ 450.00 475.00

## Posters

☐ "We Favor A Return To Jeffersonian Principles"; Liberty cap on pike with shield in front of five furled flags between laurel-bordered oval portraits (Hake 3184) red, blue, black, white ................. 150.00 160.00

☐ "For President/Alton B. Parker of New York/For Vice President/Henry G. Davis [in profile] of West Virginia"; staggered silhouetted portraits (Hake 3185) 30"h x 18"w; black, white ............. 110.00 125.00

☐ "Alton B. Parker"; silhouetted portrait of Parker in judicial robes (Hake 3186) 28"h x 22"w; black, white ...................................... 35.00 45.00

Price Range

☐ "For President/Alton B. Parker"; quarter profile in
oval (Hake 3187) 30"h x 20"w; black, white .... 35.00   45.00

☐ "For Vice President/Henry G. Davis"; oval portrait (Hake 3188) 30"h x 20"w; black, white; match
to Parker poster above ...................... 35.00   45.00

### Slogan Pinbacks

☐ "Good Bye Teddy! Good Bye!" (Hake 114) 1¼";
slogan appears in yellow decal circle with red border ....................................... 12.00   15.00

☐ "Good Bye Teddy! Good Bye" (Hake 113) 1¼";
red, white, blue .......................... 10.00   12.00

☐ "Vote For Parker. Use Maple City Soap" (Hake
134) 1¼"; black, yellow .................... 15.00   20.00

### Tobacco Items

☐ "Chief Judge" Havana Cigars cigar cutter and ashtray; cast-metal; glass-enclosed frame with Parker
bust portrait; approx. 7"h; multicolor portrait;
brass finish .............................. 350.00   400.00

☐ "Chief Judge" Havana Cigars cigar box; 9"l; multicolor ..................................... 35.00   45.00

☐ Parker–Davis jugate ashtray; crimped white metal;
oval portraits flank Capitol building; 4½"; silver
finish with black image .................... 20.00   25.00

### Trigate Pinback

☐ Davis–Parker–Charles Black (New Jersey coattail
candidate); "Hudson Co. N.J." (Hake 3007) 2";
black and white .......................... 425.00   450.00

## FRANKLIN PIERCE

Franklin Pierce, a Democrat from New Hampshire, served in the New Hampshire legislature before winning a House seat from 1833–37; he served in the U.S. Senate from 1837–42. In 1853 Pierce became the 14th President of the U.S., serving until 1857. William R. King, his Vice-President, died before entering office. In 1854, Pierce had helped Stephen A. Douglas push through the pro-slavery Kansas-Nebraska Act, and as President, upheld the rights of border ruffians to infiltrate from Missouri, a slave state, and set up a similar government in Kansas. This blunder led to the formation of a new Republican party. Pierce's candidacy will be remembered for the slogan, "We Polked 'em in '44, we'll Pierce 'em in '52." He was known for a drinking problem (the Whigs described him as "a hero of many a well-fought bottle") and is ranked in history as a mediocre President.

### *Badges, Medals*

There are fewer than a half dozen known medalets for Pierce in the 1852 race.

|  | Price Range | |
|---|---|---|
| ☐ Bust token (DeWitt FP 1852-1; Warner 55) 41mm; "United We Stand . . ." on reverse; Pierce profile; F. Leonard, engraver . . . . . . . . . . . . . . . . . . . . . . . | 300.00 | 350.00 |
| ☐ Bust token, "Gen. Franklin Pierce The Statesmen [*sic*] & Soldier" (DeWitt FP 1852-4) 28mm . . . . . | 35.00 | 40.00 |
| ☐ Collar button; portrait in circle, topped by eagle, flanked by flags; shield below; 28mm . . . . . . . . . . | 500.00 | 525.00 |
| ☐ Watch fob; "Pierce" (cannot be truly verified; may have been lapel device); half-length figure with raised arm holding rolled document; convex surface; blue paper, reverse with gilt Roman numerals, hands; looped; brass; 30mm . . . . . . . . . . . . . . . . . | 650.00 | 700.00 |

### *Mirrors*

|  | | |
|---|---|---|
| ☐ Field mirror; "Gen. Franklin Pierce, President Of The United States" embossed with bust portrait in pewter; mirror on reverse; approx. 4"; similar mirror also exists for Zachary Taylor . . . . . . . . . . . . | 300.00 | 325.00 |

## Personal Effects

☐ Personal valise, "Brig. Gen. Franklin Pierce, U.S. Army, 1847"; very battered canvas and leather case    950.00    1000.00

## Posters, Prints

☐ Franklin Pierce/Democratic Candidate for/ Fourteenth President of the United States"; half-length portrait; red curtain; 1852; from T. Dunlop daguerreotype; 11" x 8" ......................    250.00    300.00

☐ "Franklin Pierce/14th President ..." same as above except for title change; both prints Currier & Ives ......................................    200.00    250.00

☐ "Franklin Pierce/William King"; pulled-back curtain; oval portraits under winged eagle; oblong portraits of buildings below; E. B. & E. C. Kellog; 11" x 8" ...................................    300.00    325.00

☐ "Franklin Pierce/William King/For President ... For Vice President"; oval portraits under wide oval of George Washington surrounded by star border; eagle atop; Currier & Ives; 11" x 8"; hand-tinted    300.00    325.00

## Textiles

☐ "Pierce/King" jugate ribbon, 1852; $6\frac{1}{2}$"l x $2\frac{1}{2}$"w; black portraits on white; facsimile signatures ....    2000.00 plus

☐ "We Honor the Citizen and Soldier. General Franklin Pierce"; portrait; black, white ..............    850.00    950.00

☐ Handkerchiefs with bust portrait, "General Franklin Pierce"; names of past presidents and dates of administration form outer border; state seals, Capitol building, draped flags grouped under portrait; similar to Winfield Scott handkerchief; 15"sq; black, white ...............................    1000.00    1200.00

## Tobacco Accessories

☐ "Fr. Pierce President" figural meerschaum pipe, curved, with bamboo stem ...................    150.00    175.00

James K. Polk, Currier & Ives, 1844 ($175–$200).

## JAMES KNOX POLK

James Polk, a Tennessee Democrat, served in the House from 1825–39; was appointed House Speaker 1835–39. He was Governor of Tennessee from 1839–41. In 1844, Polk, an ardent expansionist who favored the annexation of Texas, was nominated for high office by the Democrats with George M. Dallas of Pennsylvania, a former Ambassador to Russia. His party cleverly linked the reoccupation of Oregon with the reannexation of Texas, thereby deflating the slavery issue, giving rise to the slogan "Fifty-four Forty or Fight" (claiming all of Oregon up to Alaska's southern boundary—54 degrees, 40'). Derisively called "Polk The Plodder" by the Whigs, he bested rival Henry Clay by a narrow margin to become the 11th U.S. President.

## RONALD REAGAN

Ronald Reagan, a Republican from California (his home town, however, was Dixon, Illinois), was a late arrival on the political scene. He was 55 when he won the governorship of California in 1966 and even topped William Henry Harrison in age when, at 70, he became our 40th U.S. President in 1981. Reagan began as a radio sports announcer; in 1937, "Dutch" (as his friends called him) went out to Hollywood to become "The Errol Flynn of the B's."

Reagan starred in 54 movies, most of them in the 1940s, including "Knute Rockne, All American" and "King's Row," as well as the film Democrats will never let him live down, "Bedtime For Bonzo." After World War II, when Reagan made training films in the Air Force, his film career faded. But it was as host and occasional star of TV's General Electric Theater that he became a spokesman and public-relations man. His patriotic homiles from that show are his trademark to this day.

In 1966 he ran for Governor. Ten years later, the two-term governor campaigned in the presidential primaries and did well. At the Republican Convention Gerald Ford narrowly edged him out on the first ballot, 1,187 votes to 1,070. 1980 was another story. After clobbering his eventual running mate, George Bush, in the New Hampshire primary, it was clear sailing. Carter's defeat by Reagan, 489 electoral votes to 49, was the biggest rout since FDR's in 1932. Reagan's defeat of Walter Mondale, four years later in 1984, proved even more devastating. His sweet sounding and simplistic mandate to the voters "to get the government off our backs" received a resounding endorsement.

**Price Range**

### *Folk Art*

☐ "Ronald Reagan Strikes Out on Foreign Policy" by Edward Larsen. Three-figure polychrome whirligig in wood and tin. Reagan as batter with catcher and umpire. When wind blows, Reagan swings at ball already caught in catcher's glove. The umpire signals "out," c. 1980 . . . . . . . . . . . . . . . . . . . . . . . . . .  2,000 plus

### *Inaugural Pinbacks*

☐ "50th Inauguration"; Ronald Reagan raising hand to be sworn in; 2″w x 1½″h; red, white, blue, black   1.00   2.00

☐ "50th Presidential Inauguration"; Regan–Bush jugate; crossed flags; "Jan. 21, 1985" . . . . . . . . . . . .   1.00   2.00

### *Jugates*

☐ "America Loves Regan-Bush/1984"; conjoining portraits in heart-shape pinback; 2″h x 1½″w; red, white, blue . . . . . . . . . . . . . . . . . . . . . . . . . . . . . . .   2.00   3.00

☐ "Bringing America Back/Reagan-Bush"; 2″w x 1½″h; red, white, blue, black . . . . . . . . . . . . . . .   2.00   3.00

Price Range

☐ "Help Keep America Great/Reelect Ronald Reagan–Bush/'84"; 1¼"; flag background; red, white, blue, black ................................:........ 2.00 3.00

☐ "Reagan–Bush" eagle over oval portraits separated by flag, shield; 1"; red, white, blue, black ....... 1.00 2.00

☐ Reagan–Bush no-name; striped shield between paired ovals; 1"; red, white, blue, black ........ 1.00 2.00

☐ "Regan/Bush/One More Time"; circle portraits on flag background; oval shape; 1½"w x 1"h; red, white, blue, black; 1984 ..................... 2.00 3.00

## *Toys and Novelties*

☐ "Reagan's Raygun/Trust Me": an updated version of 1930s paper pop guns. Equipped with instructions to aim raygun at targets (i.e., stable economy, world peace) and fire by a downward snap of the wrist. Full color ........................... 5.00 7.00

☐ "Reagan Bean Shooter/Shoot Down Reaganomics": blister pack kit with donkey cartoon on label; full bag of jellybeans and bean shooter .... 3.00 5.00

☐ "Ronald Reagan jellybean Whitehouse ceramic still bank"; 4⅝"h x 5½"w ..................... 12.00 15.00

☐ "Reagan and Bush Frankoma elephant candy container"; 4"h; white, dated 1981 .............. 10.00 12.00

☐ *First Family Paper Doll & Cutout Book;* Ronald and Nancy Reagan; 12"h x 9"w. Published by Dell, NYC, full color ........................... 5.00 7.00

## JOSEPH T. ROBINSON

Senator Joseph T. Robinson of Arkansas was Al Smith's running mate as vice-president on the Democratic ticket for 1928 (see Al Smith).

Price Range

*Portrait Pinbacks*

☐ "For Vice President. U.S. Senator Joe T. Robinson
of Arkansas" (Hake 2036) 4"h; red, white, blue,
black; companion piece to Al Smith (Hake 2028);
may also have been used as auto license attachment     150.00     175.00

☐ "Robinson"; bust portrait of a very young Robinson; may have been item from his senatorial cam-
paigns in Arkansas (Hake 2073) $7/8$"; black, white     25.00     30.00

See also Smith–Robinson Jugate Pinbacks.


## FRANKLIN DELANO ROOSEVELT

Franklin Roosevelt, a New York Democrat, served in the state legislature
from 1911–12. He was Assistant Secretary of the Navy under Woodrow Wilson from 1913–20. FDR ran unsuccessfully for Vice-President with James
Cox in 1920, losing to the Harding-Coolidge ticket. He later served as Governor of New York from 1929–32. FDR became the 32nd President of the U.S.
in 1933 and served until 1945, when stricken with a cerebral hemorrhage in
Warm Springs, Georgia. The only President to serve three terms (he started
a fourth), FDR is acclaimed for his wartime leadership, his masterful campaign technique, his New Deal measures providing social security, aid to de-
pendent children, and health services. Roosevelt is ranked among the great
Presidents in our history.

Price Range

*Automotive Accessories*

LICENSE ATTACHMENTS AND LICENSES,
PAINTED, DIE-STAMPED METAL

☐ "America Needs Roosevelt" license attachment;
die-cut circular area for smiling portrait of FDR;
approx. 11"l; red, white, blue, black painted tin;
probably 1932 race ........................     50.00     60.00

☐ "America Needs Roosevelt"; license attachment
with slanted top; small oval portrait of FDR
flanked by two stars and alternating red, white
stripes; approx. 8"l; red, white, black painted tin     35.00     45.00

"Take Off Your Cap For Roosevelt. He Kept His Promise"; donkey cartoon and figural FDR key chain bottle opener, 1936 ($25–$35).

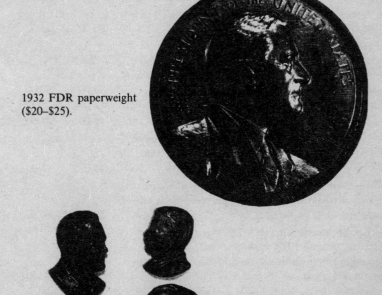

1932 FDR paperweight ($20–$25).

Paperweights: upper left: FDR "New Deal" ($20–$25), TR ($10–$15), Ben Butler ($30–$35), William McKinley "Sound Money" ($20–$25).

Price Range

☐ Democratic donkey license attachment; 1932; cartoon of donkey appears in 3"-dia area; "Democratic" appears below; approx. 4¾"l overall; Republican elephant match . . . . . . . . . . . . . . . . . . . . .     20.00     25.00

☐ "Drive Ahead With Roosevelt"; die-cut bas-relief bust figures of FDR with Uncle Sam putting hand on shoulder; approx. 11"; red, white, blue, gilt on tin . . . . . . . . . . . . . . . . . . . . . . . . . . . . . . . . . . . . . .     45.00     55.00

☐ "Drive Safely. Freedom, Democracy, Roosevelt"; license plate, full size; large eagle with wings full spread; patriotic shield; 11"l; red, white, blue, gold; made by Michigan Mfg. Co., New York, N.Y. ..     35.00     45.00

☐ "Elect Roosevelt And Wallace" slogan attachment; black, white; 1940 . . . . . . . . . . . . . . . . . . . . . . . . .     20.00     25.00

☐ "Roosevelt" name reversed out of rounded rectangle along with silhouette of donkey's head; 6½"w x 2½"h; white with red reflecting background . . . . . . . . . . . . . . . . . . . . . . . . . . . . . . . . . .     35.00     40.00

☐ Rose [rebus] "Velt For President"; illustration of large red rose at left; 12"w; red, black, white ...     35.00     45.00

☐ "F.D.R. Is Good Enough For Me. Follow Through With Roosevelt"; die-cut bust portrait; red, white, brown; approx. 5"h x 3½"w . . . . . . . . . . . . . . . .     35.00     45.00

☐ "Forward With Roosevelt. No Retreat"; 1932 race; large circular bust portrait profile of FDR on left; approx. 11"l; painted red, white, blue tin . . . . . . .     50.00     60.00

☐ "Keep Roosevelt In The White House"; oval portrait of smiling FDR appears at left; "Roosevelt" in large letters slants across entire attachment; approx. 8½"; red, white, blue, black . . . . . . . . . . . .     50.00     60.00

☐ "Re-Elect Roosevelt"; die-cut oval above rectangle; FDR bust portrait with stars and stripes background; approx. 6"w; red, white, blue, black . . . .     35.00     45.00

☐ "Rise With Roosevelt" slogan license attachment; 12" x 4½"; red, white, blue . . . . . . . . . . . . . . . . .     35.00     45.00

☐ "Roosevelt" reflecting license attachment; large letters span entire length with silver light reflecting letters with blue outline against red background and blue rim; 11"l; 1940; Willkie match . . . . . . . . . . .     30.00     40.00

Price Range

☐ "Roosevelt" bumper sticker; large white lettering across red, blue slanted panels; rectangular sepia-tone photograph of FDR at left; 11"l paper; probably 1944, as wartime austerity limited tin production ...................................... 20.00 30.00

☐ "Roosevelt" license attachment; 12½" x 5"; green, white; painted tin ........................... 25.00 35.00

☐ "Roosevelt" die-stamped letters in script; 8"l; nickel plate on brass; license attachment ....... 25.00 35.00

☐ "Roosevelt For President" slogan license attachment; 12"; black, white raised letters .......... 30.00 40.00

☐ "Roosevelt [illustration of large foamy stein of beer rebus] and Garner"; dramatic jugate license attachment with oval portraits of 1932 Democratic slate promises to repeal Prohibition; approx. 8½"; black, white, gold; considered by many as outstanding license plate attachment in the hobby ........... 125.00 150.00

☐ "Roosevelt–Garner" die-cut flying donkey; names appear across the body; approx. 6½"w; brown, black ..................................... 75.00 85.00

☐ "Roosevelt–Garner" die-cut circle with candidate's names wrapping around view of Capitol dome; approx. 4" dia; black, gray, white .............. 65.00 75.00

☐ "Roosevelt Motor Club. Victory 1932"; embossed circular license attachment or possible radiator mount; "Authorized by Democratic National Campaign Committee" imprint around circular portrait bust of FDR; 6" dia; bronze finish ............ 100.00 110.00

☐ "Roosevelt" name license attachment; 6½"; red, white, blue; 1940 race; Willkie match .......... 25.00 30.00

## RADIATOR ATTACHMENTS

☐ Die-stamped donkey with words coming out of open mouth: "Hee-Haw. Victory"; 1932; brown; red, white, blue ............................ 45.00 55.00

☐ "For President. Franklin D. Roosevelt"; light and shadow line drawing bust portrait of FDR; four punched holes in each side for attachment; Hoover match; 1932 campaign ...................... 30.00 40.00

| TIRE COVERS | Price Range | |
|---|---|---|
| ☐ "Roosevelt For President"; FDR bust portrait in circle; large lettering in border; blue, white; oilcloth | 150.00 | 200.00 |
| ☐ "Roosevelt For President" variant with slightly different pose; black, white; oilcloth; "Shelby County Democratic Committee" appears in small print under "President" .......................... | 175.00 | 225.00 |

| WINDOW STICKERS | | |
|---|---|---|
| ☐ "This Ford Votes For Roosevelt" (a response to Henry Ford's agressive support of Herbert Hoover in 1936 race) .............................. | 35.00 | 40.00 |
| ☐ "Here's A Ford That's Not For Hoover"; produced by National Democratic Campaign Committee .. | 35.00 | 40.00 |

## Banks

| | | |
|---|---|---|
| ☐ FDR bust still bank, Kenton, 1930s, cast iron, gilded paint, 6"h .......................... | 125.00 | 150.00 |
| ☐ "New Deal" Safe FDR Still Bank, Kenton, 1936, cast iron, 5"h ............................. | 75.00 | 100.00 |
| ☐ Roosevelt (FDR) "Happy Days" Barrell Still Bank, Chein, 1936, tin with slot in top, 4"h .......... | 15.00 | 25.00 |

## Cartoon/Pictorial Pinbacks

| | | |
|---|---|---|
| ☐ "A Democratic Clean Sweep"; broom illustration; 1932; (Hake 227) ¾"; yellow, black, white ..... | 10.00 | 15.00 |
| ☐ Capitol dome with "Roosevelt–Garner" names superimposed (Hake 210) ½"; red, black; lithograph | 10.00 | 15.00 |
| ☐ "Don't Change The Pilot. Re-elect Franklin D. Roosevelt"; Roosevelt at helm of ship (Hake 146) ⅞"; red, blue, white ("Fortis Non Timet," Latin phrase, in scroll) ........................... | 15.00 | 20.00 |
| ☐ Ear of corn; "Roosevelt–Wallace" (Hake 216) ⅞"; yellow, green ............................... | 5.00 | 10.00 |
| ☐ "Groundhogs Of Virginia–Roosevelt" (Hake 2026; Warner 773) 2⅛"; black, white; FDR supporter's club; 1932; key item cartoon classic ........... | 150.00 | 175.00 |

Price Range

☐ "It Used To Be A Vote Getter. Nothing In It. Grand Old Prosperity. But It's On The Junk Pile Now"; illustration of empty dinner pail (Hake 27) 1¼"; blue, white . . . . . . . . . . . . . . . . . . . . . . . . . . . . . 45.00     55.00

☐ "Kick Out Depression With A Democratic Vote"; lithographed mechanical; pull string and donkey boots elephant in backside (Hake 25) 2¾"; black, white; Hoover match from 1932 race . . . . . . . . . . 30.00     35.00

☐ "Land [on] Your [donkey rebus] For President" (Hake 309) 1¼"; black, white; Willkie match from 1940 race . . . . . . . . . . . . . . . . . . . . . . . . . . . . . . . . 125.00     135.00

☐ "Railway Employees Roosevelt Club. Stark County Ohio"; train engine illustration with circular portrait of FDR on front hood (Hake unlisted; Warner 420) 1¼"; red, black on pale green background; 1936 item ranks as perhaps best single picture pinback for FDR . . . . . . . . . . . . . . . . . . . . . . . . . . . . 700.00     800.00

☐ "Republican Roosevelt–Garner League"; illustration of large anchor and rope (Hake 211) ¾"; red, white, blue . . . . . . . . . . . . . . . . . . . . . . . . . . . . . . . 15.00     20.00

☐ "Rose [rebus] Velt" (Hake 228) ⅞"; red, green; lithograph; harks back to 1900 TR rose rebuses 20.00     25.00

☐ "Rose Velt" rebus; last four letters *(Ve* and *lt)* appear on separate leaves of stem (Hake 229) ⅞"; red, black; déjà vu time . . . . . . . . . . . . . . . . . . . . . . . . . 25.00     30.00

☐ Shield illustration, "Roosevelt-Truman, 1944"; eagle in shield with "All For One; One For All" on chest; small drawings of U.S. Navy, Army, Marines, Air Force members (Hake 219) 1¼"; red, white, blue, brown; lithograph (lithograph reproduction exists) . . . . . . . . . . . . . . . . . . . . . . . . . . . . 30.00     35.00

☐ Statue of Liberty illustration, "Draft Roosevelt For '40" (Hake 235) ⅞"; red, white, blue . . . . . . . . . . 15.00     20.00

☐ Teamster's symbol: "Team With Roosevelt" (Hake 184) 1"; red, white, blue . . . . . . . . . . . . . . . . . . . . 10.00     12.00

☐ White elephant illustration; "Get Rid Of The G.O.P. Elephant [rebus]. Turn Democratic" (Hake 225) ⅞"; red, white, blue . . . . . . . . . . . . . . . . . . . . 10.00     12.00

Price Range

☐ "Wipe Out Depression. Clean The Slate With A Straight Democratic Vote"; Democratic donkey wiping off "G.O.P." from black slate (Hake 310) 1¼"; black, red, white ..................... 35.00 50.00

☐ "Young Democrats Of Wake County," North Carolina, item; 1936 campaign; cartoon of rooster with pamphlet in beak that reads "Victory In 1936" (Hake 2082; Warner 777) 1"; red, white, blue ... 175.00 200.00

## Dolls, Games, Puzzles, Toys

☐ Franklin D. Roosevelt cloth doll; molded and painted features, cloth body, felt head, hands, suit and hat; oilcloth shirt and shoes; carries pair of canes; 19"h; white, black, blue, fleshtones; 1930s 200.00 300.00*

☐ Franklin D. Roosevelt figurine; plaster caricature study of FDR with arms akimbo (Hake 2078) 5¾"h; white, blue, yellow, fleshtones .......... 60.00 75.00

☐ "Roosevelt Garner" donkey wooden pulltoy; die-cut wooden body; leather ears, tail; wooden doweled wheels; 8"l; brown, white, black .......... 75.00 100.00

☐ "F.D.R." cloth donkey; 6"l; brown, black ...... 25.00 30.00

☐ "F.D.R./Hoover/The Presidential Puzzle—May The Best Man Win"; silhouettes of both candidates lithographed on box; red, white, blue .......... 50.00 65.00

☐ "F.D.R. Jigsaw Puzzle. World Famous Initials"; 11 blue and red pieces; 1933; made by Perry & Elliot Co., Lynn, MA ........................... 10.00 15.00

☐ F.D.R. Association wooden outhouse; dimensional novelty; headless figure appears when door is opened; 5"h; natural finish; half-moon painted on door in black .............................. 25.00 35.00

☐ "New Deal Game", 1933; Uncle Sam appears on colorful red, white, blue box; center spins to show different pictures including NRA eagle ......... 65.00 75.00

*Brought $500 at Atlanta Toy Museum Auction, October 1986.

Price Range

☐ FDR "New Deal" wooden sailboat; cloth sail; die-
cut cardboard figure of FDR at tiller .......... 35.00 45.00

☐ "The Man Of The Hour" double-vision jigsaw puzzle with 12 symbols of prosperity; multicolored
grouping includes Roosevelt bust portrait, flags of
many nations, cornucopia, montage of laborers,
students, servicemen; colorful box in red, white,
blue with illustration of Capitol building; made by
C. C. Beall, 1933 ............................ 25.00 35.00

☐ FDR head nodder; 1940; "Are You Going To Run
For A Third Term?" Tap the rockerlike head on
the chin, and it nods yes about a dozen times in suc-
cession; 3"h; hard rubber .................... 35.00 40.00

## Inaugural Pinbacks

### FIRST TERM—1933

☐ "O.K. America. You Bet I'm With You. Our President Franklin D. Roosevelt"; Capitol dome seems
to rise out of top of FDR's head; montage of other
Washington, DC buildings, including White House
and Jefferson Memorial (Hake 2014, with ribbon attachment; Warner 418, pinback only) 2⅛"; red,
white, blue ................................ 100.00 125.00

☐ "We Will Protect Our Flag, Property With Roosevelt" flag in center; small FDR portrait above
(Hake 2110; Warner 772) ⅞"; red, white, blue,
black, yellow; made by Western Badge Co., Minnesota ...................................... 250.00 275.00

### SECOND TERM—1937

☐ "Inauguration Of Franklin D. Roosevelt, Washington D.C., Jan. 20, 1937"; gilt lettering on red, white,
blue ribbon attached to no-name left-profile FDR
celluloid pinback in black, white (Hake 2018) 1¾"
cello; approx. 6" overall .................... 30.00 35.00

☐ FDR profile, "Inauguration 1937"; one of the
draped flag designs (Hake 21) 1¾"; red, white,
blue, black ................................ 25.00 30.00

THIRD TERM—1941                                        Price Range

☐ "Inauguration January 20th, 1941. Washington D.C." FDR left-facing profile in draped-flag design with no lettering on celluloid pinback but gilt embossed on dark blue attached ribbon with star (Hake 2019) 1¾"; red, white, blue, black; celluloid; 4"1 overall .................................       30.00      35.00

☐ "Inauguration January 20, 1941" in border; circular portrait of FDR (Hake 22) 1¼"; black, white       30.00      35.00

☐ "Souvenir Of The Inauguration. Jan. 20th 1941; illustration of Capitol building with "Franklin D. Roosevelt" under circular portrait superimposed on main portico and dome (Hake 23) 1¼"; black, white .......................................      15.00      25.00

## Medals

☐ 1933—left-facing bust portrait of Roosevelt with name; "1933–1937" dates; "31st President of the United States" on obverse; three-masted ship and angel embossed on reverse with "Sail On O Ship Of State. Sail On, Union Strong and Great"; silver finish ........................................     125.00     150.00

☐ 1937—right-facing bust portrait of Roosevelt with name; "Second Inauguration, Jan. 20, 1937" engraved on obverse; right-facing bust profile of John Nance Garner on reverse, with "32nd Vice President"; silver finish .........................      75.00     100.00

☐ 1941—left-facing bust portrait of much older FDR on obverse; "Franklin Delano Roosevelt, President of The United States" in border; "Jan. 20, 1941" engraved inside laurel wreath on reverse; "Third Inauguration" and stars appear around border; silver finish .......................................      75.00     100.00

☐ 1945—right-facing bust portrait Roosevelt wearing overcoat; "Franklin Delano Roosevelt. Fourth Inauguration" embossed on obverse; "Thou Too Sail On O Ship Of State" embossed around border; schooner in full sail on reverse; silver finish .....      75.00     100.00

| *Jugate Pinbacks* | Price Range | |
|---|---|---|

## ROOSEVELT–GARNER

☐ "Roosevelt–Garner" connecting oval portraits; photographs and star atop, reversed out of black (Hake 7) ⅞" black, white .................. 100.00 — 125.00

☐ "Roosevelt–Garner For Repeal And Prosperity"; large oval portraits within circle (Hake 2005; Warner 771) 1¼"; red, white, black .............. 350.00 — 375.00

☐ "Roosevelt–Garner For Repeal And Prosperity"; winged eagle atop canted oval portraits; three wide stripes in background (Hake 2006) 1¼"; red, white, blue, black, gold ........................... 250.00 — 275.00

☐ "Roosevelt–Garner" portraits conjoined (Hake 2004) ⅞"; black, white ..................... 300.00 — 325.00

☐ "Roosevelt–Garner"; eagle with wings spread; small shield; names in scroll under photographs (Hake 3; Warner 775) ⅞"; black, white ........ 225.00 — 250.00

☐ "Roosevelt and Garner" canted oval portraits reversed out of black (Hake 6) ⅞"; black, white .. 50.00 — 75.00

☐ "Roosevelt and Garner. Return Our Country To The People"; bleed portraits (Hake 4) ⅞"; black, white ...................................... 225.00 — 250.00

☐ "Roosevelt–Garner" circular portraits (line drawings); 13 stars atop; patriotic stripes below. Appeared in three sizes; red, white, blue; lithograph (Hake 11) 1½" ........................... 10.00 — 15.00

☐ (Hake 12) 1¼" ........................... 10.00 — 15.00

☐ (Hake 13) ⅞"; cello reproduction exists ........ 10.00 — 15.00

☐ Identical design in black, white (Hake 10) 1½" .. 50.00 — 65.00

☐ (Hake 8) ⅞" .............................. 35.00 — 45.00

☐ (Hake 9) ¾" .............................. 35.00 — 45.00

☐ "Roosevelt–Garner" oval portraits and lettering reversed out of black; flag bunting border (Hake 305) 1¼"; red, white, blue, black ................. 200.00 — 225.00

## ROOSEVELT–LOCAL CANDIDATES

☐ "Economic Security"; winged eagle atop oval portraits of Roosevelt and James Michael Curley, Massachusetts political kingpin; shield between names

Price Range

(Hake 155; Warner 417) $2\frac{1}{8}$"; red, white, blue, black; probably for Curley's campaign for governor in 1934 ........................................    75.00    100.00

☐ "Work And Wages," identical design to FDR–Curley above except for name change; said to be used in FDR Boston Common rally in 1932 (Hake 2020; Warner 774) $2\frac{1}{4}$"; the scarcer of the two jugates ........................................    125.00    150.00

☐ "Roosevelt–Horner"; 13 stars in blue field above circular photographs of FDR and Henry Horner, Democratic gubernatorial candidate in Illinois in 1936; stripes below (Hake 160) $1\frac{1}{4}$"; bluetone, white ........................................    50.00    75.00

☐ "Roosevelt–Horner, Peoria County. Vote Democratic"; another 1936 Illinois local FDR jugate (Hake unlisted; Warner 780) $13/16$"; red, white, blue (additional FDR–Horner jugates include Hake 161–162) ........................................    125.00    150.00

☐ "Furriers For Roosevelt–Lehman"; linked circular portraits and lettering reverse out of dark blue (Hake 157) $1\frac{3}{4}$"; blue, white; New York local item    275.00    300.00

☐ Also appeared in $\frac{7}{8}$" size (Hake 2156) .........    425.00    450.00

☐ "Vote For Roosevelt–Guffey" (Joseph F. Guffey, Democratic Senator, Pennsylvania); names appear in elaborate scroll (Hake 156) $1\frac{3}{4}$" red, white, bluetone ........................................    100.00    125.00

☐ "Me and Roosevelt For Johnson"; oval portraits of FDR and Lyndon Johnson; from Johnson's 1941 Senate race in Texas (Hake unlisted; Warner 785) $2\frac{1}{4}$"; red, white, blue ........................    550.00    600.00

☐ "Victory Parade"; oval jugate of FDR and James Michael Curley, New York Democratic leader; "July 4, 1932" (Hake 2153) $2\frac{3}{4}$"w x $2\frac{1}{8}$"h; black, white ........................................    350.00    375.00

**ROOSEVELT–TRUMAN**

☐ "Roosevelt–Truman" line drawings of candidates with a star appearing on each side of image (Hake 19) $1\frac{1}{4}$"; browntone, white ..................    35.00    50.00

|  | Price Range | |
|---|---|---|

☐ Also ⅞″ (Hake 20) ......................  30.00   35.00
    Cello reproductions of both of the above FDR–Truman jugate sizes have appeared.

ROOSEVELT–WALLACE
☐ "I'm For Roosevelt And Wallace"; conjoining portraits (Hake 15) ⅞″; black, white ............  85.00   100.00
☐ Also (Hake 18) ¾″ size ....................  65.00   75.00
☐ "Roosevelt–Wallace" circular portraits with lettering reversed out of red (Hake 16) ⅞″; red, blue; blue rim lithograph ........................  15.00   20.00
☐ "Roosevelt–Wallace" connecting oval portraits; flag bunting border (Hake 14) 1¼″; red, white, blue, black (reproduction in celluloid exists) ....  15.00   20.00
☐ "Roosevelt For President. Wallace For Vice-President"; silhouetted portraits (Hake 17) ⅞″; black, white lithograph (celluloid reproduction exists) ......................................  50.00   60.00

WARTIME LEADERS
☐ "Casablanca. Unconditional Surrender"; oval portraits of Winston Churchill and FDR with flags of their respective nations flying above (Hake unlisted; Warner 786) 1¾″; red, white, blue; celebrated World War II meeting of two leaders in 1943 ...  125.00   150.00

*Lighting Devices*

☐ FDR wooden lamp with high-relief portrait medallions, two each, of FDR and NRA eagle; walnut body; 19″h; blue, tan, black .................  200.00   250.00
☐ Roosevelt at the helm (or ship's wheel) in bronzed pot metal; three-dimensional; green glass globe; NRA eagle embossed on side of ship's wheel; 1″h including globe* ...........................  75.00   100.00

*A more common variant, minus the NRA eagle, carries slogan: "The Man Of The Hour," a design also incorporated into a mantel clock (see Timepieces); globes also in apricot color.

Price Range

☐ Roosevelt "Back To Work" theme lampshade; laurel wreath framed FDR portrait and vignettes of smoking, busy factories, farmers in the fields, symbols of transportation, and NRA shield; 5"h; brown, ivory ............................... 45.00 55.00

☐ Roosevelt lithopane candle lamp; light shines through to reveal large FDR portrait; Landon on reverse; 1936 race; 8" x 5" x 3"; white biscuit porcelain ........................................ 300.00 350.00

## Paperweights, Doorstops

☐ "F.D.R.–Garner" doorstop; deep-relief bronze figural of Capitol building and busts of both candidates with names embossed below; approx. 9"h; gilt finish ....................................... 135.00 150.00

☐ FDR "A New Deal"; die-stamped figural bust paperweight; embossed lettering; iron; 3"h; chrome finish ....................................... 15.00 25.00

☐ "F.D.R." Liberty Bell die-stamped figural paperweight; details in bell; FDR bust profile and initials incised; 3"h; chrome finish ................... 20.00 30.00

☐ "Hoover Depression Skillet 1932"; anti-Hoover cast-iron paperweight; 4"l; natural finish ....... 20.00 25.00

☐ "F.D.R." bell; cast-metal paperweight with embossed portraits of FDR, Churchill, Stalin; "Cast in metal from German aircraft shot down over Britain 1939–45. R.A.F. Benevolent Fund"; "V For Victory" embossed on handle; 6"h ............ 65.00 75.00

## Portrait Pinbacks

☐ "Brewery Worker's Choice"; Roosevelt portrait (Hake 2042) 1¼"; red, black, white ........... 100.00 125.00

☐ "Carry On With Roosevelt"; counter message to Willkie "No Third Termites"; 1940 (Hake 2012; Warner 781) 3½"; red, white, blue, black ...... 125.00 135.00

☐ "Carry On With Roosevelt"; life preserver design border in red, white, blue with message reversed out of colors (Hake 150) ⅞"; red, white, bluetone; lithograph ................................... 10.00 15.00

Price Range

☐ Similar design, with FDR facing in opposite direction in black, white (Hake 152) red, white, blue, black; lithograph . . . . . . . . . . . . . . . . . . . . . . . . . . . . 8.00 10.00

☐ "For President. Franklin D. Roosevelt" (Hake 2022) 2¼"; black, white . . . . . . . . . . . . . . . . . . . . . 75.00 100.00

☐ "Draft Roosevelt"; criss-crossed patriotic flag bunting border; bluetone circular bust portrait (Hake 50) 1¼"; red, white, blue . . . . . . . . . . . . . . . . . . : . . 75.00 100.00

☐ A variant (Hake 53) has no message; features sepiatone portrait . . . . . . . . . . . . . . . . . . . . . . . . . . . . . . 25.00 50.00

☐ "Franklin D. Roosevelt Booster Club"; FDR profile portrait; Midwest item (Hake 2056; Warner 779) 1¼"; black, white; 1936 . . . . . . . . . . . . . . . . . 100.00 125.00

☐ "For President, Franklin D. Roosevelt"; "V" (for victory with dot-dot-dot-dash Morse code designation); 1944 campaign (Hake 81) 1¼"; black, white 8.00 10.00

☐ "For U.S. Senator, Franklin D. Roosevelt" (Hake 2104) ⅞"; black, white . . . . . . . . . . . . . . . . . . . . . . 350.00 375.00

☐ Slight variant, Hake 2105, of above . . . . . . . . . . . 50.00 75.00

☐ "Franklin D. Roosevelt For President," 1936 (Hake 2060; Warner 778) 1¼"; black, white . . . . . . . . . . 75.00 100.00

☐ "He's Good Enough For My Buck" (Hake 150) ⅞"; red, white, blue; lithograph . . . . . . . . . . . . . . 10.00 15.00

☐ "I Want Roosevelt [rebus portrait] Again" (Hake 69) 1"; red, white, black; lithograph . . . . . . . . . . . 10.00 12.00

☐ "Labor's Choice. Roosevelt"; circular portrait across slanting patriotic banner (Hake 95) ⅞"; red, white, blue, black . . . . . . . . . . . . . . . . . . . . . . . . . . . 50.00 60.00

☐ "Liberal Party. Vote Row F."; pair of Liberty Bells flank FDR portrait (Hake 145) ⅞"; red, white, blue; lithograph . . . . . . . . . . . . . . . . . . . . . . . . . . . 10.00 12.00

☐ "Labor's Choice," size variant from Hake 95; (Hake 61; Warner 423) 1936 campaign; 1¼"; red, white, blue, black . . . . . . . . . . . . . . . . . . . . . . . . . . . . . . 50.00 60.00

☐ "Our Leader. Franklin D. Roosevelt"; portrait with two stars (Hake 2030) 2¼"; black, white . . . . . . . 25.00 35.00

| | Price Range | |
|---|---|---|

☐ "National Democratic Convention 1936. Philadelphia, Pa"; bust portrait (Hake 2041) $1\frac{1}{2}$"; black, white . . . . . . . . . . . . . . . . . . . . . . . . . . . . . . . . . . . . . 100.00     125.00

☐ "Our President"; portrait amid furled flags and scroll (Hake 66) 1"; multicolor; lithograph . . . . . 10.00     15.00

☐ "Member Labor For Roosevelt Club" (Hake 2057) $1\frac{1}{4}$"; black, blue, white . . . . . . . . . . . . . . . . . . . . 85.00     100.00

☐ "Our Choice. Laundry Driver's Union. No. 344" (Hake 2058) $1\frac{1}{4}$"; black, white . . . . . . . . . . . . . . 100.00     125.00

☐ "Our President. Franklin D. Roosevelt" (Hake 2044) $2\frac{3}{4}$"; black, white . . . . . . . . . . . . . . . . . . . . . 25.00     30.00

☐ "President Roosevelt"; FDR bust portrait in black against teal blue background (Hake 84) $\frac{7}{8}$"; black, white, blue . . . . . . . . . . . . . . . . . . . . . . . . . . . . . . . 20.00     25.00

☐ "Re-elect Roosevelt"; bust portrait in shield (Hake 98; Warner 427) $\frac{7}{8}$"; red, white, blue, black . . . . 50.00     75.00

☐ "Re-elect Roosevelt"; silhouetted portrait of FDR; (Hake 84; Warner 422) $\frac{7}{8}$"; black, white; steel blue 25.00     35.00

☐ Roosevelt no-name; "Bill's Buttons, Seattle, Washington"; advertising sample for button company (Hake 45) $1\frac{3}{4}$"; black, white; green rim . . . . . . . . 75.00     100.00

☐ Roosevelt no-name; "birthstone" design; months of year with corresponding birthstones border circular FDR portrait (Hake 30) 2"; multicolor . . . . . . . . 100.00     125.00

☐ Roosevelt no-name elaborate floral pattern companion to Hake 30; surrounds gold-rimmed circular portrait, giving appearance of porcelain (Hake 31) 2"; pink, green, gold, brown, black, fleshtones . . . 100.00     135.00

☐ Roosevelt no-name; four fields of blue with stars and stripes border black circular portrait of FDR (Hake 40) $1\frac{1}{2}$"; red, white, blue, black . . . . . . . . 40.00     50.00

☐ "Roosevelt" name runs vertically to border FDR's left-facing bust profile (Hake 33) $1\frac{1}{2}$"; black, white 20.00     30.00

☐ Roosevelt no-name; oval pinback (Hake 2086) $1\frac{1}{4}$"h x $\frac{3}{4}$"w; black, white . . . . . . . . . . . . . . . . . . 20.00     30.00

☐ "Support Your Commander In Chief"; 1944 race (Hake 2048) $1\frac{1}{2}$"; black, white . . . . . . . . . . . . . . 50.00     60.00

Price Range

☐ "Sweeping The Depression Out"; profile portrait
(Hake 57) 1¼"; black, white ................   25.00     30.00

☐ "The Fighting President. A Universal Picture"; motion picture promotional item (Hake 2070) 1¼";
red, white, black, blue ......................   25.00     50.00

☐ "Turn Democratic"; thumbnail-size; red, white
message area superimposed on bluetone portrait
(Hake 88) ⅞"; bluetone, red, white ...........   25.00     35.00

☐ "United Mine Workers of America. L.V. No. 473,
Sagamore, Pa." (Hake 2059) 1¼"; black, white   120.00    130.00

☐ "Veteran's Choice" reversed out of deep blue border; portrait framed by laurel wreath; possibly a
Memorial Day item (Hake 43) 1¾"; blue, white,
black, light brown ..........................   40.00     45.00

☐ "Victory 1936," no-name pinback (Hake unlisted in
this size; Warner 776) ⅞"; sepiatone ..........   250.00    275.00

☐ "Victory 1936"; 4" size (Hake 2013; Warner 421)   350.00    400.00

☐ "Vote For Roosevelt"; silhouetted portrait (Hake
2010; Warner 782) 2½"; black, white; unusual 1940
campaign centerpiece .......................   100.00    110.00

☐ "Vote For The New Deal"; dramatic 1936 portrait
item (Hake 24) 3⅛"; black, white .............   70.00     75.00

☐ "Welcome President Roosevelt"; Atlanta, Georgia,
Homecoming; 1935 FDR visit; made by Floding
Co., Atlanta (Hake unlisted. Warner 419) 1¼";
red, white, blue ...........................   125.00    150.00

☐ "We Need You Franklin D. Roosevelt"; silhouetted
portrait against pale blue background (Hake 64)
1¼"; black, robin's-egg blue (lithographed reproduction exists) .............................   15.00     20.00

### Portrait-Draped Flag Designs

☐ "Man Of The Hour. President Franklin D. Roosevelt"; draped flag borders two-thirds of circle portrait of FDR (Hake 35) 1¾"; red, white, blue, black   35.00     45.00
    The above design was issued in a number of vari-
ants:

☐ Hake 2037; FDR in profile; no lettering ........   25.00     30.00

Price Range

☐ Hake 41; FDR facing forward; no lettering ..... 20.00 25.00

☐ Hake 2036; FDR profile; "Rockland County Delegation. Franklin D. Roosevelt" .............. 50.00 75.00

☐ Hake 21; FDR profile; "Inauguration—1937" ... 25.00 30.00
See also Hake 11 for Hoover match from 1932 race.

## Posters

☐ "A Challenge For Humanity From The Nation's Capitol. America"; FDR with Capitol dome in background stands atop steps of achievement that include banking reform laws, Social Security; repeal of 19th Amendment, etc. 12"h x 9"w; red, white, blue; probably 1936 campaign ................ 35.00 40.00

☐ "A Gallant Leader. Roosevelt"; FDR line drawing within Art Deco–style stars and stripes circle; 1940 campaign; approx. 17"h x 12"w; red, black, ivory 150.00 175.00

☐ "For God And Country"; jugate poster with ornate framed portraits, canted, of "Pres. Franklin D. Roosevelt" and "Rev. Charles E. Coughlin"; a flag flanks FDR portrait; a cross, that of Coughlin; an eagle in flight carrying arrows in talons appears under scrolled legend; the pair are shown in harmony in this 1932 rendering, but later the two went in opposite directions as the famous "Radio Priest" became more bigoted and vocal in his Fascist leanings; 17"h x 12"w; black, red, white, blue ...... 125.00 150.00

☐ "Franklin D. Roosevelt"; large line drawing of FDR (Hake 2223) 15"h x 11"w; black, white; probably 1940 .................................. 20.00 25.00

☐ "Carry On With Roosevelt"; large photograph bust image of FDR in large quadruple-image tablet-like frame; red, white, blue, black; 27"h x 18½"w ... 75.00 100.00

☐ "A Progressive Candidate With Constructive Policies For President. Governor Franklin D. Roosevelt Of New York"; 1932 campaign; portrait in simulated picture frame; black on buff stock ....... 45.00 55.00

Price Range

☐ "Climb On The Band Wagon August 19"; 1936 campaign; oval picture of FDR on illustrated horse-drawn circus wagon; "Hon. James Farley, Democratic Campaign Chairman" appears in small cameo shot with donkey head protruding; vignette at bottom shows band leading large parade; names of Committee On Arrangements for the party appear at very bottom of poster; promotes a nation-wide Democratic jubilee; black, white . . . . . . . . . .    35.00      45.00

☐ "Don't Worry About The Big Boys! Give Yourself A Break. Stand by. Vote For Roosevelt And Wallace"; 1940 campaign; black, red, white . . . . . . . .    50.00      75.00

☐ "Hoover 1932. New Deal 1940. Roosevelt American Labor"; large oval FDR portrait in center with panels to left depicting bread lines and bank closings under Hoover; panels to right cite "Higher Wages, Low Rent Homes, and Social Security"; 28"h x 21"w; black, white, orange, pink . . . . . . . .    135.00     150.00

☐ "Rain Or Shine"; FDR outdoors in rain and wearing wide-brim hat; 11"h x 8"w; black, white . . . .    25.00      30.00

☐ "Forward With Roosevelt. Vote Democratic X"; appeared in two sizes: 11"h x 8"w; 14"h x 11"w; black, white . . . . . . . . . . . . . . . . . . . . . . . . . . . . .    (L) 75.00     85.00
                                                    (S) 65.00     75.00

☐ "America Needs Roosevelt. Democratic X"; multi-gate poster from 1940 race features FDR, Vice-President Henry Wallace, and three coattail candidates; 18"h x 13"w; black, white . . . . . . . . . . . . .    75.00     100.00

☐ "No World War III For Me! Mama's Going To Vote For Roosevelt And A Congress To Support Him"; 18"w x 14"h; black, white; 1944 . . . . . . . .    35.00      45.00

☐ "Register And Vote Democratic. Roosevelt. Truman For Lasting Peace. Security For All." FDR–Truman jugate poster; Democratic rooster appears at top; 14"h x 11"w; black, red, white; 1944 campaign . . . . . . . . . . . . . . . . . . . . . . . . . . . . . . .    125.00     150.00

☐ "I Want You F.D.R. Stay And Finish The Job!"; 1944 campaign; classic Uncle Sam pointing his finger (variation with Roosevelt portrait below); by

Price Range

illustrator James Montgomery Flagg; 22"h x 16"w; red, white, blue, black; by "Independent Voters' Committee Of The Arts and Sciences for Roosevelt" ...................................... 150.00     200.00

☐ "Pillars Of American Democracy"; trigate poster features Thomas Jefferson, "Founder"; Woodrow Wilson, "Interpreter"; FDR "Promulgator"; oval insets are framed between pillars; 21"w x 8"h; black, white ............................... 75.00     100.00

☐ "The Difference Between the Democrats and Republicans is 12 years of Experience"; Four Freedoms symbol and "Re-Elect Roosevelt" appear in upper left corner; 12"w x 10"w; red, black, white broadside .................................. 34.00     45.00

☐ "Roosevelt–Truman" jugate poster; stars bracket each name; 15"h x 11"w; red, black white ...... 35.00     45.00

☐ "The Democratic Party's Nominees"; trigate poster; FDR, Garner, and Miriam Ferguson, nominee for governor of Texas in 1932 race; Ferguson had been elected first in 1924 and was re-elected in 1932, the first woman governor in the United States; 38"h x 25"w; black, white .................. 250.00     275.00

☐ Roosevelt–Lehmann poster, American Labor Party, 1936; after a William Sanger painting of six people championing "shorter hours," "abolition of child labor," "collective bargaining"— accomplishments of Joint Board Dressmakers Union; 34½"w x 24½"h; multicolor; one of the most vibrant and colorful political posters of the modern era .................................. 250.00     300.00

## SENATOR/GOVERNOR CAMPAIGN POSTERS

FDR was a successful campaigner for state senator in New York in 1910, his first quest for public office. Four years later he made an ill-fated run for the U.S. Senate.

☐ "Franklin D. Roosevelt For State Senator. Counties Of Columbia, Dutchess and Putnam"; facsimile signature under portrait; black and white; photograph glued to cardboard backing .................. 100.00     125.00

**Price Range**

☐ "Franklin D. Roosevelt Candidate For Senator. His record shows that he fought for every measure asked by the farmers and the working man" (New York Senate, 1912); profile portrait; black, white; 19"h x 12½"w; ............................ 225.00 250.00

FDR was a successful candidate for governor of New York in 1928 and 1930.

☐ "For Governor. Franklin D. Roosevelt. Keep Good Government" (this slogan allied him with the Al Smith legacy; Smith was instrumental in persuading FDR to run for governor); sepiatone photo by M. B. Brown Co.; 1928 New York gubernatorial race ....................................... 100.00 125.00

☐ "Re-Elect Governor Franklin D. Roosevelt and Lieut. Governor Herbert H. Lehman. Keep Progressive Government"; black, white; 1930 campaign; portraits of FDR and Lehman .......... 75.00 100.00

## Slogan/Name Pinbacks

### 1932 CAMPAIGN

☐ "A Democratic Clean Sweep [broom illustration] 1932" (Hake 227) ⅞"; blue, yellow, white ...... 10.00 12.00

☐ "America Calls Another Roosevelt"; letters in shield outline (Hake 243) ⅞"; red, white, blue .. 15.00 20.00

☐ "America Calls Another Roosevelt. Franklin D. No Reservations" (Hake 242) ⅞"; red, white, blue .. 20.00 25.00

☐ "For Roosevelt & Repeal" (Hake 241) ⅞"; blue, white; lithograph ........................... 12.00 15.00

☐ "Goodby Hoover" (Hake 224) ⅞"; black, yellow 15.00 20.00

☐ "Have Faith In The New Deal For Prosperity" (Hake 254) ⅞"; blue, white ................. 8.00 10.00

☐ "New Deal Is Youth's Deal" (Hake 247) ⅞"; red, white, blue ............................... 8.00 10.00

☐ "Out Of The Red [white reverses out of red] With Roosevelt" (Hake 249) ⅞"; red, white, blue .... 12.00 15.00

☐ "RRR-Rally Round Roosevelt" (Hake 248) ⅞"; red, white, blue ............................ 12.00 15.00

Price Range

☐ "Roosevelt. Conditions Demand Him" (Hake 262)
⅞"; blue, white ............................ 5.00    8.00

☐ "YOUth For Roosevelt" (Hake 274) ⅞"; red,
white, blue ................................. 5.00    8.00

## 1940 CAMPAIGN

In response to a barrage of over a hundred different slogan pinbacks by the Willkieites seeking to head off FDR's quest for a third term, the Democrats responded with slogan pinbacks of their own. This is a mere sampling.

☐ "A Pauper For Roosevelt" (Hake 203) 1¼"; black,
white ....................................... 5.00    8.00

☐ "A Third Term Is Better Than A Third Rater"
(Hake 190) 1¼"; red, black, white ............ 5.00    8.00

☐ "America Wants Roosevelt" (Hake 207) 1¼"; red,
black, white ................................ 5.00    8.00

☐ "Confucius Say ... One Time Good. Two Times
Good. Three Times ... Damn Good" (Hake 189)
1¼"; black, blue ........................... 5.00    8.00

☐ "F.D.R. Carry On" (Hake 204) 1¼"; black, white,
red ........................................ 5.00    8.00

☐ "*F*riendly, *D*ependable, *R*esourceful" (Hake 193)
1¼"; black, white; red rim ................... 5.00    8.00

☐ "*F*ranklin *D*eserves *R*eelection" (Hake 202) 1¼";
black, pale blue ............................ 5.00    8.00

☐ "Confidentially I'm Voting For Roosevelt" (unlisted) 1¼"; blue, white ..................... 5.00    8.00

☐ "Keep Roosevelt In White House. Willkie In Pow-
erhouse" (Hake 199) 1¼"; blue, white ......... 5.00    8.00

☐ "I'll Bet My B.V.D. On F.D.R." (Hake 194) 1¼";
blue, yellow ............................... 5.00    8.00

☐ "If Willkie's In The Whitehouse. It's U.S. In The
Poorhouse" (Hake 192) 1¼"; blue, white ....... 5.00    8.00

☐ "Willkie No. No. 1000 Times No!" (Hake 205)
1¼"; red, white, blue ....................... 5.00    8.00

| | Price Range | |
|---|---|---|
| ☐ "Willkie For President Of Commonwealth And Southern" (Hake 200) 1¼"; blue, yellow ....... | 5.00 | 8.00 |
| ☐ "Win What? With Willkie" (Hake 201) 1¼"; blue, white ........................................ | 5.00 | 8.00 |
| ☐ "Willkie For The Millionaires. Roosevelt For The Millions" (Hake 195) 1¼"; red, white ......... | 5.00 | 8.00 |
| ☐ "Two Good Terms Deserve Another" (Hake 197) 1¼"; black, orange ......................... | 5.00 | 8.00 |
| ☐ "Willkie Gone With The Wind. Weather Forecast" (unlisted) 1¼"; black, white .................. | 6.00 | 9.00 |
| ☐ "All F.D.R. Can Get From Willkie Is Buttons" (unlisted) 1¼"; black, white .................. | 6.00 | 9.00 |
| ☐ "36 Million Americans Can't Be Wrong" (unlisted) 1¼"; blue, white ........................... | 6.00 | 9.00 |

**1944 CAMPAIGN**

| | | |
|---|---|---|
| ☐ "4th Term" (unlisted) ⅞"; blue, white ......... | 10.00 | 12.00 |
| ☐ "Happy Days Are Here Again" (Hake 2073) 1¼"; blue, white ............................... | 10.00 | 12.00 |
| ☐ "Four In A Row" (unlisted) 1¼"; red, white ... | 10.00 | 12.00 |
| ☐ "4" (large numeral in circle) (unlisted) ⅞"; black, white ........................................ | 10.00 | 12.00 |
| ☐ "Why Change?" (unlisted) 1¼"; black, white ... | 10.00 | 12.00 |
| ☐ "F.R. He Saved Our Home" (Hake 2095) ⅞"; red, white, blue ............................... | 25.00 | 30.00 |
| ☐ "Barkley–Roosevelt–Truman" (Hake 221) ⅞"; red, white, blue; lithograph .................. | 7.00 | 9.00 |
| ☐ "Roosevelt–Truman For Freedom. 44" (Hake 220) ⅞"; red, white, blue; lithograph .............. | 25.00 | 30.00 |
| ☐ "Roosevelt–Truman Save America"; small patriotic shield in center (Hake 222) ⅞"; red, white, blue; lithograph ........................... | 15.00 | 20.00 |
| ☐ "Texas For Roosevelt And Truman" (Hake 223) ½"; red, white, blue; lithograph .............. | 10.00 | 15.00 |
| ☐ "Three Good Terms Deserve Another" (Hake 2077) 1¼"; black, white ..................... | 6.00 | 8.00 |

*Trigates*                                              Price Range

MISCELLANEOUS

☐ "Forward Democracy" overlapping oval portraits
of FDR, Thomas Jefferson, and unidentified local
candidate (Hake 2155) 1¼"; black, white ......    175.00    200.00

☐ "I Am For An American"; conjoining right-facing
profile images of FDR, Lincoln, and Washington
(Hake 2085) ⅞"; black, white ...............    100.00    125.00

☐ "Let *F*reedom, *D*emocracy, *R*ing; first letter of each
word forming FDR; line drawings of Washington
and Lincoln facing left, with photo inset of FDR,
front-facing (an awkward montage) (Hake 2087)
⅞"; black, white ..........................     50.00     60.00

☐ "Mitchell Day"; Roosevelt portrait superimposed
on shield; flanked by John L. Lewis and James
Earle, labor leaders (Hake 158) 1¼"; red, white,
blue, black; 1936 item ......................    185.00    200.00

ROOSEVELT–WALLACE

☐ "A ROW Of Democrats" (first letter of each candidate's name spells out ROW: *R*oosevelt; *O*sborn;
*W*allace; conjoining portraits of all three above
their names (Hake 2003) 1¼"; black, white .....    425.00    450.00

*Timepieces*

*Note:* There are at least a dozen cast-metal clocks in various designs featuring FDR that were churned out in great quantity and often served as give-
aways and punchboard prizes; of questionable artistic merit.

☐ FDR cuckoo clock; die-stamped thermoplastic in
shape of Capitol dome, with oval portrait of FDR
in dome; clock dial is in portico area below .....    100.00    125.00

☐ FDR display clock, "Spirit of U.S.A."; FDR stands
in middle, flanked by Lincoln and Washington;
clock dial is in ship's wheel; 15"h; gilt, white metal;
electric ...................................     75.00     85.00

☐ FDR "Man Of The Hour" clock with Roosevelt at
the ship's wheel inset with clock; 13"h; gilt, white
metal .....................................     35.00     45.00

Price Range

☐ "Roosevelt At The Wheel For A New Deal"; variant of the above, except for the slogan and FDR mans ship from the right side; Windsor Electric clock; 13"h; gilt, white metal .................. 45.00 55.00

☐ Two-candle lamp clock, "The Spirit Of The U.S.A."; Roosevelt bust tops clock; Presidential advisor Harry Hopkins appears in bas relief at left below clock face; Secretary of Labor Frances Perkins at right; NRA eagle in middle; glass Christmas treelike bulbs appear in torchlike receptacles; 14"h; gilt, white metal ............................ 75.00 85.00

☐ NRA eagle atop clock with Roosevelt at helm below; 15"h; bronze finish ................... 100.00 110.00

## Watch Fobs

☐ Horseshoe-embossed brass frame with lithograph pinback inset; FDR portrait, "Franklin D. Roosevelt" (Hake 2192) 1¾"l with tab; black, white; brass finish ................................ 30.00 35.00

☐ Scrolled, irregularly shaped brass frame with lithographed FDR portrait inset; "Roosevelt" appears under portrait (Hake 2193) 1¾"; black, white; brass finish ................................ 30.00 35.00

☐ "The New Deal," inscribed die-stamped shield with embossed FDR bust and Capitol dome (Hake 2195) 1½" with tab; brass finish ................... 30.00 35.00

☐ Winged eagle atop scrolled circular brass frame with lithograph portrait inset (Hake 2194) 1¾"; black, white; brass finish .................... 25.00 30.00

☐ Watch fob, irregular die-stamped brass with embossed Capitol dome, flag, eagle, and cello inset bust portrait of FDR; 1¾" including tab; gilt finish; black, white portrait ....................... 45.00 55.00

## THEODORE ROOSEVELT, JR.

Theodore Roosevelt was a New York Republican, whose first political arena was the New York State Legislature (1882–84.) An unsuccessful candidate for mayor of New York City two years later, he served on the U.S. Civil Service Commission. Appointed New York City Police Commissioner in 1893, he weeded out corruption within the force but also alienated the citizenry by enforcing Sunday blue laws. In 1897, he accepted McKinley's appointment as Assistant Secretary of the Navy. A year later when the *Maine* was sunk in Havana Harbor, TR signed up with the Volunteer First Cavalry. The unit quickly became known as Roosevelt's Rough Riders and achieved their one great day of glory several months later when they charged up San Juan Hill in the face of intense enemy fire. As a returning military hero, TR easily won the governorship of New York, 1899–1900. TR was a sensation at the Republican National Convention in June, 1900, and when he made one of the seconding speeches for McKinley's renomination, the Republicans went wild, nominating him as vice-president by acclamation.

TR became the 26th U.S. President in September 1901 following McKinley's assassination in Buffalo. Goaded by sneering references to "His Accidency," TR swept to a smashing victory over Alton Parker in 1904. He declined to run in 1908, but his hand-picked candidate, William Howard Taft easily beat the hapless William Jennings Bryan for the third and last time. After his return from an African safari in 1910, TR grew restless and anxious to return to political life. When Old Guard Republicans insisted on renominating Taft, TR bolted the party to head a group of insurgent Progressives. The Bull Moosers lacked organization and campaign funds and with the Republicans divided, Wilson won handily. TR returned to the Republican fold and helped campaign for Hughes in 1916, but his hawkish views alienated many voters and may have cost Hughes the election. TR's military career, his African tours, and two presidential campaigns inspired a wealth of political memorabilia. Particularly desirable are the uncommon jugate pinbacks from his 1912 candidacy with Hiram Johnson; also more toys, dolls, banks and novelties than any other president (see William McKinley).

Advertising flyer for Parker Carry-Us-All shows
Taft, Wilson, and Teddy Roosevelt going for the
brass ring in 1912 race ($75–$100).

Kellogg's Corn Flakes advertising
fan, ca. 1910, features Teddy
Roosevelt ($125–$150). *(Robert
Fratkin Collection)*

Teddy Roosevelt die-stamped Lemp Beer tin stand-up display sign ($1,200–$1,300).

"Ma Bell" used Teddy Roosevelt and Charles Fairbanks to promote services in 1904; die-cut paper hanger ($50–$75).

Teddy Roosevelt intaglio tile; portrait by sculptor George Cartlidge, 1916 ($125–$235).

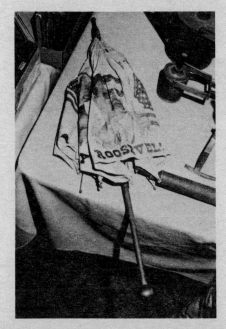

McKinley–Roosevelt, 1896 jugate umbrella ($275–$325).

Teddy Roosevelt and Fairbanks teddy bear; pinback features Clifford Berryman cartoon ($2,000 plus).

Nice assortment of Teddy Roosevelt pinbacks: McKinley–Van Sant (MN), TR trigate ($45–$55); two portrait TRs ($10–$12); "Full Dinner Bucket" jugate ($60–$65); Vermont convention ribbon badge ($85–$95); TR–Fairbanks eyeglasses ($125–$135).

McKinley–TR campaign hammer noisemaker, 1900 ($60–$65).

READY FOR THE FESTIVITIES.

Original Clifford Berryman cartoon hails the 1905 inaugural festivities for President-elect Teddy Roosevelt ($150–$200).

"Teddy and the Bear" figural ceramic match holder. Teddy kneels next to tree stump with bear cub climbing atop; German, early 1900s ($45–$55).

Teddy Roosevelt white metal bas-relief cane head, 1900 race; TR's running mate, William McKinley, featured on obverse ($125–$135).

Teddy Roosevelt dexterity puzzle, German, 1900s, mirror back ($100–$150).

Teddy Roosevelt "For Parker N.I.T. Knock Him Out" novelty toy; Scientific Toy Co., Hartford, Connecticut, 1893 ($450–$500).

Theodore Roosevelt Rough Rider pedestal bust still bank ($145–$165).

**Price Range**

## Advertising Signs, Displays, Giveaways

☐ "Citizens National Bank, Sisseton, South Dakota," tin advertising sign; portrait of TR in large oval after John S. Sargent painting; reproduced courtesy *Collier's Weekly,* © 1903, The Meek Company, Conshockton, Ohio (The Meek Company produced these as blanks for advertising messages to be localized with imprinting, so these are found featuring a variety of advertisers); 19¼"h x 13½"w; gold, black, white, gray, blue, fleshtones ............ 100.00   110.00

☐ "Lemp Beer" stand-up die-stamped tin display sign; 13"h; multicolor ........................... 1200.00   1300.00

☐ Moxie Nerve Food Company Of New England, Theodore Roosevelt stand-up counter card: "The Leading Exponent of the Strenuous Life"; die-cut cardboard full-length figure of TR; 12"h x 3½"w; browntone; © by Rockwood, N.Y., 1898 ....... 100.00   125.00

Price Range

☐ Moxie Nerve Food cardboard, self-framed sign; same pose as counter card, with figure cut off just below coat line; to TR's right is bottle of Moxie tonic, "The Necessary Support of the Strenuous Life"; 27½"w x 21"h; browntone ............. 850.00    900.00

☐ Moxie Nerve Food stand-up floor display, cardboard: oversize version of counter card above with TR "The Leading Exponent of the Strenuous Life"; 4' tall; browntone ......................... 250.00    300.00

☐ "Parker Makes 'Em Carry-Us-All Carousels"; advertising promotional flyer; cartoon sketch of carousel with Teddy Roosevelt riding a moose, William Howard Taft on an elephant, and Woodrow Wilson astride a donkey; brass ring of the "Presidency" is on pole to right of illustration; "Everybody's Doin It. Doin What? Riding Parker's Carry-Us-Alls"; 8"w x 5"h"; black, white; C. W. Parker Co. ...................................... 75.00     85.00

☐ "Philadelphia Evening Telegraph Daily Funnygraph"; TR–Parker jugate penwiper giveaway; "A Little Prize" appears above cello disk portraits; "260 Prizes a Week" under bust images; black, white disk; blue-decal felt layers ............. 40.00     50.00

☐ "Russian-Japanese Peace Commission"; painted tin advertising canister, 1903; portrait ovals of TR (who acted as mediator) and the Russian and Japanese envoys; 10½"h; multicolor .............. 350.00    400.00

☐ "T-R Havana Cigars," self-framed cardboard and tin advertising sign; oval portrait of TR; ornate "T-R" lettering in red, white, blue stars-and-stripes motif ...................................... 450.00    500.00

### Badges, Stickpins, Hangers

☐ "Big Stick" brooch; "3rd Term for Teddy" embossed along full length of club (Hake 238) ..... 30.00     35.00

Price Range

☐ "Brown Bear" figural badge with "California" on bar; blue ribbon; hanger with bas-relief portrait of TR; Progressive delegate's badge, 1912 (Hake 3373) 3″ overall; brown, blue, bronze . . . . . . . . . . . . . .    40.00    50.00

☐ "Bull Moose" stickpin, dimensional (Hake 235) ¾″l; silver . . . . . . . . . . . . . . . . . . . . . . . . . . . . . . . .    10.00    12.00

☐ Capitol dome die-cut bar; "Delegate"; blue, gold ribbon; bronze hanger with embossed portraits of Jefferson, Lincoln, Washington (Hake 3374) 3½″    35.00    45.00

☐ "Don't Be A Muck [rake] Er" rebus, die-cut leather pelt shape; tiny metal rake attached (unlisted) 3½″; black, brown . . . . . . . . . . . . . . . . . . . . . . . . . . . .    85.00    95.00

☐ Eagle bar with TR portrait hanger; portrait framed in wishbone; small metal bell attached to cello (unlisted) 1¼″; blue, black, white; Parker match . . .    100.00    110.00

☐ Gilded bar with American flag ribbon and celluloid hanger (Hake 3) 3¼″ cello; 6″l overall; cello is browntone; ribbon, red, white, blue . . . . . . . . . . .    250.00    260.00

☐ "G.O.P. Roosevelt–Fairbanks" oval cello hanger suspended from red, white, blue gilt ribbon reading: "Republican Candidates 1904"; pinback above has cartoon sketch of pipe-smoking very Irish looking Mark Hanna (unlisted); oval hanger 3¼″; pinback 1¾″; both cellos are sepiatones . . . . . . . . . . . . . .    1800.00    2000.00

☐ "It's In The Ring"; dimensional celluloid hat on pinback; 1912 (Hake 3333; Warner 642) 1″; blue, white, brown hat . . . . . . . . . . . . . . . . . . . . . . . . . .    110.00    120.00

☐ Liberty cap porcelain stickpin hanger; conjoined TR–Fairbanks images; by O'Hara Watch Co. (Hake 256) ⅞″; red, black, blue, white . . . . . . . .    35.00    40.00

☐ Miniature book stickpin; TR photo on cover; Fairbanks on reverse (Hake 3013; Warner 545) 1″; turquoise celluloid book; sepia photos . . . . . . . . . . . .    100.00    110.00

☐ "My Hat Is In The Ring" "Teddy" embossed on white metal ring with linked, suspended TR campaign hat inside ring (Hake 3102) 1¾″; bronze finish . . . . . . . . . . . . . . . . . . . . . . . . . . . . . . . . . . . . .    60.00    70.00

Price Range

☐ "Our Choice" on bar with chain and hanger die-cut in ornate flag and oval shapes; bust portrait of TR (Hake 214) 1¼"h hanger; gilt, black, white, red, blue ......................................... 50.00     60.00

☐ "Our Next President," shell pin with ribbon and mechanical pop-up of TR portrait (Hake 280) ... 95.00     110.00

☐ Pressed relief lion's head and paws; lapel or pocket tab; 1910, coinciding with TR's return from African safari; has Teddy's toothy grin with almost subliminal message across dentures: "Welcome Teddy" (Hake 3101; Warner 276) 2¼"h; yellow, black; painted tin ............................. 70.00     75.00

☐ "Roosevelt–Johnson," 1912, enameled pin; bas relief of bull moose head (Hake 240) 1"; gilt, red .. 50.00     60.00

☐ "Roosevelt" pennant stickpin; name spreads across length of pennant (Hake 225) 1¼"l; red letters on maroon background ......................... 25.00     30.00

☐ "Roosevelt–Johnson" ribbon and celluloid shield pin tab; full figure of moose in lake with waterfall in background (Hake 242; Warner 343) 1"h (with ribbon, 2"); multicolor ..................... 110.00     120.00

☐ Roosevelt spinner badge; disk spells out name when flipped (Hake 3034) 1"w; brass .............. 45.00     50.00

☐ Roosevelt–Stevenson atop elephant who has Bryan wrapped in trunk; brass pin; pressed relief; "G.O.P." embossed on blanket on elephant's forehead (Hake 3086) 1½"; gilded ............... 350.00     375.00

☐ "Rose" [rebus] "velt" dimensional brass pin or brooch (Hake 3036) 1" ..................... 20.00     25.00

☐ Rose shell mechanical; dimensional with TR bust photo in center (Hake 221) ¾"h; brass, orange, black ...................................... 35.00     40.00

☐ TR Rough Rider badge, mechanical; dimensional shell face with campaign hat; lower jaw opens, revealing red, yellow paper tongue reading: "Give them Hell Boys"; spring-held jaw (Hake 212; Warner 232) 1¾" x 1½"; gilded ................ 150.00     160.00

Price Range

☐ Rough Rider Mechanical Badge, similar image to Hake 3087 except that TR rocks back and forth on horse (Hake 3089) $1\frac{1}{4}$"h; gilded . . . . . . . . . . . . . .    300.00    350.00

☐ Teddy bear stickpin carrying small badge with TR's picture and rifle in left hand (Hake 3053) $1\frac{1}{4}$"h; gilded . . . . . . . . . . . . . . . . . . . . . . . . . . . . . . . . . . . . . .    25.00    30.00

☐ "Teddy's Our Ice Man" stickpin; die-cut ice tongs holding block of ice (words appear on ice cake) (Hake 226) $1\frac{1}{4}$"; flat gilded brass (not positively identified as TR item) . . . . . . . . . . . . . . . . . . . . . . .    30.00    35.00

☐ "Teddy Will Be There"; TR Rough Rider on horseback, brass pin; Teddy rides with raised saber; slogan is embossed across bottom (Hake 3087) $1\frac{3}{4}$"h; gilt . . . . . . . . . . . . . . . . . . . . . . . . . . . . . . . . . . . . . . . .    110.00    120.00

☐ TR bull moose pinback with ribbon and dimensional celluloid moose hanger (Hake 62) 2" pinback; 2" x 2" hanger; multicolor; brown moose    135.00    145.00

☐ TR clothing button; small circular bust portrait ringed by eight rhinestones (Hake 223) brass, sepia    25.00    30.00

☐ TR crossed-rifles badge with circular hanger; TR portrait in hanger (Hake 227) $1\frac{1}{2}$" overall; gilded brass, sepiatone . . . . . . . . . . . . . . . . . . . . . . . . . . . .    25.00    30.00

☐ TR figural campaign hat stickpin; "Roosevelt" and tassels embossed (Hake 229) $\frac{3}{4}$"; gilded brass . . .    20.00    25.00

☐ TR hat-in-ring enameled pin; hat embossed; has TR initials on crown (Hake 239) 1"; gilt, light blue; red border . . . . . . . . . . . . . . . . . . . . . . . . . . . . . . . . . . . . .    30.00    35.00

☐ TR spectacles badge; TR–Fairbanks embossed in flat brass lenses (Hake 222) brass . . . . . . . . . . . . .    75.00    85.00

☐ TR spectacles stickpin; Paper photos of TR and Fairbanks (Hake 238) $1\frac{1}{4}$"w; black, white, gilt . .    125.00    150.00

☐ TR spectacles, with paper photos of TR–Fairbanks in lenses; brass pin (Hake 3014; Warner 544) $1\frac{1}{4}$" x $\frac{1}{2}$"; sepia, brass . . . . . . . . . . . . . . . . . . . . .    125.00    135.00

☐ TR wind vane stickpin; TR portrait appears in center (Hake 224) $1\frac{1}{4}$" dia; sepia, gilded vanes . . . .    50.00    60.00

*Cartoon/Pictorial Pinbacks*        **Price Range**

☐ "Dedication of Louisiana Purchase Exposition," 1903, St. Louis; 100th Anniversary of Louisiana Purchase; portraits of TR and president of Exposition David Francis; propeller-like shape separates pictures (Hake unlisted; Warner 254) $2\frac{1}{8}$"; yellow, red, white, blue, black ...................... 600.00     650.00

☐ "De-light-ed," great word play with light bulbs representing TR's eyes, and famed prominent teeth advertise virtues of new home lighting source— electricity (Hake 3322; Warner 561) $\frac{7}{8}$"; white reversed out of black ......................... 65.00     75.00

☐ Also appeared as 1" horizontal oval (Hake 3321)    70.00     80.00

☐ "Don't Be A Maverick. Presidential Roundup, Nov. 6, 1904"; TR's symbols branded into hide of longhorn steer (Hake 196; Warner) $\frac{7}{8}$"; sepiatone   40.00     45.00

☐ "Four Years More of Theodore"; top-hatted TR and Fairbanks strolling hand in hand as teddy bear trails, bearing placard with above slogan; marvelous cartoon by Clifford Berryman (Hake 3139) $1\frac{1}{4}$"; black on white ............................ 2000.00    2200.00

☐ "Georgia Day, Jamestown, 1907"; Jamestown Exposition (Hake unlisted; Warner 270) $2\frac{1}{8}$"; multicolor ...................................... 175.00     200.00

☐ "Good Scales Teddy"; standing Uncle Sam holds balance scale (a Fairbanks scale); GOP elephant watches as TR tilts balance in his favor, while Parker is up in air (Hake 3138) $1\frac{1}{4}$" black on white, 1904; see also Parker version (Hake 3006) ...... 1300.00    1400.00

☐ GOP elephant stomping on Democratic donkey; cartoon (Hake 3312; Warner 560) $\frac{7}{8}$"; black on white ...................................... 160.00     170.00

☐ "Isthmian Canal At Panama. The Door Rosy Veldt"; overhead view showing Canal route from Pacific to Atlantic; play on word "veldt," Dutch for "lush fields" (Hake 3203; Warner 267) $1\frac{1}{4}$"; sea green, buff, black, rose ...................... 375.00     400.00

Price Range

☐ "Join The Bandwagon"; elephant beating drum with TR picture inside drum (Hake 3239; Warner 262) 1¼"; multicolor (most issues were pulled from papers years after election) ................... 125.00    150.00

☐ "Let Well Enough Alone" harks back to 1900 McKinley theme of "a full dinner pail"; shows pail side picturing TR glasses with portraits of TR and Fairbanks in lenses; 1904 race (Hake 12; Warner 248) 1¼"; black, white; also appeared as browntone .. 250.00    300.00

☐ "National Unity Prosperity Advancement. "Republican Party, 1861–1904"; Roosevelt bust portrait amid pair of flags on each side (Hake 86) 1¼"; red, orange, black, blue ...................... 175.00    200.00

☐ "Our Teddy Never Pulls Leather," cartoon of Teddy on bucking bronco; 1904 (Hake 3228; Warner 265) 1¼"; sepiatone ..................... 450.00    500.00

☐ "Railroad Employee's 20th Century Club"; cartoon of locomotive with legend "To Washington, 1904"; with TR and Fairbanks in cab (Hake 254) 1½"; black on white ............................. 1200.00    1400.00

☐ "Rooster" Roosevelt and Fairbanks cartoon (Hake 276; Warner 559) ⅞"; red, white, black; unusual adaptation of traditionally Democratic symbol .. 75.00    85.00

☐ TR as mediator between capital and labor; stands in middle with hands linked with top-hatted and blue-collar figures; "Equal Protection" (Hake 270; Warner 245) 1¼"; red, white, blue, green, black (has rarely been offered publicly and has been listed as high as $1,500) ......................... 1200.00    1400.00

☐ A variant of this rendering, "Our Candidate. Justice For All" (Hake 3233) 1¼", also was issued .... 700.00    750.00

☐ TR at the gate; TR stands at a gate with Uncle Sam, who raises first banner labeled "Prejudice" above sunburst, at top; "The Spirit Of The Republic—Success," "1904," and "President To All The People" appear on path to Capitol (Hake 192; Warner 244) 1½"; multicolor; key item epitomizing pro-equality theme .............................. 1500.00    2000.00

Price Range

☐ TR on Fairbanks scale; caricature (Hake 3232)
1¼"; black on white . . . . . . . . . . . . . . . . . . . . . . .    375.00    400.00

☐ "Teddy's Terrors—Los Angeles"; TR astride a
jackrabbit, with pistols blazing in each hand,
against shamrock background; chases an Indian, in
full retreat, out of his teepee (Hake 67) 1¼"; black,
green, orange buff . . . . . . . . . . . . . . . . . . . . . . . . . .    125.00    150.00

☐ "The Roosevelt Cabin" (North Dakota item); illustration of cabin (Hake 193) 1¼"; browntone . . . .    15.00    20.00

☐ Two fighting cocks, "Roosevelt" and "Parker,"
with feathers flying (Hake 3195) 1¼"; information
on color unavailable . . . . . . . . . . . . . . . . . . . . . . . .    225.00    235.00

☐ "You Bet They Aint Kickin' *My* Dog Around";
cartoon of bulldog with TR facial features (Hake
3288) 1¼"; black on white . . . . . . . . . . . . . . . . . . .    130.00    140.00

AFRICAN-RELATED—1910

☐ "Buano Tumbo," Swahili for "great master," appeared on numerous postcards and pinbacks following TR's return from Africa in 1910; bust portrait
appears above inscription (Hake unlisted; Warner
275) 1¼"; black, white . . . . . . . . . . . . . . . . . . . . . .    100.00    110.00

☐ "Teddy's Our Lion"; cartoon of lion with TR's face,
probably inspired by Roosevelt's return from African safari—what has been called the "Bwano
Tumbo" era (Hake 3240; Warner 568) 1¼"; white,
gold, brown . . . . . . . . . . . . . . . . . . . . . . . . . . . . . .    600.00    650.00

☐ Uncle Sam welcomes TR back from Africa; TR, just
off the boat and still in safari togs, is swept off his
feet by a jubilant Uncle Sam (Hake 3199; Warner
567) 1¾"; multicolor . . . . . . . . . . . . . . . . . . . . . . .    700.00    750.00

☐ "Welcome From Elba"; Uncle Sam with arms
around TR; refers to TR's return from self-imposed
exile to Africa (Hake 3155; Warner 274) 1¼"; mul-
ticolor . . . . . . . . . . . . . . . . . . . . . . . . . . . . . . . . . . .    250.00    275.00

☐ "Welcome"; TR portrait against draped flag pulled
back for view of two flag-topped buildings (one appears to be Flatiron Building in New York) (Hake
3252; Warner 569) 1910; 1¾"; multicolor . . . . . .    175.00    200.00

PROGRESSIVE–1912 CAMPAIGN                              Price Range

☐ Anti-TR; "Bull Moose," lively caricature depicting
TR in black cowboy hat, bandanna, sporting antlers, donkey ears, elephant tusks and trunk (Hake
281) $1\frac{1}{4}$"h; oval; red, black, gray, white .......    165.00      175.00

☐ "Bull Moose"; appears above antlers of profile of
Moose head (unlisted) $1\frac{1}{2}$"; brown, black, white    85.00      100.00

☐ "Fear God And Take Your Own Part 1916"; Bibli-
cal quote appears around silhouette of TR (Hake
3330) $\frac{7}{8}$"; black, red, ......................    100.00      110.00

☐ White; same quote was used in Hake 3329 except
TR initials replace silhouette .................    90.00      100.00

☐ "I Feel Like A Bull Moose"; 1912 cartoon bust profile of Uncle Sam; Hasson cigarette premium (Hake
248) $\frac{7}{8}$"; white reversed out of black or white on
black .......................................    12.00      15.00

☐ Also issued as multicolor ....................    15.00      20.00

☐ "If You Are Against Me, You Are A Crook";
words in script appear from mouth of TR caricature; 1912 Progressive Party allusion to "lawless-
ness" (Hake 3241; Warner 644) 1"; white reverses
out of black ...............................    210.00      225.00

☐ "Progressive. Thou Shalt Not Steal," 1916; TR rep-
resents honesty vs. government by cronyism as
symbolized by elephant and donkey (Hake unlisted;
Warner 340) $1\frac{1}{4}$"; black, white ..............    325.00      350.00

☐ Similar version (Hake 3335) is reversed out of black    100.00      125.00

☐ "Progressive" bull moose profile (Hake 208) $\frac{7}{8}$";
blue, yellow, brown (many known variants; also has
been reproduced) ...........................    5.00      6.00

☐ "Roosevelt," left-facing bull moose silhouette
(Hake 211) $\frac{7}{8}$"; black, brown, orange background    15.00      20.00

☐ "Tie That Bull Outside"; classic Ham Fisher cartoon showing Mutt (of Mutt & Jeff) pointing to TR
in uniform with donkey wearing moose antlers on
leash (Hake 246) $1\frac{1}{4}$"; multicolor ............    30.00      35.00

☐ Also $\frac{7}{8}$"; black, white (Hake 250) .............    20.00      25.00

ROUGH RIDER                                    **Price Range**

With over 35 listed TR pinbacks relating specifically to TR's famous one-day military excursion up San Juan Hill, it certainly merits its own category.

☐ "Anti-Americanism," 1917; "Remember TEDDY and San Juan Hill"; cartoon of TR from waist up in uniform and clenching fist; patriotic shield in background (Hake 251) $7/8$"; orange, blue, white    85.00    100.00

☐ Anti-TR: "I'm Brave. I Believe in Shooting. I Shot A Spaniard In The Back"; vicious caricature of TR in Rough Rider uniform, waving gloved hand (Hake 3227) $1\frac{1}{4}$"; colors not available; probably black on white . . . . . . . . . . . . . . . . . . . . . . . . . . . . .    275.00    300.00

☐ Die-cut horseshoe with uniformed TR with flag background (Hake 279) $1\frac{1}{4}$"h; sepia, red, black    95.00    100.00

☐ Flag bunting frames bust photo of uniformed TR "For Governor"; 1898 (Hake 3321) $1\frac{1}{4}$"; red, white, blue, black; see also variants (Hake 3222 and 3223) . . . . . . . . . . . . . . . . . . . . . . . . . . . . . . . . . . . . .    35.00    45.00

☐ "For President. Teddy The Rough Rider"; TR in uniform with dispatch papers labeled "His Policy. Equal Rights For All" (Hake 266) . . . . . . . . . . . .    225.00    250.00

☐ "Lieut. Col. Theodore Roosevelt"; bust portrait, hatless but wearing uniform (Hake 249) $7/8$"; black, white, red, blue . . . . . . . . . . . . . . . . . . . . . . . . . . . .    30.00    35.00

☐ Variant of Hake 249 (Hake unlisted; Warner 227) $7/8$"; issued with flag and laurel in background; multicolor; both items 1900 vice-president entries (often shows up with real rabbit's foot on key chain)    45.00    55.00

☐ Oklahoma City "Rough Riders Reunion" 1960; pair of Rough Riders on horseback with center inset a bust portrait of TR (Hake 277) . . . . . . . . .    120.00    135.00

☐ "Roosevelt" bust portrait; wearing military field hat (Hake 245) $1\frac{1}{4}$"; white, dark brown, red, bronze; 1900 vice-president item . . . . . . . . . . . . . . . . . . . . .    35.00    45.00

☐ Also $7/8$" (Hake 3315; Warner 228) . . . . . . . . . . . .    25.00    30.00

☐ "Remember San Juan Hill"; slogan appears on inset abutting portrait of TR; large bowed ribbon atop (Hake 3188) $1\frac{3}{4}$"; red, white, blue, black, bronze    65.00    75.00

Price Range

☐ "Rough Rider" TR, upper figure in full military regalia (Hake 60) 2"; sepiatone ................. 110.00  125.00

☐ "Rough Riders" slogan stickpin (Hake 3357) ⅞"; blue, white, red, black; fabric ................. 20.00  22.00

☐ TR in uniform saluting on horseback; flag on horizon with mountain labeled "San Juan" and below "For President 1904" (Hake 71; Warner 261) 1"; multicolor .................................. 110.00  125.00

☐ TR on cantering horse (Hake 73); 1¼"; multicolor  85.00  95.00

☐ TR waving on horseback, "La Fiesta"; framed by horseshoe (Hake 278) 1¼"; sepiatone; braided brass rim .................................... 165.00  175.00

☐ Uniformed TR, with one arm on hip, stands next to lion; "For Vice-President"; 1900 item (Hake 72; Warner 226) 1¼"; multicolor ................ 125.00  150.00

☐ United Spanish War Veterans, Los Angeles; cartoon sketch of smiling TR in colonel's uniform (Hake 3201) 1¼"; black, white ............... 85.00  95.00

## "STAND PAT"

☐ "Same Old Flag And Victory. Stand Pat 1904"; joined oval bust portraits of TR–Fairbanks (Hake 3161) 1¼"; black, white ..................... 240.00  250.00

☐ "Stand Pat"; hand holding four high cards labeled "Protection, Prosperity ... etc." with TR picture card as a "kicker" (Hake 127; Warner 258) 1"; black, white, red .......................... 100.00  110.00

☐ Also in 1¼" (Hake unlisted; Warner 259) ...... 75.00  85.00

☐ Still another version, 1½" (Hake 95) with braided brass trim; lithographed tin reproduction exists .. 65.00  75.00

☐ "Stand Pat"; prominent lettering outside large circle with TR portrait (Hake 80) 1¼"; black, orange  45.00  55.00

## *Cutlery*

### POCKETKNIVES

☐ "For President 1904"; standing figure of TR; celluloid over metal; brown, black, white ........... 80.00  100.00

**Price Range**

☐ "T. Roosevelt 1901" commemorative knife; oval embossed portrait of TR; all presidents and dates of office listed aslant on both sides, including TR; silver finish; made in Germany .............. 50.00 60.00

☐ Theodore Roosevelt portrait and eagle embossed (both sides) knife; silver finish; made in Germany 65.00 75.00

RAZORS

☐ "Prosperity" razor; words imprinted on celluloid handle; TR portrait and elaborate scrollwork engraved on steel blade, hand-forged ............ 90.00 110.00

## Folk Art

☐ Carved wooden figure of Theodore Roosevelt astride an elephant on upraised base, bound in tin band; four carved tortoises on four corners of lower base; red, black, yellow, brown, white; approx. 9"h; TR is wearing top hat; artist unknown; ca. 1900s 2000.00 plus

☐ "De-Lighted" pettipoint tea cozy with caricature of TR in tan suit and brandishing a big stick; green, brown, black; Peter Scanlon Collection ......... 200.00 220.00

☐ Theodore Roosevelt Rough Rider whirligig; polychromed wood; ca. 1913 ..................... 800.00 900.00

## Inaugurals

☐ Eagle atop scrolled bar with linked shield hanger; bust portrait of TR; gilded brass (Hake 3093) 1¼" shield .................................... 20.00 30.00

☐ "Inauguration. Washington D.C. March 4, '05" printed on celluloid-covered paper in gilded, framed bar; American flag ribbon; Uncle Sam stands behind TR with arm on shoulder; cello pinback is captioned: "He's Good Enough For Me!" (Hake 252) 3" pinback; black on pale green ..... 125.00 135.00

☐ "President" under bust photo of TR inside circle encased in brass badge; attached to badge is red, white, blue ribbon: "Inauguration March 4, 1905" in gold; attached to ring on bottom of ribbon is die-

Price Range

cut hanger picturing Capitol building (Hake 3176) $2\frac{1}{2}''$w badge; $1\frac{1}{2}''$ hanger; bronze, black, white          50.00          60.00

☐ "Souvenir" bar linked to heart-shaped disk; embossed bust portrait of TR against black (Hake 3094) $1\frac{1}{4}''$ heart hanger . . . . . . . . . . . . . . . . . . . . .          30.00          35.00

☐ "Souvenir" on scrolled bar linked to circular hanger; TR's bust image appears against black circle background (Hake 3092) $1\frac{1}{4}''$ brass disk; gilt, black . . . . . . . . . . . . . . . . . . . . . . . . . . . . . . . . . . . .          30.00          35.00

☐ TR bronze Inaugural medal; TR bust profile (Hake 3100) $1\frac{3}{4}''$ bronze . . . . . . . . . . . . . . . . . . . . . . . . .          180.00          200.00

☐ "Washington D.C." embossed bar with Maltese cross hanger; TR embossed portrait in center of cross (Hake 3091) $3\frac{3}{4}''$; bronze . . . . . . . . . . . . . .          30.00          35.00

## *Jugates*

### TR–FAIRBANKS, 1904

☐ Capitol dome above TR–Fairbanks; stars encircle entire image (Hake 39; Warner 538) $1\frac{1}{4}''$; gold, black, red, white, blue . . . . . . . . . . . . . . . . . . . . . .          120.00          130.00

☐ "50th Anniversary Of Republican Party"; conjoining profiles of TR and Lincoln against starlit background; gold eagle below; (Hake 160) $\frac{7}{8}''$; blue, gold, dark brown, buff . . . . . . . . . . . . . . . . . . . . . .          35.00          40.00

☐ "For President" (TR picture) "For Vice-President" (Fairbanks picture) (Hake 257) $1\frac{3}{4}''$; black on white . . . . . . . . . . . . . . . . . . . . . . . . . . . . . . . . . . .          100.00          110.00

☐ "G.O.P." tops TR–Fairbanks portraits with names in circular banner below (Hake 2) $2\frac{1}{8}''$; sepiatone          75.00          85.00

☐ "Hamilton Club of Chicago"; TR–Fairbanks (Hake 29; Warner 247) $1\frac{1}{4}''$; red, white, blue, brown . .          450.00          500.00

☐ TR–Fairbanks; large eagle with banner in beak (Hake 20; Warner 251) $1\frac{1}{4}''$; multicolor . . . . . . .          100.00          125.00

☐ Miss Liberty holding flag below; above, TR–Fairbanks pictures; mate to Parker (Hake 19; Warner 281) . . . . . . . . . . . . . . . . . . . . . . . . . . . . .          50.00          60.00

☐ "Men's Republican Club. Flathead County Montana" (Hake 3149; Warner 249) $1\frac{1}{4}''$; sepiatone          250.00          275.00

Price Range

☐ Miss Liberty (standing) with TR–Fairbanks oval portraits (Hake 7; Warner 253) $2\frac{1}{8}$"; red, white, blue, gold (often found in elaborate gold frame) 150.00 175.00

☐ Also $1\frac{1}{4}$" size ............................ 50.00 65.00

☐ "Polk County Republican Club. Des Moines, Iowa"; conjoining portrait (Hake 31501; Warner 536) $1\frac{1}{4}$"; black, white ..................... 175.00 200.00

☐ "Railroadmen's Republican Club," Indianapolis, 1904; $2\frac{1}{8}$" flag divides staggered portraits (Hake 4; Warner 541); red, white, blue, gold, black ...... 100.00 110.00

☐ "Same Old Flag & Victory. Stand Pat, 1904"; TR and Fairbanks portraits in double oval (Hake 3161) $1\frac{3}{4}$"; black on white ....................... 240.00 250.00

☐ Shield with draped flags atop TR–Fairbanks pictures (Hake 37; Warner 543) $1\frac{1}{4}$"; multicolor ... 75.00 85.00

☐ "Souvenir of Pretzel Town," Reading, PA, 1904; TR and Fairbanks portraits framed by giant pretzel (Hake 5; Warner 535); brown, rose, black ...... 425.00 450.00

☐ TR's Oyster Bay, NY, home; small round jugate in lower left-hand third of image (Hake 11; Warner 252) $1\frac{1}{4}$"; brown, cream (another version pictures Fairbanks's home in Dedham, MA) ........... 85.00 100.00

☐ "Henry Cassell" (running for Congress, 9th District, Pennsylvania); appears with TR–Fairbanks Stand Pat theme as hand holds pictured playing cards (Hake 183; Warner 260) $1\frac{1}{4}$"; black on white 110.00 120.00

TR–JOHNSON, 1912

☐ Bull moose "spread eagles" U.S. map; TR–Johnson shake hands in foreground (Hake 3167; Warner 637) $1\frac{1}{4}$"; black, white ...................... 2000.00 plus

☐ Conjoining images, TR–Johnson on brass; again with script signatures (Hake 262) 2"; black, white 550.00 575.00

☐ Conjoining TR–Johnson images with script signatures of each (Hake 3165) 2"; black, white ..... 700.00 725.00

☐ Moose head with TR–Johnson ovals nesting in antlers (Hake 3168) $1\frac{1}{4}$"; sepiatone .............. 1600.00 1800.00

Price Range

☐ "Progressive"; small circular image of bull moose appears atop oval pictures of TR–Johnson; shield and scrolled name banners below images (Hake 263) 1¼"; brown, beige ..................... 450.00    500.00

☐ ⅞" version in sepiatone (Hake 264) ........... 600.00    610.00

☐ TR–Johnson facing each other in jugate images (Hake 3166) 1¾"; black, brown, white ......... 625.00    650.00

☐ TR–Johnson portrait; almost appear to be touching noses; in partial profile (Hake 265; Warner 640) ⅞"; red, white, blue, gold, black; mates to Taft, Wilson ...................................... 900.00    1000.00

☐ "Progressive"; head-on view of moose head with antlers spread across top of image; round pictures of TR–Johnson appear beneath head (Hake unlisted; Warner 638) 1¼"; black, white ......... 1600.00    1800.00

MISCELLANEOUS

☐ TR–Robert LaFollette (Wisconsin) paired ovals under shield (1912?) (Hake 187) ⅞"; red, white, blue, black, gold .......................... 35.00    45.00

☐ "James E. March, New York, 1904" with oval pictures of March ("Our Leader") and TR and Fairbanks (Hake 3143) 1¼"; black, white, with gold rim ....................................... 220.00    230.00

## Memorial Lapel Devices

☐ "In Memoriam"; lone star appears above TR's bust portrait (Hake 3337) black, white ............. 8.00    10.00

☐ "In Memoriam"; profile bust of TR (Hake 253) ⅞"; black border; black and white image ........... 10.00    12.00

## Multigates

☐ "Pennsylvania State League Republican Clubs, Sept. 20–21, 1905"; TR, Grant, Lincoln, and McKinley portraits in clover leaf; brass-rimmed hanger; bar with "Easton" connects to "Guest" ribbon (Hake 3134) 1¾"; black, white ........... 75.00    80.00

**Price Range**

☐ "The Old Boys"; four circular portraits grouped around scepter—Fremont, Lincoln, TR, and Fairbanks (Hake 3140; Warner 246) $1\frac{3}{4}$"; sepiatone, cream ..................................... 500.00     525.00

## Noisemakers

☐ Teddy Roosevelt moose horn; same design as McKinley horn noisemaker; 1912 race; "Patriotism, Protection, Prosperity"; tin finish ............. 50.00     60.00

☐ Teddy Roosevelt "Now Knock" embossed chrome campaign hammer noisemaker; opposite side: "McKinley/Get Your Hammer Out"; 4"w; chrome finish ......................................... 60.00     65.00

## Portrait Pinbacks

☐ Alice Roosevelt portrait; daughter of TR wearing sunbonnet (Hake 244) $1\frac{1}{4}$"; red, blue, gold, black, white; name appears above bonnet ........... 30.00     35.00

☐ "Arizona For Joint Statehood" with TR bust portrait; in 1908 Republicans were pushing for joint statehood of Arizona and New Mexico; it was achieved in 1912 (Hake unlisted; Warner 650) $15/16$"; sepia, cream ........................ 120.00     139.00

☐ "A Square Deal All Around"; "T.R." letters reverse out of blue square design; 1912 (Hake 202) $\frac{7}{8}$"; red, black, white (has been reproduced) .... 15.00     20.00

☐ "Four More Years. Roosevelt"; circle portrait inside shield (Hake 3243) $1\frac{1}{4}$"; blue, black, white 75.00     85.00

☐ Moose head, straight on, with TR oval portrait squarely atop head between antlers (Hake 285) $\frac{7}{8}$"; brown, pale blue, black; gold rim ............. 120.00     130.00

☐ "National Progressive Party"; circular TR portrait in neck of bull moose head, profile view (Hake 3281) $1\frac{1}{4}$"; black on white.................. 210.00     225.00

Price Range

☐ "National Unity. Prosperity. Advancement. Republican Party 1861–1904. Elect Theodore Roosevelt For President"; TR bust portrait flanked by pair of flags on both sides (Hake 86; Warner 548) $1\frac{1}{4}"$; multicolor ............................ 225.00   250.00

☐ "Our Country's Choice For Another Term"; TR portrait completely encircled by draped flags and small shield (Hake 273) $1\frac{1}{4}"$; red, white, blue, black ........................................ 150.00   160.00

☐ "Our Greatest American"; eagle at top and twin flag banners frame TR portrait (Hake 272) $1\frac{1}{4}"$; red, white, blue, black, gold .................. 100.00   110.00

☐ "Preparedness.* 1916"; TR portrait in white circle (Hake 176; Warner 652) $\frac{7}{8}"$; white, brown ..... 110.00   120.00

☐ "Rose [rebus] veldt" (Hake 3327); $\frac{7}{8}"$; red, blue, white ........................................ 30.00   35.00

☐ "The Man Of The Hour"; Progressive candidate for president; oval portrait of TR inset in neck and body of bull moose; flag ribbon attached (Hake unlisted; Warner 636) $1\frac{3}{4}"$; cream, brown; red, white, blue ribbon ..................................... 450.00   500.00

☐ Also appears in $1\frac{1}{4}"$ and $\frac{7}{8}"$ sizes ($\frac{7}{8}"$ Hake 174; Warner 344) ............................... 100.00   110.00

☐ "The People's Choice. Roosevelt"; TR portrait along double-star ribbon (Hake 3327) $\frac{7}{8}"$; red, blue, black, white........................... 30.00   35.00

☐ "Washington Party. Come With Us"; portrait of Washington (Hake 3334) $\frac{7}{8}"$; black on white ... 12.00   15.00

☐ "Fear God And Take Your Own Part; T.R. 1916" (an aphorism for self-reliance); TR was nominated by the Progressives again in 1916 but declined (Hake 286; Warner 651) $\frac{7}{8}"$; black, yellow ..... 90.00   110.00

☐ "Preparedness. T.R. Peace" (Hake 207) $\frac{7}{8}"$; black red, white ................................... 20.00   25.00

☐ "Roosevelt Can Win All American" (Hake 206) $\frac{7}{8}"$; black, red, white ...................... 15.00   20.00

*The "Preparedness" slogan was more common to Wilson forces.

Price Range

☐ "Roosevelt 1912" (Hake 3331) ⅞"; black, red, white ....................................... 10.00 12.00

☐ Also issued as ½" variant ................... 10.00 12.00

☐ "T.R. For Me" (Hake 3336) ⅞"; black, white, gold rim ....................................... 15.00 20.00

☐ "We'll Win. Roosevelt" (Hake listed as FDR, 182; Warner 649) 1¼"; black on white ............. 65.00 75.00

☐ "For President/Theodore Roosevelt/For Vice President/Charles Fairbanks," 1904 poster; pair of flags and shield divide oblong bust portraits; names appear in large scrolls under portraits, separated by winged eagle; 36"w x 28"h; black, white ....... 85.00 100.00

☐ "For President/Theodore Roosevelt of New York/For Vice President/Charles Fairbanks of Indiana"; 1904 vertical poster; staggered photographs separated by eagle; 30"h x 20"w .............. 125.00 150.00

☐ TR 1912 Progressive Party multigate poster, Rhode Island. Includes entire Rhode Island ticket as well as TR; headed by Albert Humes for governor; 26"h x 20"w; black, white ........................ 75.00 100.00

## Slogan Pinbacks

**ANTI–TR**

☐ "Goodbye Teddy Good Bye"; slogan surrounded by ribbons (Hake 3280) 1¼"; red, white, blue, black ..................................... 20.00 25.00

**PRO–TR**

☐ "Preparedness. T.R. Peace" (Hake 207) ⅞"; black, red, white .................................. 20.00 25.00

☐ "Roosevelt Can Win All American" (Hake 206) ⅞"; black, red, white ....................... 15.00 20.00

☐ "Roosevelt 1912" (Hake 3331) ⅞"; white reversed out of black ............................... 10.00 12.00

☐ Also ½" variant .......................... 10.00 12.00

| *Textiles* | Price Range | |
|---|---|---|

☐ Cotton banner; anti-TR cartoon, "The Human Headed Calf"; Holstein calf body and TR head complete with glasses and drooping mustache; the significance of this satirical piece is anybody's guess; 65"w x 34"h; painted black, white ............ 125.00   150.00

☐ Cotton sailcloth banner: "First In War, First In Peace/First In The Hearts of His Countrymen"; TR portrait inside large heart-shape outline; at top is panorama of TR leading the charge up San Juan Hill; at bottom are Japanese and Russian ambassadors signing Russo-Japanese War peace treaty at Portsmouth, NH, in 1904; TR acting as mediator received the Nobel Prize in 1906 (Collins 869) 21¾"h x 21¼"w; maker: Campbell, Metzger, Jacobson; multicolor ......................... 225.00   250.00

☐ Cotton banner, 1912 campaign: "National Progressive Party. Roosevelt–Johnson"; dramatic bull moose head in center flanked by TR at left, Johnson at right, with names appearing under bust drawings (Collins 942) 23½"w x 14¼"h; brown on white sailcloth; one of the most appealing banners in the hobby ..................................... 800.00   1000.00

☐ Pennant, felt; 1912: "Our Next President"; facsimile signature of TR under bust portrait at left; legend in ornate Old English type (Collins 925) 26½"l x 10"w; fleshtones, red, white; dark blue background ................................ 75.00   100.00

☐ Pennant, oilcloth; 1912: "Roosevelt and Johnson"; small moose head at tapered end; large legend in white against dark blue background (Collins 930) 25"w x 12"h: blue, white .................... 65.00   85.00

☐ Pennant, felt; 1912: "Roosevelt"; irregularly shaped flag outline with moose head at top and TR bust portrait below; name runs vertically in interlinked letters (Collins 931) 29"w x 11"h; gray, white, red; made by Badge Pennant & Novelty Co., Los Angeles ....................................... 75.00   100.00

Price Range

☐ Cotton banner; 1912: "Roosevelt/Protection"; oval bust portrait of TR with draped flags surrounding portrait (Collins 950); hand-painted by C. H. Buck, Boston; marked: "Union Label Painters/ Decorations/Paperhangers"; 94"h x 57"w; red, white, blue .................................. 1000.00    1200.00

☐ Sized cotton banner; 1912: "Welcome"; winged eagle atop with 13 stars; TR portrait framed by laurel wreath against striped background (Collins 949) 94"h x 57"w; red, white, blue; black, white portrait   1200.00    1400.00

## Tobacco Accessories

☐ "Teddy And The Bear" figural ceramic match holder; see illustration with description ......... 45.00    55.00

☐ "Teddy And The Bear," U.S. guard house; shows Teddy Roosevelt inside; 4½"h; brown, yellow, blue, white; German ........................ 75.00    85.00

## Toys, Dolls, Games, Puzzles

☐ Theodore Roosevelt "African Series"; set of 15 cardboard standup figures of animals, native bearers, and TR in safari outfit; full-color lithograph figures, each approximately 6"w (or tall); © 1910, National Candy Co., Buffalo, NY ................ 125.00    150.00

☐ Roosevelt bear on bicycle, maker unknown, 1900s, lithographed tin (flat) on steel sheet bicycle, with iron weight ................................ 200.00    250.00

☐ Roosevelt on safari, Schoenhut, circa 1910, wood-jointed figure, 6"h (part of "Teddy's Adventures in Africa" set) ................................ 600.00    700.00

    *Note:* The TR safari figure is one of 25 wooden figures with jointed limbs as part of A. Schoenhut's Humpty Dumpty Circus. Set came in hinged wooden box, painted with vignettes that served as background for the figures. Human figures were 6"–8" tall; animals, 4"–5". An abbreviated version was also issued by the Philadelphia toymaker; multicolored painted wood.

| | Price Range | |
|---|---|---|
| ☐ Deluxe boxed set .......................... | 4000.00 | 5000.00 |
| ☐ Teddy Dexterity "Eyeglasses Puzzle"; lithographed tin and cardboard with metal balls; object is to place balls within center of shallow tin cups that are TR's eyeglasses; multicolor; manufacturer unknown ... | 150.00 | 200.00 |
| ☐ Teddy Dexterity Puzzle, German, 1900s; lithographed tin and glass, small white marbles; object is to place balls in indentations for Teddy's prominent teeth; 3″ dia ........................... | 100.00 | 150.00 |
| ☐ Teddy and the Lion Vanish Puzzle, maker unknown, 1900s, 3″w x 4″h (vanish puzzles comprised a geometric paradox whereby figures are dissected and rearranged and a portion of the original appears to have disappeared) ................ | 75.00 | 100.00 |
| ☐ Teddy Roosevelt "Knock Him Out" novelty toy, Scientific Toy Co., Hartford, CT; patented 1893; wood mechanical; lithograph paper-on-wood figure of Teddy pops up via spring mechanism; paper label (black on red) reads "For Parker Nit-Knock Him Out; We Want Roosevelt" (could there possibly be a Parker mate to this one?) .................. | 450.00 | 500.00 |
| ☐ Teddy Roosevelt Presidential Puzzle. "Where Are The Winners? On Top Of Course"; combination top, wheel, or badge with portraits of TR and Fairbanks (Hake 3136) 2½″; red, white, blue, black; celluloid .................................... | 360.00 | 375.00 |
| ☐ Theodore Roosevelt rag doll; TR comes complete with famed Rough Rider campaign hat with creased crown, monocle, and uniform; early 1900s; approx. 6″h; brown, black, white, fleshtones; maker unknown .................................... | 150.00 | 200.00 |
| ☐ Teddy Roosevelt Rough Rider, German, 1900s; painted tin wind-up, 7″w x 7″h .............. | 350.00 | 400.00 |
| ☐ Teddy Roosevelt Rough Rider, maker unknown, 1900s; cast-iron still bank, gold with silver and black trim, 5″h .......................... | 100.00 | 150.00 |
| ☐ Teddy Roosevelt Rough Rider gong bell, 1903; cast-iron pull toy ................................ | 250.00 | 300.00 |

Price Range

☐ Standing Teddy Roosevelt nodder, German, 1910; composition .............................. 300.00 350.00

☐ Teddy Bear still bank, maker unknown, 1900s; cast iron; "Teddy" appears on side; $2\frac{1}{2}$"h .......... 150.00 200.00

☐ Teddy's Teeth tin whistle, Teddy's Teeth Co., Chicago, IL; lithograph tin; made shrill blast, "more noise than a horn," the ultimate in political kitsch, 3"l ........................................ 35.00 50.00

MECHANICAL BANKS

☐ Theodore Roosevelt "Teddy And The Bear"; TR shoots coin into tree trunk and bear pops up; brown tree; cast-iron; yellow, blue, green, brown; ca. 1906–1907; J. & E. Stevens, manufacturer (gray tree variant, later issue) ..................... 750.00 850.00

☐ Roosevelt "Teddy and The Bear" flat-hat version; $10\frac{1}{8}$" base length; same colors as above; patent assigned to National Novelty Corporation; only two known of this scarce variant ................. 2000.00 plus

☐ Theodore Roosevelt "Lion Hunter"; Teddy in pith helmet aiming at crouched lion on rock; when coin lever is pressed, coin strikes lion in chest as it rears up and falls into receptacle below; brown, yellow, red, gilt (with mica flakes on rock for added touch of realism); patent 1911 to A. E. Cudworth & F. W. Crandall, receivers for Hardware & Woodenware Manufacturing Co., New York ........... 950.00 1050.00

# WINFIELD SCOTT

The crusty Mexican War hero, Gen. Winfield Scott was the Whig nominee for President in the 1852 race against Franklin Pierce. Nicknamed "Old Fuss and Feathers," Scott was decidedly rank-conscious and enamored of fancy uniforms. Contributing to his stunning defeat by a dark horse were the thousands of Southern Whigs who deserted Scott for his failure to support the Compromise of 1850 as forthrightly as did Pierce. This race was pivotal, in that it sounded the death knell for the Whigs as a viable independent force in American politics. A surprisingly rich lode of trinkets survive for someone who appeared so briefly on the political scene. Scott is most often seen decked out in full regalia, including saber.

Price Range

## Badges, Medals

☐ Bust token (DeWitt WS 1852-1) 41mm; "Major Genl. Winfd. Scott/A Gallant & Skillful Hero . . ." "Chippewa Lundy's Lane, Vera Cruz, Mexico" on reverse . . . . . . . . . . . . . . . . . . . . . . . . . . . . . . . . . . . . 95.00 100.00

☐ Bust token; "General Winfield Scott/The People's Choice"; small profile framed by laurels (Hake 3017) 1¼"; brass finish . . . . . . . . . . . . . . . . . . . . . . . 315.00 335.00

☐ Bust token (DeWitt WS 1852-12) "Maj. Winfield Scott. U.S.A." enclosing bust profile; W. W. Hayden engraver; reverse: "Scott Wounded," battle scene; 28mm; most are found in brass; also known in silver, copper, white metal . . . . . . . . . . . . . . . . 225.00 250.00

☐ Shell pin (DeWitt WS 1852-16) bust portrait of Scott in metallic oval frame; 47 x 38mm; multicolored portrait . . . . . . . . . . . . . . . . . . . . . . . . . . . . . . 275.00 300.00

☐ Uniform breastplate; classic Scott profile facing left; "P. H. Jacobus" on pedestal of bust; concave back with three loops; 87 x 66mm; brass finish . . . . . . 250.00 300.00

## Ceramics

☐ "General Winfield Scott" ABC plate; black transfer waist-high portrait; name misspelled "Windfield"; 4" dia; white . . . . . . . . . . . . . . . . . . . . . . . . . . . . . . 175.00 200.00

## Photography

☐ Carte-de-visite portrait of "Gen. Scott," ca. Civil War era (Warner 58) . . . . . . . . . . . . . . . . . . . . . . . . 100.00 120.00

## Prints, Posters

POSTERS

☐ "Whig Rally At Marshalltown . . ." 1852; winged eagle illustration "Mass Meeting of the Friends of Scott and Graham" (Hake 3010) black, white . . . 475.00 500.00

Price Range

☐ "Winfield Scott" lithographed poster; waist-high portrait in full military regalia, including sword in right hand; 17½" x 13½"; black, white; published by A. Winch, Philadelphia .................. 125.00 135.00

☐ Winfield Scott "Ornithology/The Great Birds of the United States not described by Audubon"; turkey with Scott's head and rooster with Pierce's head; Scott is attempting to push Pierce out of the way at Mason-Dixon line; Scott is identified with slaveholder's interest; full color .............. 350.00 400.00

## PRINTS

☐ "Winfield Scott/Whig Candidate For/Fourteenth President..."; upright, half-length, out of uniform; red curtains; Currier & Ives; 11½"h x 8¼"w ... 250.00 300.00

☐ "Winfield Scott/The People's Choice ... 13th President"; 1848 campaign; Currier & Ives (printed in 1847) ...................................... 275.00 325.00

☐ "Winfield Scott" facsimile autograph; bust portrait, slightly facing left; Currier & Ives ............. 250.00 300.00

## *Statuary*

☐ Bas-relief wall plaque; bust profile of Winfield Scott wearing general's uniform (Hake 3006) 12"l x 6"w; bronze finish ................................ 235.00 250.00

## *Textiles*

### BANDANNAS

☐ "Major Genl. Winfield Scott U.S.A."; bareheaded general standing holding reins of white horse; based on G. & W. Endicott lithograph (Collins 239) 30¼" x 27¼"; red, brown, white ............. 375.00 400.00

*Note:* Scott's image also appears in an 1848 Gen. Zachary Taylor bandanna.

### RIBBONS

☐ "Scott/Hero Of Columbia"; military bust profile within corn wreath; unusual embossed leather (Hake 3012) natural leather .................. 300.00 325.00

Price Range

☐ Scott–Graham jugate ribbon with facsimile signatures (Hake 3013) black, white ............... 1750.00    1800.00

☐ "Scott Graham Club" ribbon; "Hero of Lundy's Lane" under eagle and scroll atop; quarter bust portrait of Scott (Sullivan WS-2) ................. 250.00    275.00

☐ Scott "The Hero Of Many Battles ..."; oval military bust portrait; Vera Cruz, Mexico, battle scene below (Warner 57) black on white woven background ..................................... 375.00    400.00

### *Tobacco Accessories*

☐ Winfield Scott match safe; bust portrait; Scott in tricorn hat, bas relief; $2\frac{1}{2}$"; white metal finish .... 625.00    650.00

## JOHN SERGENT

John Sergent of Pennsylvania served in the House for three terms; from 1815–23; 1827–29, 1837–41. In 1832 he ran for Vice-President with Henry Clay on the National Republican ticket. Sergent was a friend of influential Nicholas Biddle of Philadelphia, president of the Bank of the U.S.

Jackson and Van Buren trounced Clay and Sergent so thoroughly that the anti-Jackson *Vermont Journal* announced that it "had no heart to publish the election returns" (see Henry Clay).

## HORATIO SEYMOUR

Seymour, popular Democratic governor from New York, presided as Democratic convention chairman in 1868, and after bitter deadlock was nominated as compromise candidate for president. He was defeated by U. S. Grant.

Price Range

### *Canes*

☐ Cast-iron bust effigy cane head; 3"h; natural finish    300.00    350.00

*Lapel Devices, Shell Badges* **Price Range**

☐ "Seymour-Blair" shell badge with jugate ferrotype; enclosed by eagle, shield, scroll; brass shell portrait of Seymour on reverse (Hake 3011) $1\frac{1}{4}''$; gilt brass    450.00    475.00

☐ "Seymour" shield hanger with flying eagle; craned neck with beak holding hanger loop; bust portrait in shield frame (Hake 3031) $1\frac{1}{2}''$h; gilt brass ...    200.00    225.00

☐ Seymour star shell badge; ferrotype in framed circle mounted in six-point star; $1\frac{1}{4}''$; gilt brass ......    225.00    250.00

☐ "This Is A White Man's Government"; Liberty head profile with coronet inscribed "Liberty"; bow at bottom (Hake 3054; DeWitt HS 1868-87) $1\frac{1}{2}''$; gilt brass; quote based on Nast cartoon; Democrats charged Republicans with subjecting southern states to "Negro supremacy" .................    225.00    250.00

*Lighting Devices*

☐ Parade lantern: "Seymour & Blair;" illustration of pair of hands clasped in friendship; red, white, blue, black .........................................    225.00    250.00

*Posters*

☐ "Seymour–Blair" jugate Currier & Ives print; Liberty figures; oval insets of hands on plow; arm wielding hammer; national Democratic banner; hand-tinted .................................    275.00    300.00

*Textiles*

☐ "Candidate For The Presidency," jugate ribbon, Seymour–Blair, 1869; tassel; black, white (T. Stevens Coventry specimen) ...................    300.00    325.00

☐ "Seymour & Blair/White Boys In Blue"; Seymour portrait encircled by laurel wreath (Warner 134); red, blue lettering; black on white portrait ......    650.00    675.00

*Tobacco Accessories* Price Range

☐ "Seymour & Blair/1869–1873"; rounded gutta-
percha embossed portraits on snuffbox; light brown
(anticipated candidates winning election) . . . . . . .     650.00        700.00

## JAMES SCHOOLCRAFT SHERMAN

"Sunny Jim" Sherman, a wealthy industrialist from Utica, New York,
served as a U.S. congressman for twenty years. He served as Vice-President
under William Howard Taft, 1909–12, and died a few months prior to the
Republican slate's defeat to Wilson in 1912 (see William Howard Taft).

## R. SARGENT SHRIVER, JR.

Sargent Shriver, a brother-in-law of John F. Kennedy, once headed the
Chicago Board of Education and managed the Merchandise Mart for his
father-in-law Joseph Kennedy, Sr., before taking on the newly founded Peace
Corps in 1961. He was picked by George McGovern as Vice-Presidential run-
ning mate in 1972 in mid-campaign, following the disastrous withdrawal of
Thomas Eagleton (see George McGovern).

## ALFRED E. SMITH

Alfred E. Smith went into politics as a young man, and moved up the
ladder, with the help of Tammany Hall and the New York Assembly, to the
governorship of New York. An ardent "wet" advocate, Smith became the
first Catholic to run for the Presidency, when his friend Franklin Roosevelt
nominated him in 1928 as the "Happy Warrior" and the Democrates quickly
chose him on the first ballot. When Senator Joseph Robinson, a Protestant
Prohibitionist was picked for second place, one observer later summed it up,
"The Democratic Donkey with a wet head and wagging a dry tail left Houston."

Hoover bested Smith with a lopsided victory in 1928 and Smith blamed
the religion issue. Hoover, however, was probably closer to the mark, with
his summation, "General Prosperity was on my side." Smith's four successful
gubernatorial campaigns and the quest for the presidency yielded a number
of prized mementos, most of which incorporated his famous brown derby
trademark.

Al Smith barrel-shaped Stangl pottery mug, 1932 ($35–$45). *(Ken Smith Collection)*

Al Smith brown derby, 1928: celluloid hat with ribbon and celluloid pinback ($25–$30); souvenir derby, 1933 Chicago World's Fair, "Smile With Al" ($35–$40).

Price Range

*Automotive Accessories*

LICENSE ATTACHMENTS, RECTANGULAR
☐ "Al Smith" (Hake 2123) 10″l; black, white; painted
tin ........................................ 20.00     25.00

Price Range

☐ "Al Smith For President"; die-cut brown derby (Hake 2118) 8¾"; white, brown .............. 75.00     85.00

☐ "Al Smith [in script] For President" (Hake 2122) 11½"; black, white ........................ 30.00     35.00

☐ "Boost Al Smith For President"; 10"l; black, white 30.00     35.00

☐ "From The Sidewalks Of New York. Al To The White House"; illustration of New York skyline at left; Capitol building at right; large arrow points to Capitol in Washington, DC (Hake 2119) 10"l; black, white ................................ 45.00     55.00

## LICENSE ATTACHMENTS, ROUND

☐ "Alfred E. Smith"; line drawing bust portrait in circle; chevron border; double tabs for attachment (Hake 103) 3¼"h; red, white, blue, black, bronze 50.00     75.00

☐ "For President. Alfred E. Smith"; large bust portrait (Hake 2028) 3½" dia; red, white, blue, black 150.00     175.00

☐ "Smith For President"; oval portrait of Smith flanked by furled U.S. flags; large ribbons enclose "Smith" (Hake 27) 3½"dia; red, white, blue, black 1200.00     1300.00

## RADIATOR ATTACHMENTS

☐ "Smith For President"; silhouetted portrait in circle against American flag background; lettering appears in border; 4"; black, red, white, blue; lithographed tin with four holes for affixing to auto's radiator; made by Ericson, Des Moines, IA; Hoover match ..................................... 25.00     35.00

☐ "1928" no-name deep-relief brass radiator attachment; silhouetted caricature of Smith in top hat, date embossed on crown; 9½"h x 4½"w; brass finish; hole in top of hat for insertion of flag; made by L. H. Company, Newark, NJ ................. 85.00     100.00

### *Badges, Medals, Stickpins, Studs*

☐ "Al & Joe" enameled donkey stickpin (Hake 2105) 1"; silver embossed ........................ 25.00     30.00

☐ "Al" brown derby stud (Hake 76) ½"; brown brass 10.00     12.00

Price Range

☐ "Al [Smith portrait] Smith"; lithograph bar pin
(Hake 104) 1"w; red, white, blue . . . . . . . . . . . . . .          10.00       15.00

☐ "Al" stickpin, enameled (Hake 102) ¾"w; red, gilt
brass . . . . . . . . . . . . . . . . . . . . . . . . . . . . . . . . . . . . . .          15.00       20.00

☐ "Al Smith" brass badge, embossed name (Hake 49)
⅞"; black, gold . . . . . . . . . . . . . . . . . . . . . . . . . . . .          25.00       30.00

☐ "Al Smith" derby stickpin; celluloid (Hake 74) 1"w;
brown, white . . . . . . . . . . . . . . . . . . . . . . . . . . . . . .          20.00       25.00

☐ "Al Smith" bar with dimensional brown derby cel-
luloid hanger (Hake 72) 1¼" overall; brown . . . .          25.00       30.00

☐ "Al Smith" in script; donkey badge (Hake 78)
1½"l; chrome finish . . . . . . . . . . . . . . . . . . . . . . .          18.00       20.00

☐ "Al Smith" lady's oval brooch (Hake 6; Warner
767) 2"h x 1⅜"w; black, white celluloid oval in
white metal frame; Hoover match . . . . . . . . . . . . .          75.00       100.00

☐ "Al Smith" donkey, enameled pins; these novelty
pins appeared on cards captioned: "Al's Brown
Derby. Headed For Victory" (Hake 80) ¾"l; red,
gilt (Hake 79) blue, gilt; (Hake 81) white, gilt; each          10.00       15.00

☐ Donkey with derby (Hake 82) aqua, brown, gilt          20.00       25.00

☐ Brown derby no-name die-cut brass badge with circular celluloid sepia photo inset (Hake 90; Warner
409) 1¾"; brown brass . . . . . . . . . . . . . . . . . . . . . .          100.00      125.00

☐ "For President. Al Smith. Our Favorite"; oval brass
badge (Hake 50) 1"w; black; brass finish . . . . . . .          25.00       30.00

☐ "National Democratic Convention 1924" badge;
"New York" skyline embossed on bar; gold/blue-
striped ribbon; arrowhead-shaped hanger with
large embossed star, eagle, and official New York
state seal; small medal on ribbon with bust portrait
and "Hon. Alfred Smith, Gov. New York" em-
bossed (Hake 2117) 4½" overall; brass finish . . .          50.00       75.00

☐ "Our Next President Al"; dimensional celluloid
brown derby badge (Hake 73) 1½"; brown . . . . .          25.00       30.00

☐ Smith–Robinson no-name die-cut stickpin in shape
of eyeglasses; sepia portraits in each lens (Hake 21)
1¼"w; sepia; brass finish . . . . . . . . . . . . . . . . . . . .          175.00      200.00

Price Range

☐ "Vote For Al Smith"; die-cut caricature bust portrait badge with brown derby attachment on chain (Hake 75) 1"h; gilt chrome; brown derby . . . . . . .  50.00    60.00

☐ "Wet" die-cut enameled beer stein stud (Hake 77) $\frac{1}{2}$"; brass finish; white foam . . . . . . . . . . . . . . . .  10.00    15.00

☐ "You Know Me Al. Smith and Robinson" shield badge (Hake 2100) 1"h; red, white, blue; brass finish . . . . . . . . . . . . . . . . . . . . . . . . . . . . . . . . . . . . . . .  45.00    50.00

### Cartoon/Pictorial Pinbacks

☐ "Al Smith and Robinson"; "Al" appears on brown derby, his famed trademark (Hake 51; Warner 768) $\frac{7}{8}$"; brown, black, white . . . . . . . . . . . . . . . . . . . . .  100.00    125.00

☐ "For President. American Liberty Smith"; "A" and "L" heavily outlined to make word "Al"; Liberty Bell line drawing (Hake 2060; Warner 766) $\frac{7}{8}$"; blue, white; key item for 1928 race . . . . . . . . . . . .  150.00    175.00

☐ "Hello Al. Goodby Cal"; cartoon of Democratic rooster (Hake unlisted; Warner 765) $1\frac{3}{4}$"; red, brown, white; tie-in with 1928 campaign song; Chattanooga, TN, button maker . . . . . . . . . . . . . .  225.00    250.00

☐ "Hoo Hoo Hoover For President" (Hake 107; Warner 401) $\frac{7}{8}$"; blue, brown, white; small cartoon of owl . . . . . . . . . . . . . . . . . . . . . . . . . . . . . . . . . . . . . . . .  35.00    50.00

☐ National Democratic Convention, Houston, Texas, June 26, 1928; cartoon donkey kicks sand on elephant's backside as it sits chained to Tea Pot Dome (Hake 2017) $1\frac{1}{4}$"; black, white; classic item . . . .  75.00    100.00

☐ "To New Heights With Al"; hot air balloon ascending (Hake 95) $\frac{7}{8}$"; blue, white . . . . . . . . . . . . . . .  100.00    110.00

☐ "What's Under Your Hat? Al Smith For President"; picture of derby (2061) $\frac{7}{8}$"; black, white  200.00    224.00

### Ceramics

☐ "Al Smith" ceramic liquor jug; approx. $4\frac{1}{2}$"h; glazed brown and cream; square sides . . . . . . . . .  100.00    125.00

Price Range

☐ Al Smith caricature ceramic mug; depicts Smith smoking a big cigar; 4"h; speckled tan glazed coloring; Roosevelt match; made by Stangl Pottery, Trenton, NJ ............................... 65.00    75.00

☐ "Al Smith" facsimile Toby mug; three-dimensional; has hands folded in front and big smile on face; 7"h; white or cream glazed coloring; made by Patriotic Products Association Gold Medal China ....... 65.00    75.00

☐ "Our Commodore" transfer portrait of a young Al Smith; ceramic mug; prepresidential; copy on reverse reads: "Ned Harrigan Club. Popularity Beefsteak. To Our Commodore Hon. Alfred E. Smith, October 25, 1915" ......................... 75.00    100.00

## Jugate Pinbacks

☐ "Al And Joe Let's Go"; canted oval insets (Hake 2002; Warner 405) 1¾"; black, white (item has been reproduced as lithograph) .............. 325.00    350.00

☐ "Our Choice. Smith And Robinson"; conjoining silhouetted portraits (Hake 2005) 1¼"; black, white 675.00    725.00

☐ "Smith And Robinson"; oval insets (Hake unlisted; Warner 762) 1¼"; red, white, blue ........... 650.00    700.00

☐ "Smith For President. Robinson For Vice President"; oval portrait insets in silhouette of brown derby (Hake 24) 4"; brown, white; key item from 1928 race .................................. 500.00    550.00

☐ "Smith—President. Robinson—Vice-President"; oval insets (Hake 22) ⅞"; sepia, white; lithograph 100.00    125.00

☐ "Smith–Robinson"; circle insets over patriotic bow (Hake 2) ⅞"; red, white, blue, black ......... 100.00    125.00

☐ (Hake 3) color variant of above; red, white, blue, black, gold ................................. 75.00    100.00

☐ "Smith–Robinson" shield/eagle, crossed flags in background, circular insets (Hake 1) 1¼"; red, white, dark blue, black, gold; classic key item design 500.00    550.00

☐ "Smith and Robinson" portrait insets against three-color bands (Hake 2007) ⅞"; red, white, blue, black; Hoover match ....................... 300.00    350.00

Price Range

☐ "Smith & Robinson"; small shield tops canted insets; candidates' heads almost touch; lettering conforms to oval shapes (Hake 2003) 1¼"; black, white    1100.00    1200.00

## Gubernatorial and Other Offices

In addition to being a four-time governor of New York, Al Smith held numerous minor offices, from alderman to sheriff. Items related to these earlier campaigns are avidly collected by Al Smith buffs.

☐ "Al. Smith For Governor" (Hake 2053) ⅞"; blue, white, silver rim ............................    20.00    25.00

☐ "Elect Smith Governor" slogan pinback (Hake 2081) ⅞"; red, white, blue ..................    25.00    30.00

☐ "Keep Governor Smith"; white star, slogan pinback (Hake 2052) ⅞"; red, white, blue .............    10.00    15.00

☐ "He Made Good. Smith For Governor" (Hake 2079) ½"; black, white .....................    20.00    25.00

☐ "Smith For Governor" (Hake 2078) ⅞"; blue, white ......................................    15.00    20.00

☐ "Re-elect Governor Smith" (Hake 88) ⅞"; red, white, blue ................................    10.00    15.00

☐ "Al Smith Gave Us Boxing"; bleed bust portrait; governor item (Hake 2049) black, white ........    85.00    100.00

☐ "Al Smith Gave Us Sunday Baseball"; bust portrait (Hake 2048; Warner 412) ⅞"; black, white; reference to Smith revoking Sunday Blue Laws in earlier term as governor of New York ...............    85.00    100.00

☐ "Al Smith Gave Us Sunday Movies"; bust portrait (Hake 84) ⅞", black, white ..................    75.00    85.00

☐ "For Governor. Alfred E. Smith"; bust portrait circle inset (Hake 2009) 2"; black, white (also appeared as mirror) ...........................    85.00    100.00

☐ "With Malice Toward None. With Charity For All. Governor Al Smith" (Hake 86) ⅞"; black, white    35.00    45.00

☐ "For Sheriff. Alfred E. Smith"; bust portrait (Hake 83) ⅞"; black, white ........................    80.00    90.00

☐ "For President, Board of Aldermen. Alfred E. Smith" (Hake 2047) ⅞"; black, white .........    50.00    75.00

INAUGURAL ITEMS  Price Range

☐ "City of New York" on gilt, celluloid; bar, brass; ribbon attached reads: "Alfred E. Smith, Governor State Of New York. Inaugural. January First, 1919"; ornate scrollwork-framed hanger with celluloid bust image of Smith (Hake 2091) $4\frac{1}{2}''$ overall; red, white, blue ribbon; black, white cello; gilt brass frames ..................................... 50.00 75.00

☐ Inauguration, Governor of New York: "Governor-Elect Alfred E. Smith" (Hake unlisted but companion to #2009; Warner 770) $2\frac{1}{8}''$; black, white; for Smith's first term as governor, January 1, 1910 .. 75.00 100.00

## *Portrait Pinbacks*

☐ "Al. Smith" appears in scroll (Hake 7) $1\frac{1}{2}''$; browntone, black ................................ 75.00 85.00

☐ "Al. Smith For President" (Hake 16) $\frac{7}{8}''$; black, white ....................................... 25.00 30.00

☐ "Alfred E. Smith For President" (Hake 2067) $3\frac{1}{4}''$; black, white .............................. 200.00 225.00

☐ Al Smith no-name; bust portrait, bleed (Hake 2066) $3''$; black, white ........................... 225.00 250.00

☐ "American Liberty. Smith For President"; small Smith oval portrait appears opposite Statue of Liberty; patriotic shield background (Hake 2018; Warner 408) $1\frac{1}{4}''$; red, white, blue, black (lithographed reproduction exists) ......................... 400.00 425.00

☐ "A Winner For You". "Al Smith" (Hake 2033) $\frac{7}{8}''$; black, white .......................... 75.00 80.00

☐ "Alfred E. Smith For President"; candy stripe border (Hake 89) $\frac{7}{8}''$; red, white, black; lithograph 25.00 30.00

☐ "Do You Know Al? Read The Philadelphia Record"; Smith's head in silhouette (Hake 97) $\frac{7}{8}''$; black, white; advertising giveaway ............. 60.00 70.00

☐ "For President. Alfred E. Smith"; bleed portrait with deep shadow behind bust (Hake 5) $1\frac{1}{2}''$; black, white ............................... 100.00 110.00

☐ "For President. Alfred E. Smith"; bluetone portrait (Hake 13) $1\frac{1}{4}''$; blue, white ................. 10.00 15.00

Price Range

☐ "For President. Alfred E. Smith"; circle inset, thin-line border (Hake 2011) $1\frac{1}{2}$"; black, white ..... 110.00    135.00

☐ "For President. Alfred E. Smith"; reversed out of black (Hake 20) $\frac{7}{8}$"; black, white ............ 30.00    45.00

☐ "For President. Alfred E. Smith"; Smith wearing brown derby (Hake 23; Warner 407) $1\frac{1}{4}$"; white, brown; the only pinback with Smith wearing famous trademark hat ........................ 12.00    15.00

☐ "For President. Alfred E. Smith"; white reversed out of brown border (Hake 101) $\frac{7}{8}$"; brown, white 12.00    15.00

☐ "I Gave $1.00. Won't You?" "Smith For President" (Hake 2038) $\frac{7}{8}$"; black, white ................ 275.00    300.00

☐ "I'm For Al"; bluetone portrait (Hake 37) $\frac{7}{8}$"; blue, white ................................ 45.00    55.00

☐ "Our Next President, Al Smith"; black circular portrait inset (Hake 30) $\frac{7}{8}$"; black, white ...... 115.00    125.00

☐ "Our Next President, Al Smith"; gray background behind portrait (Hake 2037) $\frac{7}{8}$"; black, gray, white 50.00    60.00

☐ Smith no-name portrait; flag bunting border (Hake 12) $1\frac{1}{4}$"; red, white, blue, black .............. 12.00    15.00

☐ Smith no-name portrait; thin white, thin black circled line around portrait (Hake 25) $1\frac{1}{4}$"; black, white ...................................... 30.00    35.00

☐ "Smith Club" (Hake 41) $\frac{7}{8}$"; black, white ...... 45.00    55.00

☐ "Smith," patriotic ribbon border (Hake 29) $\frac{7}{8}$"; red, white, blue, black ........................ 100.00    125.00

☐ Smith no-name with brass rim; bright red background behind silhouetted bust portrait (Hake 42) $\frac{7}{8}$"; black, red, white, gilt ................... 45.00    55.00

☐ "Smith [in large script] For President" (Hake 91) $\frac{7}{8}$"; blue, black, white, silver rim ............. 75.00    100.00

☐ "Smith For President"; patriotic border surrounds circular portrait (Hake 18) $\frac{7}{8}$"; red, white, blue, black ...................................... 15.00    20.00

☐ "Smith For President"; patriotic border surrounds larger bust image than above (Hake 19) $\frac{7}{8}$"; red, white, blue, black (lithograph reproduction exists) 10.00    15.00

Price Range

☐ "The Guiding Star [rebus] Of Our Nation"; star appears just atop Smith's head; six furled flags behind silhouetted head; "Alfred E. Smith of New York" appears below (Hake 2041; Warner 410) $7/8$"; blue star; red, white, blue, black (also appears with red star, but blue star is considered rarer) . . . . . . . .  125.00   135.00

☐ "Up From The Streets" "Al Smith"; bleed portrait (Hake 2035) $7/8$"; black, white . . . . . . . . . . . . . . . .  75.00   100.00

### Slogan/Name Pinbacks

☐ "Al" (Hake 96) $7/8$"; blue on gold . . . . . . . . . . . . .  15.00   20.00

☐ "Al Smith For President" (Hake 48) $7/8$"; red, white, blue . . . . . . . . . . . . . . . . . . . . . . . . . . . . . . .  20.00   25.00

☐ "Al" Smith and "Bob" Wagner; New York local item (Hake 63) $7/8$"; white reversed out of blue . .  15.00   20.00

☐ "Al Smith For President"; red bull's-eye with concentric white, blue circles; enameled (Hake 65) $1/2$"; red, white, blue, gold . . . . . . . . . . . . . . . . . . . . . . .  15.00   20.00

☐ "Al Smith's Friend" (Hake 99) $7/8$"; black, white  30.00   35.00

☐ "All For Al"; double stars (Hake 2062) $7/8$"; black, white lithograph . . . . . . . . . . . . . . . . . . . . . . . . . . .  35.00   40.00

☐ "Businessmen's Al Assn., N.Y." (Hake 2076) $7/8$"; black, white . . . . . . . . . . . . . . . . . . . . . . . . . . . . .  30.00   35.00

☐ "Downtown Tammany Smith Club. For President"; enameled stud (Hake 2102) $1/2$"; black, red, white . . . . . . . . . . . . . . . . . . . . . . . . . . . . . . . . . . .  30.00   35.00

☐ "No Oil On Al"; double stars (Hake 58) $7/8$"; black, white . . . . . . . . . . . . . . . . . . . . . . . . . . . . . . . . . .  35.00   50.00

☐ "May All Your Wet Dreams Come True"; anti-Prohibition theme (unlisted) $7/8$"; red, white . . . .  75.00   100.00

☐ "For President Alfred E. Smith"; *Brooklyn Citizen* advertising giveaway (Hake 2064) $7/8$"; black, white  50.00   60.00

☐ "Happy Warrior"; favorite Smith nickname (Hake 2065) $7/8$"; red, blue; white border . . . . . . . . . . . . .  35.00   50.00

☐ "Hello Al!"; American Legion emblem (2032) $1 1/2$"; blue, black, white; probably Legion and not campaign-related . . . . . . . . . . . . . . . . . . . . . . . . . . .  10.00   15.00

☐ "Me For Al" (Hake 2063) $7/8$"; black, white . . . .  25.00   35.00

Price Range

☐ "Member Smith, Hunt, Clarke Club"; New York local item (Hake 2081) $7/8$"; reversed out of red          25.00          30.00

☐ "Non Partisan Smith League" (Hake 2077) $7/8$"; red, white, blue ............................          30.00          35.00

☐ "Rockland County Al Smith For President Democratic Club" (Hake 2030) $1 1/4$"; black, white ....          75.00          100.00

☐ "Smith–Robinson First Voters' League" (Hake 2057) $7/8$"; blue, white .......................          30.00          40.00

## Statuary

☐ Al Smith pot-metal statuette; wears bow tie; name embossed on center front; $4$"h x $4 3/4$"w; bronze finish (shoulder, as opposed to full torso bust) .....          35.00          40.00

☐ Al Smith cast-metal pedestal, bust statuette, © Marie Appel, 1929; $8$"h; bronze finish .........          55.00          65.00

☐ "Al Smith For President," plaster deep-relief wall plaque; portrait of smiling, bow-tied Smith; $4$"dia; bronze finish; wire hanger at top; made by E. Pragge, 1928...............................          25.00          35.00

☐ Al Smith no-name zinc cast-metal bust; $4$"h x $4 3/4$"w; bronze finish; Hoover match ...........          30.00          40.00

☐ "Alfred E. Smith," three-dimensional plaster bust figure; name appears on pedestal base; approx. $6$"h; simulated bronze finish ......................          25.00          35.00

## Toys, Games, Puzzles

☐ "Al Smith Wins, Here's How," puzzle; Cahoes Novelty Co., Cahoes, New York; 1928; cardboard with wood tiles; $5 1/2$" sq .....................          50.00          75.00

☐ Al Smith whistling figure, German, late 1920s; wood-carved with clockwork mechanism and bellows; Al Smith with famed derby hat whistles tune "Happy Days Are Here Again," $12$"h (Smith ran

Price Range

on the "Wet" anti-Prohibition platform in 1928
against Hoover) ........................... 400.00    500.00*

## ADLAI EWING STEVENSON

The grandfather of Adlai Stevenson, the Democratic standardbearer in 1952 and 1956, served as Vice-President over a half century earlier under Grover Cleveland. Stevenson was a firm advocate of dispensing patronage. As first assistant postmaster general he fired over 40,000 Republican postmasters and replaced them with Democrats, thereby earning the nickname "The Axeman." Earlier in his career, he had broken a 32-year Republican stronghold and was sent to Congress from his home state of Illinois. After serving with Cleveland from 1893–97, he later ran in the second spot with William Jennings Bryan in 1900, losing to TR and McKinley (see Grover Cleveland and William Jennings Bryan).

## ADLAI EWING STEVENSON II

Adlai Stevenson, a Democrat, was running for reelection as Governor of Illinois in 1952 when he became the first genuinely drafted presidential candidate since James Garfield in 1880. Stevenson was grandson to Grover Cleveland's Vice-President in 1892–97. Always aware of the perils of running against a popular war hero like Eisenhower, the two-time loser (1952 and 1956) eloquently took his message to the American people. A political pundit once remarked, "If the Electoral College ever gives an honorary degree, it ought to go to Adlai Stevenson."

Price Range

*Automotive Accessories*

LICENSE PLATES
☐ "I'm For Stevenson"; cartoon of donkey at speaker's stand with microphone in hand (Hake 2092)
12″ x 6″; dark blue, white ................... 30.00    35.00
☐ "Stevenson" name plate (Hake 2095) 12″ x 6″; dark blue, white ................................. 20.00    25.00

---

*This toy, akin to the Charlie Chaplin whistler toy, sold for $1100 at an auction in 1985.

| LICENSE ATTACHMENTS | Price Range | |
|---|---|---|
| ☐ "I'm For Stevenson"; slogan attachment; tapered at top; 12″ x 4″; red letters, blue trimmed, on white (Hake 2094) ............................... | 20.00 | 25.00 |

### Cartoon/Pictorial Pinbacks

| | | |
|---|---|---|
| ☐ "Adlai and Estes Are Best For You"; four-leaf clover illustration with virtues such as "Maturity, Integrity..." in each leaf, "Right Will Prevail" under illustration (Hake 56) 1½″; black, white ....... | 25.00 | 30.00 |
| ☐ "All The Way With Adlai"; "Stevenson" superimposed on outline map of California (Hake 97) ⅞″; red, white, blue ............................ | 10.00 | 12.00 |
| ☐ Die-stamped silhouette of shoe with hole in sole; lapel stud (Hake 114) 1″w; silver finish; one of a number of variants ......................... | 10.00 | 15.00 |
| ☐ Donkey head cartoon, "Adlai/Estes" (Hake 47) 2¾″; red, white, blue .................... | 12.00 | 15.00 |
| ☐ "For '56," crossed-legs cartoon rebus with one shoe sole exposed to show famous Stevenson hole-in-shoe (Hake 44) 3¼″; black, white, red rim ..... | 15.00 | 20.00 |
| ☐ "I Like Stevenson"; cartoon of Joe from Bill Mauldin's famed Willie and Joe Up Front" series popular with GIs in World War II (Hake 34) 1¼″; black, white lithograph (item has been reproduced) | 10.00 | 12.00 |
| ☐ "I'm For Stevenson/How We'd Like Harry"; cartoon of Harry Truman with button on lips; Democrats were embarrassed by HST's "sounding off" on campaign issues in 1952 (Hake 8) 2½″; red, white, black ...................................... | 12.00 | 15.00 |
| ☐ "My Favorite Sun [sun rebus] Is Stevenson" (Hake 59) 1½″; orange, black, white ............... | 35.00 | 40.00 |
| ☐ "Walk To Victory With Adlai"; illustration of lady's shoe (Hake 84) ⅞″; red, white, blue ..... | 20.00 | 25.00 |
| ☐ "Why Be Fooled By The Old Bunk In A New Trunk? Vote Democratic"; elephant with trunk raised squirting water (Hake 50) 3¼″; red, white, blue ...................................... | 20.00 | 25.00 |

Price Range

☐ "We've Still Got Steve Up Our Sleeves"; cartoon of laughing Democratic donkey in circle (Hake 2009) 2¼"; black, yellow ......................... 25.00    30.00

## *Jugates*

### MISCELLANEOUS

☐ "Stevenson–Humphrey/President/Vice President/ Will Sweep The Country"; conjoining portraits under arched lettering at top; lower slogan bordered by stars (Hake 152) 2¾"; red, white, blue; produced by Humphrey Minnesota delegation at Democratic National Convention ................. 120.00    130.00

☐ Stevenson/Robert Wagner New York Senatorial; local: "Adlai And Bob/Let's Go In 1956" (Hake unlisted; Warner 463) 3½" ................. 275.00    300.00

### STEVENSON–KEFAUVER, 1956

☐ "Adlai and Estes—The Bestest/The Winning Team"; portraits in four-leaf clover design (Hake 4; Warner 823) 2¼"; green, white ............ 200.00    225.00

☐ Also 2¾" (Hake 2) ......................... 225.00    250.00

☐ "A Winning Team," Stevenston–Kefauver portraits in oval jugate (Hake 2005; Warner 464) 2¾"w x 1⅞"h; blue, white ................. 250.00    275.00

☐ "Dollars For Democrats"; conjoining portraits inside TV screen (Hake 3) 1½"; red, white, blue, black; lithograph .......................... 25.00    30.00

☐ "President/Adlai Stevenson; Vice President Estes Kefauver"; large shield between ovals at top; laurel branches in circle border (Hake 2004) 3½"; red, blue, green, black on buff .................... 30.00    35.00

☐ "T.V. Victory Committee"; conjoining jugate portraits in TV screen area (Hake 2002) 2"; red, white, blue, black ............................... 140.00    150.00

☐ "Vote Democratic"; same shield and laurel branch design as Hake 2004 (Hake 5) 3½"; red, white, blue, green, black ........................... 35.00    50.00

Price Range

☐ "Vote Straight Democratic"; large bull's-eye Stevenson/Kefauver portrait jugate, "General Election 1956" (Hake 2001) 4"; black, white ....... 175.00 200.00

STEVENSON–SPARKMAN, 1952

☐ "Go Forward With Stevenson/Sparkman"; conjoining bleed portraits with names in scroll (Hake 7) 1¼"; multicolor; lithograph (a lithographed tin reproduction exists) ......................... 20.00 25.00

☐ "Stevenson/Sparkman"; conjoining portraits with patriotic border (Hake 9) 3¼"; red, white, blue, black; celluloid reproduction exists ............ 40.00 50.00

☐ "Vote Straight Democratic"; silhouetted heads of candidates appear on red center band (Hake 6) 3¾"; red, white, blue ...................... 130.00 150.00

## *Portrait Pinbacks*

☐ "Adlai Best In View" (Hake 26) 1½"; red, white; lithograph reproduction exists ................ 35.00 45.00

☐ "All The Way With Adlai"; portrait of Stevenson in hat (Hake 31) 1"; red, white, blue .......... 8.00 10.00

☐ "For President/Adlai E. Stevenson" (Hake 2038) 3½"; black, white ......................... 10.00 15.00

☐ "Forward With Stevenson"; blacktone portrait and lettering reversed out of black (Hake 18) 1⅛" black, white; lithograph ..................... 8.00 10.00

☐ John Sparkman, running mate (Hake 19) ....... 8.00 10.00

☐ "I'm Still Madly For Adlai"; 1956 race; line portrait (Hake 2007; Warner 825) 2¼"; black, white .... 80.00 90.00

☐ "Our Next President/Adlai Stevenson"; three stars on each side of portrait (Hake 2011) 3½"; red, white, blue, black; red rim ................... 20.00 25.00

☐ "Adlai Best In View" (Hake 26) 1½"; red, white; lithograph reproduction exists ................ 35.00 45.00

☐ "All The Way With Adlai"; portrait of Stevenson in hat (Hake 31) 1"; red, white, blue .......... 8.00 10.00

☐ "For President/Adlai E. Stevenson" (Hake 2038) 3½"; black, white ......................... 10.00 15.00

Price Range

☐ "Forward With Stevenson"; blacktone portrait and lettering reversed out of black (Hake 18) $1\frac{1}{8}$"; black, white; lithograph ..................... 8.00 10.00

☐ John Sparkman, running mate (Hake 19) ....... 8.00 10.00

☐ "I'm Still Madly For Adlai"; 1956 race; line portrait (Hake 2007; Warner 825) $2\frac{1}{4}$"; black, white .... 80.00 90.00

☐ "Our Next President/Adlai Stevenson"; three stars on each side of portrait (Hake 2011) $3\frac{1}{2}$"; red, white, blue, black; red rim ................... 20.00 25.00

☐ "Stevenson–Mennon Williams" portraits flasher; "Make It Emphatic" (Hake 2080) $2\frac{1}{2}$"; black, white ....................................... 8.00 10.00

☐ "Stevenson For President 1960"; an attempt by loyal Stevensonites to get him to run a third time in 1960 (Hake 2066) $1\frac{1}{8}$"; black, white lithograph 8.00 10.00

☐ "Vote Democratic/Adlai" (Hake 32; Warner 824) 1"; red, white, blue; choice Stevenson smaller portrait pinback .............................. 90.00 100.00

☐ "We Cannot Afford A Lesser Man/Stevenson In '60"; Draft Stevenson movement (Hake 2064; Warner 466) $1\frac{1}{4}$"; blue, white ................... 80.00 90.00

☐ "Adlai" (Hake 51) 2"; vibrant red lettering on black 10.00 12.00

☐ "Adlai & Estes Are The Bestes'/Vote Democratic" (Hake 2059) $1\frac{1}{4}$"; black, white .............. 15.00 20.00

☐ "But Stevenson Is Change Enough For Me" (Hake 2044; Warner 467) $1\frac{1}{2}$"; red, white (refreshing departure from standard "outs" slogan, "Time For A Change") ................................. 25.00 30.00

☐ "Fore! We'll All Be In The Same Hole Together!" (Hake 2040) $1\frac{1}{4}$"; black, yellow (one of countless "digs" at Ike's preoccupation with golf) ........ 12.00 15.00

☐ "General Eisenhower/General Motor$/Our 2 Pre$ident$" (Hake 2051) $1\frac{1}{4}$"; black, yellow .... 30.00 35.00

☐ "Gladly For Adlai" (Hake 2049) $1\frac{1}{4}$"; black, white 20.00 25.00

☐ "I Like Adlai Better. 20th Congressional District" (Hake 43; Warner 826) $2\frac{1}{4}$"; red, white, blue; Democrats' rejoinder to "I Like Ike" ............. 60.00 70.00

Price Range

☐ "I Like Ike/But I'm Going To Vote For Stevenson" (Hake 54) 1¾"; black, white .................     15.00    20.00

☐ "Madly For Adlai" (Hake 2015) 2"; red, white blue     20.00    25.00

☐ "Nix-On Eisenhower & Nixon" (Hake 2051) 1¼"; black, yellow .............................    25.00    30.00

☐ "Now Do You Like Ike?" (Hake 2055) 3½"; red, white, blue; 1956 race (they still did) ..........     8.00    10.00

☐ "Teen Agers For TASK/Stevenson/Kefauver" (Hake 46) 1¾"; red, black, white ............    15.00    20.00

☐ "Two Strikes Are Not Out/I'm For Adlai" (Hake 2077) 3½"; black, white; 1960 ...............    20.00    25.00

☐ "Vote Gladly For Adlai" (Hake 101) ⅞"; white reversed out of black ........................     6.00     8.00

☐ "We Need Adlai Badly" (Hake 2053) 4"; black, white .......................................    25.00    30.00

☐ "Winning Team/Stevenson/Kennedy"; oval shape (Hake 2083) 2¾"w x 1¾"h; black, white; Stevenson draft attempt at 1960 Democratic Convention    125.00   135.00

## *Trigate*

☐ "The Team For You/Not Just A Few. Adlai/George/Estes"; George Rhodes, 14th District, Pennsylvania, Congressional candidate, 1956 (Hake unlisted; Warner 822) 4"; red, white, blue    225.00   250.00

## WILLIAM HOWARD TAFT

William Howard Taft, a Republican from Ohio, was appointed U.S. Circuit Judge by President Benjamin Harrison in 1892 and served on the bench until 1900. He became first civil governor of the Philippines and was appointed Secretary of War by Teddy Roosevelt (1904–08). Taft became the 27th President of the U.S. in 1909, but lost to Woodrow Wilson in the 1912 race. He later returned to his first love, the judicial system, and was appointed Chief Justice of the Supreme Court shortly after Harding's inauguration.

William Howard Taft postcard,
1912–1913 ($20–$25).

William Howard Taft Toby mug, ca. 1910;
sold in curio shops during Taft's term of
office ($55–$65).

Price Range

*Advertising, Commercial Organizations*
*Pinbacks*

☐ "Allen County Taft League"; gold eagle and stars
in blue shield (Hake 158) ⅞"; blue, gold, black,
white . . . . . . . . . . . . . . . . . . . . . . . . . . . . . . . . . . . . . . . . . .   15.00      20.00

"Taft–Sherman" 1908 celluloid cane top ($100–$125). *(Bruce DeMay Collection)*

| | Price Range | |
|---|---|---|
| ☐ Apple Festival, Spokane, Washington, 1900; Taft portrait framed by apple tree leaves and apples (Hake 97) 1¼"; red, green, black, white . . . . . . . | 50.00 | 60.00 |
| ☐ "Clothier's Legion. Our Craft Is For Taft"; bust portrait of Taft (Hake 3143) 3½"; black, white . . | 150.00 | 175.00 |
| ☐ "Commercial Men For Taft"; pair of U.S. flags project from circle inset portrait (Hake 90) 1¼"; red, white, blue, black . . . . . . . . . . . . . . . . . . . . . . | 225.00 | 250.00 |
| ☐ "Commercial Travelers For Taft"; portrait inside suitcase (Hake 3183) 1¼"; black, sepia . . . . . . . . | 275.00 | 300.00 |
| ☐ Slight variant (Hake 211) . . . . . . . . . . . . . . . . . . . | 275.00 | 300.00 |
| ☐ Kansas Semi-Centennial, Hutchinson, September 1911; Taft portrait inside center of sunflower (Hake 3145) 2"; yellow, brown black, white . . . . . . . . . . | 75.00 | 100.00 |
| ☐ "Middletown Taft Day, Nov. 12, '08" (Hake 74) 1¼"; multicolor . . . . . . . . . . . . . . . . . . . . . . . . . . . | 15.00 | 20.00 |
| ☐ "Nebraska First Voter's League"; Taft portrait (Hake 146) ⅞"; blue, black, white; one of a series issued for a number of states . . . . . . . . . . . . . . . . | 10.00 | 15.00 |

Price Range

☐ "Sixth Annual German Day, Aug. 8, 1910. Compliments of DuBois Árt Studio, Utica, N.Y."; jugate portraits of Taft and Kaiser against U.S. and German flag background (Hake 3144) 1¼"; multicolor ... 45.00 ... 55.00

☐ "Taft Day Military Tournament. Sept. 20, 1909" (Hake 3165) 1¾"; black, white .............. 25.00 ... 35.00

☐ "Taft & Sherman Businessmen's Republican Ass'n, 1908. Paper Division"; bust portrait (Hake 46) 3¾"; multicolor ........................... 175.00 ... 200.00

☐ "Taft League Of Erie County"; eagle with arrow in beak behind ballot box (Hake 3278) ⅞"; black, white ...................................... 20.00 ... 25.00

☐ "Unconditional Republican Club"; bust portrait (Hake 215) ⅞"; red, sepia, white ............ 65.00 ... 75.00

## Badges, Medals, Stickpins

☐ "Aide-de-Camp" paper/celluloid brass-framed bar; chain-linked to figural eagle framing celluloid hanger with bust portrait of Taft (Hake 3174) 2¾" overall; black, white, gilded brass ............ 20.00 ... 25.00

☐ Baseball bat wooden pin with small banner attached horizontally; "The Big Stick" with Taft's portrait appears on banner (Hake 187) 3" bat, 2" banner; red, blue, black; brown bat .................. 50.00 ... 60.00

☐ Bas-relief bust of Taft; brass hanger on stickpin; (Hake 172) 1"h; brass finish ................. 10.00 ... 12.00

☐ "For President. William H. Taft" paper tab (Hake 170) 1¼"w; red, white, blue ................ 10.00 ... 12.00

☐ "Heads-U-Win-If-U-Vote-For Taft," brass token (Hake 3036) 1¼"; brass finish ............... 25.00 ... 30.00

☐ "I-Am-For-Bill?" 1908; mechanical badge; changes candidate's portraits—Bryan or Taft (Hake 210) 1¼"; black, beige; gold rim ................. 200.00 ... 210.00

☐ "Presidential Chair" mechanical badge; brass with paper photograph portrait of Taft framed in lid to chair seat (Hake 3042) 1¾"h; silver on brass ... 125.00 ... 135.00

Price Range

☐ Standing Taft figure with spinner attachment; spin
disk and figure seems to wave greeting (Hake 196)
1″; black figure and "Taft" lettering on gilded brass    35.00    40.00

☐ "Taft In Clover" (lettering on ribbon) attached to
celluloid hanger; Taft portrait with four-leaf clover
behind it; brass frame (Hake 3166) 3½″ overall;
green, black hanger; red, blue, green ribbons ....    45.00    55.00

☐ "Taft" spinner attachment; name is spelled out
when disk is spun (Hake 198) 1″; brass finish ...    20.00    25.00

☐ "The Butting Bills. Which One Will Win?"; celluloid badge with lettering; dimensional attachment
of pair of goats locking horns (unlisted) 1¼″;
badge, black on white; gilded metal goats ......    125.00    135.00

☐ Taft Inaugural key to White House; "Souvenir"
marked on bar; die-cut brass key-shaped hanger, inscribed "March 4th, 1909"; 3½″l; brass finish ..    45.00    55.00

☐ Taft convention delegate's badge; silvered shell with
bust portrait cello (1½″; black, white); ribbon
marked: "Republican National League Conven-
tion"; 1903; 6″ ribbon; white, green ...........    65.00    75.00

☐ Mechanical badge: Presidential chair, seat pops up
to reveal bust portrait of Taft; (Hake 3042) 2½″h;
brass gilt finish ............................    125.00    135.00

☐ White House view in shield; "My Choice" under
circular pop-up portraits of Taft–Sherman; tin mechanical badge (Hake 5) 1¾″h x 2″w; red, white,
blue, black ................................    175.00    200.00

☐ White House with jugate portraits of Taft–Sherman
in ovals in foreground; cameo insets of Republican
presidential candidates from Fremont through TR;
ornate brass-framed paper hanger suspended from
brass bar with paper/celluloid insert that reads:
"Pennsylvania" (Hake 168) 1¾″ hanger; 3½″
overall; browntone hanger with brass finish .....    160.00    170.00

☐ "Who Will Wear These Shoes?" Bryan–Taft portraits with spread eagle above ovals; starred border
(Hake 14) 1½″; red, white, blue, black celluloid
pinback with metal shoes hanger; salesman's
"Safety Pin" ...............................    175.00    200.00

Price Range

☐ Inaugural badge, heart-shaped, suspended from enameled, scrolled bar labeled "Souvenir"; pendant bears embossed bust portrait of Taft and inscription (Hake 3035) 1½″ overall; red, white, blue bar; brass-finish pendant ......................... 30.00     35.00

☐ Inaugural medal; conjoining profile portraits of Taft–Sherman (Hake 3039) 2″; brass finish ..... 160.00     170.00

☐ "Inaugural Washington D.C., March 4" ribbon; "Our Pres. Taft" portrait pinback (Hake 3172) 3″ overall; gold-on-blue ribbon; black-on-white pinback ...................................... 35.00     45.00

☐ Souvenir "Inaugural" badge, "March 4, 1909. President Taft, Washington D.C."; die-cut, engraved brass (Hake 169) 2¾″w x 1¾″h; brass finish ... 25.00     30.00

### Cartoon/Pictorial Pinbacks

**ANTI-TAFT**

☐ "Smile" (Taft looking especially grim) "Prosperity" (Hake 130) brownish tan on buff .............. 75.00     100.00

☐ "What Is A Man To Do When Out Of Work, In A Financial Crisis And Starving? God Knows!" (Taft, at well over 300 pounds, obviously was never in this plight); caricature bust of a perplexed Taft (Hake 3179) 1¼″; black, white .............. 300.00     325.00

**PRO-TAFT**

☐ "From Chicago To Washington–Taft"; Taft riding elephant and waving club (Hake 3177; Warner 1¼″; mate to Hake 3279; Warner 608; red, black, white ...................................... 375.00     400.00

☐ "Hello Bill"; cartoon of man with cane extending large hand; Hassan Cigarettes premium (unlisted) ⅞″; multicolor ............................ 10.00     12.00

☐ "I Am A Tafty Kid"; Taft caricature, wearing beanie and looking even heftier than usual (Hake 3178) 1⅞″; red, white, blue, black ................. 300.00     325.00

☐ "My Billy" "For President. Wm. H. Taft of Ohio"; billy goat with Taft head caricature (unlisted) 1¼″; black on white (Billy Bryan match) ........... 250.00     300.00

Price Range

☐ "Possom Klub" [*sic*] photo of possum out on tree limb (Hake 167) 1¼"; sepiatone .............. 55.00   65.00

☐ "Race Track"; Taft rides GOP elephant and out-races Bryan on donkey, who is far in distance (Hake 3221; Warner 583) 2"; black on white; key item and one of prize cartoon pinbacks in hobby; see also Bryan mate (Hake 203; Warner 599) .......... 400.00   500.00

☐ Steamroller; caricature of Taft standing on front of steamroller ringing small bells in each hand; driver leans out from seat (Hake unlisted) 1¼"; black on white ...................................... 350.00   400.00

☐ Steamroller (photo version); Taft bust in oval atop steamroller (Hake unlisted; Warner 584) 2"h oval; sepiatone; filigreed brass frame ................ 300.00   325.00

☐ "U-N-I-T-E-D" (play on "You and I Ted"); Taft and TR shaking hands; reference to TR's support-ing Taft as Republican nominee in 1908 (Hake 98) ⅞"; red, white, blue, fleshtones ............... 100.00   110.00

## Jugates

### TAFT–DIAZ

When President Taft and President Diaz of Mexico met in El Paso, Texas, in October 1909, it inspired a number of political items.

☐ Taft–Diaz conjoining heart-shaped portrait within furled flags of U.S.–Mexico (Hake 3126) 1¼"; mul-ticolor ...................................... 100.00   125.00

☐ Taft–Diaz jugate variant with smaller crossed flags of two nations above portraits (Hake 3125; Warner 293) 1¾"; multicolor ....................... 150.00   200.00

☐ Taft–Diaz ovals with flags of respective nations waving above portraits (Hake 3124; Warner 593) 1¾"; multicolor ........................... 125.00   150.00
   See also Taft–Diaz pocket mirror.

### TAFT-SHERMAN
☐ "Bloomington, Illinois" ear of corn jugate (Hake 9) 1¼"; black on white portraits; yellow, green ear of corn ........................................ 500.00   550.00

**Price Range**

☐ Conjoining heart-framed portraits linked to a stylized balance scale (Hake 33); 1¼"; red, white, aqua, dark blue ........................... 125.00 150.00

☐ Eagle with full spread wings embraces oval portraits; star-bordered circle with "1908" and scrolls breaking out under portraits (Hake 3120; Warner 591) 1¾"; sepiatone; variants of this design appeared from 1904 to 1916; again in 1928 for Hoover 150.00 175.00

☐ Eagle with wings spread; oval insets of Taft–Sherman are linked across eagle's breast and wings (Hake 12) 1¼"; red, white, blue, gold, black 150.00 175.00

☐ "Elephant Ears"; Taft–Sherman inset portraits appear in flared elephant ears of cartoon-style pachyderm (Hake 7; Warner 287) 1¼"; red, black, gray, yellow, white; complements Bryan–Kern "Clean Sweep" (Hake 93), and both are key items for 1908 race ......................................... 800.00 850.00

☐ GOP elephant with tiny Taft–Sherman jugate on elephant's blanket (Hake 3136; Warner 590) ⅞"; browntone, cream; 1912; one of the most intricate designs from the Golden Era of pinbacks; also appeared as poster ........................... 200.00 225.00

☐ "Liberty Halo"; Miss Liberty holds portrait insets of Taft–Sherman in folds of her red-white striped skirt (Hake 8) 1"; multicolor; Warner 588 variant has Taft facing opposite way; mate of Bryan (Hake 102; Warner 603); an Art Nouveau classic ...... 250.00 275.00

☐ Liberty on shield-backed throne holds up oval portraits of Taft–Sherman (Hake 4) 1¾"; multicolor 500.00 550.00

☐ Oval Taft–Sherman flag jugate with small shield below (Hake 201) 1"w oval; red, white, blue, black, gold ....................................... 100.00 125.00

☐ "Republican Candidates, 1908"; conjoining bust portraits (Hake 15) 2"; browntone on white; lithograph ...................................... 200.00 225.00

☐ "S" and "T" entwined letters (for Taft–Sherman) frame circle insets; unusual profile view of Sherman accentuates sideburns (Hake 3130) 1¼": black, sepia, white................................. 250.00 300.00

Price Range

☐ Scepter and flags with circular Taft–Sherman portraits (Hake 11); a slight variant (Warner 586, 1½″) features smaller insets and more prominent flags; 1¼″; red, white, blue, gold, black . . . . . . . . . . . .   200.00   225.00

☐ Seated Liberty (at left) with hand leaning on lower circle inset of Sherman; Taft inset appears above; flag and laurel frames portraits (Hake 6) 1¾″; multicolor . . . . . . . . . . . . . . . . . . . . . . . . . . . . . . . . .   400.00   450.00

☐ Statue of Liberty with beacon rays from torch spotlighting oval portraits of Taft–Sherman (Hake 1; Warner 582) 1¾″; multicolor; one of the most beautiful jugates in the hobby and a key item for the 1908 race . . . . . . . . . . . . . . . . . . . . . . . . . . . . .   525.00   550.00

☐ Taft–Sherman circular insets; shield and eagle at top, small eagle presidential emblem below (Hake 26; Warner 589) 1¾″; red, white, blue, gold, black   250.00   300.00

☐ "Taft–Sherman" conjoining portraits (Hake 17) 2″; browntone . . . . . . . . . . . . . . . . . . . . . . . . . . . . . . .   75.00    85.00

☐ Taft–Sherman with scepter dividing circular insets; crossed American flags behind (Hake 11) 1¼″; red, white, blue, black, gold . . . . . . . . . . . . . . . . . . . . .   175.00   200.00

☐ Also unusual 1½″ size (Warner 586) . . . . . . . . . .   350.00   400.00

## Mirrors

☐ "Bill"; famed John De Yongh portrait of genial-looking Taft (unlisted) 2″; black, white, gold . . . .   125.00   150.00

☐ "Creme Elcaya For The Complexion" advertising mirror; Taft portrait (unlisted); vertical oval; 2½″h; brown, blue, black, fleshtones . . . . . . . . . .   85.00    95.00

☐ "For President. For Vice President. Our Candidates"; Taft–Sherman jugate mirror; 1912 race (Hake unlisted; Warner 286) 2″; red, white, blue, brown . . . . . . . . . . . . . . . . . . . . . . . . . . . . . . . . .   1000.00  1200.00

☐ "Hand Shake Jubilee"; meeting of President Taft and President Diaz of Mexico in El Paso, Texas, in 1909; cartoon figures stand atop bridge over Rio Grande; see related pinbacks (Hake 3044; Warner 293, 593) 2¾″ horizontal oval; multicolor . . . . . .   200.00   220.00

Price Range

☐ Taft–Sherman jugate mirror (Hake 3119; Warner 587) 2¼"; browntone with reverse signatures; mate to Wilson (Warner 624) from 1912 race . . . . . . . .     350.00     375.00

☐ "Tried And Safe Man." "Up To The Man On The Other Side"; appeal to vanity of voter, who sees mirror image; numerous variations issued through the years; taft bust portrait above lettering (Hake 205) 2"; sepiatone . . . . . . . . . . . . . . . . . . . . . . . . .     125.00     150.00

### Miscellaneous Novelties

☐ Bookend; elephant, three-dimensional figure with cello inset in middle; Taft bust portrait, "Taft For President"; cast-iron elephant, 7" x 5"; black finish; cello, 2¼"; sepiatone . . . . . . . . . . . . . . . . . . . . . . .     85.00     95.00

☐ Bookmark; standing bear (reference to TR's endorsement in 1908) with heart-shaped portrait of smiling Taft; loop hanger; 2¾"h; black, brown, white . . . . . . . . . . . . . . . . . . . . . . . . . . . . . . . . . .     25.00     35.00

☐ Paper holder, spring-loaded brass with marble on handle; bust portrait of Taft inside marble; holder, 2¼"w, brass finish; marble, 1¼", sepia image . . .     25.00     35.00

☐ Turtle paperweight; cello of James T. Sherman "For Representative In Congress, 27th District N.Y."; turtle, approx. 4"l; cello, approx. 3"h oval; black on white . . . . . . . . . . . . . . . . . . . . . . . . . . . .     45.00     55.00

### Noisemakers

☐ "For President/Wm. H. Taft" (obverse) "For Vice President Jas. S. Sherman" (reverse); painted tin rattle noisemaker; Taft wears top hat; two rounded halves form canister; 3½"; red, white, black, flesh-tones . . . . . . . . . . . . . . . . . . . . . . . . . . . . . . . . . .     350.00     400.00

*Portrait Pinbacks*                                    Price Range

☐ Eagle with banner in beak tops shield and arrows
in quiver to frame circular bust portrait of Taft
(Hake 204; Warner 585) 1¾"; multicolor; a classic
single-portrait item .........................   200.00     250.00

☐ Elongated oval portrait of Taft, commemorating
opening of Gunnison Irrigation Tunnel by Taft at
Montrose, Colorado, 1909 (Hake unlisted; Warner
594) 1½" x ⅝"; multicolor ..................    75.00     100.00

☐ Liberty Bell framing Taft portrait (Hake 122) ⅞";
red, white, blue, gold, black ..................    20.00      25.00

☐ Laurel wreath framing Taft portrait (Hake 72)
1¼"; red, green, orange, black, buff ...........    35.00      45.00

☐ Patriotic shield with elongated oval portrait of Taft;
lighter-colored waves of stars and stripes in background; laurel leaf frame on portrait (Hake 47)
1¼"; red, white, blue, pale blue, pink, black photo;
another striking single-portrait item ...........   150.00     175.00

☐ Taft shield portrait framed by half shield at top; laurel leaves, ornate scroll below (Hake 67) 1¼"; red,
white, blue, aqua, gold, black photo; vivid coloring    50.00      75.00

☐ Eagle with arrows projecting from both sides of
spread wings; oval portrait of Taft appears on
eagle's breast (Hake 66) 1¼"; orange shades, dark
blue background; black on white photo; Wilson
match ......................................    45.00      55.00

☐ Ruffled red, white, blue ribbon bordering sepiatone
Taft portrait (Hake 208) 1¼" .................    40.00      50.00

☐ Eagle head peers from above diamond-shaped Taft
portrait (Hake 207) 1¼"; red, white, blue, gold;
sepia photo .................................    45.00      55.00

☐ "Wm. H. Taft" appears in circular scroll under portrait (Hake 48) 2"; browntone, white, green; see
Hake 78-80 for variants of the above pinback, in
more common 1¼" size .....................    45.00      55.00

☐ "I Am For Playgrounds" appears in border around
circle portrait (Hake 142) ⅞"; white reversed out
of black ....................................    50.00      60.00

| *Slogan Pinbacks* | Price Range | |
|---|---|---|
| ☐ "Ask Bill" (Hake 3279) ⅞"; reversed out of blue | 10.00 | 12.00 |
| ☐ "Hello Bill" (Hake 16) ⅞"; reversed out of red (there has been speculation as to whether this refers to Taft or to a lodge slogan) ................. | 5.00 | 10.00 |
| ☐ "Me For Bill" (Hake 166) 1¼"; slogan across middle in blue; red-white stripes above; blue-white stripes below................................ | 20.00 | 25.00 |
| ☐ "Rah For Taft And Hap-A-Day" (Hake 161) ⅞"; white reversed out of blue; Bryan match ....... | 30.00 | 35.00 |
| ☐ "The Safest" (Hake 127) ⅞"; black and white Taft portrait; slogan mix of red, black lettering ...... | 15.00 | 20.00 |

### Tobacco Accessories

| | | |
|---|---|---|
| ☐ William H. Taft figural clay pipe; bust-shape bowl with curved shank; 7"l; made by Gambier of Paris | 60.00 | 75.00 |
| ☐ William H. Taft corncob pipe with lithograph paper jugate portraits of Taft–Sherman; 2"h .......... | 50.00 | 60.00 |

### Toys, Games, Puzzles, Dolls, Banks

| | | |
|---|---|---|
| ☐ "Billy Possum" still bank, maker unknown, 1908; cast iron, silver on black base; slogan reads "Billy Possum" and "Possum and Taters" on opposite sides of base ............................... | 250.00 | 300.00 |
| ☐ Peaceful Bill/Smiling Jim still bank, maker unknown, 1908; cast iron; bust masks of successful running mates William Taft and James Sherman appear back to back; bronze finish; 4"h ........ | 250.00 | 300.00 |
| ☐ Taft "Bill the Beamer" Roly-Poly, Bill the Beamer Co., New York, circa 1909; white composition; figure holds baseball in right hand, 4½"h, 3"dia (Taft was the first President to officially throw out the first baseball at a World Series) ............... | 150.00 | 200.00 |
| ☐ Taft "Billy Possum" Prosperity still bank, maker unknown, 1908; ceramic, caricature of Taft's head on possum's body, 5"h (Hake 3021) ........... | 150.00 | 200.00 |

Price Range

☐ Taft "The Egg" still bank, J. & E. Stevens, 1908; cast-iron, egg-shaped caricature with top hat on figure; very common bank $3\frac{1}{2}$"h ................ 900.00  1000.00

☐ Taft "Happy Billy Possum's Prosperity Puzzle," National Novelty Co., Worcester, MA, 1908; lithographed cardboard game with marbles; object is to send marbles through dimensional image of William Howard Taft and into White House Gate, 6"sq  150.00  200.00

☐ Taft Roly-Poly, maker unknown, 1900s; celluloid; stained black, green, tan; $1\frac{1}{2}$"h .............. 150.00  200.00

☐ William Howard Taft Roly-Poly, maker unknown, 1900s; papier-mâché, $5\frac{1}{4}$"h .................. 200.00  250.00

## Watch Fobs

☐ Ballot box, die-cut; "Taft" embossed under slot; "On The Lid" on front of box; $1\frac{1}{4}$"; silver finish  20.00  25.00

☐ Brass-linked fob; four chained die-cut disks; embossed figures of elephant, baseball player, army camp, and "Taft For President" portrait; $3\frac{3}{4}$"l overall; brass finish ........................ 30.00  35.00

☐ Caricature, full-face portrait, "Wm. Taft For President"; 2"h; gilt on black .................... 35.00  40.00

☐ Die-cut torso view of Taft; head-on; $1\frac{3}{4}$"h; black on brass .................................. 20.00  25.00

☐ Eagle atop shield; "Taft"; $1\frac{3}{4}$"; red, white, blue, silver ....................................... 10.00  15.00

☐ Eagle, die-cut, atop laurel leaf–bordered shell with cello inset; "Wm. H. Taft" portrait; 2"; browntone cello; gilt finish ........................... 15.00  20.00

☐ Flying eagle and shield; Taft portrait; cello on leather background; $1\frac{1}{2}$"; black, sepia, white ... 20.00  25.00

☐ Horseshoe, die-cut; embossed images of Taft–Sherman; "Our Choice. 1908"; $1\frac{1}{2}$"; gilt ....... 15.00  20.00

☐ Linked cello on brass portraits of Sherman, $\frac{3}{4}$", and Taft, $1\frac{1}{4}$"; sepia on black background linked to swivel snap; $4\frac{1}{2}$"l overall .................... 55.00  65.00

Price Range

☐ "Our Choice. Taft and Sherman, Washington D.C."; circular paper portraits of pair; 1¾"; black on white; brass finish; die-cut shield shape ...... 200.00 225.00

☐ Oval Taft–Sherman jugate; embossed portraits on gilt brass; 1¾" ............................. 40.00 45.00

☐ Padlock-shaped "Lock To White House—1912"; 1½"; etched brass .......................... 20.00 25.00

☐ Possum, seated, with tail in hand; die-cut brass; "1908. Taft"; 2"; silver finish; embossed ........ 30.00 35.00

☐ Rooster, die-cut, with crossed brooms; "Taft"; 1"; red, gold, black; enameled .................. 15.00 20.00

☐ Satchel, die cut; "Taft. Washington D.C."; 1½"; embossed on silver finish .................... 30.00 35.00

☐ Shell horseshoe, embossed, with cello inset portrait of Taft; small buckled embossed strap across base of horseshoe .............................. 15.00 20.00

☐ Silhouette of Taft; die-cut brass; profile; 1¾"h; black on brass finish ....................... 20.00 25.00

☐ Taft head, caricature; ceramic deep relief on leather background; 2½"l; white on tan leather ........ 25.00 30.00

☐ Taft portrait, bas relief in brass; irregular octagonal shape; 1½"; brass finish .................... 15.00 25.00

☐ Taft portrait; cello on die-cut shield, leather background; 2"l; red, white, blue, black cello; dark leather .................................... 30.00 35.00

☐ "Taft–Sherman 1908"; die-cut shield with etched lettering; countless variations of this prosaic item issued during 1904 and 1908 campaigns ........ 10.00 15.00

☐ Taft–Sherman cello with eagle and shield atop oval portraits on leather background; red, white, blue, black; black leather ........................ 150.00 160.00

## ZACHARY TAYLOR

Zachary Taylor, affectionately known as "Old Zach" and "Old Rough and Ready," had been a professional soldier for over 40 years and was completely lacking in political savvy, when he was nominated by the Whigs in 1848. A glorious victory over President Santa Anna at the Battle of Bueno

Vista in the Mexican war had made Taylor a national hero. Taylor defeated Democrat Lewis Cass and Free Soiler Martin Van Buren to become the 12th U.S. President. During his administration, bitter disputes erupted over the slavery question in California and New Mexico territory, and Taylor strongly advocated self-determination. If his untimely death had not occurred only two years after taking office, a number of observers, including Daniel Webster, felt there would have been a civil war in 1850. Taylor's chief legacy to collectors is a wide variety of figural whiskey flasks and one of the most massive of three-dimensional artifacts, a cast-iron parlor stove bearing his embossed bust portrait.

**Price Range**

### Cutlery

☐ Razor; "General Taylor" etched on blade; celluloid
handle; white ............................... 185.00    200.00

☐ Razor; "Bust Zachary Taylor" etched on blade;
white celluloid handle ....................... 185.00    200.00

### Lapel Devices

BRASS SHELLS

☐ "Major Genl. Taylor/Born 1790," enclosing military portrait; "Genl. Taylor Never Surrenders" on reverse; brass shell (Hake 3059; DeWitt ZT 1848-19) 27mm ................................. 275.00    300.00

Zachary Taylor Bennington pottery pitcher, ca. 1850. Tricorn hat reads "Rough/Ready" on opposite sides ($4,000 plus). *(Photo courtesy of Skinner Auctions)*

Price Range

☐ "Major Genl. Taylor/Born 1790"; Taylor left profile; "The Hero of Palo Alto/Monterey. . ." (Hake 3060; De Witt ZT 1848-20) 27mm; gilt brass shell    250.00    275.00

☐ "Zachary Taylor 1849"; 8 stars atop shell enclosing right-facing Taylor bust; "Taylor & Fillmore" on reverse; sunburst ornament below (Hake 3061; De-Witt 1848-22) 25mm; silvered brass shell . . . . . . .    265.00    285.00

## BRASS TOKENS

☐ "Gen. Taylor The People's Choice"; military left-facing bust profile; Liberty figure surmounted by 13 stars; "Untrammeled With Party Obligations" on reverse (Hake 3048; DeWitt ZT 1848-1) 42mm; white metal . . . . . . . . . . . . . . . . . . . . . . . . . . . . . .    260.00    275.00

☐ "Maj. Genl. Z. Taylor Never Surrenders" enclosing left-facing military profile; "A Little More Grape Captain Bragg" on reverse (Hake 3050; DeWitt ZT 1848-4; Warner 49) 41mm; white metal . . . . . . . .    150.00    175.00

## *Lithographs Under Glass*

☐ "Zachary Taylor" colored lithograph with pewter rim; lithograph of Fillmore on reverse (Hake 3013); see also listing under Fillmore . . . . . . . . . . . . . . .    1100.00    1200.00

☐ "Zachary Taylor," black and white, with Fillmore on reverse (Hake 3015); see listing under Fillmore    1100.00    1200.00

☐ "Major Genl. Z. Taylor"; left-facing military portrait; pewter rim as above; mirror on reverse; $2\frac{1}{2}$"; black, white; lithograph . . . . . . . . . . . . . . . . . . . . .    1000.00    1100.00

## *Mirrors*

☐ Field Mirror; "Maj. General Zachary Taylor/ President Of The United States"; embossed portrait in pewter; mirror on reverse (Hake 3019) approx. 4"; gray finish; match to Pierce mirror; French import . . . . . . . . . . . . . . . . . . . . . . . . . . . . . . . . . . . .    375.00    400.00

☐ Similar version, with smaller portrait, ornate border    350.00    375.00

## *Miscellaneous*                                    Price Range

☐ Parlor stove, cast iron; very ornate with filigreed
dome top; Franklin-type stove; large right-facing
bas-relief bust of Taylor on front . . . . . . . . . . . . . .        2500.00 plus

☐ Candy box lid, plaid border; Taylor with wide-
brimmed hat, legs crossed, leaning on rock; multi-
color lithograph under glass . . . . . . . . . . . . . . . . .    575.00        600.00


## *Pint Flasks*

Approximately 40 flasks are known to bear likenesses of Zachary Taylor.
Those not picturing George Washington on the reverse are likely to honor
Major Samuel Ringgold, with claim to fame as first American officer killed
in the first battle of the first foreign war.

☐ "Gen. Taylor Never Surrenders. Dyottville Glass
Works, Philad. A."; "Washington, The Father of
His Country" on reverse; $8\frac{3}{4}$" amber flask . . . . .    300.00        325.00

☐ Same as above, minus manufacturer's name; pale
green flask . . . . . . . . . . . . . . . . . . . . . . . . . . . . . .    250.00        275.00

☐ Busts of George Washington/Taylor; "Bridgeton,
New Jersey" embossed; 7"; pale green flask . . . . .    265.00        285.00

☐ "Gen. Taylor Never Surrenders/A Little More
Grape Capt. Bragg" embossed cannon; $7\frac{1}{4}$"; amber
flask . . . . . . . . . . . . . . . . . . . . . . . . . . . . . . . . . . . .    700.00        725.00

☐ "A Little More Grape Capt. Bragg"; embossed can-
non on reverse; $5\frac{3}{4}$"; pale green flask . . . . . . . . . .    710.00        735.00


## *Prints, Posters*

☐ Taylor–Fillmore jugate by Currier & Ives; standard
format of draped curtain; winged eagle perched on
globe, crossed flags; inscriptions on curled ribbon;
titled "Grand National Whig Banner"; hand-
colored, N. Currier . . . . . . . . . . . . . . . . . . . . . . . .    225.00        250.00

☐ "Brigdr. Gen. Zachary Taylor"; Taylor in wide-
brimmed hat astride white horse (Hake 3006)
29"h x 23"w; black, white; print by H. R. Robinson    175.00        200.00

Price Range

☐ "Zachary Taylor/The Nation's Choice for/Twelfth President of the United States"; right profile; hand rests on map of Mexico; in uniform; Currier & Ives, 1847 . . . . . . . . . . . . . . . . . . . . . . . . . . . . . . . . . . . . . . .   200.00   225.00

☐ "Rough & Ready Meeting"; West Whiteland Club broadside; eagle with scroll at top (Hake 3005) 13″ x 13″ sq; black, white . . . . . . . . . . . . . . . . . . .   325.00   350.00

## Textiles

☐ Zachary Taylor coverlet, double-weave, handmade jacquard pattern; tree border and "Rough & Ready" slogan; indigo-dyed wool yarn with natural cotton yarns; Maryland made (Collins 195) 83″l x 76″w; 1847 . . . . . . . . . . . . . . . . . . . . . . . . . . . . . . . . .   2000.00 plus

☐ Zachary Taylor glazed cotton roller print; Taylor on horseback with foot soldiers advancing before him; commemorates battle of Palo Alto, 1846; Taylor is on favorite charger, "Whitey" (Collins 199) 25″l x 15″w; brown, green, blue, white; cotton . .   275.00   300.00

### BANDANNAS

☐ "General Z. Taylor Rough and Ready/Palo Alto"; large American flag, center; Taylor's oval portrait under flag at mid-border; corner cameos of Generals Scott, John Wool, Patterson, and Lt. Col. C. May (Collins 205) 30½″ x 24½″; red, blue, white, brown (predominantly blue background); cotton   1175.00   1225.00

☐ "Neither Faction Nor Party, Nor Individual Interest/But the Common Wellfare . . ."; U.S. flag in open field; scrolled oval portrait of Taylor in cocked hat and uniform; cotton (Collins 206) 25″h x 21″w; red, brown, white . . . . . . . . . . . . . . . . . . . . . . . . . .   1250.00   1300.00

☐ Zachary Taylor "Hero of Bueno Vista" bust likeness over draped flag, shield, cannons; Bueno Vista battle scene below; silk (Collins 204) 31¼″w x 25¼″h; red, white, black . . . . . . . . . . . . . . . . . . . .   1350.00   1400.00

CAMPAIGN RIBBONS                                    Price Range

☐ "Maj. Gen. Zachary Taylor" astride horse; "A Little More Grape Capt. Bragg" (Hake 3009; Warner 50) $7\frac{3}{4}''$l x $2\frac{3}{4}''$w; black, blue (muted effect) ...    650.00    700.00

☐ "Old Rough & Ready. Genl. Z. Taylor" eagle and shield in top panel; Taylor bust portrait, "I ask no favor & shrink from no Responsibility," middle panel; "Peacemaker" cannon with slogan "A Little More Grape," lower panel (Warner 51) $8\frac{1}{2}''$l x $3''$w; black, white ..........................    600.00    625.00

☐ "For President, Zachary Taylor, Louisiana/For Vice President Millard Fillmore of New York"; bust portrait of Taylor; "I shall continue to devote all my energies ..." quotation (Hake 3010) .....    775.00    800.00

## *Tobacco Accessories*

CIGAR CASES*

☐ "Gen. Taylor" in plumed cockade hat and full dress uniform, three-quarters figure; eagle and shield at top; multicolor hand-painted portrait on wood strips joined together by pleated leather that expands; cardboard insert; opposite side is dark brown or black, with slogan; lacquered surface; $5''$l x $3''$w ...................................    1000.00 plus

☐ "General Taylor And Staff"; Taylor and staff on horseback reviewing long line of troops; multicolor; hand-painted and lacquered; approx. $5''$l x $3''$w ..    1000.00 plus

PIPES

☐ Figural bust bowl, Meerschaum, curved; Zachary Taylor .......................................    125.00    150.00

SNUFFBOXES

☐ "Old Rough And Ready/The Hero Of The War With Mexico"; right-facing waist-high portrait; "Gen. Zach. Taylor" inscribed below; metal with copper-colored finish .......................    700.00    750.00

☐ "Old Rough And Ready ..."; basically same design but hand-colored ...........................    750.00    800.00

*Skeptics contend that these cases, which fold flat, actually held calling cards.

## ALLEN GRANBERRY THURMAN

Allen Thurman, an Ohio Democrat, served in the House 1845–47 and the U.S. Senate, 1869–81. He was a popular but aging party faithful when added to the ticket with Presidential nominee Grover Cleveland in 1888, in what proved to be a losing cause (see Grover Cleveland).

## JAMES STROM THURMOND

James Strom Thurmond, a Republican from South Carolina, was a member of the U.S. Senate 1954–56 and three-time Governor of South Carolina. When the Democrats proposed a strong pro-Civil Rights stance at their National Convention in 1948, 35 delegates (all of Mississippi's and half of Alabama's) stalked out. The recently formed States' Rights Party convened a few weeks later and nominated Thurmond for President and Mississippi Governor Fielding Wright for Vice-President. The Dixiecrats (as they were called) won 1,760,125 popular votes in the 1948 race, but their defection proved far less damaging to Harry Truman than anticipated, and northern blacks gave the Missourian their overwhelming support. There is very little campaign material from the Dixiecrats in 1948. A Thurmond-Wright paper jugate badge in red, white and blue, sells in the $100–125 range.

## SAMUEL J. TILDEN

Samuel Tilden, a former New York District Attorney, was instrumental in sending Boss Tweed and his cronies to jail. As Governor of New York, he smashed the crooked Canal Ring and led a reform campaign under the Democratic banner in opposing Rutherford B. Hayes in 1876. Just 56 hours before the inauguration, the most bitterly disputed election in U.S. history was awarded to Hayes.

**Price Range**

### *Lapel Devices*

☐ "Centennial Candidates For 1876"; die-stamped shield shell; stars & stripes; circular jugate Tilden–Hendricks insets (DeWitt SJT 1876-23) 2″h; gilt brass .................................... 325.00      350.00

☐ Tilden ferrotype in oblong brass shell frame (Warner 148) 1½″h; gilt brass .................... 200.00      225.00

☐ Tilden–Hendricks die-stamped broom-shape shell; gilt ........................................ 225.00      250.00

*Textiles* Price Range

☐ "Our Candidates/Tilden and Hendricks"; jugate
paper ribbon; die-cut rooster pasted on at top; 6"l;
black on beige ............................. 250.00 275.00

*Toys*

☐ "Tilden the Statesman," one of elite group of four
extreme rarities by A. E. Hotchkiss, Cheshire, CT;
walking clockwork figure; 10"h; multicolor; cast
iron, wood; cloth costume (see Butler match); patented 1875 ................................ 5000.00 plus

## DAVID D. TOMPKINS

Tompkins, a Democrat Republican from New York, was a protege of De-
Witt Clinton. He won the governorship of that state in 1807 and served two
terms. Tompkins served under James Monroe as Vice-President from
1817–25. Unjustly accused of having pocketed money used in fund raising
during the War of 1812, he spent much time and energy trying to clear himself. Heavy drinking and stress contributed to his death in 1826, only a year
out of office (see James Monroe).

## HARRY S. TRUMAN

Harry Truman, a Democrat from Missouri, served in the U.S. Senate
1935–45. A surprising running mate with FDR in 1944 (James F. Byrnes sup-
posedly had the inside track), he suddenly found himself the 33rd President
of the United States after only two months in office. In what is regarded as
the major political upset of the 20th century, he defied all odds and was re-
elected over Thomas E. Dewey in 1948. One of the most popular Presidents
among collectors, his relatively few mementos are commanding increasingly
higher prices.

Price Range

*Automotive Accessories*

LICENSE ATTACHMENTS
☐ "Win With Truman"; die-stamped metal license attachment with rounded area for Truman likeness;
8"l; black, white ........................... 75.00 85.00

Newspapers "jumped the gun" and ran the wrong banner headline in three campaigns: Hayes–Tilden in 1876, Wilson–Hughes in 1916, and the most prized edition of all, the *Chicago Tribune* "Dewey Defeats Truman" headline in 1948, which commands $800 to $1,000.

"Protection/Prosperity" McKinley horn ($45–$55); "True Blue" Truman siren whistle ($75–$85); "Click With Dick" (Nixon) clicker ($6–$8).

Harry Truman "Behind the 8-Ball" issued by Dewey forces, 1948; one of the scarcest contemporary lithos ($800–$850).

Roosevelt–Willkie salesman's safety pin, 1940 ($10–$12); "Harry Truman For President" cello with ribbon and donkey novelty ($15–$20); "Gerald R. Ford In '76" cello ($3–$4).

|  | Price Range | |
|---|---|---|
| ☐ "Win With Truman And Barkley"; line drawings of both Democratic candidates from 1948; die-stamped scalloped top; 8"l (Hake 2005) ........ | 95.00 | 110.00 |
| **INAUGURAL LICENSE PLATE** | | |
| ☐ "Inaugural 1949/District Of Columbia"; Capitol dome reversed out of blue on left, shield on right (Hake 2044) 12"w x 6"h; red, white, blue ...... | 65.00 | 75.00 |

*Cartoon/Pictorial Pinbacks*                    **Price Range**

☐ Anti-Truman; eight ball with blacktone portrait of
HST in white circle with "8" superimposed (Hake
128) 1½"; black, white; key item and one of the rare
lithographs of modern era (also listed under
Dewey) . . . . . . . . . . . . . . . . . . . . . . . . . . . . . . . . . .   800.00     850.00

☐ "Truman Crusaders" acrostic with letters inside
red-bordered cross (Hake 28) 1¼"; red, white, blue;
another key item . . . . . . . . . . . . . . . . . . . . . . . . . . .   100.00     125.00

☐ "Truman–Barkley" with red donkey cartoon (Hake
51) 1½"; red, white . . . . . . . . . . . . . . . . . . . . . . . .   100.00     125.00

*Inaugural Pinbacks*

CARTOON/PICTORIALS

☐ "I'm Just Wild About Harry"; musical scale illustration under word "Harry"; "Inauguration, January 20, 1949/Washington D.C." (Hake 30) 2"; blue,
white . . . . . . . . . . . . . . . . . . . . . . . . . . . . . . . . . . . .    75.00      85.00

☐ "Truman/Barkley      Inaugural/January/1949";
large heart illustration in middle of design (Hake
unlisted; Warner 447) 2⅛"; red, white, blue; also
seen with "Illinois" on attached ribbon . . . . . . . .   300.00     325.00

JUGATES

☐ "Inauguration Of President And Vice President";
circular bluetone portraits of Truman–Barkley with
names under portraits; eagle and shield at bottom
with banners in beak bearing their names (Hake 6)
1½"; red, white, blue, gold . . . . . . . . . . . . . . . . .   235.00     250.00

☐ "Truman & Barkley/Inauguration/1949"; small
oval portraits of pair on body of Democratic don-
key (Hake 4; Warner 442) 2"; red, white, blue . .   350.00     375.00

SINGLE PORTRAITS

☐ "Inauguration January 20, 1949/Harry S. Truman"; portrait with red, white, blue starred border
and reverse lettering (Hake 8) 1½"; red, white,
bluetone . . . . . . . . . . . . . . . . . . . . . . . . . . . . . . . . .    10.00      15.00

☐ Same image without stars and in black, white (Hake
9) . . . . . . . . . . . . . . . . . . . . . . . . . . . . . . . . . . . . . . .    10.00      15.00

Price Range

☐ "Inauguration Of Harry S. Truman/President Of The U.S./Jan. 20, 1949"; silhouette portrait (Hake 7) 1½"; black, white ........................ 300.00 325.00

☐ Also 1¼" (Hake 2019) ...................... 240.00 260.00

☐ Also 4" (Hake 2015) ........................ 300.00 325.00

☐ "Inauguration/Washington D.C. ..." silhouetted bust portrait with patriotic flag border (Hake 13) ⅞"; red, white, blue, black ................... 35.00 45.00

### Jugates

#### TRUMAN–BARKLEY

There are but six known Truman–Barkley jugates, and two of these are Inaugural items.

☐ "For President Harry S. Truman/For Vice President ..."; oval bluetone portraits with lettering top and bottom; pair of stars (Hake 1) 1¼"; bluetone, white ...................................... 135.00 150.00

☐ "Truman And Barkley"; staggered oval portraits with border of stars, furled flag (Hake 3; Warner 448) 3½"; red, white, blue; sepia portraits ...... 75.00 100.00

☐ Also 1¼" (Hake 2) (item has been reproduced in this size) ................................... 85.00 110.00

☐ "Truman/Barkley" conjoined portraits (Hake 5) ⅞"; bluetone, black, white ................... 115.00 125.00

#### TRUMAN–LOCAL JUGATE

☐ "Missouri/Harry Truman/Jesse Donaldson"; conjoined portraits (unlisted) 2"; black, white ...... 55.00 65.00

### Miscellaneous Novelties

☐ Ballpoint pen, free-form shape with vertical rectangular portrait; 8"l; black, white .............. 20.00 25.00

☐ "Fair Deal For Harry. Lucky Foot"; leather key case ........................................ 75.00 85.00

☐ "Foe Of Privilege/Harry S. Truman"; pocket flashlight; 4"l; red, white, blue; plastic ............. 20.00 25.00

Price Range

☐ "Friend Of The People/Harry S. Truman"; mechanical pencil; 5½"; red, white, blue; plastic (probably part of set with flashlight listed above) · 15.00 · 20.00

## Noisemakers

☐ "True Blue Truman" siren noisemaker; 1½"h; silver lettering on blue plastic; "Compliments of Mo. State Dem. Com."; part of a complimentary packet given out at National Convention (see illustration) · 75.00 · 85.00

## Portrait Pinbacks

☐ "For President/Harry S. Truman"; broken-line patriotic border; graytone portrait (Hake 2017; Warner 806) 3½"; graytone, white . . . . . . . . . . . . . . . · 30.00 · 35.00

☐ "For President/Harry S. Truman" line drawing of HST with shadow background (Hake 2026) ⅞"; black, white . . . . . . . . . . . . . . . . . . . . . . . . . . . . . . . · 300.00 · 325.00

☐ Also 1¼" (Hake 2021) . . . . . . . . . . . . . . . . . . . . . · 350.00 · 375.00

☐ "For President/Harry S. Truman"; small donkeys on each side of portrait (Hake 17) 1¼"; black, white . . . . . . . . . . . . . . . . . . . . . . . . . . . . . . . . . . . · 15.00 · 20.00

☐ Also 2¾" (Hake 2011) . . . . . . . . . . . . . . . . . . . . . . · 20.00 · 25.00

☐ "Harry S. Truman"; name in scroll (Hake 48) 1¼" blue/graytone . . . . . . . . . . . . . . . . . . . . . . . . . . . . . · 20.00 · 25.00

☐ "Let's Go With Truman" (Hake 2007; Warner 443) 3½"; graytone, white . . . . . . . . . . . . . . . . . . . . . . · 550.00 · 600.00

☐ "Our President"; portrait of Truman at desk (Hake 2008; Warner 805) 3¼"; black, white; official White House photograph . . . . . . . . . . . . . . . . . . . . · 140.00 · 155.00

☐ "Our President/Harry S. Truman" (Hake 15) 1½"; black, white . . . . . . . . . . . . . . . . . . . . . . . . . . . . . . · 15.00 · 20.00

☐ "President" with Harry Truman facsimile signature (Hake 2001) 6¼"; black, gray, white . . . . . . . . . . · 35.00 · 45.00

☐ "Sixty Million People Working. Why Change?" (Hake 54) 2"; black, white . . . . . . . . . . . . . . . . . . · 675.00 · 700.00

☐ "Truman For Me" (Hake 27) ⅞"; red, white, blue, black . . . . . . . . . . . . . . . . . . . . . . . . . . . . . . . . . . · 20.00 · 25.00

Price Range

☐ "Truman/Minnesota Golden Jubilee/1949"; (Hake 2012) 2"; black, white ........................ 150.00 160.00

☐ Truman no-name portrait with laurel wreath border and crossed flags (Hake 64) 3¼"; red, white, blue 40.00 50.00

☐ Also 9" (Warner 446) ........................ 75.00 85.00

☐ "Vote Truman For President"; silhouetted portrait on white between red and blue bars (Hake 2009) 3¼"; red, white, blue, black ................... 160.00 175.00

LOCAL OFFICE

☐ "Truman For Judge, Eastern District" (Hake 2027) ⅞"; brown, white ........................... 650.00 675.00

☐ "Truman For Senator" (Hake 2028) ⅞"; black, white ...................................... 160.00 170.00

## Posters

☐ "Vote The Democratic Ticket. Guard Your Gains In State and Nation"; Truman for Senator multigate poster; illustration of Statue of Liberty and portraits of seven Democratic candidates from Missouri, plus FDR; 1940 race; 14"h x 11"w; red, white, blue cardboard ....................... 135.00 150.00

☐ "Secure The Peace. Elect Harry S. Truman President"; Truman bust portrait; stars in each corner; 16"h x 12"w; red, black, white; 1948 campaign .. 100.00 125.00

☐ "Beat High Prices. Elect Harry S. Truman President. Alben W. Barkley, Vice-President"; conjoining bust portraits; 14"h x 12"w; black, white .... 65.00 75.00

☐ "Nobody Wants War. Harry Truman Knows Why!"; silhouetted head of Truman wearing military cap with captain's bars; 1948 race ......... 75.00 100.00

## Slogan/Name Pinbacks

☐ "All 48 In '48/Young Democrats" (Hake 36) 1¼"; red, white ................................... 25.00 30.00

☐ "Confidentially I'm For Truman" (Hake 35) 1¼"; black, white (Dewey match) .................. 30.00 35.00

Price Range

☐ "Don't Tarry. Vote Harry" (Hake 2016) $1\frac{3}{4}$"; black, red ................................. 65.00 75.00

☐ "Elect Truman. No New Man" (Hake 2014) $1\frac{3}{4}$"; red, black ................................. 60.00 65.00

☐ "Give 'Em H—Harry"; souvenir of Orville Freeman Appreciation Dinner, 1955 (unlisted) 2"; black, white ............................... 65.00 75.00

☐ "I'm A Stand Pat Democrat" (Hake 2031) $\frac{7}{8}$"; red, white, blue; lithograph ..................... 8.00 10.00

☐ "Phooey On Dewey" (Hake 34) $1\frac{1}{4}$"; black, white 10.00 12.00

☐ "Forward With Truman. No Retreat" (Hake 62) $\frac{7}{8}$"; red, white, blue; lithograph; has been reproduced ................................. 15.00 20.00

☐ "Sixty Million Jobs/Ohio C.I.O./P.A.C." (Hake 2031) $\frac{7}{8}$"; red, white, blue; lithograph ......... 8.00 10.00

☐ "States Rights Or Human Rights?" (unlisted) $1\frac{1}{4}$"; black, white ............................... 35.00 40.00

☐ "The Won't Do Congress Won't Do" (Hake 2040) 6"; black, white ........................... 75.00 85.00

☐ "Think! Prevent Wallacitis" (Hake 23) $1\frac{1}{4}$"; red, white ..................................... 10.00 15.00

☐ "Truman" appears across white band in flag background (unlisted); red, white, blue, black ....... 10.00 12.00

☐ "Truman/True-Man" (Hake 2003) $1\frac{1}{2}$"; black, white ..................................... 70.00 80.00

☐ "Truman Fights For Human Rights" (Hake 63; Warner 445) $\frac{7}{8}$"; blue, white; Democratic Convention slogan ignited by Hubert Humphrey, which precipitated the Strom Thurmond walkout and subsequent formation of States Rights splinter ticket 125.00 135.00

☐ "Truman And Civil Rights" (Hake 56) $1\frac{1}{4}$"; black, white ..................................... 85.00 95.00

☐ "We Did It To Dewey Before And We Can Do It Again. Vote Democratic" (unlisted) 5"; black, white ..................................... 75.00 85.00

☐ "Westminster College/Harry Truman/Winston Churchill. [names appear in entwined circles] Fulton, Missouri, 1946" (Hake 2033) $1\frac{3}{4}$" ........ 150.00 160.00

## JOHN TYLER

John Tyler, a Democrat Republican from Virginia, served in the House from 1817–21; in the U.S. Senate 1827–36; President pro tempore 1834–35; Governor of Virginia from 1825–27. He served as Vice-President under William Henry Harrison in 1841, assuming the reins of President two months after the inauguration, following the death of Harrison. Our 10th President elected to run as nominee of a new states rights party favoring the annexation of Texas in 1844 (when his party nominated James K. Polk), but later withdrew at the urging of Andrew Jackson in order to assure Henry Clay's defeat. Later Tyler led a Peace Convention of border states to try to avert a civil war. In the end, he sided with the southern secessionists and was elected a Virginia representative to the Confederate Congress (see W. H. Harrison).

## MARTIN VAN BUREN

Martin Van Buren, a Democrat from New York, served in the U.S. Senate 1821–28; was Governor of New York, 1820; Secretary of State, 1829–31. A protege of Andrew Jackson, he served as Vice-President in 1833–37; In 1837, he became the eighth President of the U.S. Van Buren had designs on the Presidency again in 1844, but made a fatal blunder of reaching an agreement with Whig opponent Henry Clay to rule out annexation of Texas as a campaign issue. This so angered Andrew Jackson, who favored annexation, that he threw his support behind James K. Polk, the eventual winning nominee (see Andrew Jackson).

**Price Range**

### *Lapel Devices*

BADGES, TOKENS

☐ "M. Van Buren," left-facing portrait enclosed by
   olive sprays (Hake 3021) 38mm; brass . . . . . . . . .  225.00  250.00

☐ "Martin Van Buren & Democracy," left-facing portrait; reverse has scales balanced in favor of democracy over federalism, with inaugural date beneath
   eagle; pierced (Hake 3019; Warner 24) 38mm;
   white metal Inaugural token . . . . . . . . . . . . . . . .  325.00  350.00

SULFIDES

☐ "The Country Demands His Reelection/Martin
   Van Buren"; 1840 oval sulfide; bust left-facing
   (Hake 3008) 1½"h x 1¼"w; black, white . . . . . .  1600.00  1700.00

Price Range

☐ "Van Buren/Democracy," left-facing bust (Hake 3019; DeWitt MVB 12) 28mm h x 25mm w; white enamel portrait; light green background; also in black enamel surface ........................ 1450.00     1650.00

☐ "Van Buren & Democracy," cameo bust on dark orange enamel (DeWitt MVB 15) 33mm x 30mm    1200.00     1250.00

## Timepieces

☐ Split-column ogee clock with glass panel, reverse-painted color portrait of Van Buren seated before partially drawn drape; wooden clock case 30"h x 17"w x 4½" deep; portrait panel not original with manufacture of clock ........................ 750.00     800.00

## Tobacco Accessories

☐ "Martin Van Buren," full-face bust portrait with domed building in background; 3½"; black, orange, black-rim papier-mâché ................. 850.00     900.00

☐ "Martin Van Buren/President of the United States," bust portrait interspersed between heading; 2¼"; black, pale orange ..................... 900.00     950.00

## GEORGE WALLACE

George Wallace, a former Democratic Governor of Alabama, ran for President on the American Independence Party ticket in 1968. Wallace denounced the 1954 Supreme Court desegregation decision and took a strong stand in favor of law and order. His running mate was Air Force General Curtis "Old Ironpants" LeMay (also known as "Boom Boom"), who scared the daylights out of voters with his threat to use nuclear weapons in Vietnam. The Wallace forces did extremely well for a third-party entry with almost 10 million popular votes and 46 electoral votes. With the race between Nixon and Humphrey as close as it was, there was no doubt that the Wallace defection cost HHH the election. Wallace campaign material from 1968 is readily available, but has sustained little interest among collectors.

## HENRY AGARD WALLACE

Henry Wallace was a former editor (of his father's magazine, *Wallace's Farmer*) from Iowa. He served several terms under FDR as Secretary of Agriculture and in 1940 as vice-president, but was one of the most unpopular vice-presidents in history. FDR was persuaded to dump Wallace in favor of Truman in 1944. He served under HST as Secretary of Commerce in 1946, but he was later ousted for his pro-Russia stance. He ran for president under the Progressive banner in 1948, but could garner only a little over a million votes.

**Price Range**

### 1940 Campaign

☐ "Iowa's Choice. Henry Wallace For Vice President"; portrait of Wallace (Hake 2091) ⅞"; black, white ........................................ 70.00    80.00

### ANTI-WALLACE

☐ "6,000,000 Piglets Squeal. Hank Wallace's Raw Deal"; Willkie pinback refers to then Secretary of Agriculture Wallace's decision to kill 6 million piglets to raise farm prices in FDR's second term (Hake 124) ⅞"; blue, white .................. 10.00    12.00

☐ "Think! Wallace Might Be President"; Willkieites' allusion to FDR's declining health (Hake 101) 1¼"; blue, white; 1940 ...................... 5.00    7.00

Four modern oversize pinbacks: Wallace ($40–$45); Reagan–Bush ($3–$4); "I'm For Stevenson" ($20–$25); "Young Citizens For Johnson" ($12–$15).

Price Range

☐ "*W*allace *A*nd *R*oosevelt"; three-row tier of words with first letters spelling out WAR (Hake 94) 1¼"; dark green, white .......................... 6.00   8.00

### 1948 Campaign, Progressive Party

☐ "For President/Henry A. Wallace"; bust portrait (Hake TP 2076) 1¾"; black, white ............ 15.00   20.00

☐ "Seamen For Wallace" appears in large flag banner on deck of stylized silhouetted cargo ship (Hake TP 2077; Warner 809) 1½"; red, white, blue ....... 125.00   150.00

☐ Wallace no-name portrait pinback (Hake TP 2075) 2"; black, white .......................... 50.00   75.00

☐ "Wallace For President"; cartoon bust portrait full-face, with FDR shadow profile behind him (Hake TP 2074) 2"; blue, white .................... 30.00   35.00

☐ Also in black, white color variant ............. 35.00   40.00

## GEORGE WASHINGTON

George Washington, Commander of the Continental Army throughout the Revolutionary War, was President of the Constitutional Convention that drew up the Constitution of the United States. In 1789 he became the first President of the United States and the only one to be elected twice by acclamation.

## DANIEL WEBSTER

Webster ran for president under the Whig banner in 1836 in a five-sided race won by Van Buren.

Price Range

### Miscellaneous

☐ Campaign snuffbox; black transfer portrait with light tan background; 3½"; papier-mâché, enameled ....................................... 750.00   800.00

☐ Parianware bust statuette of Webster; 6"h; U.S. Pottery Co., Bennington, VT; white ........... 325.00   350.00

Daniel Webster gilt-brass medallion with daguerreotype image, 1852 hopeful ($800–$900). *(Photo courtesy of Riba-Mobley Auctions)*

| | Price Range | |
|---|---|---|
| ☐ "Hard Times" brass token; obverse shows Webster steering Ship of State; reverse shows Van Buren ship foundering in high seas .................. | 125.00 | 150.00 |

## WILLIAM ALMON WHEELER

William Wheeler, a virtual nonentity from New York, had less than two years of political experience in the House, 1881–82, when the Republicans unaccountably picked him to run in the second slot with Rutherford B. Hayes in 1876. Wheeler, who as Hayes described, "had a charactor of sterling gold and was honest" may well have been the most bored—and boring—of all U.S. Vice-Presidents (see Rutherford Hayes).

## WENDELL L. WILLKIE

Wendell Willkie, a utilities executive from Indiana, a former New Deal Democrat turned Republican, became the Republican nominee for President in 1940, opposing FDR. Willkie, a virtual neophyte, had never before held public office. Willkie constantly raised the "third-term issue" but to no avail. Voters apparently decided it unwise to change horses in mid-stream, particularly in a time of world crisis.

Price Range

## *Automotive Accessories—License Attachments*

☐ "Drive Safely. *W*isdom, *L*eadership *W*illkie"; first letters of each of last three words form Willkie monogram; large winged eagle at top; patriotic shield under right wing (Hake 2385) red, white, blue, black; Roosevelt match .................. 35.00 40.00

☐ "He Said, 'No Third Term For Me'/Win With Willkie"; slogan appears on both sides of large oval portrait of George Washington; manufactured by Wertz Novelty Company, Muncie, IN (Hake 2381) red, blue, white ........................... 40.00 45.00

☐ "Life Begins In '40/Willkie For President"; popular slogan also used in pinbacks, posters; words flanked by illustrations of two elephants (Hake 2382) red, white, blue ................................ 25.00 30.00

☐ "The Hope Of Our Country/Willkie"; semicircle metal attachment, with star above candidate's name (Hake 2384) red, white, blue ................. 20.00 25.00

☐ "Willkie" name appears above portrait in die-stamped oval metal attachment (Hake 2386) 6"w; red, white, blue ........................... 35.00 40.00

☐ "No Third Term. We Want Willkie"; die-stamped rectangle with circular rises at both corners; Willkie line drawing in left circle area; "Third Term" lettering wraps around semiglobe shape on right (Hake 2383) 8½"w; red, white, blue, black .......... 30.00 35.00

☐ "We Want Willkie"; die-stamped oval atop rectangle; Willkie portrait in shield outline within oval with stars and stripes background (unlisted) 6"w; red, white, blue ........................... 40.00 45.00

☐ "We Want Willkie"; die-stamped triple-tiered shape with line drawing of Willkie's head at top with crossed flags under chin (unlisted) 11½"w; red, white, blue, black ...................... 45.00 55.00

☐ "Willkie For President"; die-stamped shield-shape slogan attachment; words in blue field with vertical stripes below (unlisted) 6"h; red, white, blue .... 20.00 25.00

Price Range

☐ "Willkie" in large letters across die-stamped elephant's body (unlisted); approx. 6"w; white, dark blue ........................................ 30.00    35.00

☐ "Willkie & McNary"; names appear under die-stamped shield depicting elephant and three stars (unlisted) 6"h x 3½"w; red, white, blue ........ 35.00    40.00

☐ "Willkie & McNary"; variant of above within die-stamped circle; names are bolder and larger, and elephant is reduced in size in black silhouette (Hake 2388) 3½"dia; red, white, blue ............... 12.00    15.00

☐ "Willkie"; long, narrow metal attachment rounded at top with three stars on each side of name (Hake 2389) 8½"w x 2¾"h; red, white, blue ......... 12.00    15.00

☐ "Win With Willkie"; long, narrow die-stamped metal attachment that peaks just above the first two words; "Willkie" in large shadow letters with round portrait at left of candidate, with halo of stars (unlisted) 8½"w; red, white, blue ................ 35.00    40.00

☐ "Win With Willkie"; die-stamped tiered panel shape with words only (Hake 2387) 8¼"w; blue, white ....................................... 15.00    20.00

### Cartoon/Pictorial Pinbacks

☐ "On Our Way"; smiling GOP elephant is sliding to victory at the polls on an arrow that begins in Maine and ends in California; outline map of the U.S. in background (Hake 208) 2½"; red, white, black; our nomination for the best cartoon pinback in the hobby to simplify the Democratic voting process ..................................... 75.00    100.00

☐ "On The Way To Washington"; cartoon of GOP elephant racing hell-bent for election with big log in trunk* marked "Willkie" (Hake 141) ⅞"; red, white, blue ................................. 6.00    10.00

☐ "Down And Out"; silhouetted elephant stands atop defeated donkey (Hake 70) 1¼"; black, yellow .. 5.00    8.00

*The symbol of the elephant with log in trunk was used over and over in pinbacks as well as in a plaster statue issued by the Republicans in 1940.

Price Range

☐ "8 Years Is Plenty"; white reversed out of black billiard ball (Hake 69) 1¼"; black, white ......... 15.00    20.00

☐ "Gone With The Wind"; backside of large elephant "expelling" donkey (Hake 61) 1½"; black, white   45.00    55.00

☐ "I'll Bet My [donkey rebus] on Willkie" (Hake 72) 1¼"; black, yellow ......................... 5.00    8.00

☐ "I'm For Willkie. Joe Louis" (Hake 202; Warner 437) 1"; black, white; the most uncommon of Louis–Willkie pinbacks ...................... 150.00    175.00

☐ (Hake 67) 1½" sepiatone .................... 135.00    145.00

☐ (Hake 68) 1¼" black, white .................. 125.00    155.00

☐ "I'm Behind The 8-Ball" (Hake 75) 1¼"; black, white (simulated billiard ball) ................. 15.00    25.00

☐ "F.D.R. Y'r Out At Third"; umpire with raised arm as Roosevelt is tagged out sliding into third base manned by Willkie (Hake 2037) 1¼"; blue, black; one of the cartoon classics of the modern era   650.00    675.00

☐ "Life Begins In '40"; elephant with trunk raised in salute; GOP marked on blanket (Hake 2038) 1¼"; black, white ............................... 25.00    30.00

☐ Variant (Warner 799) depicts GOP elephant (same slogan) with sign hanging around neck that reads: "Win With Willkie"; 1¾"; blue, white ......... 25.00    35.00

☐ Also in red, white, blue, ⅞" version (Hake 118) 5.00    10.00

☐ "New Deal Waste Basket" cartoon shows "New Deal" in scrolled document, being tossed on trash heap (Hake 74) 1¼"; black, white, black rim ... 15.00    20.00

☐ "No Third Term"; cartoon of Uncle Sam turning thumbs down (Hake 156) ⅞"; red, white, blue; lithograph ................................... 4.00    6.00

☐ "Out At Third"; cartoon of FDR tagged out at third by Willkie (very similar to Hake 2037); umpire animatedly signals "Out" call (Hake 2036) 1¼"; black, red ............................. 575.00    600.00

Price Range

☐ "Willkie and [horse rebus] Sense"; small side view of horse outlined in white band of patriotic background (Hake 157) ⅞"; red, white, blue; lithograph    15.00    20.00

☐ "Willkie Minute Man"; Uncle Sam's high hat with candidate's name superimposed on crown (Hake 139) ⅞"; red, white, blue (one of a number of ⅞" pinbacks employing the hat device) ............    6.00    9.00

☐ "Willkie" schoolhouse; illustration of little red schoolhouse with U.S. flag mounted on cupola (Hake 114; Warner 441) 1"; red, white, blue; probably intended to espouse Willkie's pro-stand on public education and traditional values; a key item ..    35.00    45.00

☐ "Wings For Willkie"; World War II fighter plane; (Hake 116) ⅞"; red, white, blue .............    6.00    9.00

☐ "Young Republican's Club"; GOP elephant waving flag in trunk (Hake 142) ⅞"; red, white, blue ...    6.00    9.00

☐ "Willkie First Voter. N.Y. Young Republicans." Tiny elephant casting big shadow (Hake 162) ⅞"; blue, white; one of the cleverest of the low-budget pinbacks ...................................    3.00    5.00

☐ "Sure I'm For The New Deal. I.M.A.Simp" (Hake 2034) 1¼"; black, white (cartoon sketch of Alfred E. Newman type)...........................    65.00    75.00

☐ "Willkie and Chemurgy"; illustrations of factory, farm, automobile, airplane, home (Hake 2035; Warner 439) 1¼"; multicolor; key item for Willkie in 1940 ......................................    100.00    125.00*

*Note:* "Chemurgy," now a passé term, covers a branch of chemistry devoted to the utilization of agricultural raw materials—e.g., soybeans, corn—to produce industrial products as opposed to food (one assumes that Willkie endorsed the concept).

---

*Substantially above guided prices in recent years. In a 1987 mail auction, it brought a whopping $168.

**Price Range**

☐ "Willkie For President"; elephant holds up placard (which looks like a piece of Swiss cheese from afar) with initials W.C.R.P.O. (Hake 205) 2"; red, white, blue (one version of meaning of initials: "We Can Really Pull It Off") ......................... 100.00    125.00

☐ "You Lose Franklin"; illustration of a pair of dice that roll "snake-eyes" (Hake 76) 1¼"; black, white    10.00    15.00

## Jugate Pinbacks

☐ "I'm For Willkie And McNary"; bust portraits (Hake 2) ⅞"; black, white ................... 50.00    60.00

☐ "Our Next President"; conjoining portraits of Willkie–FDR; salesman's safety pin (Hake 10) 1¼"; black, white ........................... 12.00    15.00

☐ "Our Next President/Willkie. Governor/Vanderbilt"; local (Hake 2043) 1¼"; black, white    55.00    65.00

☐ "The American Way of Life"; flag waves above circular, staggered portraits (Hake 1) ⅞"; red, white, blue; lithograph ............................ 75.00    100.00

☐ "Wendell Willkie For President; Charles McNary For Vice-President" (Hake 3) ⅞"; bluetone lithograph ....................................... 45.00    55.00

☐ "Wendell Willkie For President; Charles McNary For Vice-President" (Hake 4) ⅞"; red, white, blue (portraits encircled by pair of furled flags); lithograph ....................................... 85.00    100.00

☐ "America's Hope"; silhouette bust (Hake 26) 1¼"; black, white; (reproduction exists) ............. 8.00    10.00

☐ "For President/Wendell Willkie" line drawing portrait (Hake 31; Warner 440) ⅞"; black, white ...    40.00    50.00

☐ "For President/Wendell L. Willkie"; portrait in flag banner border (Hake 21) 1¼"; red, white, blue, black ...................................... 10.00    15.00

☐ "Our Next President/Wendell Louis Willkie"; portrait with small eagles on sides (Hake 27) 1¼"; black, white (reproduction exists but minus eagles) ...................................... 8.00    10.00

| | Price Range | |
|---|---|---|

☐ "The Winner And Next President/Wendell Willkie The Hope Of Our Country" (Hake 8; Warner 793) 3"; red, white, blue; centerpiece item .......... 60.00 65.00

☐ "We Want Willkie"; three stars around portrait (Hake 5; Warner 436) 2⅛"; red, white, blue, black 95.00 115.00

☐ "Willkie"; oval portrait within circle image area (Hake 12; Warner 794) 2¼"; black, white ...... 115.00 125.00

☐ "Willkie For President" bull's-eye with letters in border (Hake 34; Warner 795) 1"; red, white, blue 20.00 25.00

☐ Also 1¼" (Hake unlisted) ................... 30.00 35.00

☐ "Willkie For President"; silhouetted line drawing (Hake unlisted; Warner 435) 2½"; red, white, blue; key item from Midwest Badge Company ....... 125.00 150.00

☐ "Willkie-ite"; circular portrait in entrance to Capitol building (Hake 42; Warner 438) ⅞"; red, white, blue, black ................................. 55.00 65.00

☐ "All I Have Left Is A Vote For Willkie" (Hake 112) 1¼"; olive, white........................... 5.00 7.00

☐ "America Wants Willkie" (Hake 2117) 1¼"; red, blue, white ............................... 6.00 8.00

☐ "Boy! Do We Need A Change!" (Hake 2118) 1¼"; blue, white ............................... 5.00 7.00

☐ "Battleships For Fishing Trips. Preparedness. Economy" (Hake 2089) 1¼"; black, white ..... 6.00 8.00

☐ "Confidentially I'm Voting For Willkie" (Hake 2121) 1¼"; red, white..................... 6.00 8.00

☐ "Confucius Say Willkie O.K." (Hake 2122) 1¼"; blue, white ............................... 8.00 10.00

☐ "Dictator? Not For Us" (Hake 2125) 1¼"; black, yellow ................................... 5.00 7.00

☐ "Don't Be A Jackass. Follow The Eagle" (Hake 2127) 1¼"; black, white ..................... 6.00 8.00

☐ "Don't Be A Third-Term-Ite" (Hake 2128) 1¼"; red, yellow ............................... 6.00 8.00

| *Slogan/Name Pinbacks* | Price Range | |
|---|---|---|
| ☐ "Dethronement Day/Nov. 5th" (Hake 2123) 1¼"; blue, yellow | 5.00 | 7.00 |
| ☐ "East Side/West Side/Wants Willkie" (Hake 2131) 1¼"; brown, white; words reverse out of outline of brown derby (alluding to endorsement of Democrat Al Smith for Willkie) | 12.00 | 15.00 |
| ☐ "Goodby Roosevelt. Hello Willkie" (Hake 2148) 1¼"; blue, yellow | 6.00 | 8.00 |
| ☐ "*Guard Our Peace*"; words running in three rows; first letters spell out GOP (Hake 2149) 1¼"; blue, white | 6.00 | 8.00 |
| ☐ "Here's Your Hat Frank. What's Your Hurry" (Hake 111) 1¼"; black, orange | 6.00 | 8.00 |
| ☐ "I'm Against The Third Term. Washington Wouldn't/Grant Couldn't/Roosevelt Shouldn't" (Hake 79) 1¼"; red, white, blue | 10.00 | 12.00 |
| ☐ "I Want To Be A Captain Too" (Hake 173) ⅞"; blue, white (refers to FDR's son Elliot's sudden, yet in this case warranted, elevation to a captaincy in the Air Corp Reserves) | 6.00 | 8.00 |
| ☐ "Napoleon Met His Waterloo. Frank You Will Too" (Hake 103) 1¼"; black, pale blue | 6.00 | 8.00 |
| ☐ "100 Million Buttons Can't Be Wrong" (Hake 104) 1¼"; red, white | 5.00 | 7.00 |
| ☐ "No Man Is Any Good The Third Time" (Hake 89) 1¼"; blue, white | 5.00 | 7.00 |
| ☐ "No Third International Third Reich Third Term" (Hake 96) 1¼"; red, white | 5.00 | 7.00 |
| ☐ "Roosevelt Is Buying The Aquacade To Keep Eleanor Holme"* (Hake 105) 1¼"; blue, yellow | 6.00 | 8.00 |

*Rather confusing play on words. Eleanor Holme was a swimming star in Billy Rose's Aquacade at the time. The "Eleanor" reference, however, is to FDR's wife. The GOP resented her overexposure in the national media.

Price Range

☐ "My Day [the name of Eleanor Roosevelt's syndicated column] When I Vote For Willkie" (Hake unlisted); one of over a dozen slogan pinbacks lambasting her ................................. 12.00    15.00

☐ "*R*oosevelt *A*nd *W*allace Deal"; words appear in a row so first three letters spell out "RAW (Deal)" (Hake 94) 1¼"; blue, white ................. 6.00    8.00

☐ "Roosevelt. Hide At Hyde" (Hake 2206) 1¼"; black, orange ............................... 5.00    7.00

☐ "Roosevelt Would Rather Be President Than Right" (Hake 2208) 1¼"; black, orange ........ 8.00    10.00

☐ "Rotten Eggs With Roosevelt. Omelets With Willkie" (Hake 2009) 1¼"; blue, yellow ........... 8.00    10.00

☐ "Score A Touchdown With Willkie" (Hake 2211) 1¼"; black, white .......................... 10.00    12.00

☐ "Third Term Taboo. 23 Skidoo" (Hake 2218) 1¼"; blue, orange ............................... 8.00    10.00

☐ "We Don't Want Eleanor Either" (Hake 2223) 1¼"; blue, white .......................... 5.00    7.00

☐ "Willkie Train" with attached ribbon that reads "Staff," used in one of Willkie's cross-country-by-rail campaign swings (Hake unlisted; Warner 796) 1¾"; red, white, blue; ribbon: blue, gold; 5¾"l overall ..................................... 100.00    125.00

## HENRY S. WILSON

Henry Wilson from Massachusetts served in the U.S. Senate for 18 years. He began as a Whig but bolted the party because of its stand on the slavery question, had a brief flirtation with the Know-Nothings and finally became a Republican, winning the nomination for Vice-President in Grant's second term in 1873. He suffered a stroke and died less than two years after taking office (see U.S. Grant).

## WOODROW WILSON

Woodrow Wilson, New Jersey Democrat, became President of Princeton University from 1902–10; his political career began as Governor of New Jersey, 1911–13. He became the 28th U.S. President in 1913, serving two terms ending in 1921. The 17th, 18th, and 19th Amendments were added during his tenure, calling for direct election of senators by the people, Prohibition, and giving women the right to vote, in that order. Wilson's strength of leadership in war and in peace rank him among the great Presidents. He was the only President to earn a Ph.D. His famous *Fourteen Points* proved to be the basis for peaceful settlement in Europe and his support of the idea of the League of Nations earned him the Nobel Peace Prize in 1920.

**Price Range**

### Badges, Stickpins, Studs, Medals

| | | |
|---|---|---|
| ☐ "Chew Messer's Charcoal Gum"; Wilson portrait, cello flip; 1"; black, white; advertising giveaway | 40.00 | 50.00 |
| ☐ "Democratic National Convention, Baltimore, 1912"; montage of White House, Capitol building, and Baltimore's Convention Hall, with large eagle and shield superimposed (Hake 3132) 1¾"; red, white, blue, gold cello; attached flag ribbon with cello bust portrait of Wilson, ⅞"; black, white; approx. 3"l . . . . . . . . . . . . . . . . . . . . . . . . . . . . . . . . . | 75.00 | 85.00 |
| ☐ "Contributor—Pennsylvania, 1912"; circular embossed image of Wilson against die-cut Maltese cross; "Wilson," "Marshall," Berry," and "Cresswell" (latter two were senatorial hopefuls) embossed on each segment (Hake 3047) 1¼"; blue, gilt | 20.00 | 25.00 |
| ☐ "For God And Our Country"; Wilson bust profile (Hake 3131) 1½"; black, white; with flag ribbon, red, white, blue; 3"l overall . . . . . . . . . . . . . . . . . | 100.00 | 125.00 |
| ☐ "New Jersey" oval bar pin with linked cello hanger; Wilson three-quarters portrait (Hake 3129) 1¾"; 2¼"l overall . . . . . . . . . . . . . . . . . . . . . . . . . . . . . . | 60.00 | 70.00 |
| ☐ Star cello, black on white (Hake 3118) with "Tammany Hall, Wilson and Sulzer" on white ribbon; 6"l overall . . . . . . . . . . . . . . . . . . . . . . . . . . . . . . . . . | 40.00 | 50.00 |
| ☐ Wilson brooch; Wilson–Marshall jugate with filigree brass frame; floral designs around sepia oval portraits (Hake 136) 1½"; sepia, ivory, gilt . . . . . | 125.00 | 150.00 |
| ☐ "Wilson," die-cut silhouette bust with scroll (Hake 123) 1"h . . . . . . . . . . . . . . . . . . . . . . . . . . . . . . . . | 10.00 | 15.00 |

Mr. Hughes–President Wilson fan gives bipartisan endorsement to Woman's Suffrage on opposite side, 1916 ($35–$45).

Selection of campaign watch fobs: H. H. Harrison lead log cabin figural ($30–$35); Taft ballot box ($20–$25); Wilson double cello ($65–$70); Taft cello ($15–$20); Bryan brass silhouette ($35–$40).

Wilson "Champion of Uprightness and Humanity" cigarette lighter. Embossed portrait on obverse; reverse shows "Gen. Foch–Allies" with portrait embossed in brass ($35–$45).

Wilson–Marshall celluloid coin bank, 1916 ($900–$1,100).

|  | Price Range | |
|---|---|---|
| ☐ Wilson spinner badge; letters engraved on both sides of coin spell out name when spun (Hake 125) 1"h; gilt metal | 20.00 | 25.00 |
| ☐ Wilson stickpin oval with black border around bust portrait; brass rim; numerous variations were issued (Hake 132) ¾"; 2½" with pin | 20.00 | 25.00 |
| ☐ Wilson stickpin circular bust portrait with gold rim backed by cloth flag bow (Hake 133) 1¼"w | 15.00 | 20.00 |
| ☐ Wilson stickpin, flag waving, "For President, Woodrow Wilson," with bust portrait; dark blue with white lettering | 55.00 | 65.00 |

### INAUGURALS—1913, 1917

☐ Eagle with spread wings atop "Souvenir" bar; linked hanger with embossed portrait of Wilson and "March 4, 1913" inscription; two versions: one in shield shape; other in diamond shape; approx. 2½" overall; gilt brass; each ............ 25.00    35.00

Price Range

☐ Scroll bar with round linked medal bearing Wilson's bust portrait; "March, 1917" also embossed, along with "Souvenir" on bar; approx. $2\frac{1}{4}$"; gilt brass ........................................ 25.00 35.00

☐ "The Nation's President, Twice Choice, March 4, 1917" and Wilson's bust portrait embossed in circle on die-cut Maltese cross; approx. 2"h; gilt brass 30.00 40.00

☐ Woodrow Wilson Inaugural Medal (Hake 3049) 3"; bronze ...................................... 25.00 30.00

☐ Wilson–Marshall Inaugural: "Democratic Party Rules 4 Years More" (Hake 3071); top cello $2\frac{1}{4}$" strutting rooster, blue on white; ribbon, 4"; gilt on black; jugate cello at end of ribbon with Capitol dome in background; "March 4, 1917"; browntone 550.00 600.00

## Banks

☐ Woodrow Wilson/Thomas Marshall Coin Bank, maker unknown, 1916, oval celluloid, slogan appears: "Our Country. Our Flag. Our President. Help Re-Elect Woodrow Wilson," with cameo portraits of Wilson and Marshall, red, white, and blue colors, 3"l ................................... 300.00 350.00

## Canes

☐ "Wilson 2nd Inaugural—1917" cane (cane head shaped like a golf putter); white metal ......... 85.00 100.00

## Cartoon/Pictorial Pinbacks

☐ "You Should Worry Woodrow"; caricature of Uncle Sam with one hand on Wilson's shoulder; the other is shaking hands (Hake 3210) $\frac{7}{8}$"; black on white ...................................... 300.00 350.00

## Ceramics and Glassware

☐ Octagon plate with full-color bust portrait of Wilson; ca. 1920s; china, unmarked .............. 45.00 55.00

Price Range

☐ Military souvenir plate; Camp Dix, New Jersey; issued during World War I; Wilson's name is in plate's border under color portrait; 9"h ........ 45.00 55.00

☐ Profile portrait Wilson plate; sepiatone image; gold rim; 5"dia ................................. 30.00 35.00

☐ "Strange Bedfellows"; blue glazed earthenware pocket flask; caricatures of Woodrow Wilson and his newly appointed Secretary of State, William Jennings Bryan (ca. 1916), snuggled together under the bedcovers; one of the most sought after of all political ceramic relics; approx. 6"h; pale blue ... 350.00 400.00

☐ Panama Canal plate; map of the Canal surrounded by oval portraits of all U.S. presidents through Wilson; American flag and shield enhance the vividness of flow; blue type coloring; 8¼"dia ........... 25.00 35.00

☐ White House plate; color view of the White House with all presidents through Wilson appearing in small cameo portraits around border ........... 25.00 35.00

## TILES

☐ Octagon-shaped Wilson profile tile; Wedgwood-type jasperware; approx. 4"h; white bas-relief bust on Wedgwood blue background; made in 1916 by Mosaic Tile Co., Zanesville, OH; a Lincoln companion tile was issued at the same time ........ 100.00 125.00

☐ Rectangular Wilson portrait tile; 9"h x 6"w; brown-tone; made in 1916 by J. H. Barratt & Co. Ltd., Stoke-on-Trent, England; Geo. Cartlidge, sculptor 85.00 100.00

## *Cutlery*

### POCKETKNIVES
Knives are approximately 3½" long, except where noted.

☐ Wilson–Marshall jugate knife; portraits appear vertically; steel with celluloid backing; red, blue, black, white ...................................... 100.00 125.00

Price Range

☐ Wilson medal knife; embossed round medal; opens at top to curved knife, bottom to nail file; profile of Wilson with "Let Justice And Progress Go Hand In Hand" inscribed around rim; 2½″; silver finish (White House on reverse) .................... 45.00     55.00

☐ Wilson silver knife; embossed portrait of Wilson with name and those of all previous presidents inscribed on a slant from top to bottom; German-made; matches are known for TR and Harding; silver finish ..................................... 35.00     45.00

☐ Wilson single-portrait ebonite-handled knife; celluloid layer in knife's center over Wilson bust photo with draped flags; buttonhook blade; black, red, white, blue .................................. 55.00     65.00

☐ Wilson trigate; vertical portraits of Washington ("Who Won Our Freedom"), Lincoln ("Who Preserved Our Freedom"), Wilson ("Who Demands More Freedom"); red, black, white ............ 35.00     45.00

## RAZORS
☐ "Wilson–Marshall" jugate razor with Statue of Liberty, flags; handle of marbleized celluloid; green, pink, turquoise, white, salmon ................ 150.00     200.00

## Fans

☐ "For The Cause Of Liberty"; heart-shaped cardboard fan depicting Washington, Lincoln, and Wilson; red, white, blue ........................ 25.00     35.00

☐ "Mr. Hughes/Pres. Wilson"; jugate cardboard fan; winged eagle and starred border; small shield between canted oval portraits; black on buff; see illustrations ..................................... 35.00     45.00

☐ "Protection Prosperity"; oblong cardboard fan with large oval Wilson portrait in center surrounded by vignettes of farms, factories, oil fields, a seaport, household views; red, white, blue, black; compliments of National Spiritual Alliance, Lake Pleasant, MA ..................................... 20.00     25.00

## Governor Pinbacks

Price Range

Woodrow Wilson was a successful candidate for governor of New Jersey in 1910.

☐ "For Governor. Woodrow Wilson" (Hake 3198) $\frac{7}{8}$"; black on white .......................... 150.00 175.00

☐ "Governor Woodrow Wilson of New Jersey" (Hake 3197; Warner 626) $1\frac{1}{4}$"; sepia on white ........ 300.00 325.00

## Inaugural Pinbacks

☐ "Inauguration, March 4, 1913" (Hake 27) $1\frac{1}{4}$"; black on white ............................. 60.00 70.00

☐ "Inauguration, 1913. Washington D.C."; bust portrait of Wilson (Hake 26) $1\frac{1}{4}$"; sepiatone ...... 35.00 40.00

☐ "Our President. March 4, 1913" (Hake 3153); $\frac{7}{8}$"; black and white portrait of Wilson; red, white, blue, gold ........................................ 50.00 60.00

☐ White House shell badge, elongated horizontal shield; red, white, blue ribbon attached as background for heart-shaped hanger with paper portrait of Wilson; ornate scrolled frame (Hake unlisted; Warner 331) approx. 5"l overall .............. 150.00 200.00

☐ Wilson–Marshall conjoining bust portraits (Hake 135) $1\frac{3}{4}$"; sepiatone on white; listed as inaugural badge (Warner 320) with attached blue ribbon with gilt lettering and second pinback at bottom picturing rooster ($2\frac{1}{4}$") blue on white; approx. 7"l overall 300.00 325.00

☐ "W"–"M," large monogram letters of candidates' names intertwined to form three diamond-shape insets for portraits flanking White House; lettering interspersed at top reads: "March 4, 1913" (Hake 3074) $1\frac{3}{4}$"; black, brown, white; a favorite among Inaugural collectors ........................ 650.00 700.00

☐ "Party Rules 4 Years More," imprinted on ribbon hanging from cello pinback illustrating Democratic rooster ($2\frac{1}{4}$"); cello hanger with Wilson–Marshall jugates ($3\frac{1}{2}$") (Hake 3071); black, blue, white; gilt lettering .................................... 550.00 575.00

Price Range

☐ Capitol dome behind Wilson–Marshall (Hake 3075) 2¼"; sepiatone . . . . . . . . . . . . . . . . . . . . . . . . . . . . . 225.00 250.00

☐ "Inauguration Club, York, Pa." jugate portraits (Hake 3072) 1½"; black on white . . . . . . . . . . . . 130.00 140.00

☐ "Inauguration March 4, 1913"; Wilson bust portrait (Hake 3126) 3"; black on white . . . . . . . . . . 60.00 70.00

☐ Initials *W* and *M* overlapping to form frames for three diamond shapes; two show Wilson–Marshall; third shows Capitol building (Hake 3074) 2¼"; red, blue, white, sepia . . . . . . . . . . . . . . . . . . . . . . 650.00 700.00

☐ Souvenir bust portrait of Wilson (Hake 3135) 2¼" browntone . . . . . . . . . . . . . . . . . . . . . . . . . . . . . . . 130.00 140.00

☐ "2nd Inauguration, 1917"; profile bust portrait of Wilson (Hake 39) 1¼"; sepiatone . . . . . . . . . . . . . 30.00 40.00

☐ "Woodrow Wilson Inauguration. 1917"; Wilson bust portrait (Hake 3154) 1¼"; black on white .. 40.00 50.00

## Jugates

☐ Capitol Dome just visible above laurels and flag top oval portrait of Wilson, square image of Marshall (Hake 3086) 1¼"; multicolor . . . . . . . . . . . . . . . . . 500.00 550.00

☐ Conjoining portrait of Wilson–Marshall; (Hake 135) 2" browntone . . . . . . . . . . . . . . . . . . . . . . . . . . 300.00 350.00

☐ "Democratic Candidates" 1912; conjoining portrait figures (Hake 3077) 1¾"; browntone . . . . . . . . . . 275.00 300.00

☐ "Democratic Club"; small oval portraits; (Hake 3095) ⅞"; black, white . . . . . . . . . . . . . . . . . . . . . . 150.00 175.00

☐ Eagle atop insets with acorn in laurel leaves topped by small cross at bottom (Hake 3096) red, white, blue, gold, black . . . . . . . . . . . . . . . . . . . . . . . . . . . 235.00 255.00

☐ Eagle sunburst above jugate insets (Hake 3083) 1¼"; red, white, blue, black . . . . . . . . . . . . . . . . . . 500.00 525.00

☐ Furled flag between jugate portraits (Hake 3082) 1¼"; red, white, blue, black . . . . . . . . . . . . . . . . . . 500.00 525.00

☐ Hand holding playing card portraits (Hake 3100) ⅞"; red, white, blue, black . . . . . . . . . . . . . . . . . . 200.00 225.00

| | Price Range | |
|---|---|---|
| ☐ Hearts overlapped frame Wilson–Marshall portraits (Hake 3085) 1¼"; red, white, dark blue, aqua, black; Taft match | 325.00 | 350.00 |
| ☐ "I've Paid My $1. Have You?" (Hake 3) 1¼"; conjoining portraits in bluetone; white reverse lettering in deep blue border | 250.00 | 275.00 |
| ☐ Shield hanger (with slot in top); oval portraits with "President" and "Vice President" arched in scroll above (Hake 137) 1¾"; red, white, blue, black | 400.00 | 425.00 |
| ☐ Shield with seven stars above circular portraits that extend beyond outline (Hake 3078) 1¾"; red, white, blue, gold, black | 425.00 | 450.00 |
| ☐ "Vote For 8-Hour Wilson"; circular portraits in figure-8 (Hake 139); 1¼"; gray, black, white (alludes to Wilson's championing 8-hour working day) | 375.00 | 400.00 |
| ☐ "Winners" inscribed on scroll that separates jugate portraits against scepter background (Hake 134; Warner 321) 1¼"; red scroll; red, white, blue, black; gold background; mates to Taft "Winners" pinback | 850.00 | 900.00 |

## WILSON–COATTAIL CANDIDATES

| | | |
|---|---|---|
| ☐ Wilson–James Cox ("For Governor") New York jugate (Hake 86) 1½"; black on white | 1200.00 | 1400.00 |
| ☐ Wilson–Gardner "Peace & Prosperity" (Hake 91) 1"; orangetone on buff | 65.00 | 75.00 |
| ☐ Wilson–Glynn "Friends Of The People" (Hake 88) 1¼"; browntone, buff | 75.00 | 85.00 |
| ☐ Wilson–Reed (Sen. James Reed of Missouri) "Champions Of The 8-Hour Law" (Hake 90; Warner 633) 1"; black, white | 75.00 | 85.00 |

## WILSON–MILITARY HEROES

| | | |
|---|---|---|
| ☐ Wilson–Admiral (unidentified); portraits above destroyer; Navy anchor insignia (Hake 3108) 1¼"; red, white, blue, black | 45.00 | 55.00 |
| ☐ Wilson–Pershing "Victory" (Hake 3105) 1¼"; red, white, blue, black | 35.00 | 45.00 |

Price Range

☐ Wilson–Pershing elongated shield behind diamond-shaped jugates (Hake 98) 1¼"; red, white, blue, black, gold background ...................... 35.00 40.00

☐ Wilson–Pershing "Victory 1918" (Hake 95) 1¼"; red, white, blue, black ....................... 30.00 35.00

☐ Wilson–Pershing "Victory, Peace" (Hake 96) 1"; red, white, blue, black ....................... 25.00 30.00

☐ Wilson–Waller; large eagle; stylized line drawings of pair (Hake 3107) red, gold, black, white ..... 35.00 40.00

## Lighting Devices

☐ Woodrow Wilson figural cast-metal lamp; large oval bas relief of Wilson; World War I doughboy, nurse, and sailor are cast in deep relief surrounding oval and up to light socket; cast-metal and slag lampshade is topped by winged eagle; approx. 24"h; gilded metal; buff-colored slag ................ 125.00 150.00

## Memorial Pinbacks

Embittered and heartbroken over the debates and intrigues that transpired at the Versailles Peace Conference and U.S. failure to join the League of Nations, Wilson died on February 3, 1924.

☐ "In Memoriam," bust portrait of Wilson (Hake 3201) 1¼"; black, white ..................... 12.00 15.00

☐ "In Memoriam," line drawing of Wilson bust, framed by laurel branches (Hake 3200) 1¼"; black, white ...................................... 15.00 20.00

## Multigates

☐ "Wilson, Marshall, Foss, Walsh"; names appear under portrait insets in four-leaf clover; Massachusetts senatorial candidates (Hake 3073) 1½"; black, green, white; ribbon is gilt lettering on olive, white; brass outline of Massachusetts appears at top of ribbon as pinback; multigate is often found unattached 150.00 175.00

Price Range

☐ "For Human Rights"; multigate of five world leaders: Wilson, King George, Victor Emmanuel, President Poincaré, King Albert. "Our Victorious Leaders" (Hake 3110) 1¼"; multicolor (also appeared in 2" size as mirror) ........................ 30.00   35.00

### Trigate

☐ "Victory, Liberty For All"; Wilson–Foch–Pershing (Hake 3104) 1½"; black, gold, white .......... 40.00   45.00

### Pocket Mirrors

☐ Bust portrait of Wilson (Hake 3123) 4"; black, blue, green, white ............................... 100.00   125.00

☐ Wilson–Marshall jugate mirror; 2¼"; sepiatone .. 250.00   275.00

☐ Wilson portrait mirror; ribbon with bow border; "The Man On The Other Side Can Help Elect Wilson" (Hake 3052) 2"; red, white, blue, black .... 175.00   200.00

### Portrait Pinbacks

☐ "America First"; large shield with Wilson's head in silhouette on shield (Hake 3159) 1¼"; red, white, blue, black ................................. 75.00   85.00

☐ "America First. Thank God For Wilson"; eagle and dove above Wilson portrait (Hake 151) ⅞"; red, white, blue, gold ........................... 50.00   60.00

☐ "An American For America. Preparedness"; small circle portrait of Wilson; eagle perched atop pair of cannon barrels (Hake 147; Warner 628) 1¼"; black, white, pale yellow .................... 450.00   500.00

☐ "Delegates Of Pennsylvania"; keystone portrait (Hake 38) 1¼"; dark blue, black, white ........ 100.00   125.00

☐ Eagle with oval portrait of Wilson on its chest; flags at top, arrows project from behind eagle (Hake 142) 1¼"; subtle shades of orange, blue; dark blue background; Taft match ......................... 75.00   100.00

Price Range

☐ "Wilson 8-Hour Club"* appears in lower half of figure-8; Wilson portrait in top half (Hake 3157; Warner 327) $1\frac{1}{2}$"l x $1\frac{1}{8}$"w; blue, brown, black; vertical oval .............................. 500.00 525.00

☐ Flag with circle-inset portrait of Wilson across part of field and stripes (Hake 42) $1\frac{1}{4}$"; red, white, blue, sepia; gold rim ............................ 75.00 100.00

☐ "For President"; life preserver design with Wilson portrait inset (Hake 47) $\frac{7}{8}$"; red, white, blue ... 25.00 30.00

☐ "For President. Woodrow Wilson"; bust portrait (Hake 46) $\frac{7}{8}$"; white reversed out of blue ...... 20.00 25.00

☐ "For The White House Bound, With A Platform Safe And Sound"; Wilson bust portrait (Hake 145) $1\frac{1}{4}$"; red, white, blue ....................... 250.00 275.00

☐ "He Proved The Pen Mightier Than The Sword"; Wilson bust portrait (Hake 70) $\frac{7}{8}$", black on white 10.00 15.00

☐ Horseshoe, tied with ribbon bow, frames "Wilson" portrait (Hake 3164) $1\frac{1}{4}$"; red, white, blue, black 50.00 60.00

☐ "I Am With Wilson" [portrait rebus] in shield (Hake 3227) $\frac{7}{8}$"; red, white, blue, black ....... 100.00 110.00

☐ "League Of Nations"; flags of many nations surround Wilson portrait; 1919, nonpolitical (Hake 3195; Warner 631) $1\frac{1}{4}$"; multicolor ........... 150.00 175.00

☐ "Our Choice"; Wilson portrait framed by curled ribbons with bunch of grapes at top (Hake 3149) $1\frac{1}{4}$"; red, blue, black, white ................. 100.00 125.00

☐ "Peace And Prosperity"; profile Wilson bust; (Hake 80) $\frac{7}{8}$"; white reversed out of dark blue ....... 10.00 12.00

☐ "Pride Of New Jersey. Democratic Convention, Baltimore, Md. 1912" (Hake unlisted; Warner 329) $1\frac{3}{4}$"; blue, cream .......................... 250.00 300.00

☐ "Safety First"; Wilson portrait (Hake 71) $\frac{7}{8}$"; red, black, white ............................. 10.00 15.00

☐ Shield with eagle and bust portrait; scrolled gilt rim (Hake 41) $1\frac{1}{4}$"; red, white, blue; sepia photo ... 75.00 100.00

*Over a dozen versions were issued in the 1916 race to remind voters of the enactment of the 8-hour day in Wilson's first term.

Price Range

☐ "Stand By The President"; bust portrait, full flag in background; braided brass rim (Hake 40) 1¼″; red, white, blue, gilt ............................. 75.00 100.00

☐ "The Man Of The Hour"; Wilson bust portrait, 1912; slogan used in his gubernatorial and two presidential races (Hake 28; Warner 330) 1¼″ orange, purple, black (sometimes identified as blue, yellow) 200.00 225.00

☐ Classic also appeared in 1½″ size ............. 175.00 200.00

☐ "The World Must Be Made Safe For Democracy"; Wilson portrait (Hake 3158) 1¼″; black on white 125.00 150.00

☐ Wilson wearing hat; oval pinback with ornate floral rim (Hake 3173) 1½″h; black on white ........ 40.00 50.00

☐ Wilson without hat; same frame as above, oval (Hake 3174) 1½″h ......................... 30.00 35.00

☐ "Win With Wilson"; bust portrait under slogan (Hake 32) 1½″; multicolor; numerous variants of this pinback, including 1¼″ and ⅞″ sizes; also as sepiatone ................................... 15.00 20.00

☐ Winged eagles, stars surround circle portrait (Hake 25) 1¼″; red, white, blue, black, gold ......... 50.00 60.00

☐ "Woodrow Wilson. His Heart Is In The Right Place"; Wilson portrait inset, gold rim (Hake 146) 1¼″; black, rose, gold, white ................... 75.00 100.00

### Slogan Pinbacks

☐ "I Am For Wilson And An 8-Hour Day" (Hake 3207) ½″; white reversed out of black ......... 25.00 30.00

☐ "Nominee And Winner" "Wilson [in large shadow type] For President," 1912 (Hake 3270) 1″; black on white ................................... 50.00 60.00

☐ "Peace With Honor, Preparedness, Prosperity Wilson. Marshall" (Hake 100) ⅞″; red, black, white (litho reproduction exists) ................... 10.00 15.00

☐ "Preparedness, Peace" above picture of mortar shell; stars reverse out of border (Hake 126) ⅞″; red, white, blue ............................ 15.00 20.00

Price Range

☐ "Remember Your Friends. Defeat Your Enemies" "Union Meeting—Five Brotherhoods" (Hake 36; Warner 630) 1¼"; black on white; rates as one of best slogan pinbacks in hobby ............... 150.00  175.00

☐ "Watchful Waiting Wins" (Hake 110) ½"; white, black; large $W$ leads off all three words ........ 8.00  12.00

☐ "We Are Neutral. Peace"; "Peace" appears on eagle's chest (Hake 127) ⅞"; red, white, blue ... 15.00  20.00

☐ "Well Done Wilson & Dunne" (Hake 3207) 1¼"; black on white ............................ 25.00  30.00

☐ "Win With Wilson"; large $W$ leads off all three words (Hake 104) ⅞"; white reversed out of red; blue border ................................ 10.00  15.00

☐ "Woodrow Wilson's Wisdom Wins"; large $W$ leads off all words (Hake 103) ⅞"; red, black, white .. 10.00  15.00

☐ "Wilson Thats All"; "Wilson" appears in large horizontal oval (Hake 3205) 1½"; black, red, white 10.00  15.00

### Statuary

☐ "Wilson" bas-relief bust portrait, copper plaque (Hake 3002) approx. 8"h x 5"w; copper finish ... 45.00  55.00

☐ "Wilson. Our President 1913"; Inaugural Tiffany-signed bronze pedestal bust figural (unlisted); approx. 6"h x 3"w; bronze finish ................ 300.00  350.00

☐ "Woodrow Wilson. Martyr For Democracy"; oval bas-relief profile bust portrait; "1856–1924" (unlisted) 5½"h x 4¼"w; brass finish; hinged bracket for standing; memorial item .................. 35.00  45.00

### Tobacco Accessories

☐ Cigar, jumbo Havana with multicolor cigar band bearing Wilson's portrait, flags, and a heraldic shield; 8"l .................................. 20.00  25.00
 *Note:* The problem with cigars is that they eventually dry out and crumble. Most examples we have seen are in a sorry state indeed.

Price Range

☐ Match holder, china with sepiatone transfer image of Wilson (the same that appears on the 5″ china souvenir plates); has hole in back for wall hanging and space for advertising imprint; (we've usually seen them promoting grocery chains and dry goods emporiums) .................................. 50.00   60.00

☐ Match safe; White House in background with Wilson portrait inset at upper right; metal case with cello image; 2¾″ x 1½″ ..................... 25.00   35.00

☐ Match safe; medal-type image of Wilson embossed with words in French; brass; 2½″h ........... 20.00   30.00

☐ Wilson lighter; bust portrait of Wilson on obverse with legend in French hailing him as "Champion of Uprightness and Humanity"; "Gen. Foch— Allies" on reverse; embossed brass; 2″h; ........ 35.00   45.00

☐ Wilson figural pipe; curved meerschaum; bowl is bust; approx. 6″l; white, black stem ........... 75.00   100.00

### Watch Fobs

☐ Golden eagle cello fob; stylized eagle profiles, stars and stripes surround circular Wilson portrait; backed by round leather cutout with strap loop (Hake 117) 2″ overall; red, white, blue, black, gold 50.00   60.00

☐ Eagle with spread wings atop wreath shell; round sepia portrait cello of Wilson; gold rim (Hake 118) 1¾″ overall ................................ 35.00   40.00

☐ Flag, Capitol dome, eagle in flight border Wilson portrait cello (Hake 119) 1¾″ overall; red, white, blue, black, gold cello; silver-finish metal ....... 40.00   45.00

☐ Minor variant of this fob (Hake 3061) ........ 30.00   40.00

☐ Keystone die-cut shaped fob with circular Wilson portrait cello inset (Hake 3055) .............. 50.00   60.00

☐ "Look To White House, Wilson 1912"; mechanical die-cut fob (Hake 3062) 1½″; silver metal ...... 30.00   35.00

☐ Double cello Wilson portrait fob (Hake unlisted); black and white bust portraits similar to Hake 35; approx. 5″l; black and white cellos; black leather cutouts ..................................... 45.00   55.00

## WOMEN'S SUFFRAGE

The American women's rights movement dates back at least as far as the Seneca Falls Convention in New York in 1848. Most collectors prefer to concentrate on the period of militant protest from 1910 to the enactment of the 19th Amendment giving women the right to vote in 1920. The two major organizations were the American Woman Suffrage Association and the National American Woman Suffrage Association. In 1907 Harriet Stanton Blatch, daughter of noted rights leader Elizabeth Cady Stanton, founded the Equity League of Self-Supporting Women. (It later became the Woman's Political Union in 1910.) Alice Paul and Lucy Burns, co-leaders of NAWSA's Congressional Union Committee, later split and founded the most militant of all the women's rights groups, the National Women's party, a worthy predecessor to today's NOW. Picketing and chaining themselves to the White House gate, waving banners on the streets of the nation's capitol and continuous heckling of members of Congress, and the mass demonstrations and parades are all reflected in the fascinating artifacts avidly pursued by today's collectors.

|  | Price Range | |
|---|---|---|

### *Cartoon/Pictorial Pinbacks*

| | | |
|---|---|---|
| ☐ "Votes For Women," 1915; sunrise on horizon; $7/8$"; multicolor | 35.00 | 45.00 |
| ☐ "Women's Rights," cartoon; lower part of two women's skirts showing legs (kicking up heels? symbolism) $7/8$"; black on white | 25.00 | 30.00 |
| ☐ "Don't Let It Suffer"; anti-Suffrage pinback; less than flattering cartoon of female singing (apparently "off key") $7/8$"; black, white | 15.00 | 20.00 |

### *Figurines*

| | | |
|---|---|---|
| ☐ Goose, porcelain figurine wearing bonnet and shawl; holds books and papers; window on house reads: "Votes For Women"; "Suffragette" appears on base; 5"h; multicolor | 325.00 | 350.00 |
| ☐ Kitten, ceramic figurine; small scroll reads: "Votes For Women"; 4"h; gray, brown | 75.00 | 100.00 |
| ☐ Sojourner Truth "Votes For Women" porcelain figurine; outlandish get-up of Truth in corset, carrying club, and holding petition for women's voting rights | | |

Kitten, Woman Suffrage ceramic figurine; small scroll reads: "Votes For Women," 1912 ($75–$100). *(Frank Corbeil Collection)*

"Votes For Women," state of Oregon, orange, blue, and white umbrella ($100–$125). *(Frank Corbeil Collection)*

Parading Suffragette woman in black cloche hat with flag ($85–$110). *(Frank Corbeil Collection)*

"Suffragette" glass candy container appears to be holding skunk ($75–$85). *(Frank Corbeil Collection)*

Demure little pewter lady figural with sandwich boards: "Votes For Women" ($125–$150). *(Frank Corbeil Collection)*

Centerpiece in Suffrage grouping is "Votes For Women," die-stamped metal window hanger produced by Massachusetts Woman Suffrage Association, 1915 ($125–$150). *(Frank Corbeil Collection)*

"Votes For Women" banner, bearing goddess ($125–$135); trigate honors Carrie C. Catt, Elizabeth Cady Stanton, and unidentified Suffragette ($85–$100); pair of variants of trumpeting suffragette ($45–$55). *(Frank Corbeil Collection)*

"Votes For Women" fan, 1915 ($25–$30). *(Frank Corbeil Collection)*

"Sarah's Thread Holder" advertising tin celebrates achievement of the Lowell (Massachusetts) Female Labor Reform Association, founded by Sarah Bagley, 1845, the first woman trade unionist of note in this country ($50–$60). *(Frank Corbeil Collection)*

Suffragette valentines, ca. 1914 ($10–$15 each). *(Frank Corbeil Collection)*

| | Price Range | |
|---|---|---|
| in one hand; the Negro activist often paraded in demonstrations in this attire; "Suffragettes" inscribed on base; 6"h; multicolor (also in larger size) | 125.00 | 150.00 |
| ☐ Woman in black cloche hat, with flag over shoulder, wearing World War I era attire; plaster figurine; she obviously is parading for "Votes For Women" .. | 85.00 | 110.00 |

## *Miscellaneous*

Price Range

☐ Carte de Visite (CDV) "Miss Tennie C. Claflin" sister of Victoria Woodhull and author of *Constitutional Equality—A Right of Woman* ........... 75.00 100.00

☐ CDV Victoria Woodhull ..................... 100.00 125.00

☐ Bronze bust of Susan B. Anthony, "National American Woman Suffrage Assn."; on reverse, tree branches: "Failure Is Impossible" ............. 125.00 135.00

☐ New York state seal; "Votes For Women" inlaid enamel pin; "Victory 1915"; $7/8''$; blue; gold .... 40.00 50.00

☐ "Votes For Women" card game; 48 cards with scenes of women parading, speaking, going to jail; final six scenes portray ineptness of male politicians and voters; various colors .................... 65.00 75.00

☐ "Votes For Women"; pennant on original parade stick; $10''$; black on gold ..................... 75.00 85.00

☐ "Woman Suffrage Party," parade sash; $18''$; blue on tan ........................................ 65.00 75.00

☐ "Votes For Women"; enameled shield pin; $1 1/4''$h; gold, blue, red, white ...................... 25.00 35.00

## *Posters*

☐ "We Give Our Work Our Men Our Lives—If Need Be—Will You Give Us Your Vote?" "Vote For Woman Suffrage Nov. 6th"; woman stands between World War I officer and enlisted man; printed by Greenwich Litho Co., New York; $21'' \times 28''$; multicolor ...................................... 450.00 500.00

## *Slogan Pinbacks*

☐ "Votes For Women"; $3/4''$; black on gold ....... 10.00 12.00

☐ "Equal Suffrage"; $3/4''$; blue on gold ........... 35.00 40.00

☐ "Suffrage First"; $1''$w oval; gold, white ......... 65.00 75.00

☐ "Vote For Woman Suffrage Nov. 2"; $7/8''$; black, orange ....................................... 75.00 85.00

☐ "Votes For Women"; "Penna. 1915"; $3/4''$; blue, white ...................................... 15.00 20.00

☐ "Votes For Women"; $7/8''$; red, white, blue ...... 15.00 20.00

| | Price Range | |
|---|---|---|
| ☐ "Votes For Women"; $7/8$"; blue, gold, 10 stars around border | 15.00 | 20.00 |
| ☐ "Vote For Women Suffrage Nov. 6th"; $1\frac{1}{4}$"; blue, orange | 35.00 | 40.00 |
| ☐ "Women Vote," reads over woman's torso as she stands silhouetted against rising sun; holds sheaf of arrows in each hand; $1\frac{1}{4}$"; multicolor | 45.00 | 55.00 |
| ☐ "Men's League For Women's Suffrage" borders stylized morning glory; $1\frac{1}{4}$"; dark blue, white | 65.00 | 75.00 |
| ☐ "Votes For Women. Patriotism"; eagle, shield, furled flags, stars; $3/4$"; red, white, blue, yellow, brown | 12.00 | 15.00 |

# MAIL AUCTIONEERS

The following hold periodic mail auctions related specifically to political memorabilia and Americana.

*Al Anderson*
P.O. Box 644
Troy, OH 45373
(513) 339-0850

*Ben Corning*
10 Lilian Road Ext.
Framingham, MA 01701
(617) 872-2229 or 872-3361

*David Frent*
P.O. Box 455
Oakhurst, NJ 07755
(201) 922-0768 or (201) 922-2753

*Hake's Americana & Collectibles*
P.O. Box 1444
York, PA 19464
(717) 848-1333

*U.I. "Chick" Harris*
Box 20614
St. Louis, MO 63139
(314) 352-8623

*Historicana*
Robert W. Coup
1632 Robert Road
Lancaster, PA 18601
(717) 291-1037

*Ohio Boys Video Auction*
The Dixeys
626 Arlington Avenue
Mansfield, OH 44903

*Rex Stark*
49 Wethersfield Rd.
Bellingham, MA 02019
(617) 966-0994

# POLITICAL COLLECTING ORGANIZATIONS

When the Association for the Preservation of Political Americana (APPA) merged with the American Political Items Collectors (APIC) in 1978, the result was one strong, unified organization under the APIC banner. The APIC now numbers over 2,000 members, and their many programs and activities are covered in detail in other sections of this guide.

American Political Items Collectors
P.O. Box 340339
San Antonio, TX 78234

There are over 30 local chapters and clubs sponsored by APIC. In addition to a chapter specializing in "cause" items, there are a Third Party and Hopeful chapter and chapters for those who collect items relating to the following hopefuls and presidents:

Carter Political Items Collectors

Gerald R. Ford Chapter

Warren G. Harding Chapter

John F. Kennedy Chapter

Franklin D. Roosevelt Chapter

Harry S. Truman Chapter

Nixon Political Items Collectors

George C. Wallace Chapter

Wendell L. Willkie Chapter

# POLITICAL MEMORABILIA PUBLICATIONS

The following publications regularly cover the topic of collecting political and patriotic items.

*The Keynoter,* Official APIC publication
Published triannually
P.O. Box 340339
San Antonio, TX 78234

*The Political Bandwagon*
Published monthly
1632 Robert Rd.
Lancaster, PA 17601

Includes *APIC Newsletter* insert. Price of subscription to the *Bandwagon* as well as *The Keynoter* is included in annual APIC membership dues ($20).

*The Local*
Published (usually) four or five times annually
Robert M. Pratt
*The Local*
P.O. Box 159
Kennedale, TX 76060

Publication began as a tabloid devoted to city, county, and state candidates across the United States; now a list of items, primarily pinbacks, available from various consigners. $5 fee for four issues.

*The Political Collector Newspaper*
Published monthly
444 Lincoln Street
York, PA 17404

*The Frontrunner Newsletter*
Published bi-monthly
Box 155, RFD 2
Peterborough, NH 03458

# PUBLIC POLITICAL MEMORABILIA COLLECTIONS

The following museums and institutions (the list is by no means complete) offer permanent collections of presidential memorabilia.

Clark Historical Library
Central Michigan University
Mt. Pleasant, MI

National Museum of History and Technology
Smithsonian Institution
900 Jefferson Drive
Washington, DC 20600

Paul Perlin Collection of Political Americana
University of Louisville
Louisville, KY

The Presidential Museum
622 N. Lee
Odessa, TX 79761

Western Reserve Historical Society
Cleveland, OH

Wisconsin State Historical Society
Madison, WI

*Note:* As of October 1988, the Museum of American Political Life will be permanently housed on the University of Hartford campus, Hartford, CT to house the renowned J. Doyle DeWitt collection.

The following is a listing of memorial foundations honoring specific presidents of the United States, that offer vast holdings of documents, paintings, and memorabilia.

Calvin Coolidge Memorial Foundation, Plymouth, VT

The Harry S. Truman Memorial Library, Lamar, MO

The Herbert Hoover Presidential Library, West Branch, IA

The Lyndon Baines Johnson Library and Museum, Austin, TX

The John F. Kennedy Memorial Foundation, Boston, MA

The Franklin Delano Roosevelt National Historic Site (with library), Hyde Park, NY

The Theodore Roosevelt Association, Oyster Bay, NY

The Dwight D. Eisenhower National Historic Site, Gettysburg, PA

The Dwight D. Eisenhower Center, Abilene, KS

The Lyndon B. Johnson Library, University of Texas, Austin, TX

The Richard Nixon Library, San Clemente, CA

The Illinois State Historical Library, Springfield, IL

(Lincolniana)

Mention should also be made of national shrines dedicated to presidents: George Washington (Mt. Vernon, New York); Thomas Jefferson (Monticello, Virginia); Lincoln's Tomb, Springfield, Illinois.

# BIBLIOGRAPHY

## POLITICAL BADGES, MEDALETS (NUMISMATICS)

DeWitt, J. Doyle. *Alfred S. Robinson: Hartford Numismatist*. Hartford, CT: Connecticut Historical Society, 1968.

*A Century of Campaign Buttons, 1789–1889*. Hartford, CT: Edmund Sullivan, 1959.

Dusterberg, Richard B. *The Official Inaugural Medals* (2nd ed.). Cincinnati, OH: Medallion Press, 1976.

Julian, R. W. *Medals of the United States Mint: The First Century, 1792–1892*. La Cajon, CA: Token and Medal Society, 1977.

Kobbe, Gustave. "Presidential Campaign Medals." *Scribner's*, September 1888. Reprinted by Charles McSorley, Closter, NJ, 1970.

MacNeil, Neil. *The President's Medal 1789–1977*. New York: Clarkson N. Potter, 1977.

Raymond, Wayte. *The Early Medals of Washington, 1776–1834*. (Coin Collector Series No. 4) New York: Wayte Raymond, 1941.

Zerbe, Farran. "Bryan Money, Tokens of the Presidential Campaigns of 1896 and 1900—Comparative and Satirical." *The Numismatist*, July 1926.

## POLITICAL CERAMICS AND GLASSWARE

Jokelson, Paul, *Sulphides, The Art of Cameo Incrustation*. New York: Galahad Books, 1968. Good coverage of glass paperweights, vases, flasks, tumblers bearing sulfide presidential images.

Klamkin, Marian. *American Patriotic and Political China*. New York: Charles Scribner's Sons, 1973.

Larsen, Ellouise Baker, *American Historical Views on Staffordshire China*. New York: Doubleday, Doran 1939.

Lee, Ruth Webb, and Rose, James H. *American Glass Cup Plates.* Northborough, MA: Authors, 1948.

Lindsey, Bessie M. *American Historical Glass;* revised and edited by Walter Risley. Rutland, VT: Charles E. Tuttle, 1967. Published originally in two volumes in 1948 and 1950 under title *Lore of Our Land Pictured in Glass.*

McKearin, Helen, and Wilson, Kenneth M. *American Bottles and Flasks and Their Ancestry.* New York: Crown, 1979.

## POLITICAL PAPER (EPHEMERA)

Blaisdell, Thomas C., Jr., and Selz, Peter. *The American Presidency in Political Cartoons: 1776–1976.* Salt Lake City, UT: Peregrine Smith, 1976.

Brodsky, Vera Lawrence. *Music for Patriots, Politicians and Presidents.* New York: Macmillan, 1976.

Brown, William Burlie. *The People's Choice: The Presidential Image in the Campaign Biography.* Baton Rouge, LA: Louisiana State University Press, 1960.

Hart, James D. "They All Were Born in Log Cabins." *American Heritage* (Vol. 7, no. 5), August 1956.

Keller, Morton. *The Art and Politics of Thomas Nast.* New York: Oxford University Press, 1968.

Murreil, William. *A History of American Graphic Humor: 1747–1865* (2 vols.). New York: Whitney Museum of American Art, 1933, 1938. Reprinted by the Cooper Square Press, 1961.

Nevins, Allan, and Weitenkampf, Frank. *A Century of Political Cartoons . . . 1800 to 1900.* New York: Charles Scribner's Sons, 1944.

O'Neal, David (compiler). *Early American Almanacs: The Phelps Collection.* Peterborough, NH: Compiler, 1978.

Peters, Harry J. *American on Stone.* New York: Doubleday, Doran, 1931.

Shaw, Albert. *Abraham Lincoln: A Cartoon History* (2 vols.). New York: Review of Reviews, 1929.

*The Puck Papers,* a quarterly newsletter devoted to the art and artists of political cartooning; edited by Richard S. West, Lansdale, PA.

Tripp, William, *Presidential Posters.* New York, London: Drake Publishers, 1976. All too brief coverage from Jackson's 1828 campaign to Carter in 1976.

Tyler, Ron (Ed.). *The Image of America in Caricature and Cartoon.* Catalog of an exhibition presented by the Amon Carter Museum of Western Art, Fort Worth, TX: Museum, 1975.

Weitenkampf, Frank. *Political Caricature in the United States . . . An Annotated List.* New York: The New York Public Library, 1953.

Zeman, Zynek, *Selling the War: Art and Propaganda in World War II.* London: Orbis Publishing, 1978. Collection of patriotic posters.

## POLITICAL LAPEL DEVICES

Albert, Alpheus H. *Record of American Uniform and Historical Buttons with Supplement.* Hightstown, NJ: Author, 1973.

Cobb, J. Harold. *George Washington Inaugural Buttons and Medalets: 1789 and 1793.* Privately printed, 1963.

———. "The George Washington Historical Buttons." *The Keynoter,* Summer 1964, Summer 1965.

DeWitt, J. Doyle. *A Century of Campaign Buttons: 1789–1889.* Hartford, CT: Privately printed, 1959.

French, Tom. *The 1972 Presidential Campaign in Buttons.* Capitola, CA: Author, 1973.

Hake, Ted. *The Encyclopedia of Political Buttons . . . 1896–1972.* New York: Dafran House Publishers, 1974. All three price guides by Theodore Hake are available from the author at PO Box 1444, York, PA 17405.

Hake, Theodore. *Political Buttons: Book II, 1920–1976.* York, PA: Hake's Americana and Collectibles, 1977.

———. *Political Buttons: Book III, 1789–1916.* York, PA: Hake's Americana and Collectibles, 1978.

   *Note:* Since 1974, when Ted Hake introduced *Political Buttons: Vol. 1. 1896–1972,* his publications have served as definitive value guides in the hobby. His latest price updating was the culmination of input from a panel of highly knowledgeable dealers and collectors.

Sullivan, Edmund S. *American Political Badges and Medalets/1789–1892.* Lawrence, MA: Quatermain Publications, 1981. Revised edition of J. Doyle DeWitt's *A Century of Campaign Buttons, 1789–1889.*

## POLITICAL MEMORABILIA—GENERAL

Fratkin, Robert. "Political Souvenirs: Reminders of Old Campaigns." *The Encyclopedia of Collectibles* (Vol. P–Q, pp. 64–75). Alexandria, VA: Time-Life Books, 1979.

Gores, Stan. *Presidential and Campaign Memorabilia.* Des Moines, IA: Wallace-Homestead Book Company, 1982.

Sullivan, Edmund. *Collecting Political Americana.* New York: Crown Publishers, 1980. The definitive work on political collecting.

Wagner, Dale. *Presidential Campaign Memorabilia: A Concise History, 1789–1972.* Washington, DC: Public Policy Research Associates, 1972.

## POLITICAL NOVELTIES

Ackerman, Donald. "Snuff Boxes: The Standard" *Journal of the Association for the Preservation of Political Americana,* Summer 1977.

———. "Thread Boxes: The Standard" *Journal of the Association for the Preservation of Political Americana,* Autumn 1977.

Collins, Herbert R. "Political Campaign Torches." (Contributions from the Museum of History and Technology) *United States National Bulletin* (Paper 45). Washington, DC: Smithsonian Institution, 1964.

Holzer, Harold, and Ostendorf, Lloyd. "Sculptures of Abraham Lincoln from Life." *Antiques,* February 1978.

Jamieson, Kathleen Hall. *Packaging the Presidency: A History and Criticism of Presidential Campaign Advertising.* New York, Oxford: Oxford University Press, 1984.

Ladd, Everett. *American Political Parties.* New York: Norton, 1971.

Leish, Kenneth (Ed. in charge). *The American Heritage History of the Presidents of the United States.* New York: Simon and Schuster, 1968.

Lorant, Stefan. *The Glorious Burden.* Lenox, MA: Author, 1976.

McKee, Thomas Hudson. *The National Conventions and Platforms of All Political Parties.* Baltimore: Friedenwald Company, 1900. Reprinted in 1970 by Scholarly Press, Saint Clair Shores, MI.

Miller Lillian B., and other editors. *If Elected . . .: Unsuccessful Candidates for the Presidency.* Washington, DC: The Smithsonian Institution Press, 1972.

Morris, Dan, and Morris, Inez. *Who Was Who in American Politics.* New York: Hawthorn Books, 1974.

Morris, Richard B., Noble Cunningham, Hugh Sidey and others. *Every Four Years: The American Presidency.* Smithsonian Exposition Books. New York, London: W. W. Norton & Co., 1980.

Myrers, William Starr. *The Republican Party: A History.* New York, London: Century Co., 1928.

Piercy, Elmer. "Watch Fobs." *The Keynoter* (Journal of the American Political Items Collectors), Spring 1970.

Porter, Kirk H., and Johnson, Donald Bruce (compilers). *National Party Platforms: 1840–1968.* Urbana, IL: University of Illinois Press, 1970.

Rossiter, Clinton. *The American Presidency* (2nd ed.). New York: Time-Life Books, 1960.

———. *Parties and Politics in America.* Ithaca, NY: Cornell University Press, 1960.

Schlesinger, Arthur, Jr. *The Coming to Power: Critical Presidential Elections in American History.* New York: McGraw-Hill, 1972.

Smallwood, Frank. *The Other Candidates: Third Parties in Presidential Elections.* Hanover, NH, and London: University Press of New England (for Dartmouth College), 1983.

Sperber, Hans, and Trittschuh, Travis. *American Political Terms: An Historical Dictionary.* Detroit: Wayne State University Press, 1962.

Taylor, Jim. *The Book of Presidents.* New York: Arno Press, 1972.

Whitney, David C., *The American Presidents.* Garden City, NY: Doubleday & Company, 1978. Brief biographies from Washington through Carter.

## POLITICAL PHOTOGRAPHS, PRINTS, HISTORICAL DOCUMENTS

Axelrod, Todd M. *Collecting Historical Documents: A Guide To Owning History.* Neptune City, NJ: T.F.H. Publications, 1984.

Hamilton, Charles. *Great Forgers and Famous Fakes.* New York: Crown Publishers, 1980. Good rundown on manuscript and autograph forgeries and how to detect them.

Holzer, Harold, Boritt, Gabor S., and Neely, Mark E., Jr. *The Lincoln Image: Abraham Lincoln and the Popular Print.* New York: Charles Scribner's Sons, 1984.

Holzer, Harold, Boritt, Gabor S., and McNeely, *Changing The Lincoln Image.* Ft. Wayne, IN: Louis A. Warren Lincoln Library and Museum, 1985. Supplement to *The Lincoln Image* . . . exhibit and book.

Meredith, Roy. *Mathew Brady's Portrait of an Era.* New York, London: W. W. Norton, 1982.

Rinhart, Floyd, and Rinhart, Marion. *The American Daguerreotype.* Athens, GA: University of Georgia Press, 1981.

Welling, William. *Collector's Guide to Nineteenth Century Photographs.* New York: Collier Books, 1976.

## POLITICAL RECORDINGS AND VIDEO TAPES

American Heritage Publishing Company. *The Invention of the Presidency.* 1968, #XB-136.

Audio Archives Enterprises. *If I'm Elected: Actual Voices of Our Presidents and Their Opponents, 1892–1952.* 1952.

————. *Election Songs of the United States.* Sung by Oscar Brand, #FH-5280.

————. *Moonshine and Prohibition.* 1962, #FH-5263.

Folkways Record and Service Corporation. *Songs of the Suffragettes.* 1958, #FH-5281.

Time, Inc. *Sing Along with Millard Fillmore.* 1964.

*Note:* Steve Russell of Belle Vernon, PA, deals in VHS political films: documentaries of all major political leaders from TR to Reagan. For catalog, write Steve Russell, 500 Perry Avenue, Belle Vernon, PA.

## POLITICAL TEXTILES

Collins, Herbert R. *Threads of History.* Washington, DC: The Smithsonian Institution Press, 1979.

Godden, Geoffrey A. *Stevengraphs.* Rutherford, NJ: Fairleigh Dickinson University Press, 1971.

Hornung, Clarence. *Treasury of American Design.* New York: Harry N. Abrams, Inc., 1976. Published in editions of two volumes and two volumes in one.

Sullivan, Edmund S., and Fischer, Roger A., *American Political Ribbons and Ribbon Badges. 1825–1981.* Lawrence, MA: Quartermain Publications, 1985.

Washburn, Wilcomb E. "Campaign Banners." *American Heritage* (Vol. 23, No. 6) October 1972.

## POLITICAL TOYS, BANKS, DOLLS, GAMES

Barenholtz, Bernard and McClintock, Inez. *American Antique Toys: 1830–1900.* New York: Harry N. Abrams, Inc. 1980.

Lavitt, Wendy. *Dolls.* New York: Alfred A. Knopf, 1983.

Norman, Bill. *The Bank Book, The Encyclopedia of Mechanical Bank Collecting.* San Diego, CA: Accent Studios, 1985.

Slocum, Jerry, and Botermans, Jack. *Puzzles.* Seattle, WA: Penary Publications International, University of Washington, 1986.

Whitton, Blair. *Toys.* New York: Alfred A. Knopf, 1984.

## CARING FOR YOUR COLLECTION

Crain, Chris. "Safeguarding Your Collection." *Political Collector,* December 1978.

Cross, Reva. *China Repair and Restoration.* New York: Drake Publishing Company, 1973.

Fall, Freeda Kay. *Art Objects: Their Care and Preservation.* Washington, DC: Museum Publications, 1967.

————. *Handbook for Museums and Collectors.* La Jolla, CA: Laurence McGilvey, 1973.

Guldbeck, Per. *The Care of Historical Collections: A Conservator's Handbook for the Nonspecialist.* Nashville, TN: Association for State and Local History, 1972.

Leene, Jentina E. (ed). *Textile Conservation.* Washington, DC: Butterworth, 1972.

McDermott, Robert, and Irwin, Theodore. *Stop Thief! How to Safeguard Your Home and Business.* New York: Macmillan, 1978.

Sloane, Eugene A. *The Complete Book of Locks, Keys, Burglar and Smoke Alarms.* New York: William Morrow, 1977.

## SOURCES OF PROTECTION AND
## DISPLAY MATERIALS

Acid-free Paper, Pastes, and Containers. The Hollinger Corporation, PO Box 6185, 3810 South Four Run Dr., Arlington, VA 22206. *Talas.* Catalog of the Technical Library Service, 104 Fifth Avenue, New York, NY 10011.

Button Frames. Wilbur R. Elling, 154 Lagoon Boulevard, Massapequa, NY 11758.

Lamination. New England Document Conservation Center, Abbott Hall, School Street, Andover, MA 01810.

Plate Hangers. T and B Sales, PO Box 30, Dept. AT, Old Hickory, TN 37138.

Riker Mounts. Edmunds Scientific Company, Barrington, NJ 08007. Ward's Natural Science Establishment, 300 Ridge Road, East Rochester, NY 14445.

## FANTASIES, REPRODUCTIONS, RESTRIKES

American Political Items Collectors. *Brummagem.* An illustrated compilation of reproductions and fantasies that appears in issues of *The Keynoter.*

Spieler, Dave. *Repro Report. The Political Collector.* A series of articles about campaign button reproductions that appeared in the January, March, April, June, and September 1974 issues.

## THE PRESIDENCY—GENERAL REFERENCE

Bailey, Thomas A. *Presidential Greatness: Image and the Man,* Englewood Cliffs, NJ; Prentice-Hall, 1966.

Binkley, Wilfred. *American Political Parties: Their Natural History,* New York: Alfred Knopf, 1966.

Boller, Paul F. Jr. *Presidential Anecdotes.* New York, Oxford: Oxford University Press, 1981.

———. *Presidential Campaigns.* New York, Oxford: Oxford University Press, 1984.

Chester, Edward W. *A Guide to Political Platforms,* Hamden, CT: Archon Books, 1977.

*Congressional Directory,* Washington, DC: U.S. Government Printing Office, 1979. Annual supplements are issued.

Congressional Quarterly Research Service (eds.). *Members of Congress Since 1789* (2nd ed.) Congressional Quarterly Inc., Washington, DC, 1981.

Cunliffe, Marcus. *The American Heritage History of the Presidency.* New York: Simon and Schuster, 1968.

Diamond, Robert A. (ed.). *Congressional Quarterly's Guide to U.S. Elections.* Washington, DC, U.S. Government Printing Office, 1975.

Frank, Beryl. *The Pictorial History of the Democratic Party.* Secaucus, NJ: Castle Books, Ottenheimer Publishers, 1980.

———. *The Pictorial History of the Republican Party.* Secaucus, NJ: Castle Books, Ottenheimer Publishers, 1980.

Goldman, Perry M., and Young, James S. (eds). *The United States Congressional Directories. 1789–1840.* New York: Columbia University Press, 1973.

Healy, Diana Dixon. *America's Vice-Presidents.* New York: Atheneum, 1984.

Hofstadter, Richard. *The American Political Tradition.* New York: Random House (Vintage Books), 1974.

Hoyt, Edwin. *Jumbos and Jackasses: A Popular History of the Political Wars.* New York: Doubleday, 1960.

## OTHER PATRIOTIC MEMORABILIA

Allen, Leslie. *Liberty: The Statue and the American Dream.* Statue of Liberty Ellis Island Foundation, Inc., published with cooperation of National Geographic Society, 1985.

Horwitz, Elinor Lander. *The Bird, The Banner, and Uncle Sam: Images of America in Folk and Popular Art.* Philadelphia/New York: J. B. Lippincott, 1976.

Isaacson, Philip M. *The American Eagle.* Boston: New York Graphic Society, 1975.

# INDEX